Women's Voices in Digital Media

Louann Atkins Temple Women & Culture Series

Women's Voices in Digital Media

THE SONIC SCREEN FROM FILM TO MEMES

Jennifer O'Meara

University of Texas Press Austin

The Louann Atkins Temple Women & Culture Series is supported by Allison, Doug, Taylor, and Andy Bacon; Margaret, Lawrence, Will, John, and Annie Temple; Larry Temple; the Temple-Inland Foundation; and the National Endowment for the Humanities.

Requests for permission to reproduce material from this work should be sent to:
      Permissions
      University of Texas Press
      P.O. Box 7819
      Austin, TX 78713-7819
      utpress.utexas.edu/rp-form

♾ The paper used in this book meets the minimum requirements of ANSI/NISO Z39.48-1992 (R1997) (Permanence of Paper).

Library of Congress Cataloging-in-Publication Data

Names: O'Meara, Jennifer, author.
Title: Women's voices in digital media : the sonic screen from film to memes / Jennifer O'Meara.
Other titles: Louann Atkins Temple women & culture series.
Description: First edition. | Austin : University of Texas Press, 2022. | Series: Louann Atkins Temple Women & Culture Series | Includes bibliographical references and index.
Identifiers: LCCN 2021038184
ISBN 978-1-4773-2443-1 (cloth)
ISBN 978-1-4773-2444-8 (paperback)
ISBN 978-1-4773-2445-5 (PDF)
ISBN 978-1-4773-2446-2 (ePub)
Subjects: LCSH: Women in mass media. | Voice in mass media—Political aspects. | Voice in mass media—Social aspects. | Digital media—Technological innovations. | Gender identity in mass media. | Sex role. | Voice-overs—Political aspects. | Voice actors and actresses—Political aspects.
Classification: LCC P94.5.W65 O44 2022 | DDC 305.3—dc23
LC record available at https://lccn.loc.gov/2021038184

doi:10.7560/324431

CONTENTS

*Introduction: Proliferating Screens and a New Vocal
Vortex*   1

CHAPTER 1. Film Voices + Time: Excavating Vocal Histories on
Digital Platforms   21

CHAPTER 2. The (Post)Human Voice and Feminized Machines in
Anomalisa, *The Congress*, and *Her*   53

CHAPTER 3. The Expanded and Immersive Voice-Over   85

CHAPTER 4. Karina Longworth and the Remixing of Actresses' Voices
on the *You Must Remember This* Podcast   119

CHAPTER 5. Meme Girls versus Trump: The Silent Voices of Subtitled
Screenshots   147

CHAPTER 6. *RuPaul's Drag Race* and the Queered Remediation of
Women's Voices   171

Conclusion   197

Acknowledgments   202

Notes   203

Filmography   233

Bibliography   237

Digital Artifacts   255

Index   258

Women's Voices in Digital Media

PROLIFERATING SCREENS
AND A NEW VOCAL VORTEX

IN OCTOBER 2004, ONE MONTH AHEAD OF the release of Nintendo's new DS gaming console, the company began to screen three brief, sexually charged advertisements in movie theaters and on television. Part of a marketing blitz centered around the slogan "Touching is Good," the ads aimed to highlight distinctive properties of the Nintendo DS device: that it incorporated a microphone allowing for voice commands, that one of the device's two screens was a touch screen, and that the device was Wi-Fi enabled, allowing users to interact with other consoles.[1] They featured a whispering, disembodied female voice that issued commands with sexual overtones to would-be users of the device: "Touch the bottom rectangle. . . . please. Go ahead, touch it."[2] The on-screen graphics were notably bland by comparison, including a static-dotted black screen and a bright blue rectangle from which the DS materialized. The woman's voice continued to offer encouragement for us to reach out and touch ("You might like it"), purposefully delivering promises of sexual satisfaction that she (and the device) would never be able to fulfill.

With these advertisements playing in cinemas and on television, as well as online, the woman's prominent, if anonymous, voice entered into a dialectical relationship with the historical treatment of the screened female voice: disembodied voice-overs in classical Hollywood cinema were rarely granted to women; indeed, women's voices were fundamentally tethered to women's on-screen bodies. In exploiting the sexualized potential of women's voices, Nintendo caused a stir. And within just a few years, new digital incarnations of feminine voices were causing other stirs. These incarnations included the strange popularity of "autonomous sensory meridian response" (ASMR) videos of women recording themselves whispering to a YouTube camera with a view to relaxing their imagined audience, or the sensation of hearing Hollywood actress Scarlett Johansson "read sexy Bible verses" via the audio streaming site SoundCloud.[3] As film and media scholar Joceline Andersen observed of the former, there is a distinct gendering to such whispering videos. They are generally performed in domestic settings and "[re-create] heteronormative models of care and intimacy directed by women toward men."[4] Although the content creators and consumers generally aim to distance whisper videos from associations with sexual fetishes, the affective use of the female voice recalls earlier incarnations of the sexualized, disembodied female voice—such as the erotic "blue disc" phonographs of the 1930s to the 1950s, or the phone sex hotlines that emerged in the United States in the late 1970s, thanks to the former porn star and magazine publisher Gloria Leonard.[5] The Nintendo DS ads similarly assumed that a woman's breathy voice would appeal to the company's main target audience of heterosexual men.

The streaming of Johansson's sexy Bible readings on SoundCloud is also enmeshed in this history. As part of a concept album by comedian Mike O'Brien, Johansson plays on associations around her husky voice while sexualizing misogynistic passages from Deuteronomy about punishments women should receive for bad behavior, such as having their hands cut off. Johansson's contribution to the album extends on disembodied filmic uses of her voice, such as in *Her* (Spike Jonze, 2013), where she voices an immaterial operating system with such charm that the male protagonist falls for her. O'Brien redirects these aspects of Johansson's voice and her persona into another medium, audio streaming, and into another genre, comedy. Previews of her vocal contribution were used in publicity for the album online across a range of websites, from *Rolling Stone* to World Religion News.[6]

The Nintendo ads, the ASMR videos, the Johansson recording, and similar offerings set the digital stage for a range of screen-based media to present the female voice in ways that were paradoxically both increasingly intimate and sensuous and increasingly processed via technological means. While distinctly digital-born in their programming and distribution, all three of these examples fit within the broader landscape of women's digitized screen voices (including voice-activated assistants, such as Apple's "Siri")—and, indeed, within a much longer history of women's technologized voices, dating back to Thomas Edison's talking dolls (1890) and Bell Telephone Laboratories' "Voder" machine (1939). The Voder (a contraction of Voice Operating Demonstrator) was the first technology to successfully approximate the objective of electronically synthesized human speech.[7] Like the Nintendo DS, the machine was intrinsically linked to both women and the sense of touch. Although it was invented by a man, Homer Dudley, an acoustic engineer, it was operated almost entirely by women, particularly Helen Harper, who

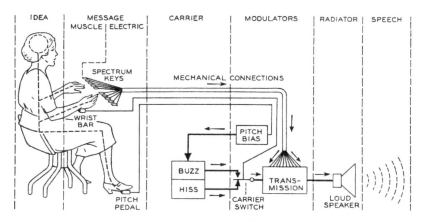

Fig. 8—Schematic circuit of the voder.

Figure 0.1. Diagram of a woman operating Bell Telephone Laboratories' "Voder," produced by Homer Dudley, in "The Carrier Nature of Speech," *Bell System Technical Journal*, October 1940.

trained some thirty other women as operators of the contraption, which was played by the hands like an organ (figure 0.1).[8]

Responses to these historically distant technologized voices can be similar to the reception of more modern examples: a mix of excitement, amusement, and anxiety at the unnerving combination of masculine machines and female embodiment. Like the controversy around blue discs, recordings of sexualized voices that were often played in public, male-dominated settings, such as taverns,[9] discourse around the Nintendo DS, the ASMR whisper videos, and Johansson's viral comedy file has highlighted the fact that they all promote distinctly gendered forms of pleasure in listening. These listening formats and environments can encourage or reflect a fetishization of the technologized female voice, particularly when its arousing properties are emphasized through performative traits such as breathiness.[10]

But what of the role of the screen in the portrayal of the female voice? Edison's dolls and the Voder typically had to be experienced in person: for example, the dolls could be purchased or viewed at the Exhibition of the Wonders of Electricity in 1890, while the Voder was demonstrated at the 1939 World's Fair in New York. But these voices might also be broadcast over the radio, and people could read about them in newspapers. In the digital era, the technologized female voice is rarely experienced without some form of screen, be it that of a computer, smart device, television, cinema screen, or virtual reality headset. Moreover, owing to the diverse archival platforms of

Figure 0.2. Screenshot of *PBS NewsHour* YouTube video, "Edison's Talking Dolls: Child's Toy or Stuff of Nightmares," May 6, 2015.

the internet, one can now also experience the likes of Edison's dolls and the Voder via short-form videos on YouTube and similar sites. Such videos are marked by the amateur qualities of grassroots digital media production, a Frankenstein-like mixing of images, video, audio clips, and on-screen text. Regardless of the video quality, streaming platforms *screen* these once-analog voices for the masses while allowing them to coexist alongside their vocal contemporaries.

Furthermore, we can now hear Edison's dolls again precisely because of digital technologies that have allowed for such voices to be reformatted. These technologies include ways of translating audio properties into visual imagery. As media archaeologist Paul Flaig explained, the voices of Edison's talking dolls were resurrected through the use of a 3D optical scanning system that "probes the grooves of recording surfaces like wax or shellac with a line scan camera, digitally reconstructing these imperceptible depths into a series of images that are subsequently mapped in 3D and converted into a WAV audio format."[11] Freed from their origins via modernity and mechanics, these voices have been reborn in digital formats, in the process becoming subject to the visual norms of internet culture. For a *PBS NewsHour* segment on the vocal resurrection of the dolls, the production team edited together still images of them and, to create a sense of movement, used basic software and rudimentary zooming to feature artificial close-ups of the dolls' "bodies" (figure 0.2).[12]

Figure 0.3. Screenshot of *Caroline ASMR* YouTube video, "ASMR Super Slowwww Hand Movements and Trigger Words for Sleep," June 14, 2020.

While the video's raison d'être may be to allow a twenty-first-century audience to hear their uncanny voices, the visual techniques inadvertently link the dolls to the closely framed shots of women in YouTube's ASMR whisper videos (figure 0.3). In the whisper videos, the body is often fragmented, with framings that go against the norms for how people are generally presented on screen.[13] In both cases, the speaking female subject is the central focal point, her microphone and mouth centered in the frame, with other parts of her face and body cropped out as unnecessary. With regard to the technologized female voice and its media iconography, these visual parallels raise crucial questions about precisely what has changed and what has stayed the same in the 120-plus years separating the two types of recordings, which sit at opposite sides of the analog-digital divide. Yet, with access to them via digital screens now ubiquitous, both nonetheless contribute to the cacophony of women's technologized screen voices in the twenty-first century. This book addresses these technological developments and their historical precursors, pioneering a transmedial approach to analyzing women's screen voices in the digital era. It explores how such voices can "travel" from one screen medium to another, in the form of verbal or vocal echoes, and how the proliferation of screens in the digital age can alter the reception of mediated voices as much as images, with substantial implications for women and culture. By examining the complexities of the vocal landscape in the digital era, we will see how contemporary screen media and cultural practices have not only amplified women's voices, including historical ones, in new ways, but also provided new ways to fetishize, police, and silence them. With a dual focus on female characters and performers in English-language media, my study shows that digital technologies are influencing how women's voices are recorded, represented, received, and remediated. It considers not only traditional screen formats (such as cinema and television) but also other digital formats and practices, detailing how voices first presented via traditional screens can travel into digital formats and practices. Finally, it theorizes the increased portability of female speech and vocal recordings as well as the gendered politics of what comes to pass when certain words or voices made famous on screen are reused in other contexts.

Susan Sontag's pessimistic account of "the decay of cinema" in 1996 linked the rapid proliferation of screens ("images now appear in any size and on a variety of surfaces") to not *really* seeing a given film. The smaller scale of nontheatrical screens and the problem of inattention in modern settings and lives were both at issue. For Sontag, the viewer was no longer "overwhelmed by the physical presence of the image" as in a traditional movie theater.[14] Subsequent discourse on the proliferation of screens has maintained this focus on the image even when the reference point is "audiovisual texts." Media studies scholar Will Straw described such screen content, for example, as "obscure, flickering imagery," and said it consisted of "murky fluctuations of movement and colour, unfolding at the margins of our vision or attention." However, the majority of devices with screens could also be understood as devices with *speakers*. And just as what is playing on the screens can be analyzed for its imagery, what plays through the speakers can be analyzed for its aural features. I contend that these aural features reflect digital media's "dissolution of boundaries" and new ways of hearing—or, more precisely, new ways of audio-viewing.[15]

It can take an extreme example to raise awareness of the impact of the proliferation of devices with screens on our everyday listening experience. Such was the case in May 2018 when social media users perplexedly debated the "Yanny or Laurel" audio illusion. A huge debate erupted over which of these two-syllable words was spoken and recorded in a viral clip. The discrepancy in what listeners heard was due to a complex intermixing of technology (in terms of both recording devices and speaker quality) and biology (with age impacting whether listeners could hear the higher frequencies). As speech and hearing sciences expert Benjamin Munson explained, those who could hear "Yanny" had "really great headphones or very good hearing."[16] The low-quality nature of the file contributed to its audio ambiguity. "Laurel" was one of some thirty-six thousand words that actor Jay Aubrey recorded for the website Vocabulary.com.[17] As the example illustrated, digitized voices can be radically shaped by conversion processes and distribution technologies. And while Sontag and Straw cited inattention to images as a problem in the late twentieth century, the "Yanny or Laurel" phenomenon shows how the opposite dynamic can take place, with images and voice recordings receiving increased scrutiny.

VOCAL (DIS)EMBODIMENT ACROSS TIME AND SPACE

The stakes involved in better understanding the gendered dynamics of digitized screen voices are high. Online discourse surrounding women in audiovisual media is increasingly structured around metaphors of the voice—from the overt silencing of female gamers in "Gamergate" to the digital sensation of the "Bechdel test." The former refers to the controversy over sexism in gamer communities. The latter concerns a measure of sexism in film and other media that rates representations of women using a simplistic formula: whether there are two or more female characters who talk about something other than a man.[18] Similar discussions stressed the need for women in the media to "speak up," as reflected in the 2014 Twitter campaign #AskHerMore, which challenged interviewers not to ask women in Hollywood superficial questions on the red carpet. Yet, within screen studies, the sustained influence of feminist film scholar Laura Mulvey's concept of the "male gaze" has channeled attention toward women's visual representation and away from women's verbal and vocal representation.[19] There have been relatively few exceptions to this prioritization of the visual aspects of the portrayal of women in screen media. Looking to cinema, in particular, in the late 1980s and early 1990s, critical theorists Kaja Silverman and Amy Lawrence focused on connections between the woman's body and voice through analysis of classical Hollywood, particularly voice-overs, using the psychoanalytic frameworks of the time.[20] They argued that women in film were frequently attributed unreliable speech, punished for talking, or silenced altogether. More than a decade later, in *Into the Vortex: Female Voice and Paradox in Film*, Britta H. Sjogren questioned Silverman's and Lawrence's influential claims in order to offer a more empowered account of how women's voices function in relation to 1940s Hollywood cinema. She reminded us of the danger of generalizing in relation to gendered forms of silencing.[21]

Sjogren's attention to the "vortexical" movement of the voice as it relates to voice-off (when we hear the voice of a character not visible within the frame) and signification provides a particularly productive entry point to the digital screen voice. For Sjogren, approaches to the gendered voice-over and embodiment by the likes of Silverman place undue emphasis on linearity and time at the expense of circularity and space: "Far from seeing the delays, the flashbacks, the holding up of time, the privileging of space, the circularity and stasis of these texts as negative attributes that lock the female protagonist 'inside' the narrative, I question the notion that 'exteriority' to the text translates into a superior subjective placement for a character."[22] My study is often concerned precisely with how screen voices, in their fragments or wholes, travel in the digital era to occupy new spaces and formats. In Sjogren's terminology, such characters and performers can be both inside the narrative and exterior to it, regardless of whether their voice (or voice-over) is embodied. Moreover, I am concerned with what it even means to refer to women's screen voices as "embodied" or "disembodied" in a cultural environment so characterized by bleeding boundaries and transmedia storytelling. Indeed, the remediation of one vocal recording in another format can frequently reverse these categories, as when separating the voice from the image of the body that produced it. This point recalls Rick Altman's famed conception of cinema as a form of ventriloquism, reliant on illusions provided by the constructed cohesion of separate sound and image tracks.[23]

In this landscape of remixed sounds and images, the soundtrack or vocal track is increasingly separated from its audiovisual format.[24] Analog films that were first redistributed on VHS, DVD, or Blu-Ray are "ripped" and uploaded as torrents that leave them vulnerable to all kinds of digital remixing and redistribution. If you're a well-known screen performer, at some stage in this process your voice (its natural sound and its recording and subsequent editing) will likely be dislocated and sent in a new direction—perhaps even ghosting a GIF or a meme that no one can technically hear. In these cases, the memory of what you said and how you said it lives on in subtitles or bold macro meme text. As even the term "ripping" suggests, visceral dislocations can take place in the process—from the analog to the digital—of the voice from the body to which it was once sutured, with significant implications for how the woman's voice and the body that produced it are experienced. What do these vocal permutations mean for the voices of female characters and performers? How and why do their voices circulate or resonate in the digital era of Twitter "echo chambers" and viral podcasts? And what are the ramifications for women, whose screen voices have historically been so tied to their visible bodies?

If you're the actress Alicia Silverstone, this can mean that, twenty-two years after *Clueless* (Amy Heckerling, 1995), memes of your character's speech might be used to critique President Donald Trump's restrictive immigration policies. If you're the actress Anna Faris, it can mean that your relationship podcast, *Unqualified* (2015–), can suddenly land you with an adjunct teaching post at the University of Southern California, a kind of cultural prestige not exactly associated with Faris's screen roles.[25] Faris's visible body is cast off from her voice on the podcast, but people recognize her without it. If you're the actress Margot Robbie, then a press junket might now involve recording an entire interview for the fashion magazine *W* in sotto voce, with the aim of pleasing the rapidly growing community of ASMR fans.[26] The description of this interview on YouTube links Robbie's performance of ASMR stimuli to her earlier, sexualized performances in films like *The Wolf of Wall Street* (Martin Scorsese, 2013) and *The Big Short* (Adam McKay, 2015). Such intertextual references to Robbie's bombshell persona—one that she herself downplays—is particularly insidious given that Robbie took part in the *W* video segment without even understanding what ASMR was.

In each of these examples, the actress's voice was overdetermined, signifying more than your average human voice, but in ways that are not necessarily empowering or authoritative for the woman in question. And while each of the above-mentioned women sounds very different (in terms of pitch, accent, and timbre), the bodies that produce the voices look relatively similar. They represent diversity as only a group of differing shades of attractive, youngish, blonde women can. Is it ultimately the similarity of their bodies that facilitates the diverse uses of their distinct voices, shrinking the available sonic space for other women, particularly women of color, and women with less conventionally "desirable" bodies and/or voices? This tendency for the voices of white women to dominate diverse digital spaces will be considered in subsequent chapters: in relation to the voice-activated assistants and their representation in cinema in chapter 2; in terms of voice-overs and podcasts in chapters 3 and 4; and in reference to subtitled memes and GIFs in chapter 5. Fortunately, there are exceptions, including popular podcasts by women of color and, as explored in chapter 6, the renegotiation of the weighty concept of the "maternal voice" by the Black drag queen RuPaul.

VOCAL SHARDS AND SPECTROGRAMS

In the transmedial digital landscape, Sjogren's metaphor of the vocal vortex gains very tangible form in a 360-degree music video featuring Icelandic performer and artist Björk. "Mouth Mantra" (2015) was filmed inside a four-foot 3D replica of the pioneering artist's mouth and exhibited via virtual reality headset as part of the 2016 *Björk Digital* exhibition in London's Somerset House. Writer Aurora Mitchell, who interviewed the director, Jesse Kanda, highlighted the unnerving experience of being surrounded by such a

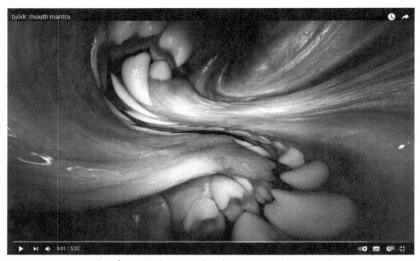

Figure 0.4. Screenshot from Björk's virtual reality music video "Mouth Mantra," 2015, directed by Jesse Kanda.

singing mouth: "The fuchsia insides of a pulsating mouth are staring back at me, sharp, shadowy white teeth warping and rotating with the surrounding flesh. Specks of saliva are dotted around, glistening with a fierce sheen."[27] Even in 2D format, the experience of watching the rapid distortions of this mouth could aptly be described as entering *into a vortex* (attaching new prescience to Sjogren's 2006 book title in the process) (figure 0.4). But unlike our previous examples, the presentation of Björk's voice is not sexualized, instead signaling toward the potential of more recent screen formats to present women's voices in ways that are increasingly immersive and graphic, even verging on the grotesque. In the hands of Björk, a multimodal artist and technological pioneer, digital innovations can thus be harnessed to provide a rendering of the source of a female voice that is, quite literally, well rounded.

The vocal vortex is not the only hermeneutic from early scholarship on the female screen voice that is capable of shedding light on the more contemporary digital mediascape. The Echo and Narcissus of Amy Lawrence's book title, *Echo and Narcissus: Women's Voices in Classical Hollywood Cinema*, also gain new meaning in relation to women's digital screen voices. Retellings of Ovid's tale from the *Metamorphoses* tend to focus on Narcissus, the young hunter who rejected Echo (although he is better known for drowning in a pool because he was so absorbed in his own reflection). Lawrence, however, refocuses attention on the nymph Echo, who loses her power to speak freely when the goddess Hera curses her; thereafter, she can only repeat the last few words that have most recently been said to her. Lawrence reminds us that the story "interweaves issues of sight and sound, vision and speech." She perceptively compares Echo's fragmented and derivative speech to cinema's representational qualities: "Like the reflection [of Narcissus] in the pool, an echo is defined by a fundamental absence: what we perceive is not an entity but an illusion, the reflection of what once was. . . . In cinema, everything we hear and everything we see isn't *there* anymore. It is an echo and a reflection." The pleasures of the fundamental absence, or "echo," are inevitably linked to gender issues, in that the various technologies used to reproduce the illusion of the live voice across history have sought "to recreate men and women according to the standards of the day."[28] What is so interesting, from the perspective of the digital era, is how the standards of the day may have largely stayed the same for at least a century, but all the while, the gendered dynamics of the mediated echo were being radically altered. This contrast, I would argue, is largely a result of the proliferation of screen technologies.

Lawrence explained that "an entire philosophy of Victorian gender relations can be read in the praises of the first telephone operators." Even here, the "dulcet tones" of the women's voices "seem[ed] to exercise a soothing and calming effect upon the masculine mind."[29] Both these tones and their effects are strikingly similar to YouTube's calming ASMR chorus of whispering women. And yet, as subsequent chapters will reveal, the mechanisms by which a female voice "echoes" have changed. While Ovid's Echo was able to repeat only the last few words that were said to her, her twenty-first-century counterparts are much more likely to have their *own words* repeated ad infinitum across digital platforms and formats (GIFs, YouTube videos, podcasts, glitch videos, and televisual lip syncs), as already signaled by the frequent references to social media "echo chambers."[30] Indeed, to revisit Silverman's focus on "the acoustic mirror," I wish to propose a new functioning for this symbolic description: if this term captures the female voice as it relates to psychoanalysis and classical Hollywood cinema, then in the twenty-first century this acoustic mirror has been shattered, dispersing vocal shards across a much broader range of screens.

Silverman's acoustic mirror is grounded in psychoanalytic theories of language and subjectivity, most notably those of Jacques Lacan and Guy Rosolato. The acoustic mirror is mapped onto Lacan's conception of the mirror stage: the maternal voice introducing the child to its mirror reflection, and the child's initiation into speech based on imitation of the mother's sounds.[31] Rather jarringly, from my contemporary sound studies perspective, such analyses make no reference to the very real acoustic mirrors developed in Britain in the early twentieth century. These huge concrete structures were built to provide early detection of aerial attacks in wartime by reflecting sound waves. Dating from the 1920s and 1930s, the mirrors—sometimes referred to as "listening ears"—were divided into two types of devices: (1) concave bowls (with a diameter of 20–30 feet), from which sound was detected using a collector wearing a stethoscope-type device, and (2) acoustic walls measuring some two hundred feet in length, from which sound was collected by an arrangement of microphones, and fed by wire to a control room.[32] Though soon usurped by radar in terms of an early warning system, most of these acoustic mirrors still stand, giant testaments to the potential of early sound technologies. They strike me as important reminders that, for psychoanalysts, tangible phenomena are too often discarded as threats to the abstract ideal. Thus there was no acknowledgment of these technologies in Silverman's book of the same name, despite the technology's precedence by some sixty years. Technology, then, has always been central to the concept of the acoustic mirror, even if it was discounted entirely from the corresponding film theory. Technology seems even more central to twenty-first-century approaches to the screen, where multiple, often distorted echoes of women's voices reverberate across screens in digital space. And much as the sound walls depended on a system of microphones, feeding noises from the wider atmosphere into a control room through a system of wires, digital screen voices are collected and reflected through a network system that allows vocal shards from cinema's shattered acoustic mirror to disperse across many different screens.

The parallels and distortions between women's traditional and digital screen voices are likely unsurprising to literary scholar Steven Connor, who noted that "the technologies of the voice are actualizations of fantasies and desires concerning the voice which predate the actual technologies."[33] In the same way, in this book I do not disregard existing theories of the screen voice based in analog media. Various historical examples can instead be considered important precursors to the digital formats under discussion here, such as classical Hollywood actresses' vocal performances on the radio, or audio guides to museums delivered by the voices of famous women and used to draw visitors into cultural exhibitions. Though the screen is absent from both setups, it is on screen that these women's voices gained the gravitas to be heard in more diverse cultural spaces. For instance, in keeping with Connor's assertion, post-synchronization technologies used to dub women in classical Hollywood have given way to digital tools that can alter the woman's voice (and its relationship to her body) in new ways.

Earlier scholars of the film voice have cited the difficulty of capturing the specifics of vocal timbre and inflection using written analysis, yet audio software packages can now make these qualities more tangible by transcodifying

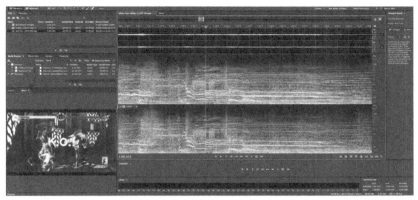

Figure 0.5. A spectrogram analysis of battle cries in *Soul Calibur*, from a research project on women's voices in video games by Milena Droumeva, Kaeleigh Evans, Nesan Furtado, and Renita Bangert titled "It Gets Worse . . . the Female Voice in Video Games," published in *First Person Scholar*, November 2017.

them into visual formats.[34] The voice, once visualized, can offer confirmation of impressions already produced sonically, much as eye-tracking software is increasingly used to confirm and revise long-held assumptions about the gaze patterns of viewers. In fact, some more digitally oriented approaches to the female voice involve the screen as a tool for vocal analysis. In order to trace the evolution of women's battle cries in video games, for example, Milena Droumeva used Adobe Audition's sound visualization tools, identifying a troubling increase in the number and duration of cries from female avatars (see figure 0.5) as well as other changes.[35] As the spectrograms of these women's battle cries help reveal, digital screens and the related technologies not only offer new ways to experience the voice, but also new ways to understand it, including its complex gendered properties.[36]

The chapters that follow discuss several other factors that influence the representation, reception, and remediation of women's voices across screen media in the digital era. These include an increased focused on identity politics related to gender, sexuality, and race as well as trends in digital culture toward more participatory approaches to making and remixing media content.[37] Such dynamics are often underpinned by the industrial and fannish workings of stardom. My approach complements that of Mary Desjardins, who in her book *Recycled Stars: Female Film Stardom in the Age of Television and Video* focused on recycled star images. I instead highlight how female film stars' *voices* can be recycled according to such a cultural logic.[38] For even though non-famous women are involved in digital incarnations of the technologized voice, there is a notable pattern for well-known actresses to be pulled into these trends, a vortex over which they have little control. Their famous bodies and/or voices can add familiarity or intertextual pleasure to a specific use of a given technology by helping to distribute new mediums such as virtual reality, or ASMR whisper videos and other subcultural trends, to mainstream users and audiences.[39]

My approach can also be positioned alongside a small number of recent studies of women's film voices that involve productive revisions of existing theories, or productive revisitings of historical examples, with the benefit of hindsight (or, perhaps more accurately, hind*sound*). Tessa Dwyer's concept of "to-be-dubbed-ness" invokes the language of Laura Mulvey's "to-be-looked-ness" in order to reexamine the dominant (but inaccurate) narrative of the dubbing of silent film star Louise Brooks.[40] While Dwyer's approach highlights the need to question "official" accounts of dubbing and other historical treatments of women's voices, Pooja Rangan has used the work of filmmaker Leslie Thornton to critique the long-held associations between voice-over and textual authority, shifting focus instead to the voice as "a physical phenomenon inflected by the matter of embodied difference." Rangan shows how prior feminist attempts "to recuperate the voice-over as a cinematic site of resistance" have come at the expense of a denial of the distinct materiality of the voice, including as it relates to traces of embodied difference (such as those related to race, gender, and national or regional identity). Her analysis presents alternative ways of examining "the interplay between looking and speaking," particularly as it relates to the sounds of racial difference.[41] In distinct but related ways, Dwyer and Rangan begin to offer fresh approaches to analyzing the (female) film voice and body in tandem, and in relation to issues and ideologies of looking that go beyond the traditional emphasis on whether a woman's voice (particularly a voice-over) is anchored to her own body in the diegesis, that is, the world as presented in the film.[42]

My analysis is similarly oriented around productive revisions of women's historical film voices and the theories used to understand them, although I situate these complex dynamics within the multifarious concepts of "the digital" and "the screen." The book is organized so as to demonstrate the diverse ways in which digital screens, and the broader media landscape of the twenty-first century, are impacting the female voice. The chapters and corresponding case studies illustrate not only how particular digital formats and platforms (including YouTube, Instagram, computer animation, virtual reality, podcasts, and GIFs) are shaping experiences of women's voices, but also how these "new media" trends relate to the historical treatment of women's voices in more traditional screen formats (such as film), as well as to the corresponding theories of voice and gender.

At a basic level, such an approach may seem purely comparative—as I offer insights into how the treatment of women's screen voices has changed or stayed the same in response to technological change. Yet, as I explain in chapter 1, the issue of what happens to mediated voices over time solidifies the dual focus on contemporary vocal practices and their historical precursors. For instance, I will argue that it is necessary to examine the manipulation of actresses' voices in glitch art alongside twentieth-century rationales for dubbing actresses' voices, because both practices subject female performers to a machine logic of discrete parts (voice, image), a logic facilitated by technological manipulation. Comparative analyses of this kind, between digital and predigital trends and practices, will feature throughout the book, as when the silenced voices of film characters in GIFs are tied to silent film intertitles, or when the remediation of women's voices on podcasts recalls radio performances of film adaptations by classical Hollywood actresses such as Hedy Lamarr and Barbara Stanwyck. In exploring the evolving nature of these practices, I build on a media archaeological approach to digital media, demonstrating how trends in the treatment and reception of women's digital voices are firmly embedded within the traditions and conventions of film and media history.[43]

In chapter 1, I examine how female voices from the twentieth century are being experienced anew through digital platforms and formats such as You-Tube and fan forums. I consider the complex dynamics between film voices and the discourses that become attached to them over time and demonstrate the role of various websites and digital archives in revising the history of women's voices. In particular, I examine the ways in which YouTube and fan forums have helped reveal the hidden history of dubbing in the James Bond series, whereby voice actor Nikki van der Zyl and selected fans worked together online to provide "evidence" of her sustained involvement, a process that required fans to reflect upon and update their memories of dubbed "Bond girls" such as Ursula Andress. In so doing, I assert the value of examining film voices using methodologies drawn from historical reception studies and media archaeology. Extending on Barbara Klinger's theorization of film history as "terminable and interminable," I propose a similar approach for film voices, one that involves a diachronic analysis of digital discourses and the historical conditions that surround a particular vocal recording.

Moving from such vocal afterlives to their in-text manifestations, chapter 2 examines films that reflect and rework the trend for artificial intelligence and androids to be coded as female through their presentation of a human woman's voice amid a technological landscape. With a focus on *Anomalisa* (Charlie Kaufman and Duke Johnson, 2015), *The Congress* (Ari Folman,

2014), and *Her*, I argue that women's voices (those of Jennifer Jason Leigh, Robin Wright, and Scarlett Johansson, respectively) are central anchoring devices to the dystopian presentation of technologically enabled diegetic worlds. The chapter demonstrates the two-directional influences between speech-bots such as Apple's "Siri" and Amazon's "Alexa" and their representations in cinema. In *Anomalisa* and *The Congress*, the storyworlds are animated in thematically relevant ways (3D printing and computer animation), thus allowing for a commentary on broader issues of performance in relation to speech technologies and digital media. I explore how, unlike in earlier cinema, where the woman's right to speak was generally linked to an audience's invitation to see her, the development of virtual screen bodies (through motion capture scanning and mapping onto 3D puppets) can create a situation in which images of the human female body can be readily replaced on screen, while the human female voice can remain crucial. With actresses' place on the soundtrack no longer corresponding to a right to be seen on screen, I identify an emerging trend: female performers are being "crowded off" the screen by their digital replacements, while their voices remain crucial for audience identification. As such, chapter 2 aims to make it clear that even in more "traditional" screen formats, such as narrative cinema, women's voices are not immune to technologically driven shifts in presentation.

Chapter 3 is also concerned with how standard conventions for film voices have evolved in response to digital technologies, but with a focus on women's voice-overs and the how their frequency and formats have expanded since classical Hollywood. Although no aspect of women's screen voices has received more attention than their narration, or lack thereof, much has changed since the 1990s, with women now providing narration across a range of genres and formats. Crucially, in the decades since classical Hollywood, audiences have become increasingly used to hearing actresses' disembodied voices in expanded formats and beyond the film or television screen, as with self-produced narration on Instagram, and, increasingly, in virtual reality. Drawing on and extending theories of "expanded cinema" and immersivity, this chapter delves into what I term the "expanded voice-over"—arguing that the traditional parameters of women's screen-based voice-overs have evolved, with digital formats and platforms providing new audiovisual spaces from which women can narrate. Voice-overs by familiar actresses are being used to help initiate audiences into newer forms of digital entertainment. Moreover, while critical theories of gender and voice-over have tended to prioritize questions around the body as they relate to the narrator (Are they embodied or disembodied, and how does that impact their discursive authority?), understanding the expanded voice-overs of the digital era can require increased attention to audiences' bodies. In virtual reality, for example, the voice can provide a grounding effect for the head-set-wearing user, who might feel disoriented, or could even be experiencing motion sickness.

Building on chapter 3's emphasis on expanded vocal space and embod-iment, chapter 4 examines how the medium of the podcast allows for the voices of female characters and performers to be disseminated in new ways. I look in particular at Karina Longworth's *You Must Remember This* podcast. Since 2014, Longworth, a film critic and journalist, has researched and shared her own interpretation of events and figures from Hollywood film history in a format that combines audio clips from films and interviews with narration of the related events. Focusing on her series "Jean and Jane" (a nine-episode section of the podcast on Jean Seberg and Jane Fonda), I examine how the particularities of this format allowed for a new understanding of the actresses' voices and their film roles. Through analysis of the podcast's remixing of film clips and recorded interviews, I consider how Longworth reorients listeners' attention to the verbal and vocal representation of women in cinema, and how the voices of female podcast hosts, such as that of Longworth herself, continue to be policed and even fetishized—a situation that inadvertently aligns her with her more famous subjects. With regard to Longworth's actress subjects, I argue that the missing images of performers' famous bodies pro-vide a structuring absence that facilitates the podcast's form of revisionist feminist historiography. Longworth is shown to pay consistent attention to Seberg's and Fonda's verbal (dis)empowerment at the hands of men (direc-tors, partners, journalists); moreover, she uses her own voice, both her literal narration and her figurative power as podcast producer, to help the women to "take back the narrative" and tell their own stories.

Chapter 5 is similarly concerned with the remediated afterlives of screen voices, this time in the form of silent but subtitled GIFs and memes based on female screen characters. The focus thus moves from one structuring absence (the absence of formerly screened bodies, in Longworth's podcasts) to another (the absence of formerly screened voices in subtitled digital imagery). Spe-cifically, I examine what such responses by female characters from certain shows—*The Simpsons, Clueless,* and *Sex and the City*—reveal about contem-porary US politics and culture, considering how feminist-oriented dialogue developed in the period surrounding the 2016 US presidential campaign. I position the practice alongside existing studies of how young women are increasingly using digital communities to participate in a feminist politics. The chapter also establishes connections between the silenced voice in GIFs and the practices of intertitles in early cinema, before the development of sound technologies, thus underscoring how digital conceptions of the voice have their origins in historical media and technologies.

Extending the analysis of chapter 5, chapter 6 addresses how the female voice is increasingly ventriloquized into another format or body in ways that allow the voice to communicate gender in revealing new ways. While questions of vocal queering surfaced as important in chapter 2, this dimension of the female voice becomes the focal point in the final chapter, in my analysis of the remediation of women's voices on *RuPaul's Drag Race* (Logo TV, 2009–). Here, I consider how the reality television show's reliance on lip syncing and vocal impersonation reworks historical discourse around queer and women's voices as both symbolically powerful and policed. By presenting head judge RuPaul's voice as a queered variation on the maternal voice, and by suggesting a voice-based symbiosis between the drag queen and the cisgender female diva, the show is found to question essentialist links between voice, gender, and body and to use expressive movement to make a visual spectacle of the re-embodied voice in ways that appeal to digital-era audiences' increased acceptance of gender fluidity. Building on cultural critic Wayne Koestenbaum's conception of "the queen's throat," and the media scholar Jennifer Fleeger's *Mismatched Women*, a study that traces the enduring figure of the on-screen female singer whose voice and body do not seem to "fit,"[44] I consider how *RuPaul's Drag Race*'s overtly queer dynamic offers a rich symbolic commentary on women's voices. I examine how the show updates the historical role of the voice in acts of female drag performance by providing hypermediated lip syncs that suit twenty-first-century audiences' appetite for YouTube's style of spectacle-based "attractions." Taken together, chapters 5 and 6 address the important influence of twenty-first-century identity politics—particularly related to gender, sexuality, and race—on women's voices in the digital era.

As these diverse case studies and conceptual approaches suggest, the screen continues to frame the female voice in complex and often contradictory ways. Underpinning all of this is a collective, culturally constructed understanding of precisely what constitutes a (cisgender) woman's voice, as well as the related issue of what constitutes a "feminine voice"—since the two do not necessarily go together.[45] To a certain degree, the sonics of a cisgender female voice are grounded in general anatomical differences between the sexes related to the glottis, laryngeal muscles, and vocal folds. Such physical differences lead to cis women's voices typically having a higher pitch and increased breathiness. Cisgender men generally have a more complete glottal closure, leading to less energy loss at the glottis, and thus less "aspiration noise"—that breathy quality.[46] Yet, as the voice-quality research of Elvira Mendoza and her colleagues have explained, these differences "may be due more to sociocultural than physiological factors."[47] Although sociocultural factors are often downplayed in frequency-based studies of gender and pitch, which can also downplay the existence of vocal outliers and nonbinary and transgender individuals, they can be highlighted in screen media. Indeed, particular case studies examined in this book lend support to the idea that vocal traits perceived as feminine can be learned, as when a drag queen on *RuPaul's Drag Race* performs the iconic breathy sound of Marilyn Monroe as part of an emulative embodiment of the Hollywood star. Similarly, analysis of Scarlett Johansson's hoarse and gender ambiguous voicing of the operating system in *Her* suggests that the screened representation of a "female" or "feminine" voice can help to deconstruct some of the essentialist assumptions around the gendered voice, including the presumed vocal markers of aging. Discourse around performers like Johansson shows how even the voices of cisgender women can fail to match up to more ostensibly anatomical (and, thus, inherently exclusionary) definitions of what constitutes a female-sounding voice—as well as a young woman's voice.

Taken together, the various assemblages—of sound and image, voice and body—considered in this book share features with the traditional film screen, reinforcing the significance of cinematic conceptions of the female voice. Yet these assemblages can also reveal how women's voices are simultaneously being shaped by broader media changes and technologies, including the proliferation of screen devices. In a cultural climate that is increasingly convergent and participatory, women's voices are subject to a forceful pull—as though in a vortex—often spinning from one screen format to another. For the individual in question, be it an actress or a character, this may manifest in a lack of control. And while they (and we) may not be able to prevent such strong forces, this book aims to at least understand them.

CHAPTER 1

FILM VOICES + TIME: EXCAVATING VOCAL HISTORIES ON DIGITAL PLATFORMS

FEMALE VOICES FROM THE TWENTIETH CENTURY ARE increasingly experienced through twenty-first-century platforms such as YouTube, fan forums, and IMDb. On such sites, videos and information related to actresses' screen voices can be shared and spread. An experimental glitch video is my chosen entry point for examining the impact of key properties of digital technologies and platforms—including the unofficial remixing of sound and image, their democratizing potential, and the quick spread of (mis)information—on women's voices. Filmmaker Thorsten Fleisch wrote, for example, in an artist statement accompanying his glitch work *Wound Footage* (2009), that "Rita Hayworth grindedly sings along."[1] Jihoon Kim described Fleisch's piece as an attempt "to blur the boundaries of celluloid-based and digital manipulations."[2] In keeping with glitch videos' aesthetic presentation of technological malfunction or distortion effects, this would have involved many processes: scratching and burning Super 8 film footage before passing it through a projector; digitizing those reels and glitching the pixels of the subsequent video using specialized software; and reshooting the digitized footage with a video camera while playing with the cables connecting the computer and the monitor. Notably, although the artist's description, as well as reviews and interviews, outline the various stages of the visual manipulation, the soundtrack and the processes by which "Rita Hayworth grindedly sings along" typically go without comment. Through careful listening, one begins to hear the distorted voice singing "Put the Blame on Mame" from *Gilda* (Charles Vidor, 1946) after around three minutes. Or, as reviewer Josh Morrall describes it, in *Wound Footage*, "The voice of Rita Hayworth sounding as if it has been filtered through a car engine can then be heard as an audio metaphor for . . . beautiful brutality."[3] But this is most likely not, in fact, Hayworth's voice, because Hayworth's singing voice for this version of the song was dubbed by Anita Ellis.[4]

In a work that Fleisch described as having an "almost humanist" goal ("unification of the digital with the analogue world"), what does it mean that the artist himself seems to be unaware of the analog manipulation of the analog voice—that it is Anita Ellis who grindedly sings along in Wound Footage, because Hayworth's voice was removed long ago, during Gilda's postproduction back in 1946? Fleisch's description is potentially more revealing when examined in relation to his lack of information than it would have been if he had been correct. Describing Wound Footage's unification of the digital with the analog world, Fleisch wrote, "They seem so far apart and yet they aren't. By exposing every material's weaknesses and injuries it [sic] was made one." Indeed, the replacement of Rita Hayworth's voice (presumably deemed materially weak by Gilda's production team) with that of Anita Ellis (for all but one song in the film) confirms an interesting point about classical Hollywood: that its analog screen outputs were highly manipulated in postproduction, even though it is digital media that are often critiqued for their highly interventionist ways (CGI, digital color grading, and so on). Morrall's description, one grounded in Fleisch's likely misunderstanding (that the voice we hear is Hayworth's), also takes on new meaning when we know that it is Ellis's voice we are hearing. To quote him once again: "The voice of Rita Hayworth sounding as if it has been filtered through a car engine can then be heard as an audio metaphor for . . . beautiful brutality."[5] It is true that the muffled voice we hear in Wound Footage is barely recognizable, sounding like it has been filtered through some kind of unnatural machine (such as a car engine), rather than a human body. But Ellis's initial voice was also *filtered* unnaturally—through Hayworth's screened body and the mechanics of suturing sound and image tracks.

Knowledge of the Gilda dubbing process lends Fleisch's supposed choice of Hayworth's voice a different audio metaphor of beautiful brutality, one that Hayworth faced repeatedly across her screen career. For, as film scholar Adrienne McLean noted, the actress "had six film singing voices over the course of about fifteen years, and few reviewers . . . ever remarked on the differences among them."[6] What is this if not a brutal message to Hayworth: that no one is really listening to you, that your voice is always secondary to your beautiful body, that no one cares if your voice changes so long as your body remains recognizably similar. Even six decades later, Fleisch did not appear to be aware that Hayworth's voice was subject to extreme manipulation in Gilda and other films. Yet a cursory Google search would have

Figure 1.1. Screenshot of 01:08 YouTube video showing Rita Hayworth in *Gilda* (1946), crediting dubbing singer Anita Ellis. Posted by "Golden Hollywood Fan," "Rita Hayworth (Voice of Anita Ellis)—Put the Blame on Mame (Gilda, 1946)," August 26, 2018.

thrown up that Anita Ellis dubbed the performance, and several YouTube clips include this detail in their titles or video descriptions (see figure 1.1)—for example, "Rita Hayworth (Voice of Anita Ellis)—Put the Blame on Mame (Gilda, 1946)."[7]

The digital afterlives of Ellis's and Hayworth's voices reveal how, within internet culture, historical voice-based information and misinformation can evolve and spread—allowing for dubbing histories once known to be forgotten, as in *Wound Footage*, and for dubbing histories previously hidden to come to light (including on YouTube). As this example suggests, such platforms are far from utopian, and yet they do have the potential to provide accurate information about women's voices, giving credit where it is due. In short, online platforms can provide new discursive spaces for women's voices.

TERMINABLE AND INTERMINABLE FILM VOICES

Writing in 1997 on the benefits and challenges of recovering the past in reception studies, Barbara Klinger described film history as "terminable and interminable" to capture the "historical excavation of meaning" as it relates to film. She was drawing on an influential new approach to literary studies that emerged in the early 1980s, wherein the object of literary analysis was redefined "from the text to the intertext—the network of discourses, social institutions, and historical conditions surrounding a work." Acknowledging the difficulty of researchers revealing "everything" that had been written about a film, Klinger nonetheless urged scholars of film reception to aim for "a cinematic version of *histoire totale*."[8] Over twenty years later, her approach has frequently been taken up. But while Klinger's object of study is the film itself, and its corresponding intertexts, I see much value in using a similar approach to examine film voices, particularly their digital afterlives, that is, to excavate meaning from the "network of discourses" and "historical conditions" that surround a particular voice.[9]

One of the key elements of Klinger's approach is that it allows for diachronic analysis: examining a film's reception in relation to a range of historical frames, and so acknowledging the ways in which the meaning of a film might develop and evolve over time. Though she was writing before the wide-scale development of digital technologies and platforms, Klinger acknowledged the growing importance of new technologies and fan cultures "in creating, maintaining and disseminating textual identities far removed from the 'official' readings offered by the production company in question."[10] As I aim to demonstrate, such technologies and unofficial accounts can be crucial to a diachronic understanding of the female screen voice. This understanding can reach beyond what the voice might have signified within the original film and during its initial release period to how it comes to be written about, discussed, remixed, and remediated in subsequent eras. And although the outputs of such unofficial processes may be disseminated via digital platforms, in many cases the voices with which these outputs are in dialogue were initially recorded and experienced through analog means and within the traditional hierarchies of the Hollywood studio system. The opening Hayworth/Ellis example is a case in point.

When Klinger concluded that "film history is both terminable and interminable," she was drawing on Freud's 1937 terminology to say that the analysis of a film (or, more specifically, its historical reception) could be ended when the analyst had "secured the best possible explanation."[11] At the same time, she stressed that in theory, reception-focused analysis of a particular film could extend indefinitely, not only because of the difficulty of detecting all the factors involved in the past, but also "because of the unpredictable concerns of the present and the future which continue to animate and otherwise affect the events of the past."[12] In extending Klinger's approach, I propose that analyses of screen voices are similarly terminable and interminable. Much as literary scholar Tony Bennett called for literary studies to examine not just the text but "everything which has been written about it, everything which has been collected on it, [and] which becomes attached to it," using the metaphor of how "shells on a rock by a seashore [form] a whole incrustation,"[13] I will consider the complex relationship between screen voices and the discourses that become attached to them over time, and particularly those emerging as a result of digital platforms, where fans increasingly share their own voice-focused remixes and theories. Here, the text-based voices of fan commentary can interject themselves into a familiar conversation, attempting to steer the reception of a particular vocal performance in a new direction.[14]

Put simply, the term *terminable screen voice* might be used to describe the vocal recording as it appears on the soundtrack in an official release of a given film. This voice is contained, at least initially, by the circumstances of its production and exhibition: the performer who delivered it, the technology used to record it, the editors and sound mixers who settled on the version to be released. This terminable screen voice may also be subject to terminable vocal analysis. This type of analysis examines it in relation to the contemporary discourse around the performer (such as comparing an accent the actor performed to others he or she had performed up until that point), as well as in relation to the broader contemporary discourse (perhaps using popular terminology of the time, such as "vocal fry" or "uptalk" in the early twenty-first century).[15] Yet such analysis is concerned only with the present or the recent past, meaning that it will inevitably become incomplete over time. As Klinger noted in relation to film history in general, the unpredictable concerns of the future "continue to animate and otherwise affect the events of the past."[16] Reapplied to the screen voice, the future continues to animate and affect the screen voices of the past—as when new information emerges regarding dubbing, or when a performer's voice changes over time, such that a performance can be contrasted with earlier ones in that performer's filmography (and vice versa). But trends in digital culture and platforms undoubtedly make the screen voice, and analysis thereof, more *interminable*. This is especially the case with partially hidden dubbing histories. Therefore, the case studies to follow largely focus on dubbing actresses (Nikki van der Zyl, Mercedes McCambridge) and actresses who were dubbed (Ursula Andress, Linda Blair, and Ann Sheridan).

In two cases I have used short timelines to highlight key moments for analysis related to the reception and subsequent resurrection or remediation of specific voices. Let us start with Katharine Hepburn's voice, bookended by fan descriptions separated by some seventy years on either side of the analog-digital divide. These represent a diverse range of discourses on her voice:

1939: A year after Hepburn's star turn in *Bringing Up Baby* (1938), Ralph Marcus wrote a fan poem titled "The Apocryphal Story of Katharine Hepburn's Metallic Voice" and sent it to the actress. The poem ended up at the Margaret Herrick Library, where I would find it in 2018.[17]

1991: Hepburn, aged eighty-four, published her autobiography *Me: Stories of My Life*, which included a chapter titled "Voice."[18]

2007: Writing on the television show *Gilmore Girls* (Warner Brothers, 2000–2007), critic Michael Ausiello described its fast-talking star Lauren Graham as "the closest thing Hollywood is ever likely to get to another Katharine Hepburn."[19]

2012: A review of Hepburn's autobiography, *Me: Stories of My Life*, was posted on e-commerce site Amazon saying, "For anyone planning in [*sic*] reading this, watch a [K]atharine Hepburn film before you start as I couldn't understand what she was on about till I imagined her saying it in her voice[,] as she obviously dictated it[,] then typed it up[,] as it is like she is speaking. Once you do that it is a great book and thoroughly entertaining."[20]

When treating Hepburn's screen voice as a temporally layered historical artifact, one sees how each of these timeline entries suggests different things about Hepburn's voice. First, it is a means of expression for the woman herself, and something she feels the need to write about in her autobiography. But it is also a cultural node, a singular point in a network at which different lines or meanings intersect or branch out in new directions. Here we have a voice-focused fan letter to Hepburn, Hepburn's own discussion of her voice, a contemporary comparison between Hepburn and another verbally dexterous actress, and an online review of Hepburn's autobiography that stresses the need to read it "in her voice." Hepburn's voice becomes a *point of comparison*: to precious metals in Ralph Marcus's poem, and as a measure of praise in relation to Lauren Graham's verbal sparring skills in *Gilmore Girls*—a twenty-first-century show that has nonetheless been positioned alongside the mid-twentieth-century screwball comedy tradition.[21] Hepburn's own discussion of her voice in her memoir raises the question of whether such an "authoritative" account should be weighted more heavily than other critical and fan-based commentaries. The 2012 Amazon review of Hepburn's book (posted by verified purchaser "PIPPA") is arguably the most incidental of these vocal branches, and yet it is perhaps also the most revealing with regard to the afterlives of a formerly screened voice. Confident in assuming that Hepburn "obviously dictated" her book, the reviewer highlighted the transformative power of bringing the memory of Hepburn's voice to a contemporary reading of her biography. By stressing the need to relisten to Hepburn's filmic voice before reading the book, "PIPPA" made readers' familiarity with recordings of Hepburn's voice a necessary precondition for enjoying the book: "*Once you do that* it is a great book and thoroughly entertaining" (emphasis added).[22] Hepburn may have died in 2003, but, as this Amazon review implies, for as long as we have her films to watch, we have the ability to play back her voice—including in our minds. Moreover, Hepburn's apparent dictation of her book—also my impression, prior to reading the Amazon review—further connects her to digital audio culture. Indeed, actresses, including Lauren Graham, Anna Kendrick, and Busy Philipps, are increasingly voicing audiobook versions of their own biographies to be distributed via the leading audiobook platform, Audible.

To what extent do these four timeline entries speak to each other? Perhaps surprisingly, Hepburn makes no reference to Marcus's evocative poem—or to a second one that he sent her in 1950, "In Praise of Katharine Hepburn's Voice"—in her memoir chapter.[23] And yet, as is clear from the detailed archival materials on Hepburn at the New York Public Library, where other Hepburn files are kept, she was moved to quickly respond to Marcus's 1950 letter accompanying the poem.[24] Instead, in Hepburn's opening reflections on her voice in the memoir, she explains the deep hurt and disappointment that can come from never receiving the kind of compliment one wants to hear: "When I was a kid, I always hoped that someone would say, 'What beautiful eyes you have.' . . . But no one ever said it to me. Or: 'What a pretty voice.'"[25] Reading this chapter after discovering Marcus's poem, I was somewhat taken aback: Had Hepburn somehow never read the poem, one so filled with lyrical adoration (of the "alchemy" of her voice) that its praise surpassed what Hepburn had desired to hear—merely that she had a "pretty" voice? Or, perhaps she had read the poem, but, writing her memoirs decades later, had simply forgotten. Either way, comparing Hepburn's published commentary on her voice with archival materials confirms at least one point: the need to reexamine existing histories of women's voices in screen media, supplementing "official" discourse with those that might be less likely to come to the surface, but that nonetheless might signal how a given screen voice has been received at different points in time. Marcus's effusive fan poem destabilized Hepburn's account of her own voice—one infused with disappointment that it never received the compliments she would have liked. Digital platforms, including archives, can equally unsettle the context for interpreting a given voice, both in its own time and over the time that followed.

"COLLECTIVE INTELLIGENCE" AND THE DUBBED FEMALE VOICE

Interactive digital platforms can allow media consumers (and increasingly media producers) to pool their knowledge, according to Henry Jenkins and other scholars, thus allowing for "collective intelligence," a term coined by the French philosopher Pierre Lévy.[26] By pooling their knowledge and research, members of digital fan communities can collectively develop their understanding of a particular shared interest. Collective intelligence operates in relation to screen voices in a similar way, particularly in those instances where there are rumors of voice-based cover-ups—such as uncredited dubbing. Dubbing rumors related to the James Bond film franchise—especially speculation that a German voice actress dubbed many of the "Bond girls"—saw a digital resurgence in forums and YouTube clip "archives," for example. A detailed analysis of this discourse can reveal how such discursive digital spaces can lead to revisions in histories of the screen voice. Such discourse can be particularly valuable to the women whose voice work was written out of "official" versions, but it can equally reveal the inherent sexism of culture in relation to how actresses are expected to sound. Such an analysis also reveals the increasingly *interminable* nature of screen voices in the digital era, including what can be a recurring cycle of voice-based criticism for the women whose voices were dubbed, especially when reasons for their dubbing are found or imagined.

Starting in July 2009, groups within the two largest James Bond fan communities spent some four years speculating on the franchise's largely hidden history of female performers being dubbed by a single woman: Nikki van der Zyl. While the inquiries appear to have started on the Commander Bond forum, it was on the MI6 Community website that the majority of the "intelligence" has been gathered. Supporting vocal "evidence" was cited from YouTube (where hosted videos allow for vocal comparisons of the voices in question), as well as from van der Zyl's own website. Van der Zyl, who was by then an elderly woman, gathered her own evidence in the run-up to her 2011 publication of a tell-all memoir, *For Your Ears Only* (she died in March 2021).[27] In a July 2009 thread with the subject line "Why were they dubbed?," an initial poster posed a number of questions related to why it would be necessary for van der Zyl to dub actresses such as Eunice Gayson and Shirley Eaton (for whom English was their first language), as well as inquiring about whether this was a common practice in film productions of the time.[28] Within an hour, the questions had been met with a range of revealing responses, including disbelief ("Shirley Eaton and Eunice Gayson were dubbed???") and harsh speculation ("Perhaps their voices were just so god-awful it would negate any physical charm?"). Significantly, members of these communities quickly encouraged (and facilitated) consultation with related materials online, particularly from YouTube: "I think Sylvia (Eunice) was dubbed alright. Just watched an original trailer for Dr No on YT [YouTube] and the clip from Bond's apartment (links to both shortly). Though similar in places, the voices are obviously different, and when she says 'I decided to accept your invitation' it sounds very much like the voice of Honeychile [sic]."[29]

The post included two hyperlinks, one to the *Dr. No* trailer and the other to the final scene on YouTube. The forum member provided further directions for viewing these videos (about skipping ahead to 3 minutes and 40 seconds, in the latter, "to compare it to the audio from the trailer"), along with a warning that the audio was a bit poor, and so listeners should turn up their speakers.[30] As such, the poster encouraged others on the fan forum not just to share their listening experiences, but also to listen in an efficient and optimal way (skipping to the right timecode, turning up their speakers). Compare this post to a hypothetical inquiry into the same topic in the predigital age: if a newspaper had reported on van der Zyl as a potential dubbing voice in the Bond films, fans would have had to congregate in person even to discuss it; or they might have shared their insights in letters to fan magazines. They would have had little or no access to extras, or to rare trailers. And even if one person turned up such materials, it would have been difficult to share them with other fans, dispersed as they would have been around the globe, perhaps in all the locations where the Bond films had been screened. It would have been much more difficult to compare the voices and to seek second and third opinions on them.

The practice of hyperlinking to YouTube videos and issuing related warnings and tips would continue on the MI6 Community, where three threads on van der Zyl and the dubbing claims were initiated between March 2011 and February 2013. Some commenters became suspicious that the forum's moderators were tampering with the threads and closing them in an effort to hush up the increasingly public van der Zyl "scandal." One thread title referred to her as a "Voice Dubber Extraordinaire" and began with a list of the films, characters, and actresses that she said she had dubbed.[31] Most of the members posting on this thread, which extended to eight pages, appeared to accept the claims and offered praise for her voice and legacy to the series. Members compared van der Zyl to other dubbing artists or "overlooked" actors, such as the Romanian dubbing actor Margareta Nistor, or even the contemporary motion capture actor Andy Serkis.[32] Some said the dubbing revelations had led them to reflect deeply on the Bond franchise. One person listed all the Bond girls they had recently learned van der Zyl had dubbed before positioning her voice as one of several defining characteristics of the early Bond series: "There are memorable characteristics of the early films: John Barry music cues, Ted Moore's cinematography, Peter Hunts [sic] editing . . . little touches that feel so familiar. Nikki's voice was one of those little familiar touches; one of those wonderful unique pieces of the early Bond films."[33]

These comments, including the comparison to the credited male contributions to the Bond music, cinematography, and editing, suggest a peculiar act of memory revision. How can this fan attach such familiarity and uniqueness to van der Zyl's voice while admitting they were unaware of her dubbing contributions (and the sameness of the voices of many women in these Bond films) until recently? Might these comments suggest that the fan rewatched some of these films with "fresh ears," paying more attention to how the various Bond girls *sounded* as opposed to how they looked? And, if so, would this suggest that van der Zyl had been successful in her quest to use her website and book to gain the voice credits that she previously had to forgo? It is such questions, and related dynamics, that warrant examining these informal channels. Fan comments can be unofficial surveys of audience response.

Verified details about van der Zyl's voice work have been slow to materialize. This is particularly the case in relation to the ten Bond films—from *Dr. No* in 1962 until *Moonraker* in 1979—that she claimed to have dubbed. (Generally she claimed not only to have dubbed the main "Bond girls," but also to have provided the voices for numerous other female characters within the same films as well).[34] Born in Berlin in 1935, van der Zyl's English accent was due to her family's moving to London when she was just four. Van der Zyl began acting as a teenager and trained at the prestigious Royal Academy of Dramatic Art. Her voice work was largely on British films and included revoicing various female characters in a number of Hammer horror films, including Ursula Andress in *She* (1964) and Raquel Welch in *One Million Years B.C.* (1965). According to Chris Fellner, an authority on the Hammer films, she never received an on-screen credit or residuals for any of her dubbing work.[35] And though major organizations, such as the British

Film Institute, have acknowledged some of van der Zyl's dubbing work (in this case, in a profile of her on its website), van der Zyl herself said the BFI credit list was incomplete.[36] It is the more contested credits—generally for Bond films—that give the discourse around van der Zyl on fan forums and YouTube added significance.

Much of the remainder of the "Voice Dubber Extraordinaire" discussion from the MI6 boards focused on why the thread appeared to be somewhat hidden on the forum, since it did not rise to the top of the section of the site as it should have when someone posted a new comment. Various members thought the moderators had intentionally changed the settings, potentially as a result of pressure from Eon Productions, producers of the Bond franchise. This reasoning was tied to news that was shared in another thread on the forum (and in some British and US tabloids) that, in September 2012, van der Zyl was uninvited to fiftieth-anniversary Bond celebrations.[37] By February 2013, various long-standing members of the MI6 Community had effectively decided that the forum moderators were trying to censor any discussion of van der Zyl: "The people running the site have put a fair bit of effort into making sure none of us talk about her."[38]

As this survey of fan discussions about van der Zyl shows, online forums provide robust spaces for debating the dubbing of women's voices (with convenient links outward to further "evidence," in the form of videos hosted on sites such as YouTube). But such spaces are still subject to regulation (or even censorship), as well as unintentional errors. Suspicions among members of the MI6 Community that the forum's moderators were meddling, or pointing out that the threads relating to van der Zyl were coincidentally the same ones that kept "glitching," were telling.[39] In an apt connection to Thorsten Fleisch's glitch work, the technology itself was being blamed for the further silencing, or at least filtering out, of van der Zyl's voice and vocal credits.

ON (NOT) HEARING "HONEY RYDER"

Having established the relative importance of online platforms as evidentiary archives for vocal mysteries, I wish to pay attention to the vocal "clues" provided on YouTube in relation to one Bond girl in particular, Ursula Andress. I will also look at another high-profile example of female dubbing—Mercedes McCambridge's dubbing of Linda Blair's demon voice in *The Exorcist* (1973). Online speculation regarding the dubbing of Bond girls is evident on YouTube, not just in the comments sections below Bond clips and trailers, but in the comments sections below other archival clips featuring the women in question as well. Andress's 1967 appearance as a "mystery guest" on the US game show *What's My Line?* (CBS, 1950–1967) gains particular relevance in this light.[40] The appearance came some five years after Andress's breakthrough film role as Honey Ryder in *Dr. No*, in the publicity period for her role as Vesper Lynd in *Casino Royale* (1967). On the long-running *What's My Line* show, celebrity panelists would question contestants with the aim of guessing their occupation. Each episode included a mystery guest whom the panelists would question while blindfolded with a view to determining their identity. Ultimately, such a setup depended on the mystery guest being visually recognizable to the audience while remaining vocally mysterious to the panel. This disjunction made Andress an apt guest. Her role in *Dr. No* made her a sex symbol, and yet her voice (dubbed by van der Zyl) remained largely unfamiliar. By this point, Andress had appeared in some nine other films since *Dr. No*, with van der Zyl also providing the voice for her characters in *She* (1965) and *The Blue Max* (1966).[41]

For the panelists, including burlesque star Gypsy Rose Lee and humorist Henry Morgan, the setup reversed the presentation of Andress's body in *Dr. No*: they had to focus only on what she was saying and how she said it, while the presentation of Honey Ryder had involved watching Andress on screen while hearing van der Zyl's voice. The interview, and subsequent reactions to it on YouTube, are revealing in light of this background information in three ways in particular: in terms of (1) the responses to Andress's voice, which was deemed "sexy" by both a blindfolded panelist and in the YouTube comments; (2) the way in which panelist questions related to Andress's visual body; and (3) the actress's self-consciousness in relation to her own voice in the segment. From the first question, asked by Morgan, the visual impact of Andress's unseen body is clear to the panelists: "I take it from the whistling that you are a lady?" Rather than answering with a yes, after a hesitant pause Andress responds with "Thank you" (in a soft and slightly husky tone). This leads to the host, John Charles Daly, to translate: "That's yes." When Bennett Cerf, another panelist, asks, "Are you a very famous movie star?," Andress responds with modesty ("Well, I don't know"), before laughing and biting her thumb while the audience loudly applauds. Again, Daly, as presenter, confirms that his guess is correct: "That has been answered by our audience. Yes." Andress had failed to provide a clear response for the second time. Briefly, the focus turns to determining Andress's origins: "Are you French?" "Are you from one of the Central European countries?" The panelists have picked up on an accent, but they cannot tell precisely what kind. And though the questioning switches back to Andress's appearance, her verbal and vocal responses continue to be intriguing. She is asked, "Are you a young dark girl?" followed by "Are you a young fair girl?" Andress responds to the latter with a drawn-out "Yes," then nervously (or playfully) sticks her tongue out of the side of her mouth. Gypsy Rose Lee, pondering her next question, comments, "She sounds terribly sexy, doesn't she?" before asking Andress, "Do you sing?" Again, Andress responds with humorous self-deprecation: "I wish . . ."

This response, and Andress's more general verbal meekness, may be grounded in her experiences of being dubbed, which may have left her with a certain insecurity about her voice. This is something audiences of the time were unaware of, but it potentially left Andress self-conscious about her "real" voice belying the truth, one the Bond producers may have asked her to conceal. As suggested by Lee's question about Andress's "terribly sexy" voice, and Morgan's off-screen confirmation that, even without seeing Andress, "I'm in love already," there is nothing inherently wrong with how Andress sounds. Yet she appears to have internalized former critiques, leading her to speak with hesitation despite appearing to understand all the questions, and to shyly bite her thumb as though afraid her real voice is not fit for a game that depends entirely upon what she says and how she sounds. Put differently, the segment's very premise would seem designed to work against Andress's persona of a classically beautiful sex symbol. It puts her before panelists who are physically prevented (through blindfolds) from perceiving Andress's most recognizable and "valuable" qualities. Instead, they must experience her only through the verbal-vocal expression that others have previously deemed substandard. It is no wonder she seems nervous.

Viewing this clip on YouTube from a contemporary perspective, we see that the question that allows the panelists to identify Andress is one that ties her fame at this time solely to her appearance: "Do you have one of the most magnificent chassis in the history of the female race?" As before, the audience erupts in approval, while Andress laughs but remains silent. Indeed, Cerf's use of the term "chassis," defined as "the framework of an artificial object," often a car, is itself reflective of the pure objectification of Andress's body in the Bond films, a process that included removing her voice as though it were an easily replaced carburetor. As in the *Wound Footage* description of Hayworth's voice (actually Ellis's voice), as sounding like it's been "filtered through a car engine," the metaphor unintentionally captures the subordination of female performers' bodies to a machine logic.

The clip of Andress on *What's My Line?* was posted on YouTube in 2009, and it continues to generate comments a decade later. The vast majority of the more than one hundred comments have been posted by users with male-identifying names. Virtually all of the comments are in praise of Andress, and they are somewhat predictable in the attention they pay to dissecting

Andress's appearance in the clip or in the Bond films. Andress's voice is also subject to attention, both in terms of general praise ("What a sexy voice") and in terms of people weighing in on the dubbing of her voice in the Bond films: "Ursula Andress [sic] real voice sounds fine. She didn't need to be dub [sic] in 'Dr. No.'"[42] Though this comment was "liked" by several other users, one commenter attempted to clarify that Andress was dubbed "not because of her voice [so] much as because of her accent."[43] Taken together, the comments signaled how information (and potentially misinformation) about the dubbing of the Bond girls remained of sustained interest to fans of the series, as well as of the related actresses. Moving beyond the specialized Bond forums previously discussed, this interest extended to YouTube, the dominant video-sharing site on the internet. The comments also signaled a retroactive desire for different vocal practices: the idea that Andress didn't *need* to be dubbed. Moreover, they showed fans' ability to simultaneously accept and reject actresses whose voices had been dubbed. *What's My Line?* featured Andress's *real* voice, and the commenters accepted that, but they previously also accepted Andress's dubbed voice—implied here to be a *fake* or *unreal* voice. The secondary comment, which attempted to separate Andress's voice *proper* from her accent, is also indicative of the enduring rumors and opacity regarding the reasons for dubbing many of the Bond girls. Even if one could separate Andress's raw vocal properties out from her ingrained Swiss accent, would this have resulted in her being allowed to appear on the Bond soundtracks? It seems unlikely, given that the Bond producers appear to have used van der Zyl to dub even a number of English-born actresses.

The fan discourse around dubbing on YouTube and the Bond forums confirms that such platforms are facilitating "collective intelligence" of the kind Jenkins identified as a benefit of interactive digital culture. To better appreciate how digital platforms have changed the dynamics of withheld dubbing histories, in particular, we now turn to a less contested example, both from the perspective of the 1970s and from the perspective of its related treatment on YouTube: that of Mercedes McCambridge's dubbing of Linda Blair in *The Exorcist* (1973).[44] On YouTube, both of their vocal performances remain subject to both digital manipulation and mass commentary. By the time of *The Exorcist*'s production, McCambridge was a well-respected actress, mostly in radio plays. She had won an Academy Award for Best Supporting Actress in 1949 for her role in *All the King's Men*. Largely owing to her expressive voice work on the radio, director William Friedkin recruited her to provide the voice of the demon-possessed girl, Regan, played principally by Blair. Though Friedkin would later describe McCambridge's vocal methods for the demon in detail—"She was chain-smoking, swallowing raw eggs, getting me to tie her to a chair—all these painful things just to produce the sound of that demon in torment"—her work initially went uncredited.[45]

Unlike van der Zyl, McCambridge mobilized quickly to have her role in the film officially acknowledged by, in the words of writer and actor Ron Lackmann, campaigning to "obtain the recognition she felt her contribution to the film most certainly deserved." Though it would be much later when McCambridge heard from sources at Warner Brothers that Friedkin did not want anything to detract from Blair's performance—particularly since he had an Academy Award in mind—McCambridge's campaign achieved most of its desired effect.[46] Her name was added on later prints of the film, albeit without the specific credit she desired, to be listed as "the voice of the demon." As Jay Beck observed, McCambridge's battle to receive credit for her contribution was a significant moment in film history because it exposed an assumption prevalent in 1970s Hollywood: that the dubbed voice "was somehow an added 'effect,'" and not the "real voice."[47]

What set McCambridge apart from van der Zyl was that McCambridge insisted that she had been promised a credit from the outset, a detail that provided her with clearer grounds for action (she sued Warner Brothers and requested arbitration by the Screen Actors Guild). Unlike van der Zyl, McCambridge had a high-profile award to her name as well as a high-profile friend and collaborator, in the form of the filmmaker and actor Orson Welles. According to Lackmann, Welles insisted that McCambridge benefited more from the publicity around her fight for credit than she would have from being credited in the first place.[48] McCambridge's campaign led to extensive coverage of her vocal contribution to *The Exorcist*, beginning in the aftermath of the film's release and continuing until her death in 2004, when a number of high-profile obituaries, including those of international newspapers, made this their focal point:

"Spirited McCambridge Had Big Voice" (*Variety*, March 22–28, 2004)[49]

"McCambridge, 85, Had Wickedly Good Voice" (*USA Today*, March 18, 2004)[50]

"Mercedes McCambridge: Big-Screen Actor Whose Tough Personality—and Voice—Matched Her Roles" (*Guardian*, March 19, 2004)[51]

In McCambridge's narrative we can see a broader history, one of how dubbing actresses have to be vocally forceful—*behind* the scenes as well as *off screen*—in order for their presence to be felt, or at least credited. But van der Zyl came before McCambridge's high-profile contestation of her right to receive a credit. As Beck noted, even in the 1970s Friedkin felt he could rightfully claim proprietorship of McCambridge's vocal performance as just another sound effect added and altered in postproduction.[52] Because van der Zyl's work dubbing the Bond girls preceded this significant moment, it is unsurprising that she did not contest her lack of credits, legally or otherwise, at the time. Decades later, however, the internet provides ways for such actresses to receive (retroactive) credit. Digital platforms are well-suited to making formerly behind-the-scenes contributions much more public, partly as a result of the chatter produced by fans' own text-based voices. If we look beyond the often awkward phrasing, the typos and grammatical errors, we can see in such fan comments a fundamental urge to revisit the production and technological contexts for given screen voices.

THE EXORCIST'S "RAW AUDIO" ON YOUTUBE

As we have seen, the discourse around McCambridge's *Exorcist* dubbing work was prominent in the 1970s as a result of her campaign to receive credit. And, perhaps not surprisingly, it has left enduring digital traces, including on YouTube. Two YouTube videos, in particular (though one of them is effectively only audio), help to show how the official (if delayed) crediting of McCambridge's work has influenced the circulation of dubbing actors' voices. The more recent and audio-driven of the two is a fourteen-minute-long recording of McCambridge's "Raw Audio Tracks," posted in December 2018, which as of this writing had almost twenty thousand "views" (figure 1.2).[53]

The video begins with what sounds like Friedkin's voice introducing the subject matter: "Here are some examples of how Mercedes McCambridge dubbed the demon voice into Linda Blair's original voice tracks." McCambridge's contribution is thus made explicit from the outset. Her name also appears prominently on the video's holding image, sitting above the familiar type of the film title in red. Below the title, the words "RAW AUDIO" appear, signaling that the content is authentic. As with the Andress YouTube video, the comments below the video from viewers can be as revealing as the content itself. In response to a question about the origins of the recording, the original poster of the video, "XSpawn13," explains that the audio track was included in the twenty-fifth-anniversary DVD release of *The Exorcist*.[54] The very presence of McCambridge's original audio on the official anniversary DVD shows a revised strategy on the part of the production company to embrace her voice work on the film, or at least to allow fans to embrace it.

Figure 1.2. Screenshot of YouTube video of Mercedes McCambridge's original audio recordings for her dubbing work in *The Exorcist* (1973). Posted by "XSpawn13," "The Exorcist—Mercedes McCambridge Raw Audio Tracks," December 14, 2018.

By the time of the DVD's release, it had been decided that fourteen minutes' worth of comparisons would be included to lay bare the process. It was another twenty years before these tracks would appear as an independent entity on YouTube, however, where McCambridge's voice work would not be presented as one of many varied "extras," but as a primary focus.

Considering this recording in relation to van der Zyl, one begins to wonder whether such "raw audio" might also exist for her, files that could answer questions and remove ambiguity about which Bond girls were dubbed. Assuming such files do exist, then the specifics of McCambridge's quick fight for recognition lend an unfortunate pathos to van der Zyl's case. How frustrating it must have been for van der Zyl to *know* such before-and-after files existed, but that she would likely never have access to them. And how frustrating that her attempts to create a website to compile lists and proof, decades later, would result in gaslighting from some Bond fans, precisely because the conditions of van der Zyl's work left her without access to the same kinds of concrete "proof" that McCambridge had. Van der Zyl could not benefit from the same access simply on account of the very different circumstances of her employment status when she did the work.

The second video of note was posted on YouTube eight years earlier, in 2010, and it includes increased creative intervention on the part of the maker, the kind often associated with the remix properties of digital fan videos. The maker describes the video, which is less than three minutes long, as an edit of the scenes with the demon voice. McCambridge's vocals are played at a slight delay, so that Blair's own voice can also be heard. Though the basic premise of the video is the same as the longer 2018 "Raw Audio" file, it bears the marks of its unofficial nature, particularly in the low quality of the video footage. The video also bears the marks of its maker's formal decisions (to play McCambridge's vocal at a slight delay to Blair's vocal, and at a higher volume, for example), decisions that reveal the video's potential as a new site of unofficial critical discourse. According to the maker, the decision not to overlap the voice was a subjectively qualitative one: "i [sic] thought it sounded better."[55] But "better" in what sense? If the aim of the video is a comparison of Blair's and McCambridge's voices, then the lag is certainly better. One can at least hear parts of Blair's original vocal performance before McCambridge's version is added in, after which she effectively drowns Blair out (though the phrasing means that Blair can still be heard at some points). Unlike the 2018 "Raw Audio" file, this video also features footage from the film, and it is helpful to see the scene while hearing it, although the video quality is compressed and poor. The comments viewers have posted below the video suggest how much McCambridge's voice helped to create the overall impression of the character as possessed. This video allows fans of *The Exorcist* to experience Linda Blair's cohesive performance (her physical presence, including her voice) and to compare that with the Blair-McCambridge hybrid, something that the "Raw Audio" version and the DVD extras cannot offer. The comments from YouTube viewers are predictably diverse, yet there is a consensus that, while Linda Blair's performance was great *in general*, McCambridge's voice was ultimately necessary. In this way, the unofficial video, remixed and offered up for scrutiny, effectively becomes another piece of concrete evidence in favor of McCambridge having made a valuable contribution through voice work. Moreover, the unquestionable differences between the two performers' bodies sets the Blair-McCambridge combination apart from that of van der Zyl and the Bond girls. Even in the comments, Blair's young age (thirteen at the time of filming) is used as justification for why she could not sound like McCambridge ("a seasoned actress in her 50s"). Their different ages thus allow McCambridge to be praised without slighting Blair's performance—as though she could have voiced the demon, if only she had been forty years older. Like the Andress *What's Your Line?* clip, both of the fan-made YouTube videos on McCambridge have discursive value. They become important sites of critical debate into what Tessa Dwyer has termed "to-be-dubbed-ness."[56]

DEBATING "TO-BE-DUBBED-NESS"

Dwyer developed the concept of "to-be-dubbed-ness" as part of an argument that post-synchronized revoicing can impact all stages of filmmaking and film reception. Invoking the language of Laura Mulvey's "to-be-looked-ness,"[57] Dwyer's concept engages with how active/passive dichotomies inflect revoicing, and in particular, with how postproduction operations of translation are regularly dismissed as inconsequential to filmmaking and meaning. As she explained, the concept of to-be-dubbed-ness encourages "a consideration of the wider cultural politics of dubbing—how issues of gender, for instance, can inform dubbing decisions and its reception." Dwyer focused on the very different dubbing setups for two Louise Brooks films, *The Canary Murder Case* (1929) and *Prix de Beauté* (1930). What is particularly notable about the dubbing in *The Canary Murder Case* is that Brooks instigated it herself by refusing to lend her voice to the sound version of the film. In doing so, she signed a release with Paramount to give away her rights (likely related to royalties) to this and all her other Paramount films. Significant to my diachronic approach to the female screen voice is how Dwyer mined the reception of Brooks's muteness, both at the time of these films and much more recently. It is notable as well how she chose to include—but without privileging—Brooks's own account of the dubbing in her memoir *Lulu in Hollywood*, published some fifty years after the film's release.[58]

As with the other dubbing scandals considered in this chapter, discerning the precise "truth" of what happened with Brooks—and why—is nearly impossible. Like me, Dwyer was concerned instead with how and why such discourse circulated and changed over time. She identified what might be seen as a broader trend in historical analysis: to deem the specifics of dubbing less worthy (or less accessible) of study than other details of a performance or production. Scholarly treatments of dubbing, and particularly the reception of dubbing practices among audiences, are relatively uncommon.[59] This absence increases the value of digital forums as samples of responses to such practices. Indeed, while Dwyer's study addressed this academic oversight, nearly a decade before she published her study the topic of Brooks's dubbing was already being discussed on YouTube. For example, in a video entitled "Louise Brooks in a Talkie," the comments point to the enduring novelty of hearing the silent star speak.[60] The fan comments include praise for her voice and queries as to why she was dubbed, along with corrections noting that Brooks *wanted* to be dubbed in certain roles. The description for the video also explains that, since Brooks only had a small part, the video provides "a couple of scenes spliced together." As with the Andress YouTube discourse, the video and comments on Brooks thus reflect a desire to hear more of Brooks, but also acknowledge complicating factors that may have prevented this from happening. Such videos, including those of Andress, Brooks, Ellis, and McCambridge, might therefore be seen as a niche genre within YouTube's substantial historical film community: a group of female performers—separated by decades and continents—united by their very to-be-dubbed-ness.

Brooks suggested in her memoir that *The Canary Murder Case* was originally intended to be a silent film. But, as Dwyer noted, Paramount's advertising campaign suggests it was always intended as a "double production," released in both silent and sound versions.[61] The discrepancy thus recalls my earlier discussion of Katharine Hepburn's memoir, in her chapter on her own voice, which excluded mention of Marcus's fan poems. In both cases, the academic-archival approach to the voice appears to provide a fuller and potentially more accurate picture of the voice-related context than the woman in question could convey through her recollections. Brooks's and Hepburn's faulty memories may justify a certain hesitancy about accepting van der Zyl's account of her voice work as completely accurate. Yet the very different statuses of these women—particularly van der Zyl's visual absence in all of her screen performances—justifies paying close attention to how she and her fans have attempted to use digital platforms to provide proof of her contributions to the Bond series.

MATERIALIZING VISUAL ABSENCE BUT VOCAL PRESENCE

It was only in 2011, decades after her work on the Bond films, that van der Zyl published a tell-all memoir, *For Your Ears Only*.[62] The title of her book, a wry twist on the 1981 film *For Your Eyes Only*, signals how she was positioned throughout her career: van der Zyl never appeared on screen or in publicity materials. She was thus both present and absent in these films, an ontological novelty, as reflected in media coverage of her around the time of the book's release—the *Independent* described her as "the Bond girl you've never seen."[63] As already noted in relation to McCambridge, dubbing actresses generally have had to be vocally forceful—both behind the scenes and *off screen*—for their presence to be felt, or at least for their work to be credited. There is, in other words, a very different dynamic at play for dubbing artists as compared to other actresses' voices in cinema, as examined by the likes of scholars such as Kaja Silverman and Amy Lawrence.[64] Coming in the aftermath of Mulvey's concept of the "male gaze," theories on women's voices in film have generally stressed how to be seen but not heard is disempowering, or, in relation to voice-over narration, to be heard and eventually seen could be disempowering—because roles with entirely disembodied, authoritative voice-of-God narrators were typically male.[65] But what of the alternative paradigm of the dubbing actress? To be heard but never seen (in the film itself, in the credits, or in the promotional campaign) is arguably more detrimental, certainly to the woman in question, if not to the abstracted theorization of what this might mean for women in an audiovisual medium more generally.

Understanding how the internet can help remedy the erasure of female dubbing actresses, an issue so central to van der Zyl, requires broader consideration of how film and media studies materialize absence. This very question was the focus of a 2018 issue of the film history journal *Screening the Past*, where editors Saige Walton and Nadine Boljkovac noted how, "just because you cannot *see* something (a heartbeat, air, a supernatural entity, freedom)[,] that does not mean that it is not present, is not forthcoming or that it is not possible to imagine." Working from the position that there remains a supremacy of presence and visibility in contemporary film and media theory, Walton and Boljkovac aimed to address "the materiality of what exists beyond the frame or perhaps at the very limits of representation."[66] This invisible space is the de facto home of van der Zyl and other dubbing artists, who exist at the limit of representation, vocally present but visually and promotionally absent, offline at least. It is for this reason that online databases and platforms such as IMDb and YouTube can serve to fulfill a valuable function by reattributing vocal credits.

RETROACTIVE VOCAL CREDITS

The internet provided van der Zyl with the means to bring her hidden vocal history partially to light decades after the fact. Before van der Zyl published her book in 2011, her website (launched in 2007) began to detail her version of events. It later also included the book's foreword, by Norman Wanstall, the supervising sound editor on many early Bond films, who substantiated her claims.[67] Perhaps more significantly, van der Zyl's voice work has been entered into the records of IMDb. According to Amazon's internet tracking site Alexa.com, IMDb is in the top fifty websites for global internet traffic and engagement. It is the twenty-fifth most visited site in the United Kingdom and the twenty-sixth most visited in the United States.[68] I argue that the very visual nature of IMDb credits, which include both text and image, are one way to materialize van der Zyl's historical absence and to finally give body to her invisible presence. Van der Zyl's IMDb page chronicles her many uncredited performances. Furthermore, as a result of IMDb's hyperlinked database structure, she now also appears on the IMDb listings for each of the thirty-something films that did not list her in their credits but for which she (apparently) did voice work.

According to these detailed entries, van der Zyl's first *credited* dubbing work came in 1969 with the film *Battle of Britain* (Guy Hamilton).[69] Of her thirty-five listed credits, just one other entry officially provided a credit for her voice work at the time, and this was in a TV movie. Maybe this is why van der Zyl would give up her vocal acting in 1979, after some twenty-two years of invisible labor. After all, she was not only invisible literally on the screen, but also invisible in the sense of her name not even appearing in the credits. Though presumably she was paid for her dubbing work, the lack of credit prevented her from building up any cultural capital and thus a typical career. Van der Zyl left the film industry and trained as a barrister, eventually working as a political researcher in the UK House of Commons. Indeed, the research skills she gained through this later career potentially were the same skills that led her to reveal her earlier hidden voice work.

On IMDb, van der Zyl is finally visualized: her name and credits are accompanied by a glamorous black-and-white portrait, one that finally places her body on the screen. Indeed, while fans of Andress on YouTube can ask why they dubbed the actress (now that they can hear her voice), fans of van der Zyl may wonder why she was never cast as both the voice and the body of a Bond girl. Van der Zyl used her website to provide images of herself in this and subsequent periods, because there appear to be none in the public domain. Similarly, unlike with the Bond girls, there are no digital archive recordings of her on YouTube, materials where Bond fans could see and hear her at once. This is undoubtedly part of the problem when it comes to proving that it is her voice appearing to emit from the various Bond girls' bodies, a historical absence that van der Zyl attempted to fill later in life. There aren't archival videos of van der Zyl at work or promoting the film because no one deemed her worth filming (either because she wasn't deemed attractive enough, or because she wasn't credited, and therefore worthy of indirect promotional attention). Instead, Eon Productions seems to have gone to efforts to not have van der Zyl visually captured, all the while recording her voice again and again. The only videos of van der Zyl available online are much more recent owing to her own efforts to tell her story. Notably, both such videos are fan produced, starting with the forty-seventh episode of the popular *James Bond Radio* podcast series.[70] Van der Zyl is the subject of a 2015 episode, lasting over an hour, that includes a twenty-two-minute interview between her and the host that ends with a plug for van der Zyl's book. The only other video of van der Zyl that I could find was one that was on IMDb's video player, a clip from the German-made fan documentary *A Bond for Life: How James Bond Changed My Life* (2016).[71] In both videos, van der Zyl discusses her voice work for the Bond series; perhaps more significantly, she is finally recorded speaking on camera. It was thus a combination of van der Zyl's own website and twenty-first-century digital fan culture that would finally put her back in the picture.

The IMDb credits materialize van der Zyl's labor through a combination of text and image. YouTube videos that declare the labor of the dubbing artist in their titles are similarly valuable. In this regard, we can return to the Hayworth example that opened the chapter. The YouTube user who posted the *Gilda* video with the title "Rita Hayworth (Voice of Anita Ellis)—Put the Blame on Mame (Gilda, 1946)" included information that Thorsten Fleisch's artist statement (crediting Hayworth) ignored. The user has posted numerous other videos in the same format, listing the visible performer and the vocal performer in the video titles: for example, "Adele Jergens (Voice of Virginia Rees)—I'm So Crazy for You," and "Donald O'Connor and Vera-Ellen (Voice of Carole Richards)—It's a Lovely Day Today."[72] The very presence of these videos serves as a correction of facts. They place the actual vocal credits on a popular forum, YouTube, listing dubbing singers such as Virginia Rees and Carole Richards who earlier went uncredited, and whose involvement tends to be detailed only in relatively inaccessible academic books.

For example, the truth about Adele Jergens's dubbed voice—in *Ladies of the Chorus* (1948) and other films—was discussed in a chapter by Laura Wagner in a 2004 edited collection: "Despite later reports from studio bios and other articles devoted to her, Adele never studied singing in her youth; she always utilized a voice double when she was called on to sing in movies." Wagner's chapter credits Virginia Rees's dubbing of "I'm So Crazy for You," in *Ladies of the Chorus*, but in a much less obvious way than the subsequent YouTube title does.[73] Discussions of Rees's voice work, like discussions of van der Zyl's and Ellis's work in scholarly research, is generally confined to footnote entries in studies of the stars they dubbed.[74] On YouTube or IMDb, they are finally given double billing. In the YouTube videos and in IMDb credits, the women's names are presented side by side in a way that they never were in the original credits. In some cases, the two women, the actress who played a role on screen and the dubbing artist, who may never have met, or who may not even have been very aware of each other at the time the films were made, thus finally share credit for the role.

It may seem implausible that an on-screen actress would not know who dubbed her voice—or even that her voice had been dubbed. However, until

1965, Ann Sheridan was apparently unaware that her singing voice in *Shine on Harvest Moon* (1944) was dubbed by Lynn Martin. According to interviewer Ray Hagen, he informed Sheridan of this when profiling her for *Screen Facts* magazine. As Hagen explained in a subsequent interview, "She said, 'but I sang them.'"[75] No one had ever told Sheridan before that her voice had been dubbed, and she had never actually watched the film. This is not uncommon: in fact, many actors do not watch their own performances, because of a tendency for self-criticism. But when it comes to the digital after-lives of a twentieth-century female voice, Sheridan is a particularly complex example. Her voice, the same one marked with to-be-dubbed-ness by the producers of *Shine on Harvest Moon*, has more recently been sold online in the form of formerly private recordings. The internet has thus facilitated the "on-demand" selling of famous voices, with this niche market signaling an enduring interest in accessing the voices of movie stars such as Ann Sheridan even without commensurate footage of her body.[76] The Sheridan example allows us to consider what changes when recordings are available for sale online, and so to examine a different way that screen voices can relate to the materiality of absence. Online marketplaces such as eBay, and even fan sites, can treat vocal recordings as commodities: something to be sold to fans or even artists. These practices might serve as something of a warning about how digital platforms and technologies can be used to exact control over women's voices, or at least recordings of them.

AN ONLINE MARKET FOR VOICES

Sheridan died in 1967 at the age of just fifty-one, having appeared in almost one hundred film and television roles. There are various ways to hear *and see* Sheridan's voice online, mostly accompanied by her on-screen performances. On YouTube, one can watch an eight-minute compilation of clips of Sheridan and Ronald Reagan in scenes together,[77] or the full video of *Nora Prentiss* (1947), with Spanish subtitles.[78] But beyond this, the owner of the fan site Remembering Ann Sheridan turned less accessible interview recordings with the actress into a money-making opportunity, thus signaling the perhaps unexpected afterlife of the female film voice, in its own right, beyond its appearance in official productions. In many ways, Remembering Ann Sheridan is a fairly typical early internet fan site: a basic webpage bringing together a range of information and media materials on the star, including scanned magazine articles and images. There are links to other sites with information on the actress, as well as a "guestbook" where visitors to the site can leave comments or thanks for the webmaster, a man referred to only as "John," whose surname is not listed anywhere on the site's "About" or "Contact" tabs.

For the anonymous John, Sheridan's appeal rests not just in her beauty but also in her delivery: "As well as being extremely appealing to the eye, Ann Sheridan also had a way with a line." Elsewhere on the site he expands on that thought: "The lines she delivered always hit their intended target."[79] Significantly, this webmaster's quest to celebrate Sheridan's life work with others extends to her voice. He procured magnetic tapes of four hours of interviews with Sheridan, which he then converted into MP3s for sale on the site for $19.95. He combines these exclusive private recordings (with interviewer Ray Hagen) with previously broadcast interviews with Sheridan on various talk shows. What is especially notable about this case is how the webmaster positions the recordings with Sheridan, as though he is selling not just a recording of her voice at a particular time, but the ability to be transported back to that time by virtue of the technological magic of digitization. In other words, he attempts to provide a retroactive mental image to compensate for the absence of corresponding visual footage:

> Wouldn't it have been great to have been a "fly on the wall" when Ray Hagen interviewed Ann Sheridan in Sardi's East restaurant in New York City in 1965?
> *Now you can be!*
> The original reel-to-reel tapes have been recently transferred to MP3 files!
> And now you can listen to Ray's historic interview with Ann Sheridan as if you're sitting at the next table![80]

While the webmaster goes on to provide further details about the recordings (their dates, lengths, expected time needed to download the files, and so on), what interests me is the selling technique. Presented in a large font, with careful spacing and use of italics, it reads as though it were an infomercial. Yet what it purports to offer is not just the opportunity to hear Sheridan and Hagen having lengthy conversations, but the promise of an intimate form of listening: it will be as if you're sitting at the next table. This practice of selling Sheridan's voice "on demand" takes advantage of a new tolerance for voices of interest to be perceived without images, or only with holding or mental images (as we saw with McCambridge's "Raw Audio" on YouTube). Yet the webmaster still attempts to find a material (if mental) image to compensate for the absence of Sheridan's physical body. Unlike the other examples explored in this chapter, which are all easily accessible via public domain platforms, this webmaster is hoping to profit from his ownership of recordings of Sheridan's voice and from his ability to master their conversion from magnetic tape to MP3.

Much as the webmaster of the Sheridan site works to provide a concrete mental image to accompany Sheridan's disembodied voice, the internet's expansive network of screen-based interfaces can also lead to complex visualizations of voices not belonging to actors and not ordinarily connected to a screen. These voices, such as that of artist Frida Kahlo, can nonetheless be received in relation to their closest cinematic counterparts— thus providing a final example of how the digital reception of female voices can rely on a transmedial logic that pulls in trends from a range of audio, visual, or audiovisual media.

SOUNDCLOUD KAHLO

1955: The pilot episode of Mexican radio show *El Bachiller* aired, including a segment where a woman read Frida Kahlo's essay "Portrait of Diego."[81]

2002: Salma Hayek starred in *Frida* (Julie Taymor), a biopic of the Mexican artist Frida Kahlo, performing the role mostly in English.

2019: Digital archivists at Mexico's National Sound Library (La Fonoteca Nacional) released the probable first vocal recording of Kahlo (on *El Bachiller*) via the SoundCloud profile of the Instituto Mexicano de la Radio. In the United States, National Public Radio (NPR) broadcasters introduced a report on the archival recording by playing a clip from the film *Frida*.

The 2019 discourse surrounding Kahlo's voice signaled the relevance of my analysis not just to film voices, but also to women's voices more generally, particularly when they enter into digital archives and become visualized and subject to mass debate. Although Kahlo was not an actor, when a recording of her voice was finally uncovered by archivists it was quickly filtered through the lens of Salma Hayek's preexisting film performance—a reverse fitting of the original as it compared to the imitation. In the United States, Audie Cornish, cohost of NPR's *All Things Considered*, introduced a segment on Kahlo's voice by describing her physical appearance in photos and self-portraits, asserting that, "until now, we were led to believe she sounded like this . . ."—at which point the show played a clip of Hayek as Kahlo, speaking in English.[82] After then playing a clip from the newly discovered and

El Bachiller/ The National Sound Library of Mexico

The Guardian

Seeing him naked, one thinks
immediately of a young frog,

Figure 1.3. Screenshot of Guardian News YouTube video with vocal spectrogram, "Is
This the Voice of Frida Kahlo?—Audio," June 13, 2019.

probable Kahlo recording, Cornish explained that one thing "we know for
sure" is that "it's not Hayek doing the reading." As a result of the digitization,
Hayek's vocal performance was suddenly up for new scrutiny: Did Hayek
sound like Kahlo in the film? Are there other Mexican actresses who would
have sounded more like Kahlo? Would the choice have been the same if the
casting director had known what Kahlo sounded like back in 2002? Hearing
the Mexican-born Hayek speaking English on the NPR clip also reinforced
how the film was predominantly in English, with only some Spanish—that
is, made primarily for Anglophone ears. This framing device again became
useful when the English-speaking media was tasked with covering the Spanish
recording of Kahlo's voice—provided without subtitles on the audio platform
SoundCloud, although the UK *Guardian* newspaper would quickly provide
a subtitled version on its YouTube channel (figure 1.3).[83]

While Kahlo's voice was initially uploaded as an audio file (an MP3),
it was simultaneously paired with visual images both on SoundCloud and
YouTube: on the former, a close-up black-and-white image was selected to
accompany the file (figure 1.4): in other words, an image is used to "confirm" that this is probably her, in the absence of any formal identification
on the recording.[84] The file also automatically generated a visualization of
the sound levels in the recording, so that Kahlo's vocal traces can be seen by
viewers, albeit abstractly, even before they click play. (On the *Guardian*'s
YouTube video, the visualization is enlarged and flickers across an image of

Figure 1.4. Screenshot of annotated SoundCloud file of (potentially) Frida Kahlo's voice, uploaded by the Instituto Mexicano de la Radio (IMER-NOTICIAS), June 2019.

Kahlo's face.) On SoundCloud, the horizontal bar of the visualization was quickly populated by tiny images representing commenters on the file. Their multilingual remarks ("doce voz!," "voz muy dulce," "sublime," "if it is her this is incredible") are now a part of the experience of Kahlo's digitized voice for whoever visits the page, much as comments on the YouTube videos with McCambridge, Andress, and Brooks have become part of their screen voices' new digital afterlives.

The ambiguity related to the speaker in the vocal recording—that the archivists are only *fairly sure* it is Kahlo—is itself a telling commentary on the relative historical weight attached to women's voices in the media. The woman in the clip is not named in the radio broadcast, beyond being identified as a female painter "who no longer exists."[85] There is, however, no doubt about the subject of the woman's speech: she is reciting an essay that Kahlo wrote about Diego Rivera, Kahlo's husband, in 1949. It is the ties between the woman's voice and *his* body—rather than her own—that have led the voice to be identified as that of Kahlo. As presented by the radio host, the speaking woman is not even granted her name. If it is Kahlo, who had recently died at the time of the broadcast, then this casual anonymity is disrespectful of her memory, or, at best, it is unprofessional practice. This significant detail aligns Kahlo with the unnamed dubbing artists—such as van der Zyl and McCambridge—whose names were equally excluded from public domain recordings of their voices. In fact, some of the comments on the SoundCloud recording opine that this is not Kahlo's voice at all, but that of an actress named Amparo Garrido.[86] Again, the very format of the digital platform encourages public debate, in this case over who this sounds like. In the absence of visual evidence, the voice credited to Kahlo might belong to any number of women. At the same time, now that Kahlo's name and image have been attached to the recording online, one can imagine that if Garrido, who is now over ninety years old, came forward to claim the voice, then the onus would be on her, as it is on dubbing artists, to provide substantial proof.

Having escaped scrutiny for so long, Kahlo's digitized voice was quickly subject to mass appraisal and critique. Many have concluded that it does not sound like what you would expect Kahlo's voice to sound like. The *New York Times* quoted the art critic Waldemar Januszczak's take on it: "I was expecting something slow and pained, dark and moody. Instead, she's as chirpy as a schoolgirl reading her mum a poem."[87] Kahlo thus becomes just the latest famous woman to have her voice dissected and deemed to be an unexpected or even unsatisfactory *match* for her image, both in terms of her public persona and her physical body. Januszczak's judgmental take on Kahlo's voice is also in keeping with a broader trend for online discourse around women's voices to be circulated—and at times controlled—by male internet users. As on YouTube and in the James Bond forums, debates around the relative merits of women's voices tend to be dominated by men, or at least internet users with male-identifying names. Recall that even van der Zyl's book included a foreword by Norman Wanstall, a supervising sound editor. While Wanstall's inclusion is fitting, it perhaps also anticipates backlash against the book by the Bond films' main male demographic.

VOCAL TOPOGRAPHIES

As this viral sensation of a vocal recording deemed to belong to Frida Kahlo has helped to reveal, users of the internet's expansive network of screen-based platforms can have an insatiable appetite for listening to, judging, and visualizing historical female voices, and not just those voices made famous via cinema. Film historian Thomas Elsaesser argued in 2019 that cinema had profoundly altered our understanding of what history is, partly owing to its "unresolvable tension between rewind and replay, between presence and absence." Exploring the new materialities of memory in relation to cinema in general, he acknowledged how such issues and boundaries had "only become more explicit, indeed self-evident, with digital imaging and 3D printing." Taking an approach grounded in media archaeology, Elsaesser drew on French historian Pierre Nora's idea of *lieux de mémoire* (sites of memory) in relation to cultural memory, citing how symbols of consumer society, including tag lines from cult movies, are "located in time, while also marking the passage of time"—and can thus "become the embodied form of a battle against forgetting," even in mediums of forgetting, such as popular culture.[88] Building on Nora's concept, Elsaesser introduced the term *historical topographies*—which, he said, "has in common with cultural memory the language of sedimentation and layering, of the past retrieved, recalled, recovered, and recollected, as the salvage of secrets, of lost opportunities, and of sunken treasures."[89] Similar to the way that literary scholar Tony Bennett invoked the metaphor of seashells encrusted on a rock to highlight the relevance of studying the discourses attached to a literary work (and which Barbara Klinger subsequently recommended in relation to historical reception studies),[90] Elsaesser compared film and photography to "barnacles, bogs and glaciers"—materials that allow us to experience history's imprint and its subsequent traces simultaneously. Referring to the "different tenses and temporal register of *visual media*," Elsaesser highlighted how such media had "affinities with the archaeological media of 'freezing' time, such as amber, peat, or ice."[91] Each of these mediums can freeze both time and the moments attached to that moment in time—thus building up to create a new formation, as in Bennett's metaphor of shells on a rock.

Much as I formerly suggested the value of developing Klinger's argument on film history as *interminable*, to address the idea of film voices as interminable, Elsaesser's ideas are useful for distilling how film voices are temporally layered, with the congregation of digital *traces* potentially as important to them as the original vocal recordings preserved far underneath. As the examples in this chapter have shown, digital traces related to the film voice are abundantly available—on internet databases, forums, and websites—in a way that earlier traces were not. To read Ralph Marcus's 1939 ode to Katharine Hepburn's voice, you need to visit the Margaret Herrick Library in Los Angeles; to read subsequent fan discourse on her voice, you need only go online. In this regard, one might extend Nora's term *lieux de mémoire*, or sites of memory, to include *websites* of memory. As already noted in relation to the YouTube videos where fans debate dubbing histories, such platforms become new sites of critical discourse as well as reflecting new knowledge—often revealed many years or decades later. On these platforms, it is then anonymous voices (of fans, with varying degrees of anonymity) that can change the direction of the discourse—namely, away from "official" histories and toward something more collective yet fragmented. On YouTube, IMDb, and fan forums, we can observe and analyze how vocal production histories and recordings are retrieved, recovered, recollected—just as Elsaesser described in relation to historical topographies. Original recordings, some released as DVD extras or uncovered by fans, become new evidence entangled in acts of vocal forgetting or revised remembering. Think here of the Bond fan who, upon learning of van der Zyl's revoicing of many Bond girls, now considers *this* voice (*these* voices) as a key element of the early Bond films. Elsaesser focuses on visual media and the traces that can attach to an image or footage over time, leading to a new formation. But as the Kahlo and other examples reveal, the very structure of digital media can lead to such formations evolving at an accelerated pace: an MP3 that is simultaneously visualized in multiple ways and rapidly annotated, each comment and image a new trace upon the recording, impacting how it is heard, viewed, and interpreted.

For Elsaesser, images in historical films and photography are "a lure and a ruse," in that they have "created and fashioned, fortified but also falsified memory and turned it into our history." Going on to note how they some-times "confer *reality of presence* to events and places which without the photographic record, might never have 'existed,'" Elsaesser asserted that "this precarious presence gives their preservation . . . a special, ethical charge."[92] To focus purely on *images* seems incomplete, however, and Elsaesser's insights are also relevant to vocal recordings. The ethical charge is arguably even greater here, given screen dubbing's combination of image and vocal recording, par-ticularly for the cultural memory of the individual dubbing artist. Because we have never seen the woman in question, and potentially do not even know her name, it becomes doubly hard to imagine her as the true origin of the voice, or to fathom how that particular voice never really existed with that particular body. We thus need critical spaces for the memories of selected film voices to be kept alive or revised: spaces where falsified memories can be revealed as such to some, if not all, who have succumbed to the "reality of presence"—of hearing Nikki van der Zyl, but seeing Ursula Andress, or any of the other Bond girls whom van der Zyl would seem to have voiced. The internet provides many such spaces, whether on niche fan forums or sites, on IMDb, or in the comments sections of YouTube, SoundCloud, and similar platforms.

At the same time, as indicated by Fleisch's glitch video, where he mislabeled Ellis's voice as that of Hayworth, there is also increased space for the original to be lost amid the layers. While such losses are likely to be genuine mistakes, one can equally imagine how the glitch video serves to underscore broader hidden histories in relation to women's voices. Indeed, as Adrienne McLean noted of Hayworth, it was well known at the time that Hayworth's voice was dubbed.[93] But what may have been well known *at the time* can become increasingly forgotten, particularly when—as in this case—the details of the dubbing are preserved only in an academic footnote. The voice we hear on Fleisch's *Wound Footage* is purposefully obscure—it is barely recognizable as a recording of *Gilda*'s "Put the Blame on Mame." And so, if the real purpose of choosing this particular vocal recording was to pick one connected to a recognizable female movie star, then Hayworth's name is of as much value as her voice, or rather, of Ellis's voice. In the twenty-first century, in particular, Ellis's name does not hold the same value in the collective cultural memory as Hayworth's, and so Ellis's vocal credit is discarded yet again. In this way, digital platforms allow for newly revised histories of female screen voices, revisions that depend on voice-based traces rising to the surface and being subject to online interpretation by cinephiles and fan communities.

THE (POST)HUMAN VOICE AND FEMINIZED MACHINES IN *ANOMALISA*, *THE CONGRESS*, AND *HER*

THE CONGRESS (ARI FOLMAN, 2013) CENTERS ON Robin Wright playing herself, an aging actress who sells her body to a production company so it can re-create a perfect digital replica of her to cast in perpetuity. In this sci-fi film set in the near future, Wright delivers nearly half of her dialogue in live-action mode, playing the human version of herself. The rest of the time, she voices a computer-animated version of herself, one that is fully aware that she has been turned into an animation in order to attend a futurist congress, which takes place in a now animated part of earth. After entering a hotel in this animated zone, Robin encounters a robot receptionist with a synthetic female-sounding voice—one that is contrasted with Robin's human voice, even though she, too, is now represented by a computer-animated character. The receptionist speaks with the unnatural intonation we have come to expect of speech-bots: largely monotone, and with ill-placed pauses. The exceptionally large robot is revealingly attired, and has oversized breasts and red lips, giving the impression of a mechanical blow-up sex doll (figure 2.1). She tells Wright that she is the sixth Robin Wright to check in that day; apparently, people in the animated zone can morph into anyone they wish. Speaking in an unnatural cadence, the robot adds, "I guess they didn't look as Robin-ish as you do." Wright seems unnerved by the fact that such a robotic and inexpressive figure can feel so qualified to make subjective judgments about her own personhood. But the scene provides a false sense of security in suggesting that vocal quality can help one distinguish humans from robots (particularly since both are in animated form). This false sense

Figure 2.1. Screenshot of the scene where the newly animated Robin Wright is greeted by a speech-bot-like receptionist in *The Congress* (2013). Produced by Pandora Filmproduktion.

of security applies to both Wright and the audience, who are simultaneously being initiated into this strange new world, where Wright's voice is the only sustained overlap with the previous live-action section of the film.

As the sequence proceeds, Wright's ontological status as still human, albeit currently posthuman (in animated form), continues to be tied to her voice and related physical processes. In her hotel room, she lights a cigarette, and we see and hear her exhale smoke. Wright's exhalation is communicative of her feelings—presumably she is smoking to relax herself—but it is also a reminder that despite the visual impression of her character (rendered using the computer animation software Harmony), she still has human organs and a respiratory system that allow her voice to sound the same.[1] By contrast, the sex-doll-styled receptionist has an overtly fake mouth and chest—visual markers of why she also sounds fake.

The Congress is one of several twenty-first-century films to use women's voices to reflect and rework the trend for artificial intelligence and androids to be coded as female, through their presentation of a female human voice amid a technological landscape. With a focus on *The Congress*, *Anomalisa*, and *Her*, I shall argue that women's voices (those of Robin Wright, Jennifer Jason Leigh, and Scarlett Johansson, respectively) are central anchoring devices to the dystopic presentation of technologically enabled diegetic worlds. In these films, the humanness of a voice adds complexity and ambiguity to posthuman female characters, whose engineering muddies the boundaries between mind and body as well as between human and machine. These characters can thus align with both theoretical imaginings of cyborgs and recent trends in transhumanism, whereby developments in science, engineering, and technology are used to develop posthumans, entities whose basic capacities far exceed those of traditional humans.[2]

Released within two years of each other, these three films are reflective of the expansion of voice technologies in the twenty-first century, along with commensurate fears for their (mis)use. In keeping with long-standing traditions for the sci-fi genre to reflect anxieties around the impact of science and technology on human identity, the films both mirror and anticipate changes to female characters' voices, as well as to the role of actresses in embodying technologically rendered characters. They do so by reorienting attention toward the irreplaceable qualities of the human voice and by intersecting with real-world uses of female-sounding voice technologies. In fact, the reasons why women's voices tend to be used for digital assistants can also be tied directly to film history. According to Tim Bajarin, a leading technology consultant, the malicious intent of HAL 9000 in *2001: A Space Odyssey* (Stanley Kubrick, 1968) is why a lot of tech companies have "stayed away from the male voice."[3] Other reasons why automated voices often sound female include the ties between virtual assistants and historically gendered roles: since women have traditionally worked as assistants, secretaries, domestic servants, telephone operators, and the like, it seems only "natural" that they would also voice their virtual successors.[4]

In the real world, this trend of giving female names and voices to devices using speech technologies (including speech-bots such as Apple's "Siri," Amazon's "Alexa," and Microsoft's "Cortana") is thought to reinforce broader cultural desires for women to be passive, agreeable, and easily dominated.[5] My approach is to reorient attention to the two-way flow between actual voice technologies and their representations in English-language cinema. This includes the tendency for a female-sounding voice to serve a male listener, and to speak, sing, or be silent on the man's demand. It involves as well the fetishization of the female voice, and often, a vocal double (a woman or feminized machine that sounds just like her). Even when the voice is presented diegetically in the film world as a synthetic one, the tendency is to use an actress's voice. In each case, the implicit requirement of the audience is that its members disavow the fundamental ruse: I know this character isn't human, yet I know that voice is.

Long before the digital age, cinema history revealed a sustained interest in presenting technologized female characters whose inception and appeal manifested in science fiction, film noir, and romance narratives and generic tropes. From Maria in *Metropolis* (Fritz Lang, 1927) through *The Stepford*

Wives (Bryan Forbes, 1975) and *Blade Runner* (Ridley Scott, 1982), such characters have reflected a legacy of artificial "women" in other mediums and myths dating all the way back to Pygmalion, the ancient Greek sculptor who fell in love with the ivory statue of a woman he had carved. Andrea Virginás has argued that the trend to construct female-presenting artificial intelligence (AI) and digital actors in films such as *S1m0ne* (Andrew Niccol, 2002) and *Ex Machina* (Alex Garland, 2014) is a "reloading" of questions of gendered ways of looking, with a focus on how the feminized digital characters (generally played by human women) remain subject to the "male gaze." Human male characters in these films tend to seek escape or spiritual redemption from digital or digitized feminine characters who "are ready to be inspected literally and figuratively by colleagues . . . whose male gaze is contrasted with the spectacle of the 'anatomical Venuses' they scrutinise." For Virginás, these films reveal how—despite the shift from analog to digital and "the apparently highly progressive medial re-encodings in a digital environment"—the depiction of digital female-presenting characters extends on earlier traditions for women to serve as spectacles for male characters and audiences.[6] But what role does the voice play in this gendered "reloading"?

Twentieth-century research into women's voices emphasized how they had to be tethered to the body—a concept used to explain the relative lack of disembodied female voice-over narrators in classical Hollywood, as mentioned in chapter 3. But in *Anomalisa, The Congress*, and *Her*, we see something that is different, and that seems tied to developments in technology: provided the voice remains, then the body can be replaced—by a 3D-printed puppet (in *Anomalisa*), by a scanned digital avatar (in *The Congress*), or by an operating system, where a body may not exist at all (in *Her*). As such, unlike in earlier cinema, where the woman's right to speak was generally linked to an audience's invitation to see her, the development of virtual screen bodies (through motion capture scanning and their mapping onto 3D puppets) can create a situation in which the female body can be readily replaced on screen even while the human female voice remains crucial. In other words, the female character's place on the soundtrack no longer corresponds to a right to be seen on screen. But being seen also translates into fully embodying a role for the actress. Taken to an extreme, this trend could be seen as leading to female performers effectively being "crowded off" the screen by their digital replacements, leaving only voice work. There are generic underpinnings to these filmic practices, with the conventions not only of sci-fi but also of the romance genre coming into play. As Jennifer Fleeger noted of the use of the expressive female voices in *Her* and *Ex Machina*, actresses' voices allow us to indulge in a sci-fi fantasy: that technological creations can love us back.[7]

My contention, then, is that films such as *Anomalisa*, *The Congress*, and *Her* provide a powerful convergence of science-fiction tropes with contemporary concerns around the actualities of scientific developments in synthetic voices and speech technologies.

THE CONGRESS

Adapted from Polish author Stanisław Lem's *The Futurological Congress*, *The Congress* combines live-action and computer animation to interrogate the dystopian possibilities of the AI body and voice as well as the value of the human performer's body.[8] Highly self-reflexive, it takes the perspective of Robin Wright as a well-known actor playing herself. Within the film world, work has dried up for this fictionalized version of Wright—as a result of both her age and her reputation as being difficult to work with. This, along with Wright's concerns about her sick son's medical treatments, leads her to accept the lucrative offer from a virtual entertainment company, Miramount, to buy her likeness and digitize her into a computer-animated version of herself. Wright signs a contract that means she can never act again. Her body is digitally scanned, and the studio begins to make films starring the computer-generated Robin Wright. Twenty years later, Robin's digital avatar has become the star of a popular science-fiction film franchise. With the initial contract about to expire, she travels to a Miramount conference, the Futurological Congress, with a view to renewing her contract. This congress takes place in an entirely animated world, and Robin has to take a compound that transforms her (and the film itself) into computer animation. But Robin's contract negotiations become fraught when it becomes clear that Miramount has developed an even more appropriative technology, which will allow anyone to transform themselves into Wright. She is torn and eventually speaks out against the congress, enraging the hosts. Over the course of the often mind-bending film, Robin is variously attacked by the hosts and protected by one of the former programmers of her digital avatar. Throughout this existential nightmare and literal out-of-body experience, she remains focused on getting back to the live-action world, to be with her son.

The Congress cleverly tackles fears around how motion capture and computer-generated imagery (CGI) increasingly shape the spaces in which actors work, leading to new kinds of hybrids between actors and technologies. Performances are increasingly subject to digital manipulation—as is the case, for instance, in films where preexisting recordings of deceased actors have been used to digitally reproduce them posthumously. *The Congress*'s

Figure 2.2. Screenshots of the animated Robin Wright experiencing the digital avatar version of herself speaking on screen, and touching her throat in response, from *The Congress* (2013), produced by Pandora Filmproduktion.

complex premise and various formats (live-action, computer animation, and live-action presenting itself as photo-realist CGI) are all anchored by Wright's voice, which provides a coherency to the different versions of her character. Wright's voice thus seems central for audiences, who might otherwise struggle to accept and follow the sudden shift from live action to computer animation. Diegetically, Wright's voice is also presented as central for the various characters whom the animated Wright meets at the congress: in a world where everyone has the power to shape-shift into Wright simply by drinking a potion, at several points people wait to hear the animated Wright speak in order to confirm that she is the "real" Robin Wright. While everyone in the animated zone has the means to transform themselves into Wright's body, they are unable to transform their voices into Wright's voice.

The CGI avatar of Wright does share her voice, however. The animated Wright's response to hearing what is recognizably her voice, emanating from what is recognizably her body, is experienced as an uncanny confrontation with the technologized voice for both the audience and Wright. In a key scene, Wright is confronted with the sight and sound of her digital avatar being interviewed on a hotel screen (figure 2.2). Notably, the voice of avatar Robin is initially presented in voice-off, as she answers a question about her role in the film franchise "Rebel Robot Robin." Focusing on the animated Wright as she listens to the interview, the sequence culminates in a crucial gesture when she raises her hand to her throat. The movement, a reflexive grasping for her voice box, signals Wright's clear unease at hearing her voice say something that she knows she did not actually say. Like her aforementioned exhalation of cigarette smoke, the moment also points to Wright's dual status as both human and animated, trapped between two ontological statuses, with her voice the only external form of expression to which she (and we) feel connected.

It is useful to examine *The Congress*'s treatment of the technologically enabled vocal doppelgänger in relation to Kim Novak's dual roles of Madeleine Elster and Judy Barton in *Vertigo* (Alfred Hitchcock, 1958). As in the Hitchcock film, in which Novak plays Madeleine as well as Judy (the Madeleine look-alike is later revealed to actually be Madeleine), the film's plot rests on a conceit: that the audience will, at least initially, consider the two characters as distinct, despite being embodied by the same performer. In *The Congress*, the conceit is even more complex, and involves a three-way separation between the human Robin Wright and her two technological doubles: animated Robin (still human) and digital avatar Robin (a synthetic reproduction). The moment when the animated Robin grasps at her throat upon hearing digital avatar Robin speaking in human Robin's voice can be compared to the moment in *Vertigo* when Judy completes her visual transformation into Madeleine. Despite agreeing to serve as a double, both women experience the encounter with their own double as highly disconcerting. In *Vertigo*, the shift from potential double to verified double is based entirely on the visual match and its confirmation by Scotty (James Stewart), the character who has motivated the transformation. For Scotty, as for Robin, the transformation is also experienced as uncanny. Yet *The Congress* attaches much of the uncanny effect to the voice. Animated Robin has already seen her digital avatar appearing in film trailers, and her reaction to that was minimal. Her response to seeing her body replicated on screen is thus presented as less disturbing, less traumatic, than hearing her voice emit from the avatar: of hearing her voice say things she has not said.

Threats to Wright's human voice as a marker of individual identity recur throughout, including a singing performance that is used to signal a play for power by Robin. Here, the animated Robin's dreamed performance of a song reveals her sustained will to perform, even twenty years after signing the Miramount contract that prevents her from engaging in any kind of public

performance. Presented as a dream turned nightmare, her somber performance of the first verse of Leonard Cohen's "If It Be Your Will" is violently
cut short by a group of men who berate her for breaking the rules of her
contract, while using guns to disperse the crowd watching her perform in a
darkened theater. The choice of this particular Cohen song is most notable
for the lyrical focus on the voice and silencing:

> If it be your will
> That I speak no more
> And my voice be still
> As it was before
> I will speak no more
> I shall abide until
> I am spoken for.

Discussions around the Cohen song tend to interpret it as a synagogue prayer,
positioning it as one of the Jewish Cohen's most overtly religious songs. Cohen
is presumably addressing God as the powerful figure for whom he would
"still" his voice by speaking no more. Within the context of *The Congress*,
Wright's singing of this verse redirects these sentiments to the Miramount
executives who have prevented her from acting for two decades, and who
are suggested to be all-seeing and all-hearing in the preceding sequence. But
while Cohen's song has been interpreted, by Cohen biographer Maurice
Ratcliff, as "a prayer expressing total surrender to the divine will," Wright's
performance of it is an act of rebellion.[9] There is a subtle irony to the way
the lyrics suggest a surrender to silence at the request of the higher power,
while Wright's singing of them reveals her unwillingness to actually let her
"voice be still." At the same time, given that the guards violently cut off her
performance by shooting at Wright's audience and arresting her, the scene
suggests that even in her subconscious Wright has lost most of the control
of her voice. As in the song lyrics, she is "spoken for."

ANOMALISA

In *The Congress*, Wright's voice is sharply contrasted with that of the monotone robot receptionist who speaks in the fragmented style of a machine.
In *Anomalisa*, however, the characters of Lisa and a mechanical Japanese
sex doll uncannily share the same voice (that of Jennifer Jason Leigh), if not
the same language and delivery. *Anomalisa* was written and codirected by
Charlie Kaufman, who adapted the story from his 2005 audio play of the

same name. It focuses on Michael, an isolated customer service expert who travels to a Cincinnati hotel to give a speech and promote his book at a convention. Despite being married with a child, Michael arranges to meet up with an old girlfriend who lives in the city; later he becomes infatuated with a sweetly shy woman, Lisa, who has traveled to the hotel to hear him speak.

Anomalisa was created in stop-motion animation and used 3D printing to efficiently allow for a photo-realist human style of puppets, though visible joins on their faces purposefully signal their nonhuman status.[10] The film combines this with a high concept merging of the puppets'/characters' bodies and voices: only two characters in the film have individual voices—the protagonist Michael (voiced by David Thewlis) and Jennifer Jason Leigh as Lisa and an animatronic Japanese doll that Michael buys for his son early in the film. Michael responds to both the doll and Lisa with wonder, though it is only in the closing scene that we hear the former sing—a Japanese nursery rhyme ("Momotarō's Song") in what is recognizably Jason Leigh's voice. All other voices are supplied by actor Tom Noonan, a premise used to gradually suggest to the audience that Michael is experiencing some kind of mental breakdown. Or rather, as the film suggests in subtle ways, he is suffering from the "Fregoli Delusion," a rare and real condition in which an individual perceives everyone as the same person. Within this narrative setup, the voice of Lisa (and Jason Leigh) becomes central.

It is the individuality of Lisa's so-called "miraculous" voice that attracts Michael to her, and which the film uses to reveal his inability to otherwise hear a range of voices. *Anomalisa* thus suggests the profundity of the human voice as a marker of identity, folding this into the film's existential questioning of what it means to be human. Furthermore, Michael, and, by association, the film, engages in a kind of fetishization of Lisa's (and Jason Leigh's) voice. This leads to two central scenes in which Lisa is persuaded to sing for him, sequences that become troubling from the perspective of the female voice being coached or coerced for the personal gain of the central male character. In this way, *Anomalisa* (like *The Congress*) invites comparison to *Vertigo*, where there is a similar grooming of a female character (who also has a double) to satisfy the man.

Michael's attraction to Lisa is based singularly on the qualities of her voice (in this case, that she sounds different from the everyperson voice of all the other male and female characters), rather than her personality. At various points in the film, Michael urges her to keep talking—about anything. He wants to hear her not because he is interested in the content of her speech, but because the uniqueness of her voice provides him with a sense of relief and satisfaction. In this regard, Lisa's voice functions like those of the women in YouTube's ASMR whisper videos, where women's whispering addresses to the camera and microphone re-create "heteronormative models of care and intimacy directed by women toward men."[11] However, in a departure from the situation with YouTube's whispering women, Michael directs Lisa to use her voice as he desires. This dynamic is clearest in the scenes where he persuades Lisa to sing despite her clear discomfort about doing so, as well as in those showing Michael's sudden disinterest in Lisa after they have slept together and she begins to sound like everyone else. At this point, Jason Leigh's voice begins to merge with Noonan's, and is quickly replaced by it.

Michael's urging of Lisa to sing or speak recalls the blunt remarks of Scotty in *Vertigo*, when he aggressively pleads with Judy to dye her hair and wear Madeleine's clothes, despite her protests: "Judy, please, it can't matter to you . . ." While Scotty knows what he wants to see in the woman, Michael knows what he wants to hear. In both cases, the woman's agency and desires are presented as secondary—and ones they must ignore in order to please the men in question. *Vertigo*, alongside much of Hitchcock's filmography, is frequently analyzed in relation to a scopophilic pleasure in watching (as in Mulvey's theorization of visual pleasure in narrative cinema).[12] *Anomalisa* sets up an aural equivalent. Michael's fetishization of Lisa's voice is both subtle and obvious, most notably when he urges her to sing when they get back to his hotel room after a night of drinks. For Michael, the performance serves as a kind of foreplay, but for the shy Lisa the song serves to stall other physical acts for which she is not yet ready, and which also come with vocal directions from Michael (who asks her if she talks during sex and urges her to "make noises, like moaning"). Though Lisa knows that Michael is invested in her voice, unlike the audience she has no understanding of why. This lack of understanding lends her various vocal performances for him an uncomfortable dimension, as when Michael accepts that they aren't going to have sex, and he tells her they can just lie on the bed and she can tell him about her day. From Lisa's perspective, talking is a welcome alternative, but for the audience—experiencing the film from Michael's point-of-audition—the remark demonstrates that he is still trying to get a version of what he wants (to hear her voice), even while seeming to put her needs first.

Michael's sexualization of Lisa's voice culminates in the scene where she speak-sings for him a second time. Lying on his bed, she recites lines from an Italian translation of "Girls Just Want to Have Fun." Michael intensely gazes at her mouth as she recites the song; indeed, the film's most extreme close-ups are reserved for his point of view in this scene, with reaction shots as he watches her mouth move. Meanwhile, most of her face and the background are in shadows or out of focus (figure 2.3). And the simultaneously

Figures 2.3. Screenshot of Michael gazing at Lisa in *Anomalisa* (2015) as she speak-sings on his bed. Produced by HanWay Films and Starburns Industries.

human-like and puppet-like details of their embodiment are never more apparent than here. The texture of Lisa's skin and lips, and the sheen on Michael's eyes, are uncannily lifelike, yet the mask joins around Michael's eyes and the imperfect timing of Lisa's moving lips remind us of their artificiality. In this intimate framing we also hear Michael's close-miked exhale as he listens to, and gazes intensely upon, the singing Lisa. As in other scenes, there is an uncomfortable sense of her voice being fetishized, never more so than when Michael momentarily gasps in wonder and/or arousal.

The rough approximation of matching between Lisa's 3D puppet mouth and Jason Leigh's voice also becomes a visual focal point when the Japanese doll sings in the closing scene. The animatronic doll's red-lipped mouth opens and closes to a consistent timed rhythm, one that does not match the sound of the song supposedly playing within her (figure 2.4). Of course, such a loose matching of mouth and voice is similarly the case with all the "human" characters in *Anomalisa*, given that they, too, are ventriloquized puppets. David L. Smith called the Japanese doll just "another member of the puppet family," noting the coincidental timing of Michael hearing Lisa's voice so soon after he buys the doll and brings it back to his hotel room, "almost as if the doll had called her into existence." Much as I noted the blow-up-doll-like quality of the fembot receptionist in *The Congress*, Smith also observed the specifics of the Japanese doll's mouth in *Anomalisa*: "Its mouth is accommodatingly round and open, making its presence in a sex

Figure 2.4. Screenshot of the Japanese sex doll in *Anomalisa* (2015), merging mechanical parts and womanly chest. Produced by HanWay Films and Starburns Industries.

shop plausible."[13] Indeed, in this and other ways, both films recall the feminized mouth as a locus for sexual activity (as in fellatio, or commercials for sex hotlines).

The fact that the animatronic doll sings in Japanese, and that Michael seems even more taken with Lisa's Italian rendition of the song, further aligns *Anomalisa*'s presentation of the female voice with those of ASMR whisper videos. Indeed, the film has been received as such in certain ASMR circles: certain scenes have been edited to provide heightened ASMR effects on YouTube, and *Anomalisa* was included in *Dazed* magazine's guide to films that also work as ASMR.[14] As Joceline Andersen noted in relation to the YouTube whisper videos, there is a strong audience demand for videos in languages listeners do not understand, and for "nonstandard pronunciations of language by second-language speakers." In these instances, "rather than focusing on the meaning of speech, the listener's attention can turn more easily to the quality of the voice itself as a carrier of meaning." Andersen thus surmises that "the popularity of foreign-language ASMR videos demonstrates that the voice, rather than language, is the primary carrier of attentiveness as an ASMR trigger."[15] This is not to say that *Anomalisa*'s writers and directors were necessarily directly influenced by trends in ASMR videos—although other filmmakers, such as Peter Strickland, have explained that they included ASMR elements in their sound design prior to learning about the phenomenon and terminology.[16] Either way, the overall impact of having Jason Leigh sing in Japanese, and voice a Japanese sex doll, is to use an Asian language to create an exotic vocal "other," for both Michael and the audience, and to do so in ways that parallel elements of ASMR sound culture, thus further aligning the film's treatment of the female voice with digital voice culture.

As mentioned earlier, *Anomalisa* waits until the final scene to reveal the vocal link between the purportedly human (but 3D-printed) Lisa and the animatronic Japanese doll. This revelation encourages the audience to retroactively reconsider the whole narrative, by implying that Lisa may be a mere projection of Michael's imagination: enamored with the Japanese doll's distinctive voice, he mentally built a more human woman to embody it before reverting to the original version (when he breaks up with Lisa and returns home to his family with the doll). Various critics have noted the significance of Lisa and the doll sharing a voice, yet no one has yet considered the implications of this for Michael's fetishization of the voice, and, more importantly, for Lisa's vocal agency.[17] If Michael's interest in Lisa is based entirely on her "miraculous" voice, then the fact that he owns this singing doll is presumably a cause for elation. But it is also a cause for concern when it comes to understanding the film's representation of gender, technology, and embodiment. Unlike Lisa, whom Michael had to gently coerce into singing, the doll can sing on his command with the touch of a button—and much like the women in YouTube ASMR videos whisper on command with the touch of a digital button. Furthermore, although Jason Leigh's delivery of the doll's song is machine-like in its rhythm, it is nonetheless a human voice. In other words, Michael is left with the best of both worlds: a voice that reassures him, and/or sexually stimulates him, and a voice over which he has full control. This new control over the female voice can be understood as a solution to his earlier frustration with some of Lisa's all-too-human vocal sounds: the morning after they have sex, he berates her for clinking her fork against her teeth, and for speaking with food in her mouth.

HER

Many of the tropes and uses of the voice in *The Congress* and *Anomalisa* are also present in *Her*. In certain ways, however, *Her* raises the most complex issues around the female technologized voice, because Scarlett Johansson's voice in the film has no physical presence whatsoever. Crucially, this setup also allowed for the voice work of Samantha Morton, who was initially cast as the voice of the AI, to be replaced entirely with Johansson's voice in postproduction. Written and directed by Spike Jonze, *Her* is set in a near-future version of Los Angeles. Like *Anomalisa*, it focuses on a lonely man. This one is Theodore (Joaquin Phoenix), who works as a writer of intimate letters for couples who cannot write such things themselves. Depressed about his impending divorce, Theodore upgrades his operating system to one that includes an AI-driven virtual assistant. After selecting the option for his virtual assistant to have a female voice, who decides to name herself

Samantha, Theodore grows fascinated with the virtual assistant's ability to learn information and to respond to things—and to him—emotionally. Effectively, this is a romanticizing of Samantha's machine learning capacity. They become closely bonded, to the point that he refers to Samantha as his girlfriend and introduces her (in the form of her voice and smart devices) to his friends and his ex.

Samantha and Theodore's growing—if impossible—intimacy includes a duet called "The Moon Song," one of the film's original musical numbers. Though *The Congress* and *Anomalisa* also foreground acts of singing by animatronic or digital "women," the duet in *Her* most directly references the intersection of art and technology. In so doing, it builds on the experimental work of Joseph Olive, a computerized speech researcher. Olive used electronically synthesized human speech and computers in a 1976 opera, *Mar-ri-ia-a*, a precursor to the three films under discussion.[18] The opera features a female scientist, Maria, who builds a computer with whom she falls in love during her efforts to make the machine speak with emotion. On completion of the project, the scientist turns off the machine, but it manages to turn itself back on and begs for her affection. The computer and scientist sing a duet, one based on the theme from Verdi's *La traviata*, but Maria eventually dismantles her creation. Within Olive's opera, Maria is unable to cope with her love for this machine. For Olive, the inspiration and theme for the opera was "our desire for computers not just to speak but to speak with feeling."[19]

Her departs from *Mar-ri-ia-a* by making some notable shifts in motivation and gender dynamics. In Olive's opera, the machine itself was apparently not explicitly gendered as either male or female. Unlike Samantha, the talking and singing machine did not have an identifiably male or female name. As the spelling of *Mar-ri-ia-a* in the fragmented title of the opera suggests, the machine's attempts to deliver words are difficult and marked with clearly audible signs that it is nonhuman. Samantha in *Her* experiences no such vocal struggles; nor does Theodore have the kind of reservations that Maria does about entering into a relationship with a posthuman creation. This notable development can be related back to Olive's own discussion of his opera as exploring the human desire for computers to speak *with feeling*. This was also the aim of Maria's character. Using Johansson's human voice not just to speak with feeling, but to sing with feeling, seems central to *Her*'s revised take on the opera's themes. In *Her*, Samantha and Theodore's duet begins with Theodore telling Samantha, "Let's make up the words to this one." She responds with a laugh and agrees before beginning, thereafter leading the song both in terms of lyrical weighting and volume. Samantha's supposedly improvised lyrics position her spatially far away from Theodore ("I'm lying on the moon"), although he is nonetheless her focal point and object of affection ("My dear I'll be there soon"). Theodore joins in, so that his singing is layered over Samantha's, but she remains the close-miked vocal focal point while Theodore (here and throughout the film) is the visual one. Although *Mar-ri-ia-a* traces the synthetic speech training process, and the machine's desire for its creator and teacher, *Her* begins—almost four decades later—with a perfectly expressive technologized voice. We might therefore link Samantha's voice, which is more rather than less expressive than Theodore's, to their equally doomed relationship. But while Maria dismantled the machine in order to end her relationship with it, Samantha dismantles her relationship with Theodore by removing his access to her voice. There is a notable shift in who holds the power (Maria, the human; Samantha, the posthuman operating system), but in both cases the power seems tied to the woman's use of her voice—to teach the machine, in Maria's case, and to support and soothe the human Theodore, in Samantha's case.

In the film, Samantha appears to hold the power. Yet the same cannot be said for the actresses who provided her voice. Consider the relatively hidden account of how it was initially Samantha Morton who voiced the operating system (and lent it her name), only for the role to be recast with Johansson after Spike Jonze decided that Morton's voice was unsuitable. Musicologist Laura Tunbridge explained how this significant change took place: "Apparently Morton had been on set every day and it was only during the editing process that Jonze decided her voice was not suitable. The replacement of Morton's voice with Johansson was because the producers thought something more characterful was required. In order for the protagonist to fall in love with 'just' a voice, it seems one has to imagine that voice as having a body; specifically, a desirable body and preferably a real one—ideally, for mass appeal, Johansson's."[20]

Beyond the question of *why* Jonze switched Morton's voice for Johansson's, it is important to stress *how* this change is tied to the broader representation of Samantha: the removal of Morton's voice in postproduction was made possible only because of the character's complete confinement to the soundtrack.[21] Or, as Fleeger put it, "Samantha exists only in Theodore's ear."[22] As such, no reshoots were required. Although Morton had been on set every day—presumably voicing Samantha's dialogue to which Theodore responds—Johansson did not need to provide on-set labor. This troubling production anecdote highlights the danger of assuming that it is inherently problematic for women's voices *to be* anchored to their bodies in the mise-en-scène (as scholars such as Silverman would have it).[23] While the appeal of using human voices is that the presence of the body in the voice remains—the unseen but recalled presence of Johansson's body in her voice—the removal of Morton's vocal performance highlights how easy it is to completely remove a voice when it is only anchored to technologically rendered "bodies" or devices. *Her*'s mediating technologies are the earpieces and smart devices through which Theodore hears Samantha, while these "bodies" take the form of 3D-printed puppets in *Anomalisa*, and computer-animated characters (also virtual avatars in the film world) in *The Congress*.

To understand precisely what is at stake when it comes to films that present a human female voice that ventriloquizes a new technologically rendered "body," we can imagine another alternative: instead of Johansson voicing Theodore's operating system, Jonze could have used a synthetic technological voice. Tunbridge noted that "a more radical presentation of the simulated female persona [in *Her*] would have given Samantha a synthetic voice, rather than a human one," because, as it stood, "the romance of *Her* founders on the deceit of the haptic voice." Tunbridge's discussion of the haptic voice alludes to qualities such as texture and the sense of intimacy that are generally associated with a sensory, haptic orientation. In *Her*, this includes Johansson's close-miked sighs. As Tunbridge implied, the film depends on the human qualities of Johansson's voice (ones further enhanced through recording and postproduction technologies), yet this is effectively a trick—one played on both Theodore and the audience. Thus, a synthetic voice would have been a more radical choice.[24] And since a synthetic voice would also have been a more *realistic* choice, it begs the question of why Samantha doesn't sound like "Siri," or "Alexa," or any of the other female-sounding AIs. Is it because of the presence of both the body and the soul "in" the voice, factors that would make a synthetic voice too robotic to engage the male character, and to convince the audience that she is a technology worth falling in love with?

EVERY *BODY* SINGS

The emphasis all three films place on scenes of singing is another reason why using synthetic voices would be much less effective than using human ones. *Anomalisa* sheds the most light on the broader issues related to singing as a distinctly human activity. The technical challenges of getting machines to sing come down to embodied differences between human speech and singing, resulting in what electronics and communications engineers specializing in speech technology have summed up as the "different characteristics of glottal excitation and the vocal tract system" involved in the two expressive modes.[25] For example, singing requires active breathing during exhalation, as well as a smooth and soothing pitch variation. It is often variation in pitch, in particular (such as vibrato), that "adds expression" to singing.[26] The different and complex bodily changes involved in singing are harder to program than standard speech, and thus require different methods. By foregrounding singing scenes, the films discussed here therefore use their actresses to represent what is technologically impossible: machine characters who can sing like a human. The *Anomalisa* scene leading up to Lisa's singing of "Girls Just Wanna Have Fun," where Michael asks Lisa if she sings, is particularly notable for two things she says that signal what I see as central to all three films' treatment of the technologized voice:

> Michael: Do you sing?
> Lisa: What? No . . . God. You're weird. [beat] I mean, of course I sing. Everybody sings. I just don't sing well. I sometimes sing along with the radio.

Lisa's initial negative response is emphatic, but it is coupled with a telling pause before she clarifies that yes, she does sing, because everybody (or every *body*) sings. Through her amended answer, Lisa signals a fundamental connection between the human body and the process of singing—one she realizes should be distinguished from qualitative self-judgments about how well one sings. Her point can be read as confirmation of the fact that it is very difficult, nearly impossible, to program a machine to express a melodic singing voice.

Lisa's comment about the radio is also a telling precursor for the nature of her "Girls Just Wanna Have Fun" singing performance. Crucially, it is also significant in light of Jason Leigh's voicing of both Lisa and the animatronic Japanese doll. When Lisa sings the Cyndi Lauper song later in the scene, she does so as though singing along to the radio, with her voice dipping in volume at different parts—mimicking the varying fade ins and outs of Lauper's audio mix. It is an inward, introverted performance that contributes to the impression that Lisa is a human with complex thoughts and feelings (the corollary of having a body, since "everybody sings"), despite presenting as a 3D-printed puppet. Michael is moved to tears, and during a break in the melody he comments, "That was beautiful"; however, Lisa does not appear to hear him. Her eyes still closed, she begins to sing again—perfectly matching the breaks in the singing track in the Lauper recording. She will sing the song until the very end, fading out and vocalizing the postproduction effects of the original song. When first experienced in the film, these quirks of Lisa's performance come across as humorous and endearing. Yet, when considered alongside the concluding scene—wherein Jason Leigh voices the looping Japanese nursery rhyme of the animatronic sex doll—Lisa's delivery can be seen as foreshadowing her connection to the doll. Lisa also being mechanical would explain why she so perfectly matches the breaks in the singing track, as well as why her singing fades in and out as though she is vocalizing the song's postproduction effects. It would also explain why she doesn't appear to hear Michael's comments, and continues to sing as though he is not there right until the very end of the unheard track that Lisa appears to be playing from memory in her mind. Like the animatronic doll, who sings for a predetermined time at the press of a button, once Lisa begins to sing, she cannot stop.

Anomalisa, *Her*, and *The Congress* all imagine a future wherein machines can be made to sound so human that their difference from us is imperceptible even to the human ear (whether on the part of the audience, or on the part of the characters). As my analysis so far would suggest, their treatment of the topic reflects the growing anxieties around an increased societal dependence on voice technologies in the twenty-first century. The films thus go beyond drawing attention to some of the audible signs of technology in such voices. One remarkable link between real-world speech technologies, such as "Alexa" and "Siri"—typically styled as "personal assistants"—and the female voices in these films is that, at least in *Anomalisa* and *Her*, the voices' narrative function is to serve as support for the male protagonist by providing emotional or fetishistic assistance to him. The voices of Lisa (in *Anomalisa*) and Samantha (in *Her*) seem to exist purely for the value they can offer to the men who want to hear them. In Samantha's case, this is the very purpose of the voice-operated software, but with Lisa it is more complex: in the film, her character's trajectory and worth emerges not from who she is but from how she sounds.

Differences between human voices and synthetic ones, of course, stem from technological challenges that engineers have not yet overcome. The development of more convincing synthetic voices would mean correcting flaws in technologized voices that are central to humans' perceptions of them as sounding synthetic and nonhuman. One of these flaws is fragmentation, which is due to a process that speech technology engineers call *concatenation*—whereby a voice is recorded saying complete phrases or fragments of phrases with a view to their later being reconstituted by a second technology. Cultural critic Nina Power eloquently captured the everyday experience of concatenation as part of a study of women's technologized voices that are used in everyday spaces, such as on public transport and in self-service checkout kiosks: "Think about those announcements you get that are ubiquitous but contingent, such as an announcement regarding the 'late running' of a particular train. Here you are likely to hear a female-sounding voice that seems more fragmentary than usual: 'Due to signal failure the . . . 9.52 . . . to . . . Penzance . . . will be approximately . . . 17 . . . minutes late. We apologise for any inconvenience this may cause.'"[27] We experience this fragmented style of delivery in *The Congress* with the fembot receptionist, which contrasts with the animated Wright's much more fluid delivery.

Virginás discussed *S1m0ne*, a film that shares *The Congress*'s focus on a digital female actress. But in the *S1m0ne* narrative, she is entirely programmed rather than based on an existing actress. Virginás noticed how the film contrasts a close-up of the digital actress S1m0ne (Rachel Roberts), on a computer screen, with the face and expressions of a human woman watching a film in the subsequent sequence: "The strange uniqueness of the digital woman is emphasised by her comparison to images of female bodies coded as human, non-fragmented and caught in the midst of affectively charged activities such as bewilderment and attention." Virginás explained how the qualities that signal humanness can be more easily identified when they are experienced "as something lacking" in, say, robots and monsters. So whereas *S1m0ne* captures the contrast between the blank digital entity and an expressive woman by means of visual close-ups, *The Congress* achieves a similar effect by using vocal markers, framing the same type of contrast in terms of vocal expressiveness.[28] In the scene where the animated Wright talks to the fembot receptionist, the receptionist, as noted, looks like an animatronic blow-up sex doll, but she also speaks with an unnatural, robotic intonation (monotone, with ill-placed pauses). Given that the recently animated Wright also appears, visually, as nonhuman, it is the contrast in voice that signals her sustained status as human—albeit one temporarily trapped in a computer animation. *Anomalisa*'s central vocal structure also relies on contrasts and comparisons to separate the human from the nonhuman, or posthuman—at least as presented to the audience from Michael's point-of-audition. The one character (Lisa) whose voice sounds different is also considered the most human. Yet even she has a synthetically reproduced vocal double in the form of the animatronic doll.

Perhaps the most remarkable way that the films engage with issues around the technologized voice is by suggesting the possibility of using preexisting media recordings to develop synthetic voices. Recall the aforementioned moment where Robin Wright's animated character grasps at her throat upon hearing her avatar character saying something that she did not actually say. More than any other scene, this one calls upon audience members to disavow preconceived notions about the character who looks like a human, and who sounds like a human, being the one that is human in the film world (they must reject the one that looks and sounds human as an avatar, and accept the animated character as actually being human). In this regard, it uses Wright's actual voice to far exceed the current realities of synthetic, technologized voices. Although, in this particular case, the real-world actress Robin Wright did deliver these lines, in the years to come actresses may actually be subjected to the unnerving experience of having their preexisting vocal performances reworked to utter things they did not in fact say. Such reedited vocal recordings could be put into the mouths of digitized characters or technologies and, as with the aforementioned process of concatenation (whereby a voice is recorded saying complete phrases or fragments of phrases with a view to them later being reconstituted by a second technology), the actress could be turned into a kind of technologized ventriloquist's dummy.

Like Johansson's notably expressive rendering of the operating system Samantha in *Her*, *The Congress* may indirectly set up expectations for synthetic female-sounding voices that the tech industry uses as direct inspiration. This possibility manifested in popular and tech-focused discourse around the time of *Her*'s release. For example, in an article titled "How Do You Teach a Computer to Speak Like Scarlett Johansson?," the computer-generated voice scholar Janet Cahn suggested that "all female voices should sound like Scarlett Johansson, I guess."[29] These films thus provide apt reminders of the dangers of voice-based technologies, such as speech-bots and voice cloning software, as they relate to vocal data and identity theft. Johansson is already a prime example with regard to digital editing software, with her face and/or body increasingly used in so-called "deepfake" porn.[30] Johansson's body even served as a blueprint for a Chinese designer, who unveiled his completed Johansson robot in 2016.[31] With comments like Cahn's, it is easy to imagine a near future in which consumers can program their "Siri," "Alexa," or GPS to sound like Johansson, or Wright, or Jason Leigh, or any other actor. This type of "advance" seems particularly achievable given that the raw data for computer-generated voices is high-quality audio recordings, which are readily accessible via digital video files. The necessary data for subsequent manipulation already exists. One voice cloning company, CereProc, typically requests approximately two hours of recordings—a voice uttering over six hundred sentences that are designed to capture the full range of sounds needed for an effective vocal clone. But it can also work from archival recordings, provided they are of high quality, and "preferably studio-quality"—that is, equivalent to files of actors' vocal performances.[32] CereProc's services received considerable media attention in 2010 when the company used DVD commentaries by film critic Roger Ebert as the basis for re-creating his voice, after he lost it as a result of a cancer-related tracheos-tomy. Since then, several other, more streamlined voice cloning technologies emerged, such as Adobe VoCo (previewed in November 2016), and Lyrebird (which premiered in April 2017). Both require much shorter lengths of vocal recordings than CereProc. VoCo requires approximately twenty minutes to generate a sound-alike voice, and Lyrebird requires just one minute. Even though Lyrebird issued a statement of ethics alongside its publicity release, the samples and discourse surrounding such technologies highlight the ease with which they can be misdirected.[33] Indeed, when it comes to the risk to actresses, in particular, a *Vice* article on Adobe VoCo jumped straight to this possibility. Journalist Matthew Gault opened his piece on the subject with a loaded question—"Ever wanted to make Natalie Portman yell obscenities at your neighbors?"—and continued with the assurance that "Adobe has you covered."[34]

Comments about teaching a computer to sound like Johansson reflect a certain tendency for the voices of female celebrities to be held up as positive or negative examples of the ideal feminine voice, not just in the media but also in the medical profession. In relation to the latter, head and neck spe-cialist Reena Gupta has discussed the damaged voices of Emma Stone and Lindsay Lohan in relation to the effects of colic and smoking (respectively) on the voice.[35] Terminology referencing the so-called Bogart-Bacall syn-drome, signifying the impact of vocal fatigue and dysphonia in professional voice users, dates from the late 1980s. Focusing on musculoskeletal tension disorder involving the larynx, clinicians James A. Koufman and P. David Blalock explained in 1988 how "most of the [affected] men sounded like Humphrey Bogart and the women like Lauren Bacall."[36]

There is a certain irony to Johansson's voice being held up as an ideal by the technology industry, given that her voice bears many of the same signs of damage that Bacall's did. The implication is that filmmakers and audiences are attracted to sounds of damage in an actress's voice, something that would appear to go against anatomical modeling of the average pitch and vocal traits for cisgender women's voices. The explanation for this lies, perhaps, in the sonics of vocal damage and how they relate to gender norms and film casting. Stone, Lohan, and Johansson are examples of how dam-age manifests in a hoarser sound and a lower pitch. They thus sound older and more conventionally "masculine" than other actresses in the same age demographic. Indeed, as film scholar Donna Kornhaber noted, Johansson's contralto voice "explodes" biological signals related to qualities that are typical of male and female voices, old and young, which is how Johansson could convincingly play older women when she was still a teenager.[37] Both

Stone and Johansson are frequently cast as romantic interests for men decades older than them, and their vocal qualities can mask their youth, distracting from the potential inappropriateness of such casting decisions—ones that underscore how women in Hollywood are much more likely to struggle to find major roles after a certain age.[38] A damaged voice also speaks to what Roland Barthes termed "the body in the voice."[39] Unlike synthetic technologized voices, these actresses have vocal chords that can amass damage that is perceived audibly. The sounds of damage in their voices testify to their off-screen bodies and corresponding vulnerability.

EMBODIMENT AND VOCAL GHOSTING

The fetishized vocal presence of women, rather than men, as the voices of many machines and posthuman characters can be linked to broader associations around softness as something that is (1) registered aurally, and (2) a trait stereotypically gendered as female. Despite significant developments in computer-generated voices, it is still almost impossible to create a voice that can convince humans it is natural over a sustained period—and this is due to the softness of humans. As Cahn explained, "Our bodies, they're made of a lot of soft parts, so they're not going to work like clockwork, and it's that irregularity that lets you know that this is a live biological organism."[40] The role of flesh, or "soft parts," in this impossibility can again be linked to Barthes's description of "the body in the voice" in his discussion of vocal grain.[41] Though not explicitly gendered, the quality of *softness* is one that resonates with different critical approaches to the machine voice in general and to the films under focus in particular. Nina Power tied softness to gender when explaining the "softly controlling" nature of collectively experienced female voices that instruct us. She asked, "Is the implication that a male-sounding voice would sound too dictatorial, too bossy, too 'serious?'"[42]

The directors of *Anomalisa* commented on a tendency for audiences and critics to discuss their puppets as appearing "soft," as if they might be made of felt, for instance, when in reality their 3D-printed faces were composed of hardened gypsum powder, with the rest of the body made of silicon.[43] With *Her*, on a technical level, softness relates to Kornhaber's distinction, that Samantha is *software* rather than hardware—meaning she does not have any physical presence but depends on "concrete intermediaries to commune with the humans who created and who employ her."[44] Another reason why critics and audiences might refer to *Anomalisa*'s puppets as seeming "soft" has to do with the physicality of the puppets. Unlike the waifish animated Robin Wright in *The Congress*, Lisa has some meat on her silicone "bones":

her puppet body is that of an average-sized, middle-aged woman, rather than exhibiting the idealized shapeliness of many animated women, such as Betty Boop and Jessica Rabbit, or Barbie-doll-like measurements. The appearance of the Japanese sex doll—Lisa's vocal double—further supports the significance of both soft parts and clockwork mechanics to the film's thematic foregrounding of the human—and technological—voice. The doll's chest presents us with both at once: a womanly breast on the left side of the doll's chest, and a series of mechanical cogs on the right side (see figure 2.4). In each case, by casting women as machine voices—rather than using synthetic voice technologies—the filmmakers bring vocal manifestations of the actresses' "soft parts" to the screen.

In her discussion of the soft coercion of women's technologized voices in public spaces, Power makes a historical comparison to a famous maternal film character: "We feel reassured we know where we're going, but also faintly controlled and guided by some sort of invisible Mary Poppins."[45] The wording here implies that in hearing a Mary Poppins–like voice we still recall the embodied presence of such a figure even though she is no longer visible. The premise is similar to Tunbridge's description of Samantha in *Her* as "some spirit from another dimension who only ever appears in séance."[46] This sense of the voice, where the body is not present, and yet not entirely absent, finds a partial explanation in Scott Balcerzak's discussion of the ghostly aspects of motion capture performance: "The entire philosophy behind the technology is not about a digitisation of the human, but the humanisation of the digital through the addition of supposedly real movement." Balcerzak used the term "ghosting" to describe the traces of the actor that remain—traces of an actor's recorded performance that was subsequently turned into a 3D animated puppet, and then converted into a CGI creature.[47] The actor's presence on screen might be experienced as a kind of "ghosting," even if the body itself is absent. For the viewer, this process can provide the images with a kind of heightened spectral quality.

Balcerzak also argued that motion capture "is a process developed to make the special effect perform realistically[,] as opposed to, as suggested by many, digitally [enhancing] the actor."[48] In a similar way, I would argue that the actresses' voices humanize their technology-driven, posthuman characters. Balcerzak's point, that a human actor's motion capture performance makes the *special effect* perform "realistically," might equally be applied to the various kinds of digitally or technologically produced bodies in *Her*, *Anomalisa*, and *The Congress*. For example, with *Anomalisa*, it is potentially the audible presence of the body in the voice that led to the film's publicized hook—that the stop-motion animation was "the most human film of the year, and it doesn't contain a single human."[49] While the visual track may not contain any humans, it is difficult to imagine the film's "humanness" being achieved and singled out if the 3D-printed puppets were voiced by speech-bots instead. As with motion capture performers, the "flesh and blood" bodies of the actors are not included, yet traces of their personhood—in the form of their voices—might still be experienced as a kind of ghosting.

Another way that the concept of ghosting applies to these voices relates back to Power's discussion of "an invisible Mary Poppins," where the disembodied voice is still tied to an embodied performer or character, despite the body not being visible. In relation to *Her*, we can think about Johansson's body as unseen but remembered—at least by those audience members who recognize her famously husky voice. It is perhaps this distinctiveness that led Spike Jonze to recast Johansson as Samantha after Samantha Morton had finished her vocal recordings for the role. Since Morton's disembodied voice was less easily identifiable, such a switch seems to confirm the significance of Johansson's unseen but remembered body to the overall impact of Samantha as a de facto character.

With *Her*, there is also the troubling ghost of Morton's initial vocal performance as Samantha, as later replaced by Johansson. While all traces of Morton's voice may seem to be gone, she is arguably present in Theodore/Phoenix's reactions to Samantha's voice. Theodore is the visual focus throughout the film, and the audience watches him respond with a range of emotions to Samantha's every word. But since Phoenix was on set with Morton, rather than Johansson, what we are seeing is Theodore responding to Morton's voice. It is thus only the audience that does not hear Morton: her presence is no longer tangible, and yet it still leaves its trace on the production in the form of the impression her voice made on Theodore/Phoenix—not to mention Morton's first name remaining as that of the operating system. Changing this in postproduction would have been more difficult than removing Morton's voice, given that it would have required reshoots and script rewrites. So although *Her* appears to be the only film out of the three under discussion not to employ a female vocal double as part of its treatment of the technologized voice, the production history reveals Morton to be a ghostly double: with her voice unheard in the final film, she is present only to those who know she was once there.[50]

Since Jonze and the producers are the reason she was vocally vanquished, it is hard not to question the ethics of the approach: Why not decide earlier that Morton's voice was not suitable? Was the option to use technology to make substitutions just too tempting? In a parallel to chapter 1's dubbing histories, Jonze became the latest in a long line of filmmakers to decide, after filming, that a woman's voice was substandard and must be technologically substituted. Like a person choosing the voice for a GPS system, he took advantage of software that allowed him to switch easily from one woman's voice to another.

In light of Morton's uncredited voice work for *Her*, it is also worth noting that Jason Leigh's voicing of the Japanese doll is similarly hidden. In the credit sequence, Tom Noonan is credited as "all other voices" beyond those of Michael and Lisa. This omission provides yet another reminder of the tendency for women to have their vocal performances removed or uncredited. Technology is what makes it so easy to silence them.

NORMALIZING THE "UNMARKED" WHITE VOICE

Another worrying trend to emerge is for films to reflect the norm for voice technologies to record and replay the voices of white women. As Joan K. Peters pointed out in her discussion of "Siri," "Alexa," and GPS voices, "though you can program your robot to be an American male, an Australian, or a guy with a plummy Masterpiece Theater accent, our default . . . is the American female of the pre-liberation flight attendant variety, ever accommodating and there to serve you." Peters raised questions about what this default female voice might lead to, including the possibility that women who sound "ethnic or edgy or loud" will begin to make people nervous, or that we will gradually all start to sound like Amazon's "Alexa."[51] Indeed, looking at "Alexa" in relation to the history of domestic servants in middle-class homes, Thao Phan problematized the aesthetic coding of her voice "as a native-speaking, educated, white woman." As she argued, these racialized dynamics can romanticize the historical conditions of domestic servitude, erasing the memory of the middle-class home as a site of exploitation for women of color in particular.[52] Adding to these concerns, we should thus note the potential silencing of ethnic voices even in relation to representations of digital futures in cinema. For in voicing *Anomalisa*'s Japanese doll, delivering a Japanese song, Jennifer Jason Leigh could be described as engaging in a form of racial ventriloquism or vocal "whitewashing."

This element of the film recalls Pooja Rangan's discussion of how voices are scanned for "audible evidence of racial identity." Rangan had a particular focus on the work of Leslie Thornton, whose film *Adynata* (1983) used mimicry of Asian speech patterns and cadences to comment on vocalized forms of racism.[53] For Rangan, Thornton's strategy was purposely discomfiting. With *Anomalisa*, however, Jason Leigh's mimicry of an Asian accent appears more appropriative, in part because it raises the question of why

Lisa (or any of the other "human" characters) could not be puppets of color. Instead, by having the inanimate sex doll be Japanese, and voiced by a white actress performing a mock Asian accent, the doll becomes another example of the stereotype for Asian women (and their Hollywood characterizations) to be passive, quiet, and sexually exotic, and often love interests for white men.[54] Perhaps it would have been less appropriative for *Anomalisa* to include a white animatronic doll, or to cast a Japanese woman in the role of the doll's voice (though this would naturally remove the central vocal link between Lisa and the doll). As it stands, the Japanese doll becomes an exotic vocal "other" for both Michael and the audience—much as YouTube's ASMR whisper audiences seek out voices speaking in languages they do not understand in order to have a more intense sensory experience unburdened by linguistic meaning.

The casting of Robin Wright in *The Congress* also reflects and reinforces the tendency for white American women to be seen and heard over all others, even in a film made by an Israeli writer-director, and largely funded with European financing. *The Congress* was an Israeli-German-Polish-Luxembourg-Belgian-French-US coproduction, and yet the casting seems symptomatic of the tendency in the film industry to resort to using American women by default, much as Peters identified them as the speech-bot default. Perhaps this is why Samantha Morton, who is English, was ultimately replaced with the American Johansson. But while Peters identified the American-sounding voice as the default, Power noted both US and UK reference points in relation to the "soft coercion" by female-sounding voices in public spaces, referring to them as having "the regionless accent of BBC Radio 4."[55] Indeed, as I will discuss in further detail in chapter 3, in 1996 the British actress Joanna Lumley was hired as the UK voice of the internet service provider AOL. Her voice was then used to deliver prerecorded messages such as "You've got post." Thus a trend for (white) actresses to lend their disembodied voices to digital speech technologies was established very early in the digital era.

With white voices—and white listeners—historically determining the desired vocal norms and their remediation, there is an unfortunate predictability to all of this. Speech technologies are maintaining racialized vocal hierarchies with much earlier precedents.[56] A two-way flow of influences is evident between everyday uses of technologized voices and their representations and uses in English-language cinema—and it is clear that both are generally modeled on the relatively neutral voices of white and often American women. There are only rare exceptions in cinema, such as the comedian robot briefly voiced by Chris Rock in *A.I.* (Stephen Spielberg, 2001). As

Fleeger surmised, "There are not many black robots in Hollywood films, which should not be all that surprising given there is not a lot of black speech in American cinema in general."[57] In keeping with many of the dominant speech technologies, the films under discussion re-create this hierarchy by casting white voices to accompany the various diegetic technologies and puppets. Perhaps the film directors and casting agents are merely taking their cue from the tech industries—and if *Her*'s voice-activated operating system does eventually come to pass, then it seems likely to continue the norm of modeling the voice on those of white women, particularly white actresses.

QUEERING THE (FEMALE) TECHNOLOGIZED VOICE

In some ways, the films discussed here seem to represent highly technologized worlds in which women's voices continue to be fetishized by, or subordinated to, those of male characters and patriarchal structures. However, in other ways, they can be seen to interrogate essentialist treatments of the voice as something that inherently reflects (and is reflective of) gender. The voices could be described as "queered," in terms of their liminal combination of masculine and feminine bodies. For music scholar Freya Jarman-Ivens, the voice's queer potential—in terms of providing queer spaces and possibilities for queer listening—ultimately relies on its liminality. Indeed, for Jarman-Ivens, technology can be central to the queering of an otherwise gender normative female voice. Following the view that cyborgs are inherently queer, owing to their status as boundary figures (positioned at the intersection of nature, culture, and technology), she has argued that production practices that artificialize the voice of even a heterosexual person through external technological means can imbue that voice (and person) with a partial cyborg status.[58]

This kind of technological vocal queering is most sustained in *Anomalisa*, owing to the sixty-four-year-old Noonan's voicing of the film's approximately 150 supporting characters, male and female—everyone from Michael's young son to his ex-girlfriend, Lisa's female friend, waiters, and taxi drivers. As a baritone, Noonan was able to alter his voice to reflect different genders as well as a range of ages, providing a convincing rejoinder to theories of voice as innately revealing of biological markers. The choice to use Noonan's voice in all of these roles sets *Anomalisa* apart from, say, *The Polar Express* (2004), which also has one actor voice numerous roles, but only the men: Tom Hanks voices six of the male characters, while other actors and actresses make up the rest of the cast. Commenting on the range of characters he voiced for *Anomalisa*, Noonan explained how "each character had their own persona and are in different situations, but I did the scenes like I would any other movie. I didn't worry about sounding like a girl here or a kid there."[59] As in *RuPaul's Drag Race*, explored in chapter 6, this concern signals the importance of on-screen visual markers in terms of perceiving a specific voice as male or female. Arguably Noonan didn't need to worry about "sounding like a girl here or a kid there" because, when his baritone voice was combined with the animated figure of a girl or child, it may have sounded slightly unconventional, in terms of gendered vocal norms, but not overtly so. This queering of Noonan's voice as gender fluid is particularly apparent in his performance of diegetically mediated voices: members of the hotel staff, to whom Michael speaks on the phone, for example, and, significantly, Michael's operatic personal music, which he listens to on the airplane. The "Flower Duet" from Léo Delibes's 1883 opera *Lakmé* is particularly significant to *Anomalisa*'s queering of the voice through a destabilization of traditional gender associations. The duet is traditionally performed by two women, a soprano and a mezzo-soprano. In *Anomalisa*, the piece is heard twice, both times sung by one man (first Noonan, then David Thewlis in the role of Michael). So even though, as David L. Smith argued, Michael's purchase of the animatronic doll might be read as the act that wills Lisa and her "miraculous" voice into being, we might instead interpret Michael's choice of the *Lakmé* duet for his listening material, and later for his performance of it in the shower (not to mention humming it in the taxi), as a foreshadowing of the fetishized voice that he experiences with Lisa and the Japanese doll. Michael appears similarly obsessed with this song, and yet he cannot hear it as it was meant to sound (sung by two complementary female voices), and so its reoccurrence anticipates his interest in hearing Lisa and the animatronic doll sing. Again, it is the singing voice—the one less easily replicated via technology—that helps when piecing together *Anomalisa*'s complex rendering of gender, digitality, and embodiment, including a willingness to break down boundaries between stereotypically male and female voices.

The performance of womanhood by men is also facilitated through the voice in *Her*. In one scene, Theodore describes himself as a "girl" via an interior monologue voiceover, when ghostwriting on behalf of a woman. Referring to the voice-over narration of a letter Theodore wrote to a man, from the subject position of the female partner, Kornhaber described both the letter and its narration as "a kind of deadpan drag act." She tied this observation to Theodore/Phoenix's vocal delivery, noting that the gender switch is "unmarked by any fluctuation in Theodore's largely flat delivery."[60] In this regard, Theodore's job is similar to Phoenix's, and, even more so in relation to *Anomalisa*, Noonan's. While Phoenix and Noonan technically (if temporarily) voice female characters, they do so without making explicit attempts to sound more like women, such as by raising their pitch or engaging in vocal fry or uptalk (considered elsewhere in this book as commonly critiqued aspects of the twenty-first-century female voice).

The Congress's extreme posthuman vision of the world also presents a scenario allowing for cisgender male voices to emerge from identifiably cisgender female bodies—but ones that are in fact synthetic, technological machines. In a climactic scene, the head of the futurist congress delivers his speech about a new chemical substance to a crowd of attendees. To demonstrate how the new substance will allow everyone to shape-shift in more radical ways, he sniffs it and begins to morph into different bodies: that of a cowboy, a Jesus-like figure, and finally the animated Robin Wright, dressed in her "Rebel Robot Robin" costume. Presented in lip sync from Robin's body, his male voice booms, "You have a dream? Be your dream, for God's sake." The scene's reference to God provides a dark irony, given that the man who says this is effectively using scientific and technological developments to play God—and to present as a cisgender woman.

The fact that Scarlett Johansson's voice includes some stereotypically masculine qualities may help to explain why she was brought in to replace Samantha Morton. Like Theo's voice, Samantha's could be described as queer in terms of its gender fluidity and liminality, particularly given her status as a disembodied operating system. Her role thus aligns with Jarman-Ivens's observation that otherwise gender normative voices can become queer once they are artificialized through technological means. The technological mediation lends them some of inherent queerness of liminal cyborg figures.[61] In effect, then, all three films employ the voice in ways that suggest increased gender fluidity, destabilizing the gender dynamics that might otherwise be gauged based purely on visual representation, as in Virginás's argument that female-presenting AIs constitute a "reloading" of the historical "male gaze." Mulvey's initial theory of the "male gaze" was critiqued for taking the heterosexual man as the default voyeuristic viewer (disregarding the implications for both queer men and women). But factoring both male and female voices into the overall presentation of male and female characters in these films can reveal the more ambiguous, and more queer, dimensions of gender dynamics contained in them. Setting aside Johansson as Samantha, in these instances the "male gaze" is not so much "reloaded" (Virginás's term again) as it is reworked—partly because of scenes where men's voices ventriloquize animated female bodies. At the same time, these moments point to a future where women (and their voices) might be seen (and heard) less often, at least on screen, than they are today. Digital technologies might replace them visually, and vocally androgynous male performers could replace them vocally.

THE VOICE AS SOUL

Voice is a kind of sound characteristic of what has soul in it; nothing that is without soul utters voice.
STEVEN CONNOR, *DUMBSTRUCK*

In various ways, the films under discussion here all align with Connor's fore-grounding of the voice as an ensouled form of expression, a manifestation of presence. These ideas connect right back to the work of Aristotle.[62] Connor noted that for a sound to be "recognized as a voice rather than as a sound," it had to be "assumed to be coming from a person or conscious agency."[63] Similarly, for Walter Ong, a historian and philosopher of orality, "voice is not *peopled* with presences. It itself is the manifestation of presence."[64] *Anomalisa*, *The Congress*, and *Her* all center their futuristic worlds around such distinctions. Each film presents its audience with characters who are either posthuman within the filmic world (Samantha as operating system; Robin Wright's animated self and her digital avatar), or who are explicitly coded as mechanical (*Anomalisa*'s 3D-printed puppets, with visible joins on their face plates). But the films confuse the characters' status as posthuman, or artificially intelligent, by providing them with human voices—voices that are automatically accompanied by the souls of the actors who perform them, and which thus serve as manifestations of human presence. Considered from this perspective, it seems clear that although using synthetic, computer-generated voices would be more radical, it would likely destroy an audience's ability to suspend enough disbelief to buy into Theodore falling in love with his operating system, or Michael falling for Lisa and the animatronic Japanese doll, or Robin Wright as a human who has been technologically captured and multiplied across new digital formats. The overall impact of all three films thus depends on a fundamental, voice-based disavowal—a human voice, emitting from a posthuman character.

At certain points, these narratives orient themselves quite directly toward questions of difference between humans and their technologically determined surrogates. During an animated segment of *The Congress*, a Miramount executive tells Robin, "You might have sold your image as an actress, but the actress never left your soul." Significantly, he refers here to Robin's *image* only and, indeed, in all but the scene of digital avatar Robin being interviewed on screen, scenes of the avatar Robin do not include her voice (the scanning process itself is focused on the visual aspects, though with reference to an attempt to capture her laughter). Even if "the actress never left [Robin's] soul," what is an actress without the ability to express a performance through her body, including through her voice? This scene, along with two others in which the animated Wright is pulled off a stage where she holds a microphone, seem to suggest that without the ability to use her voice as she desires, her life is not a free or meaningful one.

The complex narratives of *Anomalisa*, *The Congress*, and *Her* all suggest that there will be a continued demand for "ensouled" voices: when it comes to digitally rendered characters, actresses currently seem more likely to be visually rather than vocally replaced. Even within *The Congress*'s otherwise somber account of the future of the film industry, Wright's voice is central to her various technological doubles. In these films, the female voice is rendered uncanny not just through the use of character doubles, but also through strategic uses of digital animation, including *Anomalisa*'s merging of 3D-printed puppets with traditional stop-motion animation. Both *The Congress* and *Anomalisa* complicate existing understandings of animation's uncomfortable "uncanny valley" effect, which tend to focus on visual shortcomings in animated characters. As Stephen Prince observed in relation to photo-realist animations such as *Beowulf* (Robert Zemeckis, 2007), animated characters' faces and expressions are subjected to unconscious but intense scrutiny by audiences, and this can lead to criticisms of characters' photo-realist eyes as "vacant and lifeless" relative to those of real humans.[65] And yet, as revealed by the importance of the expressive human voice to *Anomalisa* and *The Congress*, vocal markers can similarly reveal when characters are convincingly human and when they are not.

Prince argued that the danger of a photo-realist film entering the uncanny valley (by attempting to make animated characters look as human as possible) is why many digital animators at Disney and Pixar present characters as stylized and cartoonish.[66] *Anomalisa* and *The Congress* instead use voices to deal with this danger. Both draw explicit attention to their animated worlds—through the very visible lines on the puppets' faces in *Anomalisa*, and by having Wright willingly agree to be turned into an animated version of herself in *The Congress*. The burden is then placed on the voices of the actresses, Jason Leigh and Wright, to imbue their characters with the humanness required for the narrative focus on personhood and identity in their respective diegetic worlds, where humans are being threatened by their technological replacements.

Considered together, the treatment of women's voices in these three films reflects current trends in speech technologies and assistants. They also anticipate where these technologies may be going. In particular, by placing the audience in the point-of-audition of the central male character, *Anomalisa* and *Her* can suggest—and even encourage—a world in which technology intensifies the fetishization of an actress's voice that is simultaneously cast off from her body. As the ongoing issues around "deepfake" porn would suggest, the increased use of creative technologies may lead to digital recordings of vocal performances being fed into software that creates "deepfake" voices, thus appropriating actresses' bodies in a different way. The issues with these technologies, particularly for performers, are especially well rendered in *The Congress*. The scene where the animated Wright grasps for her throat, upon hearing her digital avatar speak with her own voice, offers a powerful moment for reflection on whether this might be possible in the future, and if so, when that will happen, as well as why female actors may be particularly affected (as with "deepfake" porn). Wright's performance of Leonard Cohen's song reinforces the film's inherent commentary on such issues: she will speak no more, as she is spoken for. As "deepfake" voice technologies such as Adobe VoCo and Lyrebird continue to emerge on the consumer market, such lyrics may prove eerily prescient. As mentioned, the voice of HAL 9000 in *2001: A Space Odyssey* influenced many programmers, causing them to create voice technologies with feminine-sounding voices instead of masculine-sounding ones. And those working on speech technologies and in the film industry continue to negotiate questions around voice and gender. Science fiction and the science of real-world technologies remain entwined, like two strands of DNA coiling around each other. The double helix that results contains instructions for the development and representation of voice technologies now and in the future.

CHAPTER 3

THE EXPANDED AND IMMERSIVE VOICE-OVER

BACK IN 2017, I VISITED THE MUSEUM of the University of St Andrews, MUSA, part of an ancient university in a Scottish seaside town where I was lecturing at the time. Inside I saw a black-and-white headshot of the actress Joanna Lumley with a pair of headphones framing her face. The sign was an invitation to "join" Lumley on a tour through the galleries using the museum's free audio guide. A few months later, just a few streets over, I had my first go at virtual reality using an Oculus Rift headset. A hand-drawn animation, *Dear Angelica* (2017), had been downloaded for staff and students to try out. After donning the headset, I heard the voices of two other actresses: Geena Davis as Angelica, and Mae Whitman as her daughter.

The similarities between the two experiences were hard to miss: while they did not take place in a cinema, or even on a screen, both involved listening to famous actresses whose voices were familiar to anyone who has sampled their film and TV work. Both setups also required becoming immersed in their voices, and both the headphones and the headset blocked out almost all background noise to deepen this immersion. My immediate impression was that Lumley, Davis, and Whitman had provided variations on the traditional screen voice-over. I began to consider how these examples were tied to the various other new media formats where we increasingly listen to actresses narrate stories: Instagram videos, web documentaries, audiobooks, podcasts, visual albums—all those spaces beyond the traditional big screen (where they are now also heard). The very number and nature of these narrating women provide a jarring contrast to much of twentieth-century film history, urging reflection on whether it is the technology, the industry, or the women themselves driving the trend.

No aspect of women's screen voices has received more attention than their work in narration—or lack thereof—particularly in relation to

mid-twentieth-century cinema. Writing on women's voice-overs in classical Hollywood and other mid-twentieth-century cinema, scholars such as
Kaja Silverman and Amy Lawrence are unlikely to have anticipated the
sheer ease with which women could record, edit, and distribute their own
narrated videos in the digital era. Whether the final destination is YouTube,
or, increasingly, for actresses, Instagram, the near ubiquity of smart devices
with in-built cameras and microphones has made narrating episodes from
one's personal life a popular way to communicate with fans and a broader
audience. And significantly, these modes allow for increased control over
that narration, including control over whether to speak from an on-screen
or an off-screen space. Silverman stressed the rarity of disembodied female
voice-overs and demonstrated how the typical female narrator was tied to
her body much more than the typical male narrator was tied to his. She also
identified various strategies for keeping female voices "overheard," and
therefore less authoritative than men's voices, such as framing them within
the constraints of a letter.[1] But much has changed in the subsequent decades
since "New Hollywood," particularly since the 1990s. Women now provide narration across a wide range of film genres and media formats, from
romantic comedies to documentaries and television shows.

Even prior to the emergence of streaming sites and social media platforms,
in the postclassical Hollywood period audiences became increasingly used to
hearing actresses' disembodied voices in a range of formats. Drawing on and
extending theories of "expanded cinema" and intermediality, in this chapter
I trace these changes. In particular, I consider how digital formats and platforms such as Instagram and virtual reality provide new audiovisual spaces
from which women can narrate, and how voice-overs by familiar actresses
are being used to help initiate audiences into various new forms of digital
entertainment. As part of a broader shift toward women's voice-overs that
are notably reflexive and intermedial, their narrations can be hyper-aware
of the high stakes involved in the female voice-over.

To date, theories of expanded cinema overwhelmingly focus on images
and visual culture.[2] As such they risk repeating the historical trend within
film studies to discuss cinema as a visual medium. Image-focused approaches
to expanded cinema can thus disregard the significant developments in film
sound scholarship since the 1980s. They are also out of step with efforts
by other digitally oriented film scholars who have, for instance, pushed
for the term *audiovisual* essay over video essay in relation to videographic
criticism. Locating, or inserting, the voice in theories of expanded cinema
is just as important.

But first, what is "expanded cinema"? According to media theorist Gene

Youngblood's influential definition in a 1970 book, the term refers to a shift away from traditional cinematic spectacles toward forms of screen culture that are more immersive, interactive, and interconnected.[3] In this and subsequent scholarship, Youngblood discussed expanded cinema in terms of moving images and visual culture, albeit with the occasional audio reference.[4]

Sound, including the ways in which voices can function in expanded cinema, is also of rare concern for Youngblood's critical successors. In thinking about the narrative and aesthetic aspects of the voice-over from the perspective of expanded cinema, I was thus struck by a rare and revealing mention of a narrator in *Expanded Cinema: Art, Performance, Film*, edited by A. L. Rees and fellows from the British Artists' Film and Video Study Collection at Central Saint Martins.[5] The collection focuses on narrative in expanded cinema, but it largely ignores sound, including the voice and voice-over.[6] Yet the very first entry in the book's opening four-page historical timeline mentions vocal narration, summarizing the tradition of the "barker" in pre-sound "cine-lectures," whose role was to "narrate over the top of silent film." In this format, the timeline says, "often control of the 'narrative' belonged to the exhibitor rather than the filmmaker or distributor."[7] The timeline ends with a brief entry on virtual reality. And although there is no overt link between the pre-sound barker and VR, I will consider how they connect in terms of the voice and narrative control. These two narrative modes might be considered analog and digital versions of the expanded voice-over—an expansion of voice beyond the traditional film screen. As Rees and his coauthors suggested, because barkers provided commentary on the silent film (as directed by the exhibitor who hired them), they ultimately could control the narrative more than filmmakers could. As my subsequent analysis of the female voice in the VR experience *Dear Angelica* will explore, despite being associated with placing narrative control in the hands of the individual user, VR can give narrative authority to the voice that "narrates over the top" of the immersive experience. Meanwhile, the spatial properties of VR can shift the parameters for examining the female voice as it relates to the traditional screen.

Other dimensions of expanded cinema, especially its emphasis on immersivity and interactivity, are similarly instructive in understanding the workings of women's digital-era voice-overs. By examining Busy Philipps's and Sarah Jessica Parker's distinctive use of voice-over on Instagram, for example, I explore their ability to self-cast themselves as narrators and to decide when they will appear on and off screen while narrating moments from their everyday lives. By further connecting Parker's use of Instagram to her earlier narratorial roles across television, digital documentaries, and museum audio guides, I will show how she exemplifies the intermedial narrator as it is grounded in Youngblood's work on the "open feedback system," which he said can facilitate expanded cinema's diffusion across media formats.[8] The workings of such narration can seem indebted to the historical practices of the film-based voice-over, as when spoken words are tied to textual sources. In the digital era, however, the voice-over can be tied to things these women have typed into a smart device, rather than written as letters. In keeping with broader digital aesthetics, fragments of the women's speech can be superimposed over their videos, with the built-in editing functions on the various platforms helping them to rework historical trends (for example, for female narrators' voices to be tied to textual sources such as letters). In the VR experience *Dear Angelica*, lines of speech from a letter float around the three-dimensional space, providing another way for the user to become immersed in the women's voices.

The examples considered here are symbolic of the many branches extending from the trunk of the traditional screen voice-over. By examining how these different voice-overs present an embodied or disembodied form of narration, as well as how they address the audience's own body, I aim to identify the complicated patterns of growth emerging from this particular vocal organism.

MORE VOICE-OVERS, MORE REFLEXIVE

Since the end of the twentieth century there has been a strong trend toward a self-reflexive treatment of the female narrator. Such voice-overs can depend less on technological shifts than on a broader embracing of intertextuality and postmodern play, shifts attuned to audiences assumed to be highly familiar with traditional film and media tropes. In 1995, the critical and box-office success of Amy Heckerling's *Clueless* demonstrated the comedic potential of the knowing young female narrator. From *Clueless*'s Cher we might trace a line through to independent films such as *The Opposite of Sex* (Don Roos, 1998), with its sardonic narrator Dedee (Christina Ricci), and *In a World* . . . (Lake Bell, 2013), with voice-over artist Carol (Lake Bell), among others. And although there are examples of male voice-overs that engage playfully with voice-over conventions—such as Charlie Kaufman's screenplay for *Adaptation* (Spike Jonze, 2002)—the shift is more apparent in relation to female narrators. Sarah Kozloff began her 2012 article on voice-over in contemporary romantic comedy by acknowledging changes both in relation to voice-over in genre cinema and in relation to her previous accounts of it: "When I wrote *Invisible Storytellers* in the mid-1980s, romantic comedy was not one of the genres that leapt out at me. *Noir*, of course, with its use of first-person detectives; adaptations of famous novels replicating the narrator's commentary (whether first-person or third); semi-documentaries with epics with their god-like scene-setters—all appeared more prominent. . . . However, voice-over has become—to varying degrees, and for different purposes—a staple element of *contemporary* romantic comedies."[9]

Kozloff's subsequent analysis of a range of romantic comedies spans a roughly fifteen-year period, from *Clueless* to *(500) Days of Summer* (Marc Webb, 2009). And though she is right that narrators appear frequently in such romantic comedies, in this period female narrators also appeared more often across all forms of US cinema than in previous periods. In *Secretary* (2002), for example, Maggie Gyllenhaal narrates her character's self-harm and sadomasochistic relationship with her boss, and in *The Good Girl* (2002), the jaded Justine (Jennifer Aniston) recounts her disappointments with small-town life. At the end of the century, Winona Ryder provided a voice-over in nearly every film in which she appeared, regardless of genre: from the dark teen comedy *Heathers* (1988) to the coming-of-age family drama *Mermaids* (1990), and the adaptation of *Girl, Interrupted* (1999). More broadly, since the 1990s women's voice-overs have appeared with increased frequency across various modes of English-language filmmaking, including documentaries. Furthermore, although Kozloff's case studies were of young women (late teens to early thirties), late twentieth and early twenty-first-century dramas and documentaries have frequently been narrated by more mature actresses, including Holly Hunter in *The Piano* (Jane Campion, 1993), Patricia Clarkson in *Regarding Susan Sontag* (Nancy Kates, 2014), and Rachel Weisz in *The Lobster* (Yorgas Lanthimos, 2015).[10] Since Derek Jarman's *Blue* (1993), Tilda Swinton has also continued to provide narration for experimental documentaries and films, including *When Björk Met Attenborough* (Louise Hooper, 2013) and Jóhann Jóhannsson's *Last and First Men* (2017). The female narrator is no longer the rare species she once was.

The Opposite of Sex is a significant example of the newly reflexive uses of women narrators in this period. As Kozloff explained of sixteen-year-old Dedee's distinctive voice-over, "She is completely unruly both as a person and a narrator. Cynical, angry, and totally unscrupulous, she talks about herself, but she also wields a god-like omniscience in terms of her range, communicativeness, and a wry self-reflexivity."[11] Consider how Dedee addresses the viewer at the beginning of the film:

If you're one of those people who don't like movies where some person you can't see talks the whole time and covers up all the holes in the plot and at the end says, "I was never the same again after that summer," or whatever, like it was so deep they can't stand it, then you're out of luck. Things get very complicated here very quick. And my guess is you're not gonna be up to it without me talking.

Right from the start, Dedee positions herself as an ambivalent narrator: explicitly reluctant to use the clichéd device, and yet equally explicit that it is necessary that she speak to us directly—and that we listen. Unlike many other narrators who directly address the audience, Dedee does not welcome us into her world so much as she acknowledges our codependence on one another. As Kozloff noted, Dedee's narration wryly mocks the use of voice-over in the 1950s.[12] Moreover, she provides a much more droll and reflexive voice-over than that of the middle-aged Lester Burnham (Kevin Spacey) in *American Beauty* (1999), released a year after *The Opposite of Sex* to much more critical acclaim and commercial success. Burnham's voice—quickly revealed to be speaking to us posthumously—largely repeats the narration style of classical Hollywood noir films, such as *Sunset Boulevard* (Billy Wilder, 1950), which also begins with a dead man talking.

Dedee's knowing deconstruction of the voice-over as a cinematic device is perhaps most notable in relation to her final words and actions, which bring together her intra- and extra-diegetic voices, and her visible and invisible body, to enact control over when we can hear her versus when we can see *and* hear her. After an emotive montage sequence of Dedee and other characters, she closes the film with the following narrated passage, as Kozloff transcribed and described it:

I'll tell you one thing. I'm not gonna go back to Bill's house and be this big changed person for you. I told you right off I don't grow a heart of gold. And if I do, which is, like, so unlikely, give me a break and don't make me do it in front of you! [*Dedee glares and the camera and motions it away*] Come on, guys, go, okay? Go! [*Black screen.*] I'll give you this much, though . . . [*Fake dreamy tone of voice*] I never was the same again after that summer.

The setup is remarkable in its reflexivity, particularly in the way it seems to acknowledge and rework the gendered power dynamics that Silverman and Lawrence described in relation to how the female film voice is tied to her synchronized body. As Dedee's remarks make clear, she has not only been aware that we are listening to her throughout, but she is also aware that we've been watching her. It is only in this closing moment, however, that the diegetic version of Dedee acknowledges the audience and she uses her voice (as a character spatially and temporally split from her narrator-self) to demand visual privacy: "Don't make me do it in front of you!" Moreover, the film could reasonably have ended on the directly parting word—"go!"—and the corresponding shift to a black screen—as such, there is significance to her final, narrated lines, which return Dedee/Ricci to her role of disembodied narrator. With Ricci's delivery shifting to what Kozloff described as a "fake dreamy tone of voice," the final impression is of voice-over not just as a narrative device, but as a performative one, wherein vocal traits are "put on" for the audience's benefit. Dedee (and Ricci) takes pleasure in her mastery of the performative rules of the voice-over game, as do many of her screen contemporaries.

Dedee and *Clueless*'s Cher are only part of the story of this shift toward mostly white female voice-overs that are self-aware and veer toward the unapologetically self-centered. For the director of *Just Another Girl on the I.R.T.* (1992), Leslie Harris, the decision to make sustained use of a voice-over and direct address was tied to a different kind of objective, a desire to provide Black teenage girls with a voice, as well as a chance to undo stereotypes about them and inner city life.[13] Discussing the film in 2018, twenty-five years after its release, Harris noted that the film was "maybe a little bit ahead of its time," an assessment that certainly applies to the narration by seventeen-year-old Chantel (Ariyan Johnson).[14] Chantel's attitude and unsympathetic nature are similar in some ways to Dedee's, whose film came six years later. Film scholar Paula J. Massood described her as at times "rude" and "self-centered" and noted how facets of Chantel's character were off-putting for some audiences, but provided a strong point of identification for others.[15]

Voice-overs performed by Black women are at this time generally cast by Black creators, usually women. Noteworthy examples include Julie Dash's *Daughters of the Dust* (1996), and digital expansions, such as Beyoncé's visual album *Lemonade* (HBO, 2016), and Issa Rae's web series *Awkward Black Girl* (2011–2013). *Precious: Based on the Novel "Push" by Sapphire* (Lee Daniels, 2009) also follows this trend. It was adapted for the screen by two Black men (director Daniels and screenwriter Geoffrey Shawn Fletcher), but the full title of the film nonetheless highlights the underlying creative force of Sapphire in the character brought to life by Gabourey Sidibe, whose racial identity is foregrounded from Precious's opening voice-over.[16] Unfortunately, the pioneering techniques used in such voice-overs can be largely overlooked, especially in the popular media, meaning that a narrator such as Chantel, in *Just Another Girl on the I.R.T.*, will be mostly forgotten, while *Clueless*'s Cher leaves an enduring cultural legacy (as we will see in chapter 5, in relation to the use of her voice in contemporary political memes).

Figure 3.1 Screenshot of Carol (Lake Bell) giving voice lessons to young women in *In A World . . .* (2013). Produced by Stage 6 Films and 3311 Productions.

Though the trend toward an increasingly self-aware female narrator emerged with these films in the 1990s, it came to full fruition in the 2010s with *In a World . . .*, a comedy written and directed by Lake Bell and also starring her as a voice-over artist. *In a World . . .* places a narrative focus on gender discrimination in the niche world of voice-over acting, thus deriving its very premise from historical assumptions that film voice-overs—and those in film trailers, in particular—privilege the sonorous hypermasculine narrator. The very existence (and critical success of) *In a World . . .*—a film largely *about* gender and the voice-over—reflects the evolution of women's voice-overs in film and related media since the time of classical Hollywood. Like Dedee in *The Opposite of Sex*, Carol (as well as her performer, Bell) uses a voice-over to showcase her vocal versatility and ability to use narration for her own pleasure and to achieve her goals. Carol makes a living from her ability to transform both her own voice and those of others—working as a vocal coach as well as a voice-over artist. The film's treatment of the female voice, and voice-over, treads a fine line between delivering playful critical commentary and reinforcing or policing gendered vocal stereotypes, particularly since Carol feels compelled to give "voice overs" (vocal makeovers) to women she hears speaking in high-pitched, questioning tones (figure 3.1). Hyper-aware of the vocal qualities that can lead to young women, in particular, being taken less seriously, or listened to less, Carol eventually attempts to help them. Yet earlier in the film she uses her vocal range to mimic and mock them. Indeed, it is easy to imagine young women with similar voices watching the film and feeling indirectly critiqued for having a voice that is too hesitant or too babyish. Such viewers may conclude that they, too, need a vocal makeover. Other elements of the film are more progressive. Like *The Opposite of Sex*, *In a World . . .* suggests that a productive way to address women's historical marginalization as film narrators is to "call out" the conventions and playfully deconstruct them. With *In a World . . .* , the deep male voice of the film trailer is taken up as the historical trend to be wryly mocked.

THE INSTAGRAM NARRATOR

In *The Opposite of Sex*, Dedee uses her awareness of her own omniscience to demand visual privacy (directly addressing the camera and telling us to "go!"). Fast-forward some eighteen years, and social media platforms such as Instagram now allow for more organic forms of both sharing and putting boundaries on sharing, by actresses who script or improvise narration for themselves. Social media has become the soapbox of choice for many celebrities with news to share or causes to publicize. In particular, Instagram's two main options for video sharing—either on the profile "feed" or via the daily "Stories" function, where content disappears after a day—have resulted in some unprecedented trends for actresses. Busy Philipps and Sarah Jessica Parker are just two actresses who publicly narrate their own videos, and lives, in real time. Philipps's use of Instagram's ephemeral videos quickly drew the attention of the *New Yorker*, which declared her "the Breakout Star of Instagram Stories" in a 2017 profile.[17] Accompanying Marisa Meltzer's article was a roughly two-minute compilation of some of Philipps's Instagram Stories—captioned "Busy Philipps's World." As the credit sequence signaled, with an explicit credit to Philipps, these videos are no longer accessible via her Instagram profile, because they "disappeared" from public view twenty-four hours after being posted. (Users can save their own videos, but not those of others.)

When Philipps addresses her followers, often beginning a new story with a direct address ("You guys . . .") she appears to be candid and unscripted, recounting something that has just happened to her, or, as is often the case, commenting on what is currently happening in the space around her. Pivoting the camera to give viewers glimpses of the "action" before returning to a direct address, she is like an adult version *Clueless*'s omniscient narrator, Cher: more self-aware, and with more responsibilities (including two daughters), but with a similar "Valley girl" accent and flair for narrating the everyday ups and downs of Los Angeles life.

Philipps's videos revealed her to be a candid conversationalist, capable of developing an engaging rapport with her audience—so much so that the US network E! hired her for a late-night talk show, *Busy Tonight* (2018–2019). With executive producers including Tina Fey and Philipps herself, media critics were quick to point out how Philipps was joining a very small group of women hosts "who've broken into the boys' club of late-night television."[18] Philipps's show was discussed alongside *The Late Show Starring Joan Rivers* (a short-lived show running in 1986 and 1987). Indeed, the rarity of women in late-night television in the United States was abundantly clear in *Vanity Fair*'s 2015 profile on "the titans of late-night television," a piece focusing on ten men—the vast majority of whom were also straight and white.[19] Though E! is not the same kind of major network, and the network canceled the show after just 105 episodes, Philipps's trajectory from Instagram narrator to talk-show host was still remarkable. It is a reminder of the increased influence of social media and digital celebrity culture on the traditional media industries of film and television. This trend has also seen the multi-hyphenate Issa Rae (an actor-writer-director-producer) move from her low-budget *Awkward Black Girl* web series to cocreating the award-winning series *Insecure* (2016–) for HBO, a show that—like the web series—grants Rae's character Issa Dee her own voice-over.

Like Rae, Philipps followed a trajectory that demonstrated the substantial power and influence that a woman can acquire by developing her own (digital) space from which to narrate. Philipps found a way to employ the structural rules of an existing platform, Instagram, for her own purposes. For example, aside from disappearing after twenty-four hours, videos in Stories initially had to be recorded in short fifteen-second segments. Philipps's verbal-vocal style was largely in keeping with the norms of video blogs: a direct address to a camera and a heavy use of vocal emphasis (overstressed or long vowels, for instance) in order to retain the audience's attention.[20] Her various talks have a focus, however marginal, but they are (or at least seem) unscripted. Particularly notable are the variations in Philipps's visual appearance across her Instagram videos: she has recorded herself sitting in her car, lying on her kitchen floor, and watching television in bed, for example, where she live-narrates reruns of the sitcom *Friends* (NBC, 1994–2004), directing her iPhone camera to the TV screen while commenting on the scenes. Compared to the posts on her main feed, which are generally high-quality portraits of herself and her daughters (often taken by Philipps's film director husband, Mark Silverstein), the Stories posts are often less polished: she appears without makeup, and in her bed or wearing workout clothes. The impression is that of a woman who sees the value or power in what she has to say and show, however incidental the narrative or subject matter—a power that is not dependent on her looking her best when she talks to her captive audience of followers. And so even though Silverman might suggest that Philipps's voice on Instagram is still tied to her body (when she records in selfie mode

or posts polished portraits of herself on her main profile), Philipps's nat-
uralness—conversationally and physically—belies a confidence. Philipps
casts *herself* as Instagram's preeminent celebrity orator and, unlike on *Busy
Tonight*, she does not see the need to go through hair and make-up for the
"job." Nor can she be fired from it. Instead, she brings a sense of liveness
to her narration—alternating between being in and out of the frame, for
example, in order to cover the subject at hand, like an on-the-scene reporter
of the absurdities of everyday life.

Philipps's adaptation of her Instagram voice to that of a television talk-
show host reflected the increased influence of social media and digital celebrity
culture on the traditional media industries. This influence is also a crucial
feature of *Ingrid Goes West* (Matt Spicer, 2017), a dark comedy about an
unhinged young woman, Ingrid (Aubrey Plaza), who moves to Los Angeles to
stalk an Instagram influencer named Taylor (Elizabeth Olsen). Ingrid copies
Taylor's Instagram aesthetic and learns how to perform her own heightened
digital identity. Notably, the film highlights certain connections between
the traditional female voice-over and the social media voice, and allows for
specific elements of the stereotypical female social media voice to be heard
in a more traditional screen format: narrated over the big screen. Like *In
a World . . .*, *Ingrid Goes West* engages playfully with audiences' assumed
familiarity with screen-based vocal norms. And while *In a World . . .* holds
up the film trailer, with its sonorous male voice-over, as its familiar subject
for soft ridicule, the female voice-over in *Ingrid Goes West*'s trailer (and a
related segment of the film) parodies the pseudo-sincerity of social media
influencers—both in terms of their content and its delivery. In performing
Taylor's voice-over, Elizabeth Olsen uses an inflection that seems purposefully
vacuous and different from Taylor's diegetic delivery of dialogue throughout
the rest of the film. The voice-over, implied to be that of Taylor narrating her
own life via her Instagram profile, signals the distance between her everyday
existence and her performed social media identity. Taylor's inflections in the
voice-over also require Olsen to depart from her natural vocal register (and
tendency to play thoughtful young women) to instead signal how a vacuous
woman might sound, as though Instagram's digital editing filters could be
applied to voices as well as images.

In *Ingrid Goes West*, the voice-over is tied to a textual source, things the
young women have written, and in this case typed via smart device. The film
updates the trope, however, by providing vocalized versions of a distinctly
digital vernacular. We hear Taylor verbalizing the # symbols posted in her
Instagram captions ("hashtag blessed"; "hashtag California"), as well as
the clichéd wisdom of "inspirational" captions, as when Ingrid's bride-to-be

Figure 3.2. Screenshot of a Busy Philipps Instagram "Story" from September 22, 2019, complete with a superimposed text excerpt from her speech in the video.

friend quips, "The couple that yogas, stays together." What we hear in voice-over is implied to be intra-diegetic, things the characters have typed and posted but not necessarily said aloud. And the audience is positioned to hear things from Ingrid's obsessive perspective as she becomes haunted by the familiar captions and voices of women whose (digital) lives seem so superior to her own.

This technique, of vocalizing digital text and thus smoothing distinctions between the typed and the spoken, is also found in Philipps's Instagram Stories posts, as she uses the platform's built-in editing function to super-impose fragments of her speech over the videos of her speaking. Acting like the editor of her own improvised script, Philipps picks out key soundbites, emphasizing what she deems the key points of a given spoken segment, or superimposing text to add emphasis (figure 3.2). Given that her followers may be watching the videos with the sound off, these visualized soundbites serve as partial subtitles, becoming motivators to turn on the sound and listen to what Philipps has to say.

THE INTERMEDIAL NARRATOR

These audiovisual formats—social media and film, exemplified here by Philipps's strategies as an Instagram narrator and the filmic presentation of the social media voice in *Ingrid Goes West*, respectively—are distinct, and yet they can mutually influence one another when it comes to the verbal, vocal, and visual presentation of the female screen voice. Elsewhere on Instagram, Sarah Jessica Parker provides a very different kind of self-styled voice-over. We can see the seeds of Parker's disembodied Instagram narration in her voice-over on *Sex and the City* (HBO, 1998–2004) as well as in her various other roles as narrator, such as for *Vogue*'s online documentaries, or in museum audio guides.

Parker's ties to screen narration date back to her career-defining role as sex columnist Carrie Bradshaw in *Sex and the City*. Though best remembered for its focus on fashion, and for its boundary-pushing depiction of the sexual lives of single women, Carrie's voice-over—framed as an interior monologue as she types up newspaper articles—helped launch a trend for female narrators on US television. When ABC's *Desperate Housewives* (2004–2012) began to be aired, its posthumous narrator Mary Alice (Brenda Strong) reworked the doomed noir narration of *Sunset Boulevard*, yet the interlinking "wisdom" of her observations also suggested the influence of Parker's voice-over as Carrie. With *Gossip Girl* (2007–2012), television's increased reliance on narration by a female voice (Kristen Bell) was both confirmed and denied when—in the final episode—the mysterious but omniscient blogger, "Gossip Girl," is revealed to be one of the male characters. Though in keeping with the novel on which the show was based, this revelation could be seen to confound the trust that audiences have in omniscient narrators.[21] In this case, we must consider the impact of hearing Bell's voice throughout the series, and then retroactively reconcile this with the fact that the "true" authorial voice of the narration belonged to a man. A more recent, but similarly revisionist, use of narratorial tropes can be found in *Fleabag* (BBC, 2016–2019). Phoebe Waller-Bridge, as writer, creator, and star of the show, has received considerable critical acclaim for her experimental and restrained use of direct address. As cultural critic Clem Bastow put it, "From a screenwriting perspective, this repurposing of hoary narrative tools is part of Waller-Bridge's sly feminist genius: she shows how good they can be, then walks away from them."[22]

While Parker's narration on *Sex and the City* helped usher in a new trend for female narration on television, it also led to off-screen opportunities for Parker to lend her voice to a range of other endeavors, beginning in 2008 with a Metropolitan Museum of Art exhibition tour for "Costume: The Art of Dress." Taking advantage of Parker's (and her character Carrie's) strong connections with New York and clothing, the audio tour looked at the historical costumes in the museum's permanent collections in order to explore the cultural significance of fashion through the ages. According to The Met, "Costume: The Art of Dress" became one of the most popular guided tours in the museum. Curator Harold Koda spoke of the added value that Parker's voice brought to the experience: "Walking through the galleries listening to Sarah Jessica Parker's narration [brings] a sense of discovery and delight to the experience."[23]

Up until Parker started posting Instagram voice-overs, her narratorial roles had typically had an educational focus, concentrating on different elements of fashion and costume. In 2011, she contributed to another Metropolitan Museum audio guide, this time for the high-profile exhibition "Alexander McQueen: Savage Beauty," which would later show at London's Victoria and Albert Museum. Excerpts from Parker's audio guide would be reproduced in publicity materials for the London version along with summaries. When Blaire Moskowitz, a marketing manager for the company that produced the audio guide, recounted Parker's interactions with the deceased McQueen, she said, "Sarah Jessica Parker revealed how . . . when the two of them rode together to the Met's ball, they remained respectively shy of one another."[24] And, as in her subsequent Instagram videos, one can see a certain introversion in how Parker talks about her interactions with McQueen and her predilection for making intimate revelations. The format allows her to be vocally present but visually absent.

Even more than Philipps's posts, Parker's Instagram voice-overs reflect digital developments in women's screen voices, and especially how they can shift from one audiovisual format to another. Parker's voice is a multi-platform one. On Instagram, she does not post video Stories, instead opting to upload thematically linked short videos with her own voice performing disembodied narration. Working within Instagram's sixty-second limit for profile videos, she tends to capture small slices of life, some in her home, others in the city or in nature. Parker never turns the camera on herself; nor are people her focus, although occasionally we hear a family member. Parker's soundtrack of choice tends to be the atmospheric sounds of the natural world (birds singing, wind, waves) or diegetic music. We listen to what she's listening to—be it the Beatles or the musician she describes in a caption as a "neighborhood flautist unintentionally scoring falling petals."[25] Like Philipps, she creates videos and narration that can feel very intimate, albeit in a different way. While Philipps tends toward comedic observation and action (her personal sitcom life), Parker's videos are contemplative, often reflecting on moments of stillness.

Of particular interest is Parker's use of a serialized structure where on the first day of the month she posts a video in which she whispers the words "Rabbit, rabbit," in keeping with a Western superstition that to do so brings good luck.[26] She started this practice on September 1, 2016, and the videos themselves are minor moments—often filmed in a garden or on a beach, showing the greenery or the sky. The implied premise is that Parker records one of these on the first day of every month regardless of where she is in the world.[27] Sometimes the location is identifiable, or identified in the caption, but often these are anonymous non-places—without identifiable markers, or even an identifiable creator—until we hear Parker's voice. Generally it comes at the very end of the short video, when she utters "Rabbit, rabbit." These words have become increasingly familiar to Parker's 5.6 million Instagram followers.[28] The whispered tone feels purposeful: a volume chosen as though to be heard by her phone microphone and Instagram followers, but not so loud as to drown out the atmospheric noises that she is taking care to record. It is a voice of intimacy, one that—in terms of the audio properties—would not be out of place among the hundreds of thousands of ASMR videos with which Parker's posts coexist online. Yet the context in which she delivers these words is quite different from that of ASMR videos. Unlike the whispering women of the latter, Parker's voice is used minimally, if in an intimate way.[29] Furthermore, unlike most ASMR voices, Parker's voice is loaded with familiarity. It builds on her long history of delivering various kinds of embodied and disembodied narration.

By 2017, shortly after posting her first series of "Rabbit, Rabbit" Instagram videos, Parker had also provided the narration to *Vogue*'s eleven-part digital documentary series *Vogue by the Decade*. Released as part of the magazine's 125th anniversary, the videos streamed simultaneously on *Vogue*'s website and YouTube, with Parker narrating over the two- to four-minute accounts of each decade, an intertwined history of fashion and the magazine.[30] In descriptions of the series, *Vogue* tied Parker's involvement to her personal fashion persona ("narrated by the stylish Sarah Jessica Parker"), yet there are also implicit intertextual links referring back to her character on *Sex and the City*. Carrie Bradshaw once gushed, "Sometimes I would buy *Vogue* instead of dinner. I felt it fed me more." By the end of Season 4, Bradshaw was writing freelance articles for the magazine.

In these ways, Parker's selection as narrator for *Vogue*'s documentary shorts was likely influenced as much by her role on *Sex and the City* and her subsequent audio guides for The Met as it was by her personal style. Equally notable, however, is how Parker's narration of the series also influenced her personal Instagram usage, particularly her "formula" of providing a "Rabbit, Rabbit" video on the first day of each month. Much as the *Vogue by the Decade* series was released as a staggered series of shorts rather than a single longer documentary, Parker has chosen a structured approach and a consistent yet minimal script for the personal series of videos she narrates for her followers.

Parker's Instagram narration thus exemplifies what I term the *intermedia voice-over*. *Intermedia* is another key term connected to the three qualities of immersivity, interactivity, and interconnectedness in Youngblood's formulation of expanded cinema. Youngblood conceived of cinema as part of an "intermedia network of cinema, television, radio, magazines, books and newspapers," stressing that "cinema isn't just something inside [this] environment"; instead, it is one of various "mediating channels between man and man, man and society." Later drawing a useful comparison between intermedia and energy systems in the Second Law of Thermodynamics, Youngblood connected this intermedia network to open feedback systems: "In the strictest sense, there are no truly 'closed' systems anywhere in the universe; all processes impinge upon and are affected by other processes in some way."[31] In this way, one cannot realistically disentangle the experience of hearing Parker's self-recorded voice on Instagram from prior experiences of her narrating, whether that be on *Sex and the City*, in the *Vogue* series, or via a museum headset. Unless one is hearing her voice narrate for the first time, then a given voice-over can thus be considered as an open feedback system affected by the memories of her voice across a variety of times and spaces.

Beyond Youngblood's own use of the term "intermedia"—which was also the name of his column in the *Los Angeles Free Press* from 1967 to 1970—this concept simultaneously developed a meaning in relation to science and technology. As defined in the 1960s by the American media arts collective USCO, "Intermedia refers to the simultaneous use of various media to create a total environmental experience for the audience. Meaning is communicated not by coding ideas into abstract literary language, but by creating an emotionally real experience through the use of audio-visual technology."[32] As this chapter suggests in relation to digital technologies and voice-over narration, the intermedia environment is indeed *audiovisual*—despite the tendency to disregard the audio elements in the aforementioned expanded cinema literature. For audiences in the twenty-first century, the experience of a narrator is often inflected with properties of its open feedback system.

Such properties are also characteristic of the transmedia nature of much digital content, whereby a single story or experience is told across multiple digital platforms and formats.[33]

Through their use of Instagram as a channel for vocal narration, both Philipps and Parker rework earlier channels through which female performers have navigated technological and industrial change. Gloria Swanson, for example, attempted to negotiate a transition from film to what was then the new broadcast medium of television in the late 1940s and early 1950s, in her short-lived talk show *The Gloria Swanson Hour* (WPIX, 1948). For Mary R. Desjardins, Swanson's glamorous film-star image was something of a hindrance to her transition to television. Traits such as spontaneity, intimacy, and ordinariness seemed better suited to the medium of television, and successful radio and comedy stars tended to exhibit these more than Swanson's brand of glamour.[34] These traits are arguably even more important to celebrities' use of Instagram, where seeming "relatable" to fans has become a priority for many. Parker and Philipps (particularly the latter) provide content, including video voice-over, that suggests a certain ordinary intimacy.

There are only a few overt links between Philipps and Parker that might explain their similar embracing of Instagram narration. Despite both women being blonde and slim, their appearances have been subject to similar critiques—for having faces that are longer or more angular than Hollywood's softly feminine ideal, for example. For a time in the mid-2000s, Parker's face was cruelly compared to that of a horse, or even to a foot, in memes and sketches, including on shows such as *Family Guy* (1999–).[35] Indeed, the originator of the "Sarah Jessica Parker Looks Like a Horse" meme was inspired by a line of Parker's dialogue in *Ed Wood* (Tim Burton, 1994), when her character asks, in response to a theater review, "Do I really have a face like a horse?"[36] Thus, while Philipps seems comfortable talking directly to her followers, even without makeup, and from the unflattering perspective of a front-facing camera, Parker's version of digital media authorship is grounded in the freedom to narrate over them but not appear *in* them, to be vocally present but visually absent. To be sure, Parker is visually present in some of her other Instagram posts. Yet, when it comes to her most intimate posts, where she is creating personal content rather than promoting her official work, she has the freedom to whisper to us from an off-screen space. She prevents the viewer from gazing upon her private self by staying behind the camera entirely. When Philipps narrates videos without make-up and while wearing her pajamas, she suggests a disregard for orienting her body to a critical gaze. Although working within Instagram's interface and structural constraints, both narrate their lives on their own terms.

HEADSETS AND VOCAL IMMERSIVITY: FROM AUDIO GUIDES TO VR

Much as Instagram videos can be considered a contemporary successor to the way that many actresses—including Swanson—migrated from film to television in the 1940s and 1950s, it is important to acknowledge the links between voicing VR and earlier vocal practices tied to immersive speakers, such as celebrity audio guides in museums by the likes of Parker, Joanna Lumley, and Susan Sarandon. With the latter cases, the actresses' suitability for such audio guide "roles" seemed tied to their sustained casting as narrators, which means that these, too, could be considered intermedial forms of the disembodied voice. Lumley, an Indian-born English actress, recorded the aforementioned audio guide for the Museum of the University of St Andrews in 2012. Sarandon recorded the audio guide for a Frida Kahlo exhibit at the Dali Museum in Florida in 2016. While Lumley and Sarandon are not the only famous performers to be cast in such roles, by looking at these two in more detail we can explore the links between audio guides narrated by mature actresses and their cumulative body of voice work for the screen, particularly their roles as documentary narrators.

"PICK UP A HEADSET AND DREAM"

Lumley's and Sarandon's long careers include sustained strands of vocal work. As journalist Tracy McVeigh put it in an article on Lumley in the *Guardian*, "Her voice is so loved that computer company AOL has long used it as their log-on welcome to their customers."[37] (This was in the United Kingdom; the AOL welcome and mail alerts were voiced by a man, Elwood Edwards, in the United States.) Thus, long before "Siri" and "Alexa" had made their virtual assistant debuts, Lumley was recording messages for a technology platform, and this precedent set up a certain conflation between digital voice technologies and actress voices. Since around 2010, Lumley has also produced and presented travel and geographic documentaries for the British broadcaster ITV.[38] She has taken a number of other narration roles as well, such as for the domestic violence short *The Audition* (2006), and the environmentally oriented *Restore the Earth* (2010). Collectively, these examples of her work imbue Lumley's disembodied voice with educational and authoritative qualities.

Despite her association with travel, Lumley has described how she recorded her audio tour for MUSA in London without ever visiting the museum in St Andrews (though she did visit the remote university to accept an honorary doctorate in 2006). Lumley noted the dreamlike potential of hearing a disembodied (female) voice in a headset. As such, the setup inadvertently anticipated VR's use of women's voices in *Dear Angelica* and *Arden's Wake: Tides Fall* (Eugene Chung, 2017), showing how the disembodied voices of museum spaces can constitute another form of expanded cinema's interest in screen-based installations. Lumley's voice (familiar from screen media) oriented the museum visitor to the 3D exhibition space. In noting her pleasure at providing the audio guide, Lumley spoke of how her voice could travel into headsets without her: "As I sat in the dark of a Soho recording studio I found myself yearning to be in the Museum, following my own instructions, as it were, unravelling the history of the marvels contained in every room and cabinet and case. One thing is sure: as soon as I possibly can, I shall visit what is now my alma mater, pick up a headset and dream my way through the treasures this ancient and glorious establishment guards for Scotland and for future generations."[39] Lumley's wistful description is filled with emotive language as well as an understanding of the voice's transportive properties. A voice—in all its specificity—can be captured and sent from London to MUSA, where it can be played over and over again for an indefinite period of time. Lumley grasps how she can be both the source of the voice and someone in need of hearing it, and its messages, anew. Her description of the voice as enabling listeners to "dream [their] way through the treasures" speaks to its potential to open up the mind's eye, to evoke what can no longer be seen or touched, although, in the museum, some things can be experienced via other senses, too. But although her statement was passionate, its lack of specificity about the museum or the items on display within it perhaps signals the relative superficiality of her task: to read lines from a script. In fact, Lumley was not the only person to provide a voice for the audio guide. According to a press release from MUSA, Lumley explains "the University's story" in the guide, and "at the end of each section the visitor can choose to continue with the story or to dig deeper." The "dig deeper" parts have been recorded by members of the university staff and current students and alumni.[40] Framed in this way, Lumley might be described as the vocal maître d', the one who greets guests and makes a good first impression, but not the one who is directly involved in serving a restaurant's food, or, in this case, the museum's main offerings. And just as definitions of maître d's tie them to public spaces, or the "front of the house," Lumley's role is partly about getting people into the museum, rather than about delivering the goods and services themselves.

   This is not unlike Lumley's AOL role, where she delivered prerecorded messages such as "You've got post." In a January 1996 article alluding to

Lumley's television role in *Absolutely Fabulous* (BBC, 1992–2012), the author describes Lumley's voice as though it were a luxury item: "AOL has gone to the expense of having Joanna Lumley's voice welcome the user and prompt them with information about mail and downloading. A support center in Ireland with 60 staff will deal with technical queries."[41] In both cases, Lumley is the appealing spokeswoman—who speaks little but often, and with an aspirational, upper-class British accent—while the informational details are outsourced to those who are informed but whose voices do not bear Lumley's marks of familiarity and glamour. At the same time, we should not discount the casting of a mature woman in the role of explaining "the University's story." The decision suggests a faith in Lumley as an oral storyteller, one likely grounded in the cumulative effect of her substantial voice work for a range of screens: television, film, and, in relation to her AOL role, the computer screen. Lumley's age when she was cast thus suggests that her maturity is a distinct benefit within the historical space of an ancient university's museum.

Responses to Susan Sarandon's audio guide for a Frida Kahlo exhibit at the Dali Museum reveal a different dimension of aging and vocal intermediality—where, for some, Sarandon's personal use of her voice in the political media should prevent her from providing narration in the expanded space of the gallery. Such responses to Sarandon's narration in one space, in other words, were influenced by past uses of her voice in other spaces, both in terms of content and context, in ways that were similar to the cumulative development of an intermedial voice in the cases of Lumley and Parker. Like Lumley, Sarandon's career has included a significant number of narration roles, some of which might be classified as political or activist in subject matter.[42] But these were not the politics referenced in relation to the Kahlo audio guide, when Sarandon's political views led to criticism across a range of interactive social media platforms. Sarandon shared her involvement on Twitter in December 2016 ("Happy to have narrated the audio tour of Frida Kahlo @TheDali. Check it out starting 12/17").[43] But her political position in relation to the 2016 US presidential election quickly led to scathing responses. Sarandon had not supported the candidacy of Hillary Rodham Clinton, and a number of Twitter users therefore criticized her as a choice for an exhibition on the work of a person of color. Many of those who commented on her work for the Kahlo guide conflated her politics with the subsequent oppressive treatment of immigrants on the United States' southern border by President Donald Trump.[44]

The example shows another way that vocal intertextuality and reflexivity can emerge on social media. For celebrities, in particular, anything they say can be repeated back to them, and completely out of context. As the online responses to Sarandon reveal, there can be publicity risks when hiring actresses whose voices would then be granted the authority of an expert in an off-screen space. Equally important, however, is how the comments critiqued the use of a white woman's voice to narrate an exhibition on work by a woman of color. As the examples in this chapter have already shown, female voice-overs in English-language film and media have typically been white women's voices. To a lesser extent, Black women have done voice-over work. But narrators of Hispanic, Asian, and Middle Eastern descent remain particularly rare in mainstream Anglophone screen media. Documentaries such as *Anna May Wong: In Her Own Words* (Yunah Hong, 2013)—in which Wong's words are narrated by the actress Doan Ly—are often reliant on distribution by Women Make Movies, an invaluable but relatively niche distributor of independent films by and about women. Issues with easily accessing such films, which do include voice-overs by women of color, underscore the problems that people had with Sarandon's audio guide. Casting a white woman to narrate over the life and work of a Mexican artist was particularly fraught given that the museum is a public space.

These issues are possibly compounded by the lack of access to recordings of Kahlo's actual voice (as discussed in chapter 1). The backlash to Sarandon's voice can thus be considered a sign not of sexism, or misogyny, but of the increased desire for intersectional forms of feminism. It is not enough to have a woman provide the narration for the life of another, now deceased, woman. The desire is for a suitable "match" along multiple lines, including that of race. At the same time, it is encouraging that Sarandon, like Lumley, was not subject to ageist critiques. And again, the casting of a mature actress as a narrator suggests an acknowledgment of the cumulative weight attached to the (female) voice on screen: Lumley's and Sarandon's diverse vocal portfolios could pay dividends in the form of more voice work.

VR AND THE ANCHORING, AFFECTIVE VOICE

Vocal guides accessed via headset and virtual reality have some things in common when it comes to the use of women's voices to anchor us in a cultural space. Much as the museums used actresses' voices (Joanna Lumley and Susan Sarandon) to draw visitors into their exhibitions, the VR companies, Oculus Story Studios and Penrose Studios, have used actresses' voices to provide a comforting familiarity helpful for initiating audiences into a new technology. As a format, particularly in its twenty-first-century manifestations, VR is frequently discussed in terms of its spatial and immersive qualities, its potential for interactivity, and, in comparison to cinema, its expansion beyond the traditional frame of the screen.[45] When VR experiences feature vocal narration, each of these properties impacts upon the experience of sound and voice. Indeed, the term "voice-over" immediately comes to seem inadequate. What a given voice speaks *over* is not a predetermined image track, but a more open combination of moving images and sounds, partly determined by the user's own bodily movement, particularly head movements. And yet, in other ways, the voice or narration operates in ways more in line with cinema than VR's visual elements do. In Oculus's *Dear Angelica*, the voices of Whitman and Davis remain consistent no matter who is operating the VR headset; there are no options in terms of the voices. What users see will depend, however, on where they direct their attention. At the same time, the space over which the actresses narrate is less stable than in cinema. The two female voices thus become central anchoring devices for the VR user. The voices also function as affective devices: they can build on traditional film and radio conventions in relation to melodrama, for example, a genre strongly gendered as female.

Briefly described, *Dear Angelica* is a fourteen-minute animated narrative VR experience about a young woman's memories of her now deceased mother, Angelica, a movie star. As signaled by the title, it is narratively framed by a letter from a young woman (Whitman) who addresses her mother (Davis). It is thus already grounded in traditions of the filmic voice-over, since, as Silverman noted, the trope of having women's narration anchored to a letter has been common.[46] The daughter narrates in the present (we overhear excerpts from her letters), but we also hear Angelica's voice, an indistinguishable mix of recordings from old films and her daughter's memories of things she said. The significance of the voice-over as narrative frame and device becomes apparent from the outset when the daughter addresses her mother by her first name, almost as though writing a fan letter: "Dear Angelica, I've been watching all your movies again. You were such an incredible actress. I miss you so much." By depicting a bittersweet relationship between a now separated parent and child, the story shares a melodramatic arc with Penrose Studios' *Arden's Wake: Tide's Fall*, a thirty-minute animated VR experience. Here, recognizing the affective properties of the daughter's voice—performed by Alicia Vikander—also seems key to understanding descriptions of the two VR films as being "emotionally draining" for the audience.[47] In both VR experiences, women's voices become central to the emotional impact. Furthermore, both experiences are set mostly in diegetic spaces (outer space in *Dear Angelica*, and underwater in *Tide's Fall*) where the spatial aspects of the expanded cinema label come to the fore: these VR voices can have vast diegetic spaces to "fill."

Understanding the difference between hearing voices via a VR headset and hearing voices via, say, a surround-sound speaker system in the cinema can be explained through an extension of Julie Woletz's classification of three different degrees of media immersion. In considering how different interfaces of spatial media "create effects of immersion by addressing the body in different ways," she called such experiences *non-immersive* when the device only enables a viewpoint from outside the environment; *semi-immersive* when the viewpoint is inside the environment, but there are still other stimuli available; and *fully immersive* when they require devices, such as a head-mounted display, that show a viewpoint inside the environment and at the same time block out other sensory information.[48] Hearing a film voice via a surround-sound speaker system might be considered a semi-immersive audio experience, because the voice can be placed in different speakers to create some sense of being surrounded by it. A VR headset can instead provide a fully immersive audio experience. Provided the headset is suitably placed over the ears, and the volume is set at a suitable level, all other noises are blocked out, along with all other visuals.

With the VR voice, as with other trends in digital culture (such as ASMR whisper videos), the performer and the technology thus work together to present a particular kind of "vocalic space," the term Steven Connor used to capture "ways in which the voice is held both to operate in, and itself to articulate, different conceptions of space." Connor referred to the example of a crooning singer whose voice "appears to be at our ear, standing forward and apart from the orchestral background."[49] I am interested, however, in how the voice in VR relates to the expanded and individuated visual space provided in experiences such as *Dear Angelica*, a setup that creates the impression that the voice has more space to fill—more space to express the voice *over*. In an article about *Dear Angelica*, reviewer Adi Robertson described its unique staging: "It's grasping at something VR film in general hasn't quite reached. For lack of a better term, it mounts a brute force attack on your emotions. The music and voiceover overwhelm you with a pathos the story hasn't quite earned, leveraging two characters you don't get to know all that well."[50] Although Robertson and other reviewers have not used the term "melodrama" to describe *Dear Angelica*, her word choices (pathos, emotions) and the identified channels for achieving this impact (music, voice-over) align well with critical theory on melodrama in film and related media, including melodrama's tendency to stimulate bodily responses (such as tears) from the audience. Moreover, while a large number of VR horror films and games have been released, we should remember that melodrama is also classified as a "body genre."[51]

Robertson is not the only reviewer to have drawn attention to *Dear Angelica*'s visceral bodily impact on the user. Duncan Bell described it as a "heartstring-tugging . . . sob-fest" and an "overwhelming virtual reality experience." Reflecting on his individual experience, Bell explained that it left him "with a unique double-jeopardy." He was "perilously close to both bursting into tears and being sick" while standing "in a bare-walled basement in front of a couple of PR people, wearing the familiar, comically oversized Oculus Rift headset."[52] Here, in keeping with Woletz's emphasis on the relationship between the interface and bodily engagement in fully immersive media, Bell drew attention to the unique physicality of the VR experience, in terms of how it can potentially affect the user's body (tears, motion sickness). But he also referred to what it requires of the user: wearing a headset in order to explore a VR world by yourself. By describing how *Dear Angelica*'s combination of sound and images transported him from a bare-walled basement, and the company of others, to a different space where he was both emotionally moved and physically impacted, he invokes VR's distinctly singular and immersive properties. Indeed, one is immersed in a way not possible in a traditional cinema theater. Unlike when watching a film with others in a theater, in a classroom, or at home (where the voices playing through the speakers may have to compete with background noises and talking), when engaging in VR one typically finds that the voices become more prominent. The experience is more akin to listening to music, podcasts, or a museum guide via headphones.

But the emotive language found in reviewers' responses to *Dear Angelica* is only the beginning of its relationship to melodrama. In addition, its use of women's voices—particularly Whitman's voicing of the daughter—is notably in line with an interpretation of the voice's significance to melodrama in radio and film explicated by Jacob Smith, whose scholarly work focuses on the cultural history of media, particularly in relation to sound.[53] Smith has written about the quality of "nearness" in relation to the melodramatic voice, noting how the microphone allows listeners "to hear people in ways that normally [imply] intimacy—the whisper, the caress, the murmur."[54] Smith's distinctions between the use of voice in radio versus film melodrama holds relevance for *Dear Angelica*'s combination of the women's voices and often abstract hand-drawn animation. Comparing Barbara Stanwyck's radio and film performances of *Stella Dallas* (Lux Radio Theater, 1937; King Vidor, 1947), Smith considered the significance of reaction shots in film melodrama and determined that, since reaction shots are impossible on radio, then a different strategy had to be used: "Vocal expressions of emotion are mobilized to replace not only gesture but also reaction shot and expressive mise-en-scene." In the case of Stanwyck's self-sacrificing mother in *Stella Dallas*, "the expressive lighting and lonely silhouette of the film are replaced by Stanwyck's choked sobs."[55] Notably, although *Dear Angelica* is an audiovisual experience, its fleeting and sparse animation style departs from film melodrama's use of expressive reaction shots and gestures, relying instead on the kind of vocal expressions of emotion that Smith identified in relation to radio melodrama.

As might be predicted, based on an understanding of melodrama's narrative and affective tropes, Angelica's death is accompanied by a dialing up of the performers' vocal expressiveness. Key here is how *Dear Angelica*'s narrative is linear rather than interactive. While users do not get to make choices about what happens, or what they hear, their gaze influences some visual elements. As *Wired*'s pop culture editor Angela Watercutter explained, "Some images animate if viewers move in and look closely at them . . . and other illustrations fill in with more color if you focus on them."[56] However, viewed from the perspective of identification with the characters and melodramatic conventions, these responsive visual elements do not provide the emotive weight of reaction shots, and so can be more in line, in accordance with Smith's analysis, with radio melodrama than with film. We hear the sadness in the daughter's voice as she describes her mother's death, addressing her in the present: "I remember the hospital. Mom, you look so small. Real life doesn't look anything like the movies. Goodbyes in movies? [*sniffs*] Well they're just so much better." Whitman speaks slowly, and with the occasional quivers and choked intonation of someone struggling to articulate difficult memories. One quick but clear sniff invokes the mental image of the young woman crying, but it is not the overt sobbing of Stanwyck's radio performance in *Stella Dallas*. Earlier in the film, other sound and vocal effects point to Angelica's strained body—panting, for example, or the sound of a throbbing heartbeat as she fights "monsters," both on screen and off. And even as the daughter relives Angelica's death, we hear Angelica's voice, this time whispering, vocally signaling the gradual withdrawal of life from her body. After the familiar tone of a flat-lining heart monitor, Angelica visually morphs into an astronaut, whispering, "Everything is so beautiful out here." The statement captures both her character's position, in outer space, and her daughter's hope that her spirit has departed to a better place. Davis's whispered lines are notably lower in volume than other elements and are at times difficult to hear, but they end up—rather predictably within this maternal melodrama framework—focusing on her daughter: "Houston? Can you read me? Did you hear me? Anyone? My life. My world. My daughter."

In terms of identification, our subjective alignment with Angelica—and

Figure 3.3. Screenshots of lines of voice-over in the immersive visual space of *Dear Angelica* (2017), which would appear 3D when in VR format. Produced by Oculus Story Studio.

particularly with her daughter—is much more firmly anchored in what they say and how they sound than in how they look. This is partly because of the style of hand-drawn animation, but it is also because of the individual user's freedom to explore the visual space. The most notable aspect of the animation is how it was created—by using Oculus's "Quill" tool, which was developed especially for *Dear Angelica*. The tool allowed the illustrator, Wesley Allsbrook, to render immersive 3D animations directly within VR. The result plays, as Angela Watercutter describes it, "like a fever dream, all brilliant floating images and fleeting memories."[57]

The relationship between *Dear Angelica*'s experimental animation style and its use of largely traditional verbal-vocal generic tropes seems central to understanding its overall impact. While Adi Robertson and the *Dear Angelica* producers do not directly allude to it as a VR *melodrama*, they nonetheless highlight the value of "draw[ing] heavily on broad themes and archetypes," such as mother-daughter relationships and film stardom. As *Dear Angelica*'s director, Saschka Unseld, explained, this means there was "more freedom for experimentation" with other aspects of the production. Robertson said that its artistic style "abandons realism": nothing we see appears to be "solid enough to pick up"; Allsbrook's illustrations instead provide "painted shapes floating in air . . . inviting you to take in every line from every angle."[58] Significantly, since certain words spoken in the voice-over are also visualized as text in the vast black visual space, the drawn lines to be taken in from every angle include the spoken lines of dialogue (figure 3.3). *Ingrid Goes West* and Philipps's Instagram Stories merged digital text with narration; similarly, *Dear Angelica* uses 3D animation techniques to make voices tangible, rendering melodramatic speech anew in the VR format.

Yet, in terms of content, speech in *Dear Angelica* is strongly in keeping with the dialogue norms of film melodrama that Kozloff identified: the tendency to explicitly express feelings, both for "emotional revelation and sincerity," as well as the tendency for dialogue to be "charged with metaphor." The last of these norms manifests, for instance, in the daughter's opening description of her mother: "You were a knight, my knight." Such allegorical language is sustained, and other melodramatic tropes introduced, in ways that conform to Kozloff's point when she said that, although characters in melodrama often openly discuss their emotions, their responses can also "hinge around the not said, the words that cannot be spoken."[59] This is precisely the case with *Dear Angelica*, where the cause of the mother's premature death is hinted at through metaphors and the daughter's unfinished sentence: "And that monster you were fighting . . ." The reference to fighting monsters connects to Angelica's preceding line, from a film ("I am the defender of the world"), and to a subsequent sound effect—the sound of screaming from whomever Angelica's character is battling. Through the combination of a carefully crafted script, vocal performances, and sound effects, the daughter's unfinished line skips the narrative forward to Angelica's untimely death. In keeping with melodrama's strategy for mixing open declarations with the verbally withheld, then, *Dear Angelica* draws on certain archetypal aspects of the genre—in this case, the tragic death of a mother—without ever articulating the nature of Angelica's demons. The precise cause of death—whether some form of addiction or suicide—is less important than the narrative function of the unfinished sentence, a verbal ellipsis that allows *Dear Angelica* to transport us from the daughter's memories of her mother when she was alive to her death.

In certain ways, Angelica's characterization as a screen actress is central to the overall functioning of the VR experience. The mother's and daughter's respective statuses (author/subject, alive/dead) are conveyed in part through the qualities of Whitman's and Davis's voices, and in particular by their relative clarity and perceptible closeness. Whitman speaks in the present in a close-miked setup that allows us to hear what Smith and others, in relation to melodrama, have termed "the sob in the throat."[60] When we hear Davis, we are meant to hear her voice as the daughter does—via recordings of her films on a VCR—a premise that reinforces Angelica's distance. Her voice is less clear, supposedly because it is being filtered through a dated playback device—though, presumably, the creators achieved this impression of older technology in a digital sound-mixing suite. When audience members hear snatches of Angelica's film performances (and see these scenes in fleeting animations), they gain a sense of the kinds of roles she played: action heroine, astronaut, and so on. The vocal differences create a textural layering effect while also signaling the very different statuses of the women who are speaking: one is an interior monologue based on letters, the other a merging of Angelica's real-world conversations with her daughter and her film roles as heard through predigital recording technologies (or at least simulated to sound that way).

Overall, the uses of the voice are thus much more conventional (in terms of the historical norms of genre and gender) than might be expected of a VR experience that uses pioneering techniques. The expressive uses of the voice in melodrama are applied to a new audio format, with the archetypal verbal-vocal elements grounding the user in an otherwise abstract immersive space. *Dear Angelica* succeeds in adapting melodrama to VR, injecting a genre that is often derided for its ties to women and emotions with a new kind of expressive capacity that is heavily reliant on the female voice.

(SELF-)CASTING THE EXPANDED VOICE-OVER

If we look beyond the narrative and the affective significance of women's voices in *Dear Angelica*, we can see how Davis's voicing of Angelica connects to her broader work as a gender activist. In 2004, over a decade before the #MeToo movement saw women in Hollywood push for shifts in industry practices and gendered power imbalances, Davis set up the Geena Davis Institute on Gender in Media, a "research-driven organization collaborating within the media and entertainment industry to expose gender imbalance, identify unconscious bias and creatively remodel content to achieve gender equity."[61] The institute's innovations have included pioneering software, the Geena Davis Inclusion Quotient (GD IQ), that measures characters' screen time and speaking lines according to gender. When it came to casting the role of film star Angelica, the producers appear to have factored in such inter- and extra-textual connections. Davis's role as Thelma in *Thelma and Louise* (Ridley Scott, 1991) is even invoked in a *Dear Angelica* scene where we hear her saying to the driver beside her (another character, implied to be her daughter), "They'll never catch us. We'll keep going like this forever."[62]

Davis's awareness of the power associated with both her own voice and women's voices more generally extends to a cameo in the aforementioned *In a World . . .* , where Davis plays a powerful executive who hires the voice-over artist Carol to narrate a franchise. Davis's decision to lend her voice to *Dear Angelica*—as well as Bell's independent film—came from a desire to influence the gendered dynamics of both media representation and production—in the case of *Dear Angelica*, in the developing field of VR. As Davis put it, "I've always obviously been interested in women's representations in film and television and I've always loved new technology. And I thought this is a great opportunity to try to have some influence to say, 'Let's start this one off with some gender parity, let's make this a conscious effort to have that in our thinking as we're creating this brand new medium.'"[63]

In a similarly dual role, actress Alicia Vikander not only provided the voice of Meena in *Arden's Wake: Tide's Fall*, but also served as executive producer on the project. In both cases, voicing the central VR character seems part of a broader strategy for actresses-cum-producers to influence the direction of the emerging storytelling format. Vikander's voice, like Davis's, has been a popular focal point in reviews and publicity material. Penrose Studios released a photo of Vikander recording the voice, and director and Penrose founder Eugene Chung's praise for her voice was shared in media reports. His comments stressed how her work had brought the sequel to 2017's *Arden's Wake* "to the next level," and especially how her voice had been able to "infuse the whole piece." Noting that "everyone outside of the sound booth gave a standing ovation" after Vikander had recorded her take, Chung implied that Vikander's vocal acting skills were a feature that made this VR worth seeking out over others.[64] Again, a screen actress's voice is used to coax potential audiences into trying out the technology.

FLUIDITY AND THE NETWORKED NARRATOR

In the years since the heyday of classical Hollywood, and particularly since the 1990s, the female narrator has become more common, more self-aware, and more diffused. Though Sarah Jessica Parker's voice, for example, is often still anchored diegetically to her body, the screens she speaks over are diverse—they go beyond television to include digital platforms such as Instagram, as well as *Vogue*'s digital documentaries. But female voices also provide narration for cultural spaces that are not screen based, even if the woman in question has most often been heard in screen-based media: you can hear her via headset in the expanded space of VR, or in an art gallery or museum. The familiar voices of well-known actresses are used to guide visitors through exhibitions, or to initiate audiences into unfamiliar immersive media. At the same time, as part of an increasingly intermedial landscape, women cast as screen-based narrators have sometimes earned their vocal authority or impact through singing. This is the case in a number of music documentaries that focus on women, such as *Janis: Little Girl Blue* (Amy J. Berg, 2015). Here, Chan Marshall (best known by her musical moniker "Cat Power") narrates Janis Joplin's letters. Her voice is a convincing substitute—in part because of a similar southern accent, but also because Marshall has been mimicking Joplin's singing voice since high school. In the documentary, she channels that vocal familiarity into the narration.[65]

In another example, *Lemonade*, Beyoncé directs the storytelling properties of her singing voice to the newly emerging format of the visual album, a kind of feature-length music video. Musical superstardom allows her to defy the tendency for Black women to be marginalized when it comes to screen narration (as attested by the predominantly white women's voice-overs considered in this chapter). Diversity continues to be constrained in narration by the fact that white writers and directors dominate the field. Beyoncé, naturally, cast herself as *Lemonade*'s narrator. The album was influenced by *Daughters of the Dust*, Julie Dash's nonlinear feature film about three generations of Gullah women in South Carolina at the turn of the twentieth century. Particularly influential was that film's heavy use of a mythical voice-over—and here we can again see clear links between traditional film narration and new media formats.[66]

Somewhat optimistically, the examples considered here suggest that while young women have often been the pioneers or performers of expanded forms of narration in the digital era, there are also opportunities for more mature women, particularly when they cast themselves in such roles. Davis (b. 1956) was sixty when she recorded the titular voice of *Dear Angelica*; Parker (b. 1965) was fifty-one when she began her "Rabbit, rabbit" Instagram videos (2016). Indeed, even Philipps and Bell (both born in 1979) are outside the age bracket for "millennials," suggesting that their grounding and familiarity in traditional predigital media and generic norms have been useful when developing their own voice-based content for digital platforms.

Writing on "The Networked Screen" in relation to expanded cinema, film and media scholar Haidee Wasson invoked conceptions of space in her discussion of the diversity of large and small screens in contemporary culture. With a focus on the visual rather than the audiovisual properties of screens, she referred to "the endurance of screens paired with the flows of images that fill them," asserting that audiences were "invited by these screens to look in particular ways," and "become witness to the abstractions attendant upon [the] meeting between screens of an unchanging size and the fluid images which grow or shrink to fill them."[67] As I argue in this book, we are equally invited to *listen* to these diverse screens in particular ways. More specifically, many of the qualities of the networked screen *voice* relate to the "meeting between" screen interfaces and fluid voices, which can seem to grow or shrink in response to the dynamics of the specific screen interface. In most cases, this is not a direct response—after all, unlike with the images, the possibilities of various speakers and personal headsets mean that the voices do not always *have to* grow or shrink as a result of screen size. Yet the indirect influence of digital visual culture on digital vocal culture is unquestionable (and explored elsewhere in this book in relation to podcasts, memes, and GIFs).

From the narrower perspective of the expanded voice-over, the audiovisual properties of VR depart from Wasson's description of fluid images that "grow or shrink" to "fill" screens of an unchanging size. In *Dear Angelica*, it is the women's voices as much as their ephemeral, animated images that appear to grow to fill the frameless visual space. Despite the significance of Whitman's and Davis's voices to *Dear Angelica*'s overall VR experience, present in the publicity materials is a certain familiar and worrying tendency to disregard the soundtrack, to describe VR as a means "to tell visual stories."[68] After decades of sound scholars making strides to draw attention to the crucial significance of the soundtrack to all aspects of cinema, this marketing focus serves as a reminder of what is at risk in discourse around VR: that it is most often discussed and theorized as a *visual* medium, even in those instances where (women's) voices are crucial to the narrative and the overall affective impact, and when *Dear Angelica*'s vocal conventions are adapted from both film and radio melodrama. Historically grounding these techniques, which date back to pre-cinema barkers, helps to ensure a degree of continuity despite the sensationalist attention to VR's technological newness.

At the other end of the expanded voice-over spectrum is Parker's minimalist and whispered Instagram voice-over—a voice that is barely there, but that her followers know to listen for carefully because of her previous videos. Parker purposefully "shrinks" her voice to correspond to the short duration and square frame required by Instagram. But she may also imagine the intimate setting in which her followers will hear her voice-over—via their smart device, at home, or through headphones while in transit. These listening conditions are not unlike those for Parker's museum audio narration for The Met: where the screen is the three-dimensional gallery. Narrated Instagram videos can increase impressions of intimacy between an actress and her fans, while allowing an actress to script and direct her own short productions. They therefore can allow for more organic forms of narration and visual-vocal representation.

Wasson's analysis of the networked screen posits that we should set aside questions of medium specificity to explore currents of contemporary visual culture that require us "to consider the attendant specificities of these screens and of the networks that link them."[69] I agree with her underlying descriptions of screens as "nodes in complex networks." But the cultural and technological networks alluded to here are equally impacted by—and have an impact on—*vocal* culture. Screen-based narration is particularly enmeshed in this. Youngblood conceived of expanded cinema in relation to an intermedia network with an open feedback system. In relation to the history of the screen voice, voice-overs are arguably its most open manifestation, because they exist both within and beyond the world of the screen itself. Digital technologies have consolidated such properties, not least through their ability to establish social media networks that can distribute the voice "over" screens on any number of computers or smart devices—or through headsets, in more immersive media spaces.

Critical theories of gender and voice-over have tended to prioritize questions around the body as they relate to the narrator (Are they embodied or disembodied? And how does that embodiment or disembodiment impact their discursive authority?). But understanding the expanded voice-overs of the digital era can require increased attention to *audiences'* bodies. Instagram followers are often "on the go," casually browsing social media on smart devices. Philipps seems to understand this potentially distracted consumption environment when she superimposes text excerpts from her narration onto her Instagram stories. In virtual reality, in contrast, the voice can provide a grounding effect for the headset-wearing user, who might be disoriented, or even suffering from motion sickness. In these and other cases, the screens themselves are no longer stationary. The onus thus rests on the voice to help anchor audiences as they experience narrators within increasingly diverse and interactive audiovisual spaces.

KARINA LONGWORTH AND THE REMIXING OF ACTRESSES' VOICES ON THE *YOU MUST REMEMBER THIS* PODCAST

IN WHAT WOULD BECOME A NOTORIOUS MEETING of politics and star power, in 1972 the actress and activist Jane Fonda made several announcements to US pilots via Vietnamese radio, imploring them to stop their bombings and describing the war's damage to civilians. At the end of this same trip to Vietnam, Fonda live-narrated her own footage from Vietnam at press conferences in Paris and New York, choosing to improvise after the original soundtrack was held by customs. Despite her various attempts to articulate her misgivings about the US handling of the war, Fonda's efforts were largely undermined by a photograph of her sitting on an antiaircraft gun in Hanoi, since the image implied that she thought it was acceptable for the Vietnamese to shoot down American planes. It was used repeatedly to symbolize and criticize her activism as naïve and unpatriotic. The nuances of what she had said were largely lost.

Decades later, but extending on the traditions of radio, the podcast format now offers great potential for women, including actresses such as Fonda, to be heard without the corresponding gaze of a camera. This is the case with Karina Longworth's *You Must Remember This (YMRT)* (2014–) podcast series. Here I examine Longworth's treatment of the voices of female stars and discuss how this presentation can serve to reorient listeners' attention to the verbal and vocal representation of women in Hollywood—including Fonda. It does this, moreover, partly by liberating their voices from corresponding images of their bodies.

For the past eight years, Longworth has researched and shared her interpretation of events and figures from Hollywood film history in the podcast, which combines audio clips from films and interviews along with her narration of the related events. My primary focus will be "Jean and Jane," a nine-part comparison of Jean Seberg and Fonda from the 1950s to the 1980s, and, in particular, how the podcast format allows for a new understanding of these actresses' voices and their roles in the film industry.[1] I argue that the "Jean and Jane" series uses archival materials to provide a form of revisionist feminist historiography. In this historiography, Longworth pays consistent attention to Seberg's, and particularly Fonda's, verbal (dis)empowerment at the hands of men (directors, partners, journalists). Longworth uses her own voice (both literal narration and figurative power as podcast producer) to help the women to "take back the narrative" and tell their own stories.

Furthermore, the missing images of performers' famous bodies in the podcast format can provide a structuring absence in the series, temporarily allowing the actresses to escape the camera's objectifying gaze. In this respect, *YMRT* is similar to other podcasts helmed by actresses, such as Anna Faris's *Unqualified* (2015–) and Abbi Jacobson's *A Piece of Work* (July–August 2017). *Unqualified* is a well-received relationship-based podcast in which Faris gives advice and talks to celebrities about their relationships. In *A Piece of Work*, a high-profile collaboration between Jacobson, the Museum of Modern Art (MoMA), and New York Public Radio, Jacobson talks gallery art with various guests. In both cases, the actresses' screen-based fame provides them with a ready audience, people familiar with their voices (from film and television comedies) and willing to listen to them without also watching them.

Though the remixing of actresses' voices on *YMRT* is a central focus of this chapter, I also pay attention to both Longworth's production processes and her multiplicitous presence as researcher, narrator, and overall producer of the podcast. Both Longworth's delivery and the podcast's foregrounding of emotional narratives are connected to women's work in found-footage cinema, a setup I relate to Longworth's emphasis on the creation of a podcast that *sounds* cinematic, but that casts off the image track. Although *YMRT* replaces the archival audiovisual material of found-footage cinema with archival *audio* (or soundtracks for which the image tracks are absent), the podcast uses a similar collage-like method to critically reflect on both earlier history and media. I thus historicize Longworth's various roles in relation to the reception of women's voices in early US radio and the generic conventions of voice and affect in women's films and film noir. In doing so, I consider how the female voice of a contemporary podcast host is still policed, and even fetishized, when it comes to the relationship between her disembodied sound and the body that produces it.

"BE PRETTY BUT SHUT UP": HELPING JEAN SEBERG AND JANE FONDA TAKE BACK THE NARRATIVE

Released weekly from June to August 2017, Longworth's nine-part series on Seberg and Fonda charts the various professional and personal parallels in the actresses' lives over some three decades. *YMRT* covers a range of Hollywood players, not just female figures. But "Jean and Jane" followed another of Longworth's actress-focused seasons: "Dead Blondes," a thirteen-part series on "blonde actresses who died unusual, untimely or otherwise notable deaths." In "Dead Blondes," Longworth explored the circumstances surrounding the deaths of women such as Peg Entwistle and Barbara Loden, which led to them becoming more famous in death than in life.[2] She introduces the series by discussing the crucial role that blondness, natural or artificial, can play in Hollywood. And yet this crucial aspect of the presence of these women must remain absent from the audio medium of the podcast. A line of Veronica Lake's dialogue from *I Married a Witch* (René Clair, 1942)—"Would you rather I be a brunette?"—is part of the montage that opens every episode in the series. But here, blondeness becomes an absent signifier. We must listen to these women—and to Longworth's accounts of their tragic lives or deaths—without looking at them. "Jean and Jane" is similar, in that, by playing audio clips of Seberg and Fonda speaking in character and in interviews, the podcast refracts key moments from their lives through the prism of the voice. And the opportunities for their stories to be heard are substantial, because only two women are covered in the series. Here, I focus in particular on Fonda.

In "Jean and Jane Part 2," the voice, and especially Seberg's accent, are presented as important bones of contention in the tumultuous relationship between Seberg and director Otto Preminger. As Longworth tells it, and supported by research, Preminger took credit for catapulting Seberg from small-town girl to international star. In the process, he also attempted to control her voice. Longworth quotes Preminger's triple insult prior to filming *Bonjour Tristesse* (Otto Preminger, 1958): "I don't like the way you talk, walk or dress." She also details how Preminger made Seberg take French lessons and diction classes in an effort to replace her midwestern US accent with a more "neutral" sound. Longworth suggests that issues of inflection were important to the changeable power dynamic between director and actress—Seberg eventually asserted her own authority by mimicking Preminger's far from neutral Austro-Hungarian accent. The eighteen-year-old Seberg had begun to "openly rebel" on set in Paris, including verbally, as she repeated a line of Preminger's directions in what Longworth calls "a mockery of Preminger's accent." Seberg's courage to challenge the director thus depended on her vocal skills: Preminger wasn't able to disguise his accent when directing Seberg, but she could mimic his.

Listeners hear how Preminger routinely critiqued Seberg's voice and accent. And worse, the director ignored her cries for help when she was accidentally set on fire during the filming of *Saint Joan* (Otto Preminger, 1957). Longworth recounts how Seberg pleaded, "I'm burning," while "not in character," and then how Preminger used parts of this footage in the final film. For Preminger, Seberg's cries for help were extraneous—easily edited out, like any other outtake.[3] In using this footage, Preminger forced Seberg into an uncomfortable dialectic with Joan of Arc herself, the character and historical figure Seberg was playing in the film. Joan is portrayed as being silent as she is burned at the stake, and through sound editing, Seberg, too, is forced to stoically accept her punishment, one that, albeit accidental, left the actress with permanent scars.

A he-said-she-said dynamic underpins the podcast's retelling of Seberg's and Fonda's experiences in the film industry. Longworth's historiography works to support the women by allowing them to be heard—and, ultimately, believed. At the start of "Jean and Jane Part 3," we hear Seberg on *The Mike Wallace Interview* (ABC, 1957–1958). We also hear Wallace belittling her. Longworth frames the clip—which seems scathing by contemporary standards—as one of several instances in which Seberg "had her very right to exist called into question by men like Wallace." Longworth also discusses *Pendulum* (George Schaefer, 1969), and costar George Peppard's comments about Seberg wanting to have sex with him (episode 4), but she counters Peppard's remarks. In an amused and incredulous tone, Longworth states that she would "never trust a man who says a woman's aura wants to fuck him when the woman says she does not." In these examples and throughout the series, Longworth's use of archival audio materials is particularly important to her style of revisionist feminist historiography, one grounded by a film studies background. Consider the components of the fifty-second montage of Seberg and Fonda speaking, or being spoken about, that plays at the start of each podcast:

- Five seconds of music from the score for *À bout de souffle* (Jean-Luc Godard, 1960).
- Four seconds of the *Barbarella* (Roger Vadim, 1968) score.
- Patricia/Seberg's dialogue extracted from *À bout de souffle*: "I don't know if I'm unhappy because I'm not free, or if I'm not free because I'm unhappy."

- Fonda speaking about the Vietnam War on *The Phil Donahue Show* in 1972: "I say our responsibility as Americans is to be concerned about what our country is doing."
- BBC Broadcaster Alistair Cooke discussing Seberg's death in an episode of *Letter from America* titled "Jean Seberg and the FBI, 1979": "The suicide of Jean Seberg . . . the young actress from Iowa . . ."
- Fonda addressing her audience in her exercise video "The Workout" (1982): "Are you ready to do the workout?"

In its brevity and repetition across each of the nine podcasts, this montage primes listeners to think about the women's vocal lives and afterlives. For instance, by preceding a news report about Seberg's suicide in 1979 with a clip of her character Patricia in *À bout de souffle*, talking about her unhappiness and lack of freedom, Longworth conflates Seberg's developing personal troubles with an earlier character portrayal. With Fonda, audio clips of her in activist mode (in the early 1970s) and instructional mode (in a 1982 exercise video) underscore her many uses of her voice beyond the big screen.

Fonda's vocal empowerment is more prominent than Seberg's, and it is presented as developing in spite of notable attempts by men (family members, directors, the FBI) to silence her. Fonda grew up in the shadow of her father Henry's stardom and her mother's depression (which led to suicide). *YMRT* takes a chronological approach to the material, implying a somewhat seamless transition from Henry Fonda's public attempts to control what Jane said about him to male directors' and partners' subsequent attempts to control her. In "Jean and Jane Part 2," Longworth reads out things that Fonda has said about her father's many marriages, along with his controlling response in an interview: "It's okay for her to think it but not to say it. That's disrespectful." Henry Fonda's comments, particularly invoking the idea of "respect," seem grounded in the kind of patriarchal and infantilizing structure that his daughter rallied against.

Longworth uses stories about the director Jean-Luc Godard (and several other men) to unite Fonda's and Seberg's negative experiences in the film industry, revealing that the two women had discussed Godard and his misogynist ways. She includes a twenty-two-second audio clip from Fonda's English-language monologue in *Tout va bien* (*All's Well*, Jean-Luc Godard and Jean-Pierre Gorin, 1972) in which the voice of an unseen Frenchwoman, translating over Fonda, drowns out her voice. By playing this clip, Longworth provides listeners with enough time to consider how the translation displaces Fonda's vocal presence. Ironically, the scene undermined Fonda's desire at that time to work primarily with other women.[4] On the one hand, this might be explained away as one of Godard's many formalist interventions into the standard use of the voice on the soundtrack. Like *Pierrot le Fou*'s (1965) antiphonal use of voice-over, or the deliberate drowning out of a name (through the sound of passing planes or cars) in *Made in U.S.A.* (Godard 1966), the layering of Fonda's voice in *Tout va bien* works as a distancing technique. Yet the technique, which allows Fonda to both work with—and be vocally displaced by—another, unnamed woman, is an indirect and disempowering situation, one implicitly tied to Godard's reflexive desire to tap into the star value of Fonda's image in both *Tout va bien* and its postscript film, *Letter to Jane* (Jean-Luc Godard and Jean-Pierre Gorin, 1972). So, although Godard's work can provide a critical commentary on sexism and gender—and, in the case of *Tout va bien*, the film's politics are equally about US-European relations and filmmaking—zooming in on Fonda's vocal treatment reveals certain unbalanced power dynamics that the actress was unable to control. Furthermore, as already explored in relation to dubbing artist Nikki van der Zyl in chapter 1, the clip signals toward the broader history of film actresses being disempowered as a result of overdubbing practices.

Beyond the cinema screen and soundtrack, Fonda's antiwar activism becomes all the more evident once it is removed from the familiar and often controversial imagery of her protesting in the United States and Vietnam. In "Jean and Jane Part 7," an episode that examines Fonda's antiwar activities, we are told that after she broke up with Donald Sutherland, she "[jumped] headfirst into feminism." Fonda started holding "struggle sessions, where women confront[ed] men about the difficulties [they'd] faced as a result of their gender." The account underscores how Fonda began to use her platform as a film star to become a spokesperson for women's issues, an aspect of her activism that has been largely overshadowed by popular media attention to her antiwar stance. The episode emphasizes Fonda's unusual degree of vocality, first when she asked to address US pilots via Vietnamese radio, in broadcasts that were recorded (and used against Fonda in both the United States and Vietnam). We hear a clip of Fonda explaining her decision to use the radio to inform the pilots of the real-world damage the bombings were causing: "I know of no other way to reach them," she says. Although the FBI would use her broadcast as evidence that Fonda had committed treason, Longworth takes care to explain that she never requested that the pilots stop following orders, simply that they think about their targets and the impact of the bombs. The radio address was risky for Fonda, both in terms of her career and in terms of the potential legal repercussions she might experience because of her political beliefs, as substantiated in a later episode, when Longworth details how President Richard Nixon ordered the FBI to study transcripts of the broadcast in Vietnam.

Listeners also learn how, in 1972, Fonda live-narrated her own footage from Vietnam at press conferences in Paris and New York, since the actual soundtrack was held at customs in Paris. As Fonda biographer Patricia Bosworth noted, despite Fonda's hope to distribute the footage widely, "the soundtrack remained in Paris and after the New York press conference the film mysterious vanished."[5] This anecdote gains added significance in the subsequent episode, when we learn how, in *Letter to Jane*, directors Godard and Jean-Pierre Gorin dissected a single news picture of Fonda in Vietnam. The two setups, including the relationship they present between Fonda's body and voice, are virtual opposites in every sense. In *Letter to Jane*, an image of Fonda is effectively pinned down when it is subject to critical, authoritative commentary by the two male filmmakers. They talk over her image, commenting on the meanings behind her expression. Fonda has no opportunity to respond or to articulate what she was actually thinking at the time of the photo. The problematic dynamic of an unseen (and unacknowledged) Frenchwoman speaking over Fonda in *Tout va bien* is thus taken to an extreme in the postscript film. By contrast, not only does Fonda's personal footage of Vietnam focus on something other than herself, but we learn of Fonda's pragmatic solution to the problem of how to provide commentary after customs took away the soundtrack. Her sense of urgency with regard to sharing this material led her to deliver an unplanned, ad hoc narration. As such, she is revealed not just as a guerrilla filmmaker—chronicling her anti-war visits—but as a guerrilla orator, whose close attachment to the footage meant she could provide a live soundtrack to the visuals. Similar to her radio address to US troops in Vietnam, this risky act of live narration (substituting for the lost, prerecorded narration) prioritizes politics over persona.

Though Longworth never explicitly puts it this way, episodes 8 and 9 of the series contrast Fonda's treatment in *Letter to Jane*—silent, pinned down by male narrators—with her increased confidence in her own voice both on and off screen. Despite, or perhaps because of, her brief but frustrating experience working in the male-dominated world of the *Nouvelle Vague*, she appears in Delphine Seyrig's documentary *Sois belle et tais-toi* (*Be Pretty but Shut Up*, 1981). Already known in France for her women's rights activism, Seyrig filmed Fonda and other European and US actresses discussing their experiences of sexism in the film industry. Its premise and title alone speak to the experiences that Fonda and Seberg endured, as Longworth demonstrated.

The dual narrative that Longworth assembles makes it clear that Fonda, and to a lesser extent Seberg, were unwilling to conform to the directive of simply being pretty and shutting up.

The impression built up over the course of Longworth's series is of Fonda as an effective spokesperson for women and other marginalized groups. This strategy helps to round out Fonda's image as a star in the popular media at the time and right up to the present day. For although Longworth's series only chronicles Fonda until the mid-1980s, her portrayal of Fonda as an articulate, educated activist provides a new narrative for younger generations, whose contemporary impression of Fonda, who is now over eighty, is often guided by popular media attention on her "age-defying" body.[6] Or, at least this was likely the case until October 2019, when Fonda's series of high-profile arrests for her protests against political inaction on climate change led to renewed attention to her long history of protest and activism.

Despite all this, as the final episode of "Jean and Jane" makes clear, the Fonda of the mid-1980s still had certain reservations about the political uses of her voice, possibly as a result of media backlash against it. Longworth provides a clip of Fonda saying, to Barbara Walters in 1985, "The media called me shrill. I was. I was new to activism." The quote confirms her sense that there was ongoing policing of her outspokenness. But it also implies Fonda's agreement with the assessment that she was "shrill," suggesting a degree of internalized self-criticism. That is troubling, given the historical connotations of the word "shrill" as relating to women's voices. Yet Fonda also defended herself, explaining that her "dues [had] been paid" for any errors in judgment related to her work in Vietnam: "I do not apologize for my opposition to the war. I am proud that I was against the war." As we'll consider later in the chapter, there are parallel tensions between Fonda's ambivalent descriptions of her mediated voice (self-criticism mixed with understandings of its power) and Longworth's self-description of her own voice in relation to the *YMRT* podcast. Furthermore, given Fonda's willingness to broadcast her voice on the radio and to provide live narration, we might speculate that—had the technology existed—she, too, might have started a podcast in this period. Through the "Jean and Jane" series, Longworth effectively crafts such a podcast retrospectively.

RESURRECTING FILM VOICES VIA PODCAST

In surveying recent studies of the voice in podcasting, digital culture, and cinema, one is struck by the difficulty of examining the multitude of voices available. In *YMRT*, for example, there are archival voices from film and television along with Longworth's contemporary narration and occasional vocal impersonations of historical voices.[7] In their study of the distribution of the voice through podcasting, Virginia Madsen and John Potts include an intriguing reference to a filmic voice, noting, in a discussion of UbuWebs's archive of voices, that in a 1960s radio recording Truman Capote's voice "is remarkably like the voice Philip Seymour Hoffmann resurrected in the film *Capote*" (Bennett Miller, 2005). Madsen and Potts use the term "resurrected" to denote Hoffman's ability to accurately impersonate the deceased author, in order to play him in a biopic four decades later. Yet Longworth's sustained use of archival audio in *YMRT* could equally be described as a form of vocal resurrection, one that takes advantage of two of the podcast's defining characteristics: time shifting and mobility.[8]

Podcasts allow listeners to consume audio items when and where they choose, particularly given the mobility provided by the near ubiquity of audio-enabled smart devices. This can have important ramifications when considered in light of film performers and associated forms of stardom. Much as fans of given movie stars might hang posters of them on their bedroom walls, Longworth's remediation of filmic performances demonstrates a new possibility: of effectively pocketing star voices for daily access—a form of consumption previously connected with singing rather than with speaking.

Madsen and Potts use the term "voice-cast" to refer to how podcasting "opens up a new sphere of voicings and words in motion and 'in suspension' . . . await[ing] activation as they find their listeners." They also propose that one of the "revolutionary" attributes of podcasting is its "creation of a new and extended sphere for the performance of the essentially *acousmatic* voice," wherein voices are transmitted and received "without their origin being visible."[9] Following from this, the term "voice-cast" could be used to describe instances when an image track is deliberately cast off from recorded voices. That is, when the podcast format incorporates audio from audiovisual media (such as cinema), it can effectively turn *any* screened voice into an *acousmatic* voice of sorts. In the process, it invites reflection on existing conceptions of the acousmatic voice—such as that of prominent film sound theorist Michel Chion.

In distinguishing between the "radio-*acousmêtre*" and that of cinema, Chion defined the former as inherently acousmatic, but asserted that "one cannot play with showing, partially showing, and not showing," given that there is no possibility of seeing the radio-*acousmêtre*. While the podcast medium may generally be aligned with such an *acousmatic* voice, *YMRT*'s "Jean and Jane" series (along with others, such as "Dead Blondes") continually toys with our familiarity with images and embodied voices. Although the website (youmustrememberthispodcast.com) includes supplementary images and links to online videos, most listeners access the podcast via audio streaming sites, such as iTunes and Spotify. As such, the podcast can function much like Chion's cinematic *acousmêtre* does, where "what we have seen and heard makes us prejudge what we don't see." But while a familiarity with these actresses' appearances may allow their voices to trigger images of their bodies (a kind of memory-driven playback function), the podcast format precludes the idea that we interpret what we hear in relation to "what we might see."[10] Knowing, for instance, that in Longworth's "Jean and Jane" series we are never going to see Seberg and Fonda while they speak, the format primes us to listen more intently. Furthermore, through mentions of instances when actresses such as Hedy Lamarr were hired to do vocal performances of film roles for radio (as in episode 29), the series reminds us that screen actresses have long been heard without simultaneously being seen.[11] Indeed, this is the case even if such instances complicate screen-based conceptual frameworks, such as Kaja Silverman's focus on voice-over narration.[12]

REVISING THE DEFAULT WHITE MALE PERSPECTIVE

The revisionist potential of remixing preexisting filmic voices in the podcast format becomes even more apparent in light of Helen Macallan and Andrew Plain's study of the digital filmic voice. They discuss Walter Murch's 2001 remastering of *Apocalypse Now* (Francis Ford Coppola, 1979), which altered the delivery of the voice-over narration by spreading it across all three loudspeakers behind the screen. Macallan and Plain situate this as an exceptional departure from historical practices, noting that since the 1950s there has been resistance to moving the voice away from the central loudspeaker, because of a fear that it would be "perceived as floating free of the body, hence rupturing the film's narrative."[13] Their insights are useful in relation to *YMRT*, since "rupturing" Hollywood narratives is one of Longworth's precise aims. While Macallan and Plain's discussion of narrative refers to the film's plot, this idea can be reapplied to the cultural narratives that have led to women's experiences being written out of popular histories of Hollywood. In reference to *YMRT*'s tagline—Longworth says that the podcast is "dedicated to exploring the secret and/or forgotten histories of Hollywood's first century"—Longworth explains, to *Jezebel's* Kelly Faircloth, how this often means correcting for the default framing of events: "When you start reading a lot of news stories that were written in the 1930s, '40s, '50s, you really become aware of the extent to which the default perspective of mainstream reporting used to be the white male perspective, even when the reporter was female."[14] Longworth's awareness of this history, and the complicity of (white) women (such as columnist Hedda Hopper) in shaming women in the film industry, informs her use of her podcast to retroactively support many of the women who were formerly dismissed or silenced by cinema's sexist power structures. By resurrecting women's voices, including in episodes that focus on women of color, Longworth purposely and productively ruptures aspects of the popular Hollywood narrative. There are individual episodes on the Black actresses Lena Horne (2015), Dorothy Dandridge (2019), and Hattie McDaniel (2019), for example, as well as on the Mexican actress Lupe Vélez (2018).

Released as episode 33 in February 2015, Longworth's segment on Horne was the first to make substantial use of archival audio materials with the aim of allowing Horne to tell as much of her own story as possible. Through the careful curation of recordings of Horne's voice, Longworth (as a comparatively privileged white woman) thus shares information about Horne's experience of discrimination in Hollywood without speaking unnecessarily on her behalf.[15] Her incorporation of Horne's voice is particularly important, given the extensive history of Horne's scenes being cut from films, or her voice being removed from soundtracks, as a result of her race. Longworth weaves these stories throughout the episode, including Horne's recollection of how MGM cast Ava Gardner in the role of Julie in *Show Boat* (George Sidney, 1951). The part went to the white Gardner despite the fact that Horne was under contract at MGM and felt destined to play Julie, and that she had already played the role in the compressed adaptation of parts of *Show Boat* in *Till the Clouds Roll By* (1946)—as well as the fact that the character was supposed to be a light-skinned Black woman.

Notably, the podcast includes a 1982 recording of Horne describing how Gardner's vocal performance was heavily reliant on Horne's preexisting recordings of some of Julie's songs: "Ava had to practice moving her lips with my records I'd made" [*sic*]. As Horne recounts here, MGM told Gardner to listen to Horne's recordings of the songs and mimic her delivery when recording the album soundtrack. Gardner explained elsewhere that, after deciding they still didn't want to use Gardner's voice, "they took my record imitating Lena and put earphones on her so she could sing the songs copying me copying her." When MGM discovered that it would have to use Gardner's voice on the album if it wanted to use her name and image on the cover, they asked Gardner to layer her voice over Horne's voice, which had been recorded over Gardner's voice imitating Horne's voice.[16] The farcical arrangement naturally frustrated Horne. And yet, as we hear Horne jokingly explain in an interview, Gardner took out her frustration (at having to listen to and sing over Horne) *on Horne*: "I'm so sick of hearing you!" Gardner and Horne were friends before and throughout this process, but the podcast suggests that Gardner lacked both self-awareness and sympathy for Horne's plight. Longworth, by contrast, is not only sympathetic to Horne's situation, but used this episode as a catalyst for including more archival recordings, so as not to speak unduly on others' behalf.

The podcast on Horne, particularly the details around Ava Gardner, help to retroactively address broader issues around race and Hollywood dubbing practices. In fact, just three years after Horne's experience with *Show Boat*, *Carmen Jones* (1954), directed by Otto Preminger, worked to consolidate the use of dubbing technologies in order to merge the on-screen bodies of one race with the vocal recordings of another. In the adaptation of Billy Rose's 1943 Broadway show of the same name, Dorothy Dandridge's singing voice was replaced by that of the white opera singer Marilyn Horne (similar treatment was used for two of the male actors). As Jeff Smith has explained, Preminger was fully aware of Dandridge's musical background when he cast her as Carmen—meaning that the decision to dub her, and to sever "the link between voice and body" through the "technological separation of image and sound," can be considered a way of "[enabling] a white performer to speak through the black body that is seen on screen." In terms of the Horne-Gardner situation, by requiring the white singer to selectively mimic a vocal trait associated with a Black dialect, the dubbing in *Carmen Jones* created a curious spectacle: "a black actress voiced by a white singer trying to sound black." As such, it undermined the distinct premise of the theatrical production, which claims to be an "all-Black" musical, at least according to producer Billy Rose and lyricist Oscar Hammerstein.[17]

As already noted in relation to Jean Seberg, Preminger was willing to take directorial control of actresses' accents. With Dandridge and several other performers in *Carmen Jones*, his desire for a kind of vocal mastery led, significantly, to an all-Black on-screen cast being undermined by potentially racist and classist ideas around how Black performers should sound when singing, and in particular, to the notion that they were not convincing as opera singers. Technology was ultimately the enabler. In moving from the theater to a screen adaptation of *Carmen Jones* (the former was also an adaptation, of Georges Bizet's opera *Carmen* [1875]), Preminger took advantage of cinema's separation of sound and image tracks. Longworth does something similar with the *YMRT* podcast, albeit for a very different purpose.

Beyond Longworth's occasional focus on people of color (explored most thoroughly in *YMRT*'s 2019 series on the Disney film *Song of the South* [Wilfred Jackson, 1946]),[18] there are other positive signs that podcasts can allow for a more diverse range of voices to be heard. Success stories include *2 Dope Queens* (WYNC, 2016–2018), hosted by actresses and comedians Phoebe Robinson and Jessica Williams, who were already known from the screen for their work on the likes of *Broad City* (Robinson) and *The Daily Show* (Williams). When their twelve-episode season launched in April 2016, it topped the iTunes podcast chart for seven days, something Robinson has attributed to its humorous aspects: "The huge amount of diversity is just icing on the cake because what matters to Jess [Williams] and I number one is that the show is top to bottom funny. . . . We don't consider our show a niche show or this other thing that is left of center. We're straight down the middle comedy."[19] While aiming for a broad appeal, *2 Dope Queens* nonetheless recognizes the significance of its hosts' racial identity, saying, in a matter-of-fact podcast summary, "Phoebe Robinson and Jessica Williams are funny. They're black. They're BFFs. And they host a live comedy show in Brooklyn."[20]

Many other podcasts hosted by women of color are similarly upfront about their racial identity, in some cases making it their unique selling point. An Asian American example is *Culture Chat with Mimi Chan* (2017–). Chan says, on the webpage describing the podcast, "I am thrilled to be representing as a female POC podcaster since 2017."[21] In her 130-plus podcasts, she explores a variety of topics, such as pop culture and film. One episode is dedicated to her role as the live-action model for Disney's *Mulan* (Niki Caro, 1998). Given the troubling history of Disney's representation of, and engagement with, race and actors of color, Chan's ability to use a podcast to tell this particular story on her own terms is notable. Indeed, Asian women of color are involved in two other podcasts dealing explicitly with issues around Asian American representation and opportunities in the film industry: *We're Not All Ninjas: The Podcast* (2016–), a movie review podcast about Asian American representation in Hollywood films cohosted by Melissa Slaughter, Rachel Liu, and Alex Chester; and *Asian Oscar Bait (No More Excuses, Hollywood)* (2016–2017), cohosted by Melissa Powers and Andrew Eng, which aims to "[tell] true stories of Asians throughout history—and [pitch] them to Hollywood." While none of these podcasts have achieved the acclaim or listenership of *2 Dope Queens*, or, indeed, of *YMRT*, their very presence is a sign of the increased sonic space available to voices of color online. Notably, in 2018 the audio streaming giant Spotify launched an accelerator program to support US-based women of color in developing new podcasts, a program it has repeated and expanded ever since.[22] Such programs may help to sustain this momentum.

EDITING FILM HISTORY, FROM FOUND-FOOTAGE CINEMA TO ARCHIVAL AUDIO

Historically, women's "cameraless" (found-footage) cinema can be tied to their lack of access not just to cameras, but to the institutions of cinema that would rarely employ them. In a similar way, Longworth's decision to start the *YMRT* podcast involved a move away from her art school practice of narrating over remixed imagery, partly because she was concerned about exhibiting reworked film material without institutional support or permissions. Although there are strict laws regarding the use of copyrighted music in digital outputs (for example, with platforms such as YouTube employing software that automatically detects and limits this practice), film soundtracks are not generally subject to such restrictions. Before exploring the parallel between the podcast and cameraless cinema, however, I want to return to the fear that Macallan and Plain identified, of how a free-floating voice could "rupture" a given film's narrative.

One could argue that Longworth's method of extracting audio clips from films and other archival audiovisual materials, and remixing them in a podcast, is productive in doing just that. As well as rupturing the film's narrative by rupturing its soundtrack (in part by casting off the corresponding image track), Longworth uses the remixed structure to assemble a revised narrative, one that incorporates gendered production and cultural contexts. Longworth has acknowledged that these revised narratives are also partial and subjective, and she has referred to *YMRT* as more of "a work of historiography" than history: "History is all written from a point of view and I see it all as just stories, whether it's proven to be true or not; it's all just a tapestry of public ideas." Her podcast provides a kind of tapestry of women's voices in Hollywood. In this way it challenges the place of "powerful white males" as providing the "default voice of American popular culture."[23] Longworth's own voice provides the thread that weaves these disparate voices together. Though her literal and authorial voice is crucial, however, digital editing equipment and streaming platforms provide a facilitating fabric, allowing for the featured women's voices to be intricately held together for mass consumption.

In discussing digital filmic voices, Macallan and Plain stressed that increased flexibility is one of the most important features of digital sound editing (along with speed and precision): "Now the various options for a relatively unorthodox sequence . . . can be rehearsed without penalty, because decisions can be made offline."[24] In relation to *YRMT*, this situation, and its benefits, are complicated by the fact that Longworth is able to apply digital sound editing techniques to archival soundtracks, ones that were cut manually at the time of the films' initial production, but which have now been converted to digital format. With this newfound flexibility, Longworth remixes these women's voices in meaningful ways. Indeed, in describing her technical process, which was self-taught, she has revealed the importance of freely available digital audio software, such as GarageBand, to her development as a podcast creator. Released by Apple in 2004, GarageBand was designed for both music and podcast production, allowing users to easily make multiple-track sound outputs. In a 2015 interview, Longworth explained the relatively ad hoc arrangements for producing the series and spoke about the very domestic nature of her operations:

> I record and edit everything in my house. There's a possibility in the future—working with American Public Media—that I would start recording in a studio. They have offered that, and I've turned it down at this point. As soon as I finish a script, I want to start recording[,] because the emotional aspect of it is fresh for me. Sometimes that's at nine in the morning, and sometimes that's at 10 at night. It would be difficult for me at this point to stick to a weekly recording schedule.[25]

The podcast later became less of an individual DIY endeavor and more "professional," with Longworth joining the Panoply podcast network in September 2015. She introduced a Patreon-based monthly subscription version of *YMRT*, where subscribers pay $5–$25 per month to gain access to a range of additional podcasts and materials, in May 2019.[26] After editing the first fifty-five episodes herself, she made use of professional sound editors in the ones that followed. Yet Longworth continues to strongly shape the editing process, including the use of archival audio clips. As Lindsey Schoenholtz, Longworth's assistant on the podcast, explained, "Karina always identifies the sections of films, etc., to include in the podcasts. She is very meticulous and detail oriented in this regard."[27]

Longworth's rationale for recording at home, as well as her description of history as a "tapestry of public ideas," intersects rather meaningfully with the history of women's found-footage cinema. Longworth's approach to archival audio materials builds on her experiences from art school, where she often narrated over an assemblage of video clips:

> I went to art school and studied experimental film and video with the idea of making nontraditional, nonfiction films. . . . I was inspired by people like Chris Marker and Mark Rappaport but was

also kind of inventing my own style. It was very full of my own
voice, most of it with me writing a script and reading it and using
found footage for the images. This was like 2002, 2003. It was
pre-YouTube. That stuff didn't really fit into the art world. Because
I was using so much stolen material, it wasn't appropriate for film
festivals.[28]

Longworth tied her process, and this emphasis on her own voice, to her subsequent move to the podcast format. And even if she cited Chris Marker and
Mark Rappaport as college inspirations, her description of her collage-like
process, and of cutting out the visual element, links her work to women's
nontraditional, nonfictional film, particularly found-footage practices.

As film scholars Monica Dall'Asta and Alessandra Chiarini have explained,
since the origins of cinema "women's interest in found footage and compilation has been extraordinarily intense." Historically, this interest can be seen
in a wide range of examples, from the Soviet director Esfir Shub's work to
that of French archival filmmaker Germaine Dulac and the American feminist
filmmaker Barbara Hammer, whose film *Nitrate Kisses* (1992) combines stock
footage with original shots. Discussing women's collage films since the 1960s,
Dall'Asta and Chiarini noted the growing number of women "involved in the
deconstruction of the codes of contemporary culture—and often particularly
of its sexist stereotypes—through the reworking of pre-existing footage."
Yet, for them, women's ability to creatively manipulate "inert materials" is
only part of the explanation. They place similar emphasis on the realities
of film production, and, "more precisely, the difference that exists between
labor involved in editing and researching and that involved in shooting."[29]

Of particular relevance to Longworth's approach to material in *YMRT*
are Dall'Asta and Chiarini's comments on the place of research, rather than
direction (in the standard sense of the word, meaning to direct performers and
technicians on a set), in cameraless cinema. They observed that found-footage
work "more closely resemble[s] conducting a research project, including
the immersive sessions in archives and philological interrogations about the
material." Furthermore, they noted how "the lack of means can be coun-
tervailed with patience and flair," saying that such cinema could "even be
executed at home at the kitchen sink."[30] In other words, like Longworth,
who stressed her ability to record from home, perhaps late at night after
finishing her research, Dell'Asta and Chiarini were interested in how women
working in found-footage cinema could very literally work autonomously,
without a crew, in their personal space of choice.

Beyond these general parallels, there are some other notable overlaps between Longworth's remixing of audio and the kind of work presented in found-footage films. Both formats can critically reflect on history, for example—as Chiarini explored in relation to Barbara Hammer's *Invisible Histories Trilogy*. Beginning in 1992, with *Nitrate Kisses*, Hammer used archival images and original shots to productively "re-edit" selected cinema, with "the double goal of rediscovering twentieth-century lesbian and gay history and reflecting on the concept of historical research itself."[31] Hammer was in search of an alternative style to the linear narration of mainstream cinema and interested in exploring the movement of thought and emotions that could spring from the flow of images in *Nitrate Kisses*. Chiarini identified a method of assemblage reminiscent of Maya Deren's theorization of "vertical cinema": "Found footage and original shots are combined in counterpoint to offer a critical reflection about history that calls into question the casual and chronological linearity of official historiography, thus revealing unforeseen connections between past and present, individual and collective."[32]

This use of assemblage to reveal connections between the past and the present is similarly evident in *YMRT*. Frequently, the podcast's presentation of women's verbal and vocal influences (or lack thereof) benefits from Longworth's more contemporary knowledge. In particular, the actress-focused series resonates strongly with the contemporary context of the podcast's 2017 release—just months before the revelations of sexual abuse allegations against film producer Harvey Weinstein and the subsequent flood of discourse around the #MeToo movement, including Hollywood's veiled history of mistreatment of women, particularly actresses. In the aftermath of these revelations, relistening to Longworth's "Jean and Jane" and "Dead Blondes" series inevitably leads the listener to further comparative exercises.

For both Longworth and Hammer, the process and aim of remixing existing material is also tied to the emotive potential of editing. Hammer conceived of her cinema "as a means for the expression of 'feeling-images,'" that is, "an inseparable unity of emotion and thought/idea/image and internal bodily states of excitement."[33] Similarly, we can consider how Longworth's assemblage can achieve emotive effects through a combination of the constructed content and her narratorial delivery. Longworth's opening montage sequences for the "Jean and Jane" and "Dead Blondes" series are a case in point. In these sequences, a diverse range of voices coalesce, united by their thematic relationship to each other. Although the various vocal clips in the montages are provided without explicit identifying markers (such as names and dates), they nonetheless prime the listener for the series' focus. Because the precise origins of the vocal clips are generally revealed in different episodes, the montages are rewarding examples of seriality: they become more meaningful over time. The "Dead Blondes" opening montage, for example, can be considered a pool of evidence supporting Longworth's introduction to the series in the first episode, where she explains how blonde women in visual culture have historically "symbolized exceptionalism in a variety of ways. They've been coded as hypersexualized, icily frigid, and presexually pure." The series discusses eleven blonde (white) actresses from the 1920s to the 1980s. We hear a number of them speaking in character, or being spoken about, in such symbolic terms—such as when Dorothy Stratten exclaims, "I'm better than a human woman!" in *Galaxina* (William Sachs, 1980), or when Veronica Lake asks, "Would you rather I be a brunette?" in *I Married a Witch*. We also hear a man's voice telling Lake's character, "It's just a shock to see you dressed." Here the audio montage supports Longworth's broader commentary on Hollywood's treatment of women without the crucial criterion (blondeness) actually having to be confirmed. So while Dall'Asta and Chiarini described found footage as cameraless cinema, parts of *YMRT* might instead be conceived of as imageless cinema: a situation that reflects the freedom and constraints of digital remix culture as well as Longworth's own vision for the podcast as something that "sounded cinematic," but does not have an image track.[34]

"A VALLEY GIRL WITH A GRADUATE DEGREE": LONGWORTH'S MULTIPLICITOUS (DIS)EMBODIED PRESENCE

While Longworth's processes and aims can align her remixing of women's voices with female-made found-footage cinema, in other ways the reception of her personal presence on the podcast reveals her ties to actresses and to historical reactions to women on US radio. In the process of lending her voice of support to women such as Fonda, Seberg, and Horne, Longworth herself becomes subject to some of the same media scrutiny, especially with regard to her vocal delivery and the relationship between her voice and her body. This reception of Longworth's own voice is further complicated by certain shared features with the voices of women in early radio—and so draws attention to the fact that women working in diverse, vocally expressive broadcast formats can face similar situations. As *YRMT* became more and more popular, Longworth, and the series, started to be profiled—often in an interview format—in popular (digital) media outlets, including *Rolling Stone*, *Variety*, *Vanity Fair*, the *Guardian*, and Jezebel, among others. Longworth's voice—as well as her appearance—are frequent points of discussion for journalists. In fact, there is a distinct tendency to compare both Longworth's physical appearance and her vocal qualities to the Hollywood women whose experiences she chronicles.

Nell Frizzell's piece for the *Guardian*, for example, begins with an anecdote about a man in London who interrupts her interview with Longworth after hearing Longworth speak: he taps her on her shoulder to ask if she does the *YMRT* podcast and screams, "Oh my God, I love it," when she nods. Frizzell observes, "It's a strange kind of fame when your voice is recognisable enough for you to be stopped [in this way]." But her attention quickly turns to a description of Longworth's clothing. Longworth, she says, "turns up to meet me dressed in a gold cardigan and full skirt, like something straight out of a 1950s edition of the Hollywood Reporter."[35]

Other interviewers, and some fans of the show, have similarly connected Longworth's voice and appearance to her audio persona. At times, this tactic implies that Longworth's off-mike identity is inseparable from her work, or that her Hollywood-influenced performativity extends into her everyday life. This rhetoric is a historically familiar one. As media history scholar Michele Hilmes explained with regard to the "disembodied woman" in early US radio, anxiety about women's roles and voices have often manifested in public discourse around their appearance and their impact on people off-air: "The woman who could speak without being seen controverted a more traditional feminine role—to be seen and not heard—and any article featuring a woman operator felt obliged to include comment on her physical appearance and/or effect on men, usually including age, attractiveness, and marital status (not normally a feature of profiles on male amateurs)."[36]

Although Hilmes was speaking in reference to women on wireless radio, she and broadcast historian Jennifer Hyland Wang have charted how these anxieties continued after the introduction of broadcast radio in the 1920s. Hyland Wang commented on the pioneering radio serial *Clara, Lu 'n' Em* (1931–1937), featuring and produced by Isobel Carothers, Helen King, and Louise Starkey. Journalists' comments on the women, who were college graduates but relied heavily on a working-class vernacular, reflected, wrote Hyland Wang, "cultural anxieties about the disconnect between the aural and visual regimes of knowledge in radio." Hyland Wang asked, "Without visuals, how could an audience determine the precise 'otherness' of the voices coming into their homes?" Such anxieties led to comic-strip-style visualizations of the women of *Clara, Lu 'n' Em*—for example, in a print advertising tie-in for "Super Suds" soap in 1933.[37] The visualizations, theorized Hyland Wang, alleviated anxieties around not knowing how these women looked. Nearly a century later, popular discourse around Longworth suggested that the physicality of female podcasters is equally an important part of their personae.

Frizzell's comments on Longworth's clothing are just the beginning. Fan comments—for instance, on Longworth's Instagram account—often suggest a desire for the podcast host to *look* as she *sounds*. In January 2018, Longworth posted a picture of herself dressed for the Art Director's Guild awards. The caption said her floor-length red dress was from the Los Angeles vintage store The Way We Wore. One follower commented, "Wow. Now I will always picture you in my mind like this, when I listen to your podcasts."[38] That same month, Longworth posted a black-and-white picture of herself with her longtime partner (and now husband) Rian Johnson, a film director. Of the seventeen comments on the picture, three compared Longworth (or the couple) to characters from a film noir, as when one follower noted, "You look like a film noir femme fatale."[39] Longworth's body is sometimes surveyed as an (un)suitable match for her voice, by fans making complimentary comments about her ability to visually channel the period(s) in Hollywood history with which she most connects. Given Longworth's control over her personal social media, and the publicity pictures she provides on the *YMRT* website, as well as to interviewers, it seems reasonable to conclude that she was happy to "play along" with listeners' desire for her to look like a classical Hollywood film star, or, as Frizzell suggests, "like something straight out of a 1950s edition of the Hollywood Reporter."

Considering Longworth's evident understanding of performance, stardom, and publicity materials, it even seems strategic that the pictures she shares on the site (or Instagram) are often in black and white (figure 4.1), while other official portraits for the podcast show her in color, wearing a glamorous red lipstick and a red dress. So although Longworth—like women in early US radio—may not be able to prevent public discourse from foregrounding her appearance, she does appear to have more control over the imagery on which this discourse is based. At the same time, the Instagram follower's comment about wanting to "always picture" Longworth in a vintage evening dress, when listening to *YMRT*, suggests the pressure that female podcasters may feel to look as "impressive" as they sound, if only in those instances when listeners *are* able to see them. Writing about Longworth after conducting a series of interviews with her for *The Atlantic* in 2018, journalist Sophie Gilbert said Longworth told her she left Instagram "because she disliked feeling pressured to present herself for public consumption, and she didn't think what she looked like should have anything to do with what she did for a living."[40] She has since returned to the platform.

Figure 4.1. A black-and-white promotional image of Karina Longworth recording the *You Must Remember This* podcast. Photo by Meghan Lee.

Although journalists and fans comment on Longworth's appearance, it receives less attention than her voice.[41] Perhaps coincidentally, it is also male journalists who draw the most attention to her voice and the specifics of her delivery. *Rolling Stone*'s Justin Ravitz introduced her as "the honey-voiced Longworth—a charismatic, details-obsessed film critic and historian."[42] In the interview, he tells Longworth, "People love your speaking voice, which sounds like Old Hollywood itself"—a loaded but ambiguous compliment. For another writer, Calen Cross, "Longworth's voice fits the drama of the offscreen antics of the podcast's subjects."[43] And Brent Lang, writing for *Variety*, focuses on one of Longworth's introductory tag lines ("Join us, won't you?"), which he describes as an "invitation . . . delivered in a tone that's ever so arch."[44]

Both Ravitz and another journalist, Scott Porch, inquired into the degree to which Longworth consciously altered her voice when recording, recalling anxieties around the level of contrived performance that circulated among journalists covering *Clara, Lu 'n' Em* in the 1930s. Ravitz asked whether she had any formal training or elocution lessons, while Porch noted, "Your voice on the podcast is a little different than the way you talk in conversation." He then asked, "What would you say you're doing in the podcast?" Longworth responded that she had no formal vocal training, but that she had taken some acting classes as a teenager. Notably, she added that her voice actually "kept me from pursuing acting professionally: I was constantly being critiqued over the fact that I couldn't control my voice very well." The irony in this—that

Longworth's voice is what kept her from pursuing acting, but that she was now performing almost exclusively with her voice—was further complicated when Longworth explained her vocal technique on the podcast to Porch: "I try to bring my voice down [lowering the pitch] and make it slower. I'm a Valley girl. I've never enjoyed the sound of my voice—especially when I've heard myself on the radio or in a soundbite—so I knew wanted to rein myself in like an unforgiving director."[45]

Longworth's comments indicated a degree of self-policing when it came to her delivery, one that recalled Preminger's critique of Seberg's accent, as well as Fonda's agreement with media descriptions of her as "shrill." By attempting to rein her voice in, "like an unforgiving director," Longworth suggested that she had internalized former critiques of her natural voice as unpleasant, as well as taking in the broader cultural contempt for the San Fernando "Valley girl" accent. Since the term's inception in the early 1980s, the accent has been associated with a certain kind of white girlhood—one characterized by uptalk and filler words and what musicologists Jacqueline Warwick and Allison Adrian have described as "narcissistic, immature femininity."[46] Indeed, prior to the more recent disdain for women whose delivery includes "vocal fry" or "uptalk," labeling women as sounding like Valley girls was one of the most enduring vocal insults. It is notable, then, that listeners have criticized Aminatou Sow, the Black and accented podcast cohost of Call Your Girlfriend (2014–), for her "uptalking" rather than for her other vocal qualities.[47] Sow is from Guinea but grew up in West Africa and Europe. Both she and her white cohost, Ann Friedman, were subject to the same critiques when, as journalist Nora Caplan-Bricker noted, "listeners mansplained that Friedman and Sow needed to tamp down their 'likes' and ramp up their enunciation." While drawing conclusions from this one example would be overly speculative, it may signal that the vocal stereotypes associated with young white women are subject to particular contempt, to the extent that they are less accepted than the other, more ethnically diverse vocal qualities of given disembodied women (such as Sow). Fortunately, both Friedman and Sow ignored requests to change their delivery.[48]

Despite Longworth's vocal self-criticism, she does seem to understand that "reining in" her natural expressiveness too much would be counterproductive, particularly when it comes to engaging listeners in the often melodramatic Hollywood stories she recounts. Instead, Longworth seems to have found ways to productively harness her self-proclaimed lack of vocal control to signal authenticity, and a closeness to the material she researches. Her emotive delivery is a central feature of episode 28, on Carole Lombard and Clark Gable, wherein she can audibly be heard crying when recounting the story of Gable, Lombard's husband, waiting for news of Lombard's accidental death.[49] What may be perceived negatively, as a lack of vocal control, can simultaneously be perceived positively, as a sign of vocal authenticity, an affective response that deepens the impression of intimacy between Longworth and her listeners. It further contributes to the emotive links between the podcast and feminist found-footage cinema and women's pictures.

Interviewing Longworth in 2015, Porch noted that she "broke up a little bit" in the Lombard episode, and asked why she decided to keep that version (rather than re-recording it). In the sequence in question, Longworth was discussing an incident where Gable was drinking in a hotel room, waiting for confirmation that Lombard had died in a plane crash. Longworth's response was a telling acknowledgment of the role of melodramatic vocal affect in the podcast more broadly:

> I didn't plan to start crying when I was reading the script that I wrote. (*Laughs*) There's just something about the idea of Clark Gable, cinema's icon of masculinity, sitting in a Las Vegas hotel room drinking [and] waiting for someone to confirm what he already knew, which is that his wife is dead. That just kind of destroys me. I left it in because it felt really honest. I try to walk the line between trying to get as close to the truth as possible and telling it in a cinematic way with my personal stamp on it. It would have been dishonest to cut out the part where my voice broke.

Longworth's laugh, on recalling how she cried when reading aloud a script that she herself had recently written, is revealing. This emotive reaction at the time, coupled with her amusement at how odd it might seem to someone else, signaled her simultaneous attachment to, and distance from, the material she narrates, as well as her immense sympathy for her subjects—in this case, Gable and Lombard.

Reading this section of the interview—including Longworth's description of telling this nonfiction story "in a cinematic way with my personal stamp on it"—I'm reminded of similarities between Longworth's response and existing conceptions of (female) audience's responses to "women's films," such as those that have been dubbed and derided as "weepies." Judith Mayne described women's films as Hollywood products "designed to appeal to a specifically female audience," particularly in the 1930s through the 1950s. These films were "usually melodramatic in tone and full of high-pitched emotion, from which came the pejorative title 'the weepies.'"[50] Although Longworth was reading about film stars, rather than watching a film, her emotional response to the narrative that *she herself had crafted*—albeit from the nonfiction details around Lombard's death—recalls and complicates the kind of melodramatic tone that similarly elicited tears from (female) audiences of Gable and Lombard's time.

Mayne described Barbara Stanwyck's character in the closing of *Stella Dallas* as a "pathetic spectator who peeks longingly through the window," in order to watch her daughter's wedding.[51] Similarly, Longworth is positioned both inside and outside of the events she narrates. Indeed, Longworth's description of her aim—of telling the truth "in a cinematic way [and] with my personal stamp on it"—crystallizes in this light. Telling the story cinematically means bringing forth a layer of heightened emotions that fits the tragic events of the Hollywood couple's lives. In this case, Longworth's "personal stamp" comes in the form of her own affected response—tears and a breaking voice. By not editing this out, she sacrifices a moment of private vulnerability (one otherwise captured only by her laptop, on which she records in her own home) for the sake of her listeners.

Women's films and found-footage films are not the only film genres or modes that *YMRT* channels. Frizzell's description of the podcast's remixing of early media was particularly apt, since she described the show's sound as "like a dreamy mix of film noir voiceover, 1940s gossip column and Pathé news broadcast."[52] This description implicitly draws our attention to Longworth's merging of vocal and literary styles that have traditionally been associated with one gender or another: (1) the hard-boiled *male* narrators of film noir, and (2) *female* Hollywood gossip columnists such as Hedda Hopper, whom, as already noted, Longworth criticized for her tendency to shame female stars. In noir films, voice-over is almost exclusively attributed to male characters, who frequently use the format to lament their conflicted relationships with a femme fatale.[53] How fitting, then, that, as part of Longworth's revisionist approach to film history, she casts *herself* in this role. And the reflective interviews with Longworth provide support for considering this as something of a conscious effort to revise some of noir's historical gender dynamics. In terms of more recent influences on *YMRT*, Longworth namechecks what she labels the "lowbrow" E! network show *Mysteries & Scandals* (1998–2001). The performance style of the host, A. J. Benza, was evocatively described at the time as "butch noir."[54] Longworth referred to him in an interview with a *Jezebel* reporter:

> When I was in college, the E! Network had two shows about old Hollywood: *E! True Hollywood Stories* and *Mysteries & Scandals*. I preferred the latter because it was campier and less morose. I've re-

visited a lot of the episodes recently on YouTube, and . . . they're really not badly researched, and some of them have some really good interview clips. . . . I feel sort of like the dirty secret of *You Must Remember This* is that we're a *Mysteries & Scandals* cover band, with the masculine vibe of that show and its host [Benza] replaced by me, a Valley girl with a graduate degree.[55]

Mysteries & Scandals' focus on celebrity self-destruction clearly aligns it with *YMRT*. And Longworth is right to describe Benza's show—rather than just the host himself—as having a "masculine vibe." For example, in an episode on Bette Davis (Season 4, episode 18), one is struck by the large number of male talking heads brought in to discuss her, as well as by Benza's sardonic, sexist remarks about Davis. Narrating over moving imagery of Davis in films and on set, he refers to her as "burning through four disastrous marriages." His direct address to the audience—as when he describes Davis as "I want to say witch, but that's not quite right"—involves a tongue-in-cheek misogyny that was presumably expected to be entertaining to those already subscribing to the view that Davis was a "difficult" woman. Thus, when Longworth compared *YMRT* to *Mysteries & Scandals*, her description of supplanting the show's (and host's) "masculine vibe" was crucial. As she jokingly implied, *YMRT* does not just have any old feminine vibe; its style reflects its creator's (and narrator's) status as an underestimated "Valley girl," one with a master's degree in cinema studies. And this feminine, often feminist, "vibe" also extends to Longworth's treatment of her female subjects, the likes of Davis—whose fundraising efforts during World War II Longworth examined as part of her 2015 series on stars during the wars ("Star Wars")—who are talked about in much more measured terms. Overall, *YMRT*'s noirish qualities are diverse, and they are disruptive of the genre's typical gendered conventions. Although fans may compare Longworth visually to the femme fatale character, her guiding narration and knowledge align her more closely with the male hard-boiled detective.

A TAPESTRY OF WOMEN'S VOICES

Analyzing *You Must Remember This* from the perspective of gender and the voice has proven revealing in its complexity, including the various kinds of voices—new and old, scripted performances and unscripted interviews—that make up the proliferation of voices and their effect in the podcast. Longworth's influences, like her roles, are manifold: the original films, film journalism and gossip columns, film noir and its postmodern televisual counterparts. Then there is the contextual weight of other historical precursors:

earlier responses to women's voices on US radio, the montage processes of found-footage cinema, and the emotive nature of "women's weepies," each of which helps to shed light on how *YMRT* resurrects Hollywood voices and revises historical narratives for the digital era. These diverse media outputs all contribute to Longworth's aims, processes, and performative strategies. In many respects, Longworth seems empowered by the opportunities provided by the podcast medium, which can allow podcasters to exert control over all aspects of the production and distribution process and manage the content on their chosen subjects.

Longworth's approach encourages listeners to learn from Hollywood's past, in order that these histories do not repeat themselves. It is unsurprising, then, that as the 2017 #MeToo revelations and social media campaign began to gather momentum, Longworth identified connections to certain episodes of her podcast. This is not to say that *YMRT*, and related women-led entertainment podcasts, are utopian sonic spaces. They can, however, provide valuable forums for documenting women's previously unheard accounts of Hollywood and popular culture, along with a format for (temporarily) separating women's voices from their fetishized and commodified images.

In various ways, *YMRT* is representative of women-driven podcasts more generally, at least in the English-speaking Western media. Data from 2013 suggested that the majority of the most popular podcasts on iTunes and the podcast app Stitcher were helmed by men.[56] And yet feminist scholars such as Raechel Tiffe and Melody Hoffmann have expressed hope about the potential of the sonic space of podcasts to allow for "traditionally-oppressed voices" to be heard. Though they warned that "as long as there is an internet, so too will there be trolls disparaging the sound of feminine/feminist voices," Tiffe and Hoffman identified a trend for the voices of women on podcasts to "reflect the exact qualities that are policed and criticized by contemporary society," including vocal fry, uptalk, and cursing. Furthermore, comparing women's voices on podcasts to those in traditional radio broadcasting, they noted how journalism courses train reporters and radio hosts to "speak with little emotion," in sharp contrast to feminist podcasting, where "embracing one's 'authentic voice' is a defining and foundational trend."[57] This move toward an emotive and authentic delivery is heard clearly in Longworth's podcast—including in her decision to retain the occasional sounds of her own sobs and vocal breaks.

While independent podcasts may allow for more women's voices, and voices of people of color, to be heard than in traditional broadcasting, analysis of the entrepreneurial discourse surrounding US-based podcasting reveals some limitations. As John L. Sullivan explained, based on his attendance at the 2016 edition of Podcast Movement (an annual convention on the medium), podcasters are increasingly preoccupied with molding the format "into a reliable revenue-generating medium." Attracting advertising revenue is the only real option for doing so, and independent producers are at a distinct disadvantage in this regard: "The message to amateur podcasters was clear," Sullivan noted. "Without any data about the size and character of your listeners, or without the visibility and cross-promotion that came with carriage on one of the podcast networks, advertisers would likely pay them little attention." With regard to cross-promotion, Sullivan refers here to "intensive relationship-building labour," similar to those techniques employed by female bloggers who have reported a need to brand themselves in subtle ways, to continually engage in relationship building with their online audience, and to maintain visibility on social media, often by putting their private lives on display.[58] Indeed, we can certainly observe these tendencies in relation to Longworth's promotion of *YMRT*, as it seems to be good business sense for Longworth to display herself on social media in ways that fit with the podcast's themes, such as by posting black-and-white images of herself, or photos in which she is wearing vintage dresses that costume her as though she were part of old Hollywood.

With the "Jean and Jane" series, and some of *YMRT*'s other female-focused podcasts, Longworth curates a particular kind of women's film history through her selectivity. This historiographic approach depends on the figures she chooses, the dialogue and soundtrack clips she uses to represent them, and her contextualization of the words heard in them, both in terms of narration and through the use of supporting materials available on the podcast's website and social media accounts. Throughout the "Jean and Jane" series, listeners are provided with audio clips and narrated examples that emphasize the significance of vocal modulation and manipulation to Seberg's and Fonda's working lives, including instances where Seberg's accent was critiqued, or where Fonda was spoken over. *You Must Remember This* draws attention to, and at times deliberately reverses, these dynamics, to help these actresses reclaim their vocal agency. In one episode, Longworth refers to Seberg's attempts to "take back the narrative" from the press when reporters cruelly fixated on the race of her unborn baby. More broadly, this concept of reclaiming the narrative can be used to describe what Longworth, as digital historiographer, facilitates through the podcast format when she uses this new audio medium to allow Fonda, Seberg, and a host of other women from Hollywood history to redirect popular understandings of their lives.

CHAPTER 5

MEME GIRLS VERSUS TRUMP: THE SILENT VOICES OF SUBTITLED SCREENSHOTS

DONALD TRUMP'S JANUARY 2017 PRESIDENTIAL INAUGURATION SPEECH lasted roughly sixteen minutes, but a single line received the most attention online: "We are transferring power from Washington, DC, and giving it back to you, the people." As Timothy Burke, video editor at the website Deadspin, quickly noticed, Trump's wording and delivery echoed a line of monologue delivered by the villain, Bane, in the Batman film *The Dark Knight Rises* (Christopher Nolan, 2012): "We take Gotham from the corrupt! The rich! The oppressors of generations who have kept you down with myths of opportunity, and we give it back to you . . . the people." Burke posted a ten-second mashup of the verbal parallel on Twitter, and the video was retweeted roughly sixty-four thousand times, half of these within three hours.[1] News of Trump's so-called plagiarism spread quickly, with bloggers and journalists jumping at the opportunity to repost video comparisons or to contextualize the irony of Trump channeling a fictional villain. During his time in office, Trump continued to merge politics and pop culture to jarring effect, often sharing media objects mimicking film and television promotional materials. These include several memes inspired by *Game of Thrones* (HBO, 2011–2019), one of which featured the words "Sanctions are coming," for example—a play on the show's "Winter is coming" line, along with a Hollywood trailer–like video that Trump showed North Korean leader Kim Jong-un in 2018.[2] Trump not only shared the *Game of Thrones*–inspired imagery on his Twitter account but also printed them out as posters. HBO eventually issued a statement saying it would prefer that its intellectual property not be used for political purposes.[3] With the trailer, the video's aggrandizing voice-over cast Trump and Kim as two leaders

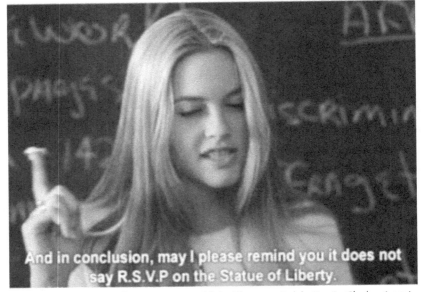

Figure 5.1. Screenshot of Cher Horowitz (Alicia Silverstone) debating in *Clueless* (1995), as posted on the Instagram account of "The Wing" in January 2017.

with "one destiny." For Trump, then, the job of US president often seemed interchangeable with that of a PR agency. His apparent goal was to craft a narrative and create hype.

Social media users responded in kind—frequently putting Trump in dialogue with a fictional screen character. In January 2017, dialogue from *Clueless* was so appropriated. In light of Trump's restrictive immigration policy, a New York–based women's club, called "The Wing," shared a subtitled still from Cher's school debate on Haitian immigrants on its Instagram (figure 5.1).[4] Standing in front of a blackboard on which words such as "discrimination" and "suffragette" are scrawled, Cher (Alicia Silverstone) delivers her closing statement: "And in conclusion, may I please remind you it does not say R.S.V.P. on the Statue of Liberty." In the full speech, Cher improbably compares the plight of Haitian refugees to her father's fiftieth birthday party.

Here, the women of The Wing used Cher's pro-immigration comments from 1995, as written and directed by Amy Heckerling, to speak for their position on Trump's new policies. Cher has replaced Hillary Rodham Clinton as Trump's opposition. Subtitled stills and GIFs of this line were picked up and shared on other sites, which supplied a range of imagery with superimposed text. These image-text combinations emphasized how, as Jordan Bassett of NME explained, Cher "nailed the refugee debate in one minute." In drawing a comparison between Cher's impassioned 1995 argument on behalf of Haitian refugees and the minority groups being targeted in 2017, commentators thus retroactively praised the character's words for their articulation of the pro-immigration stance. As with the Bane-Trump comparison, there is a glibness to the accompanying commentary. Bassett stated, "Basically, if Cher were in power, politicians would all get a lot more stuff done."[5]

These Trump-focused moments are just two examples of how digital media is allowing new discourse to be created between current political events and preexisting film and television dialogue. This chapter is concerned with the afterlives of scripted screen dialogue and how it is reused in different contexts on the secondary screens of the internet. I focus on what responses by female screen characters reveal about digital identity politics and culture; what motivates social media users to circulate this particular format of remixed media; and how the use of feminist-oriented dialogue has developed in tandem with meme culture and what has been termed the "online culture wars," which played out on sites such as Twitter, 4chan, and Tumblr in the period before and after the 2016 US presidential campaign.

Using three main case studies drawn from US film and television—the opening *Clueless* example, a "Feminist Lisa Simpson" Tumblr page, and digital exchanges between President Trump and women from *Sex and the City* (HBO, 1998–2004) on the "everyoutfitonSATC" Instagram account—I argue that this use of a range of female characters in memes responding to social and political issues served a valuable purpose, acting as surrogate voices for those frustrated with the political climate of the Trump era while aligning with the rise of what Sarah Banet-Weiser, among others, has termed "popular feminism."[6] As case studies, I chose not only examples that were significant in terms of their popularity (measured via metrics such as shares and like counts), but also ones that allowed me to trace something of a genealogy in the trend for sharing the dialogue of female characters via subtitled memes. Along these lines, Tumblr's "Feminist Lisa Simpson" helped to establish a vernacular that was developed in a more political direction several years later on Instagram. In particular, I connect the use of pop cultural spokeswomen expressing outrage to Trump's inauguration as president despite the substantial number of women who had accused him of sexual misconduct, and to his administration's rollback of women's and immigrants' rights.[7] Though my analysis takes gender politics as its focus, it also allows for the consideration of broader issues of voice as related to the practice of sharing film and television dialogue in the form of subtitled stills and GIFs. These formats can be considered as something of a return to the text-based speech of silent cinema.

A REVISED RETURN TO SILENT FILM INTERTITLES

Subtitled still or looping screenshots constitute a return to silent film intertitles and early expressions of the screen voice as forms heard through mental enunciation. Emerging scholarship on GIFs discusses their relationship to early cinema—such as the looped media of optical toys and the near-fetishization of simple moving imagery. GIF analysis tends to focus on visually "pure" examples: those where the looped movement, often of a character's facial expression or gesture, is not accompanied by superimposed text. Yet, much as critiques of dialogue in early sound films disregarded how silent cinema often included unheard—but read—conversations between characters, GIFs can equally depend on superimposed dialogue for their appeal or effect. That is, a substantial number of GIFs are not "pure movement" (Hampus Hagman's term), or "pure affect" (per Michael Z. Newman).[8] Instead, they can be some combination of movement and affect moderated by the accompanying superimposed text. And although characters' voices are automatically silenced by the limitations of the subtitled GIF or screenshot format, the corresponding images of the character's expressions encourage readers to "hear" the text in certain ways when mentally enunciating the words, a linguistic process known as *endophony*.[9] As pointed out by various "read this in my voice" memes—featuring the faces of performers or characters who have distinctive voices—when we read a caption over the image of a familiar figure we can mentally enunciate it in their voice.[10] The phenomenon has led to numerous variations on this style of meme, including ones with Morgan Freeman (figure 5.2) and *The Simpsons* resident narrator Troy McClure.

Such memes draw attention to the process of endophony, but it is a practice that is equally present when reading subtitled screenshots. With the *Clueless* meme, the widespread circulation of Cher's subtitled dialogue likely depended on Alicia Silverstone's initial delivery of the speech back in 1995. This includes the memory of her Valley girl accent as well as of the yellow gum visible on her index finger as she raises it for emphasis. Acknowledging the power, or at least the presence, of endophony is one reason why this form of political communication should not be written off. When scrolling through the political commentary of non-famous social media users whom we have never heard speak, we must infer the tone and inflection of their typed words. When the words are tied to the image of a popular fictional character, there is more potential to find those words engaging, or at least to hear those words in the tone in which they were originally spoken. This

Figure 5.2. A sample "Read this in my voice" meme featuring Morgan Freeman. Uncredited.

level of identification likely increases the chance that the message will be "spread," or at least be read.

If the trend for subtitled screen imagery can be considered as a second coming of the intertitled voice, there are some fundamental differences in the digital version. Most obviously, the contemporary demand for them emerges from the removal of sound from film and television programming that was made to be audiovisual: the sound of voices delivering dialogue is shifted into a text format in the self-contained frame(s) of the screenshot(s). The fact that the text is read simultaneously, rather than after a cutaway to a black screen, also marks a shift from the dominant silent cinema style. However, silent films also sometimes experimented with more efficient ways to integrate dialogue. *The Chamber Mystery* (Abraham S. Schomer, 1920), for example, incorporated speech bubbles rather than cutting away to intertitles, thus providing something of a precursor to the digital text-on-image format (figure 5.3).

The nature of the voice-as-text in internet memes also differs from intertitles in silent films in that, in the latter, the text generally served an expositional purpose (clarifying the plot or establishing a character's motive), while in the former, the lines of dialogue chosen for digital sharing are often inconsequential to the original narrative. Indeed, this lack of connection to the original narrative is a feature that memes with text share with movement-focused, text-free GIFs. As Hagman noted of such GIFs, "cinematic movement is rebooted—given a second life as it were—outside the strictures of the narratives from which they originate."[11]

Figure 5.3. Screenshot showing the use of superimposed speech bubbles rather than intertitles in the silent film *The Chamber Mystery* (1920). Produced by Schomer-Ross Productions.

People often repeated favorite lines from movies even before the internet era, and this practice has become particularly common when (re)watching cult films and television shows. The online sharing and resharing of lines of dialogue is an apt update to this practice. GIFs, in particular, offer an effortless way to repeat lines (albeit without the voice), because the looping format replicates how individuals previously took pleasure in repeating certain lines themselves. In looping GIFs, a line that is deemed worth repeating can now repeat itself. While the individual might previously have repeated a given line out loud, the format of the GIF makes an unknowing parrot of the original character. The original soundtrack of the voice is missing, but we lip-read along with the printed words. Assuming our familiarity with the original performer, we can mentally enunciate the words using the character's tone and inflection. This process provides a reverse dynamic to the way that women's formerly screened voices are remediated in the *You Must Remember This* podcast (chapter 4). On the podcast, the voice is present while the visible body is absent, but the body can seem present for listeners who have experienced these voices via audiovisual screen media. With the subtitled meme, the visible body is present, and the voice is now absent—but it can seem present for viewers who remember hearing the voice while also seeing it.

PLAYFUL ACTIVISM AND FICTIONAL "SOCIAL JUSTICE WARRIORS"

Recycling screen dialogue is not a strictly gendered practice: both male and female characters are quoted by social media users who identify as a range of gender and sexual orientations. Yet it is female characters' dialogue that is increasingly being employed as a tool for women's rights activism. Indeed, girls and young women are harnessing the power of networked communities such as Instagram and Tumblr to spread playful but meaningful messages, potentially in an effort both to challenge the opposition and to comfort one another. As such, I position the practice alongside existing evidence of how young women are using digital communities to—as digital feminism scholar Jessalynn Marie Keller put it in relation to blogging—"participate in a feminist politics, drawing on opportunities that the internet provides to embrace new understandings of community, activism, and even feminism itself."[12] Recyclers of scripted speech can differ in their motivations: more commercially oriented women-led groups also employ this tactic as part of an affective brand-marketing strategy.[13] By considering different points on the spectrum of grassroots to commercial forms of activism, my analysis aims to highlight how these politicized meme practices can be channeled in a capitalist direction.

Keller coined the term "playful activism" to capture how young feminist bloggers include "fluffier fare" alongside their more serious political analyses in an effort to get their message to a mainstream audience.[14] This sentiment also applies well to the practice of sharing recycled film dialogue. Understanding precisely how subtitled screenshots function as a kind of voice involves acknowledging various complexities: (1) the changing content, including the original dialogue and its remixed form; (2) the changing context, which includes political and social changes that may have given way to the remixed form, as well as the new silent format in which the voice is presented; and (3) the factors motivating those who create and/or "like" and/or share the new content. With the interconnectedness of these factors in mind, let us now examine the digital dialogue between Cher from *Clueless* and President Trump more thoroughly, considering why this particular example was contrived, why it proved particularly "spreadable," and how it connects to broader trends in the recycling of women's screen dialogue and voices.[15]

Writing on convergence culture in 2006, Henry Jenkins examined the new relationship between politics and popular culture through the use of a Trump example—only this time, George W. Bush was the presidential subject of ridicule. Jenkins was referring to a 2004 video that was made by the voter participation group TrueMajority, which mashed up news footage of Bush with clips from Trump's reality show, *The Apprentice* (NBC, 2004–2017). The mock preview for the show presented Bush as an incompetent president whom Trump should "fire" for his poor performance. Jenkins asked, "Who would have imagined that Donald Trump could emerge as a populist spokesman, or that sympathetic images of corporate control could fuel a movement to reclaim democracy?" The video serves as an unnerving point of contrast to the *Clueless* and Trump discourse that emerged thirteen years later: Who would have imagined that Cher, a fictional character—a superficial sixteen-year-old from Beverly Hills—would emerge as a spokeswoman against Trump, a populist president? Explaining the success of the 2004 video, Jenkins noted that "*The Apprentice* provided a perfect metaphor" for expressing "a widespread desire to end a failed administration," adding that the metaphor helped to bring that decision closer to home.[16] To understand why the 2017 *Clueless* response was a similarly effective metaphor for expressing dissatisfaction, it is necessary to consider what Cher, as a popular fictional character, signifies to the masses, as well as her relationship to online communities on the political left and right wings in the run-up to the 2016 election.

Gender politics are undoubtedly important to the spreadability of Cher's recycled dialogue: now that Trump's Democratic Party opponent, Hillary Rodham Clinton, could no longer take to the podium to debate him, the women of The Wing chose a different woman to speak for them, a character they assumed would be familiar to their followers. In a class debate titled "Should All Oppressed People Be Allowed Refuge in America?," Cher uses a personal example from her privileged Beverly Hills life—having to reallocate food and seating at her father's birthday party—as evidence that Haitian refugees should be granted entry to the United States despite the potential impact on resources. Cher wins over her peers with her approach and closing statement: inconsiderate party guests had shown up to her father's party after failing to respond to her invitation, but she reminds her classmates that "it does not say R.S.V.P. on the Statue of Liberty." In other words, refugees and immigrants should be facilitated in the United States. Here, the R.S.V.P. stands for the kinds of policies and administrative bureaucracy that can work to turn them away.

Cher's display of a welcoming tolerance remains relevant and still resonates today. But there is another, and perhaps more significant, reason why Cher has been a fitting spokeswoman for frustrated US citizens, and for women in early 2017 in particular. In October 2016, a video was leaked of Trump boasting about controlling women by grabbing them "by the pussy." Cultural theorists Florian Cramer and Ana Teixeira Pinto posited that this infamous statement energized rather than repulsed Trump's supporters because of a phenomenon identified by the twentieth-century philosopher Mikhail Bakhtin. Bakhtin's theories included notions of the carnivalesque, ideas of how high ideals are often reduced to the materiality of the lower stratum of the body. The alt-right has used the term "meme-magick" to describe this phenomenon. Cramer, however, coined the term "weaponization of carnival" to capture the energizing impact of such memes.[17] Those outraged by Trump's grotesque phrasing and behavior began using the rejoinder #pussygrabsback. The writers Amanda Duarte and Jessica Bennett hoped the slogan would inspire women to "grab back" by voting for Rodham Clinton, and the hashtag was often accompanied by an aggressive cat meme along with an #ImWithHer endorsement.[18] The Cher *Clueless* meme became another variation on this. And if, as Cramer maintained, a "meme-producing machine" was at the center of the alt-right's online power at this time, then it is fitting that more liberal, left-leaning groups would respond in kind.[19] Film-based memes, in particular, can have a broad appeal.

Trump's election success was closely intertwined with the use of social media platforms by oppositional groups, including a deep divide—largely based on gender and identity politics—between the often misogynistic forum 4chan and the microblogging site Tumblr.[20] As the writer Angela Nagle saw it, "Tumblr-liberalism" was a source of contempt for Trump supporters. Members of the alt-right frequently overlapped with 4chan posters, at least in terms of their extreme views and taste for ironic and faux-ironic in-jokes, which often had a sexist or racist slant. Of particular relevance to the subsequent *Clueless* rejoinder were the fictional male characters who became central to 4chan culture. Nagle noted the significance of *American Psycho*'s Patrick Bateman (played by Christian Bale), and *Fight Club*'s Tyler Durden (Edward Norton / Brad Pitt). In this way, Nagle wrote, 4chan "was not only deeply and shockingly misogynist, but also self-deprecating in its own self-mockery of nerdish 'beta' male identity." Bateman, for instance, is presented in the film (and original novel) as a sociopathic killer of the homeless and an abuser of women, behavior that made him a popular cultural touchstone on "alt-right, alt-light and anti-feminist forums."[21] Narrative ambiguity about whether these events were merely Bateman's delusions made him an even more suitable figure for the more self-aware and ironic trolls on the forums. They, too, when criticized, would claim that their shocking misogynistic remarks were satire, much as Trump often denied his culpability or made light of serious allegations by calling them "fake news." As Pinto noted, there was a tone of transgressive irony to the online behavior of many alt-right groups. She went so far as to use the term "fascist-curious" to describe a sensibility that is "not outright fascist," but that often flirts "with far-right tropes and racist idioms ironically, in order to maintain plausible deniability."[22]

If *American Psycho* and *Fight Club* provide the alt-right with virtual mascots, then *Clueless*'s Cher and *The Simpsons*' Lisa might be seen as mascots for the liberal left. An ironic and sympathetic figure in Heckerling's cult teen rom-com, Cher is humorously vain and superficial but also generous and quick-witted. Indeed, with her Beverly Hills mansion and endless designer wardrobe, she effectively embodies the kind of "shallow, vain, clueless girl with mainstream tastes" whom Nagle identified as a "hated" figure in geeky subcultures like 4chan.[23] In other words, Cher is the ultimate "basic bitch" (a term that has since been reclaimed ironically by women with mainstream tastes), but one who is nonetheless revealed throughout the film, including in her Haitian refugee speech, to be liberal and charitable. Like the Tumblr "SJWs" (social justice warriors) who are so criticized by the alt-right, *Clueless* sees Cher spearhead donations for a disaster relief fund. By the film's close, she has also coupled up with her hippieish stepbrother, who is studying environmental law.

The cultural legacy of *Clueless*'s dialogue, including Cher's trademark expression, "As if," is another reason why she was a fitting interlocutor for Trump.[24] Among other functions, digitally shared dialogue can reveal the depths of verbal cinephilia tied to certain films and shows. The tendency for favorite lines of dialogue to be remembered and repeated has long been considered a feature of cult media. Audiences' interest in film dialogue—rarely shared by film scholars, who tend to disregard verbal analysis, in order to focus on the visual—has become increasingly apparent online. The superimposition of dialogue over screen imagery is widespread. Once saved, text typed over the image or GIF becomes an embedded element of the image, meaning the quoted dialogue will not show up in search engines. This limitation nonetheless cements the relationship between the screen image and the dialogue it quotes, allowing users to simultaneously share favorite scripted lines and recontextualize them alongside the original context, which remains present through the image of the character and the memory of the character's now absent voice. Dialogue from *Clueless*, in particular Cher's, has been circulating in these ways on the microblogging site Tumblr for close to two decades. Given these various factors, it is perhaps unsurprising that Cher's voice reemerged as relevant to digital politics in early 2017. As a *Guardian* headline observed, "Pussy Grabs Back" became a "rallying cry for female rage against Trump" in October 2016.[25] Cher's pro-immigration speech provided a tongue-in-cheek reminder that Trump's behavior should not go unchecked, whether on- or offline. Yet in certain ways it was the animated character of Lisa Simpson (voiced by Yeardley Smith) that paved the way for women's screen dialogue to be fruitfully recycled online for activist purposes.

The "Feminist Lisa Simpson" Tumblr account was active between July 2014 and January 2016, with seventy-six original or shared posts in total, some of which now have close to a million comments or shares.[26] The posts, drawn from episodes of *The Simpsons* (Fox, 1989–), can be loosely divided into two types: remarks or exchanges in which Lisa "calls out" sexism or makes feminist statements, and remarks or exchanges in which Lisa is patronized as a result of her gender and/or age. An example of the latter is when father Homer congratulates Lisa for her successful biology experiment by telling her, "If you were a boy, you'd be a scientist."[27] With only a few exceptions, each post displays one or more subtitled images, either in GIF or in still form. Unlike much of meme culture, which is associated with self-contained messages, some of the most widely circulated Lisa Simpson Tumblr content requires scrolling through subtitled imagery.

This is the case with a post drawing on a scene from Season 5 (1994), when Lisa is infuriated about her new "Talking Stacy Doll."[28] The ten-part post (with 1,108,575 notes as of July 2021) charts Lisa's excitement and anger about what her doll has to say: "A hush falls over the general assembly as Stacy approaches the podium . . . to deliver what will no doubt be a stirring and memorable address" (subtitles 1 and 2). We read Stacy's first remark: "I wish they taught shopping in school." After a text-free shot of Lisa's disappointed face, we read Stacy's second remark: "Let's bake some cookies for the boys." This is followed by Lisa's disappointment, spread across two images: "Come on, Stacy. I've waited my whole life to hear you speak. Don't you have anything relevant to say?" (figure 5.4). Stacy's next response is: "Don't ask me, I'm just a girl." This is followed by Bart's endorsement of Stacy's underestimation of girls: "Right on. Say it, sister." The sequence ends with Lisa's angry summation of the issue: "It's not funny Bart. Millions of girls will grow up thinking that this is the right way to act." Through the aforementioned process of endophony (mental enunciation of text), readers familiar with *The Simpsons* can read these lines of dialogue with voice actress Yeardley Smith's distinctive voicing of Lisa in mind. Lisa's expressions can also be used to inflect how the text is read. For example, in the image reproduced in figure 5.4, Lisa's expression allows us to mentally hear the despair at her Stacy doll's superficial speech as we read her words.

Figure 5.4. One segment of a subtitled sequence from *The Simpsons* (1989–) on the "Feminist Lisa Simpson" Tumblr, posted in 2015.

Smith's voice has migrated to Tumblr, where she inspired digital natives to speak out against gender discrimination.

Though imagery of Lisa Simpson (with or without subtitled dialogue) also appears on other social media sites, including Instagram, the practice of promoting certain lines of dialogue through subtitled screenshots or GIFs is part of Tumblr's aesthetic. The comments accompanying the "Feminist Lisa Simpson" also usefully highlight the perceived value of the character's comments long after her inception in 1989 (much more so than on Instagram, where comments tend toward tagging friends rather than providing commentary). In many cases, bloggers engage in a kind of reflective, biographical commentary about how a given scene or episode resonated with them. Even though there is no reference to Lisa being a feminist in the dialogue exchange itself, the context of the "Feminist Lisa Simpson" Tumblr means the scene is to be read as an example of her general alignment with feminist ideas. The next comment on this post refers to Lisa as the "voice of reason." Indeed, comments on these posts often highlight Lisa's preternatural wisdom, or note that she was meant to be only eight years old. Within the diegetic world of *The Simpsons*, her youth is an additional barrier to her gender when it comes to why no one will listen to her. Conversely, on Tumblr, Lisa has a captive audience of hundreds of thousands of like-minded individuals.

The "Feminist Lisa Simpson" Tumblr, as well as the broader trend for resharing gender-empowered dialogue, can thus be considered another example of what Ednie Kaeh Garrison has referred to as the "technologic" nature of third-wave feminist networks. One feature of such networks is that they combine diverse technologies to construct oppositional cultural expression.[29] This definition applies well to the practice of sharing subtitled screenshots that draw on familiar mainstream media (such as *Clueless* and *The Simpsons*), but depend for their impact on the selectivity of the person who makes and/or shares them. In this way, the practice becomes an example of how digital environments are making it easier for young women to renegotiate their status as so-called passive media consumers. By recycling and/or remixing the products of audiovisual culture that can speak for them in response to political issues that are being debated online, they become more active participants in public debate.

COMMODIFYING OLD SCRIPTS AND NEW PUBLIC SENTIMENT

There is a certain timelessness to much of the recycled Lisa Simpson dialogue. Her subtitled comments capture general gender-based frustrations that have endured for decades. These sentiments align well with the mood of online identity politics during the period under discussion (2014–2016), when the "Feminist Lisa Simpson" Tumblr page was most active. Yet, as the US political climate began to shift divisively in the run-up to the 2016 election, the meme-able potential of female characters' speech became more closely tied to overt politics—as well as to the increased commodification of female empowerment by profit-oriented producers and retailers. This is the case with The Wing when it revisited the *Clueless* dialogue, as well as with the "everyoutfitonSATC" Instagram page when it revisited speech from *Sex and the City*.[30] The "everyoutfitonSATC" Instagram account was set up by Chelsea Fairless and Lauren Garroni in June 2016 with the purpose of documenting, and mocking, characters' sartorial choices on the popular HBO show. Diverging from this initial motivation, however, the creators subsequently used its viral popularity to address their some 689,000 followers with political commentary in the run-up to, and aftermath of, the US election.[31] Although each post includes a carefully selected screenshot from *Sex and the City*, generally with subtitled dialogue, much of the account's appeal lies in the satirical captions. This combination proved suitable for

everyoutfitonsatc ⊙ • Following   ···

everyoutfitonsatc ⊙ Happy (not my) President's Day, love Samantha Jones 🐆 (S3/EP2) #SamanthaJones #LeopardMoment #Nixon

214w

The country runs better with a good-looking man in charge

Look at Nixon. No one wanted to fuck him, so he fucked everyone.

FEBRUARY 20, 2017

☺   Add a comment..

Figure 5.5. Samantha Jones (Kim Cattrall) from *Sex in the City* (1998–2004) has her political views recycled in 2017 on the "everyoutfitonSATC" Instagram. Screenshot.

creatively selecting scenes from the show to remind their followers to vote, and, subsequently, to make Trump the butt of their jokes.

At the time of the election, Fairless and Garroni urged followers not to be like Carrie Bradshaw (Sarah Jessica Parker) by not registering to vote (a fact about Carrie that another character had revealed).[32] The creators later posted a number of subtitled stills quoting the political views of Samantha Jones (Kim Cattrall) and recontextualizing them with tongue-in-cheek commentary. For example, on President's Day in February 2017, Samantha's comment about the country running better with a good-looking man in charge was accompanied by a "Happy (not my) President's Day" caption (figure 5.5).[33]

Samantha's comment seemed fitting in 2017—given the shift to President Trump after eight years of President Obama. Almost like a verbal "Kuleshov effect"[34] for the digital era, those who were unhappy with the Trump administration could derive renewed meaning and pathos from Samantha's remarks (comparing Presidents Richard Nixon and John F. Kennedy). The insult builds on mockery of Trump's physical appearance by a variety of commentators and talk-show hosts—such as references to the size of his hands and his artificially orange skin, as well as his public preoccupation with sex.[35] These connections, and Instagram users' potential to appreciate them, no doubt benefited from the fact that in 1999 Trump made a cameo appearance on Season 2 of the show, in an episode titled "The Man, the Myth, the Viagra." As Refinery29 writer Carolyn L. Todd said of the episode, even though "the man" in question was not Trump, the title later lent itself to "creative reinterpretation."[36] The creators of "everyoutfitonSATC" thus used these subtitled images to share the political frustrations of its creators in a light and "on-brand" way. Samantha Jones is revealed as having a clairvoyant political moment alongside her hashtagged, clothing-related "#LeopardMoment." Indeed, such moments align with writer Jay Owens's observation that meme culture has an uncanny ability to provide "unexpected, witty truths" from photo content that is inauthentic, borrowed, or stolen.[37]

Fairless and Garroni later sold merchandise in the form of slogan T-shirts and bags. The decision to do so raised questions about branding and about merging fashion-based critiques with cultural and political discourse. The slogans reflected one of the Instagram account's overriding views about the show: that the main protagonist, Carrie, was too judgmental and narrow-minded to be a sex columnist, and that the lawyer on the show, Miranda Hobbes (Cynthia Nixon), was the smartest, sanest character. On the merchandise webpage, Miranda Solidarity, fans could purchase "We Should All Be Mirandas" T-shirts, with 10 percent of the proceeds going to the National Immigration Law Center, because, as Fairless noted in a September 2017 interview, "it's the Miranda thing to do."[38] Fairless also explained why they chose to parody the Dior slogan T-shirt reading, "We Should All Be Feminists," a sentiment Dior took from Chimamanda Ngozi Adichie's 2012 TED talk of the same name.[39] "It's hard being a Miranda in the age of Trump and $700 feminist slogan tees. But if Mirandas ruled the world, the world would be a considerably less fucked up place."[40] Here, Fairless matter-of-factly equates Trump-era politics with the mainstreaming and commodifying of feminism in the form of $700 Dior T-shirts. Not only did the "everyoutfitonSATC" T-shirts sell for only $32, but the proceeds were donated to a cause that aligned with both the ongoing political climate (a protest of Trump's anti-immigration policies) and the fictional character's legal training.

In these recontextualizations of preexisting dialogue, there are notable similarities and differences between the *Sex and the City* examples and the examples using *Clueless*. In both, for instance, it led to claims that the fictional female characters (Miranda and Cher) would be more effective presidents or "rulers" than Trump. Indeed, in terms of their ability to forcibly speak back to Trump, the women in both fictional universes were experienced debaters, either by profession (the Miranda character was a lawyer), or through education and familial connection (Cher learned to debate and negotiate from her father, a litigator). The examples depart somewhat, however, in their eagerness to recycle female screen voices as a part of a strategy to commodify feminism. The Instagram profile for The Wing described it as "a co-working and community space for women" and provided a link to the club's merchandise shop, where one could buy a wide range of products, such as logoed pillboxes and $17 keyrings (reading "GIRLS DOING WHATEVER THE FUCK THEY WANT IN 2017"). Yet this merchandise presumably only provided petty cash for the organization, which was simultaneously charging $2,350 for annual memberships at one location. That membership fee provided access to "open-plan and private workspace plus amenities designed with women's needs in mind," as well as "a robust and unique calendar of events & a community of women dedicated to living their best lives."[41] As the Instagram photos made clear, for $2,350 a year one could expect to work and socialize in a luxurious penthouse with plush furniture in millennial pink and rooftop gardens. In other words, while there are undoubtedly benefits to women's clubs, this particular one was also selling an exclusive kind of lifestyle that was out of reach for the average woman, and especially for those whose circumstances might benefit most from connections with such a space.

In different but related ways, then, The Wing and everyoutfitonSATC Instagram accounts used subtitled screenshots of familiar female characters as part of a branding strategy that commodified their followers' support for women's rights. In this way, they aligned well with Sarah Banet-Weiser's discussion of the strong relationship between culture and economics in contemporary brand culture. In her book *Authentic™*, Banet-Weiser examined how cultural spaces that are generally considered to be "authentic"—such as self-identity, politics, and religion—are increasingly "structured by brand logic and strategies." As part of that theme, she noted how, through the use of social media, contemporary marketers have learned to assume and exploit consumers' relationships with cultural products, and to "emphasize an affective exchange between corporations and consumers." She explores, for example, how brand cultures can "authorize consumption as praxis," a process in which individuals buy goods that have a politics attached to them.[42] In the two cases discussed here, the timely, creative content of Instagram accounts served to catch the attention of Instagram users who felt unhappy and perhaps powerless regarding the political situation in the United States. And while this frustration could extend to a large number of issues and policies, the Instagram accounts generally highlighted women's rights issues; or, in the case of *Clueless*, they used a female spokeswoman with a distinctive voice as a surrogate for Hillary Rodham Clinton, the sharers' desired forty-fifth president. Even if buying a slogan keyring or a T-shirt from such a group is not going to directly alter the political climate, it can provide a sense of solidarity for the purchaser with those individuals with whom they agreed, at least as based on the views articulated playfully online. Buying a product from a group that openly condemned President Trump's policies—such as policies to decrease funding for Planned Parenthood, or those assuming that pregnancy and sexual abuse were preexisting, uninsurable conditions—was thus a small but tangible act of support for consciousness-raising.

In certain ways, the Instagram account of The Wing seemed not unlike those of feminist magazines, such as *Bitch Media* and *Bust*, that also recycled women's screen voices in various subtitled forms. For the January 2017 women's marches on Washington, DC, and elsewhere, *Bust* provided downloadable posters that they urged attendees to print out. Two of the three images featured an original or amended line from a film—*Grease* (Randal Kleiser, 1978) and *Mommie Dearest* (Franky Perry, 1981)—along with the image of the character associated with that line. The character of Rizzo (Stockard Channing) from *Grease* is presented, open-mouthed, beside the words "KEEP YOUR FILTHY LAWS OFF MY SILKY DRAWERS,"[43] an update of her original line, "Keep your filthy paws off my silky drawers."

In this way, Instagram's interface, particularly the image-focused format, played an important role in revealing or concealing activist-cum-capitalist motivations. Someone posting content may contextualize their content with detailed captions and/or hashtags, but the emphasis on images means that users may choose to scroll through a feed paying attention only to the images, without fully understanding the nature of the organization behind them. In other words, one could easily follow The Wing based on its account's images related to women's empowerment, without realizing the exclusivity of its corresponding offline women's club.

THE BENEFITS AND LIMITS OF SUBTITLED VOICES

The memes considered here allow for some wider reflection on the benefits and limitations of subtitled experiences of the voice as a form of playful political discourse. Writing on digital politics in *Activism or Slacktivism?*, tech philosopher Tom Chatfield outlined digital activism's "potentially unholy trinity of ineffectiveness," which he said included "wasted effort, false reassurance and alienation from truly effective activism."[44] But when it comes to recycled scripted dialogue, understanding the benefits of this playful form of activism involves first recalling that a substantial portion of

President Trump's campaign played out on social media. Addressing what she termed "the Trump Twittersphere," sociologist Zeynep Tufekci described her attempts to understand "the power of the Trump social media echo chamber." As she noted, while Trump received criticism for not conducting internal polls with a view to adjusting his message, he instead "[used] Twitter as a kind of gut focus-group polling to pick up and amplify messages that resonate[d]."[45] The metaphor of an echo chamber recurs in discourse around social media communities. It refers to an environment where users can easily seek out and subsequently engage with like-minded individuals, largely filtering out dissenting voices. Even if Trump supporters could filter out dissenting opinions, at least to some degree the presence of dissenting opinions was nonetheless crucial; without them, social media platforms would only reflect a subset of extreme individuals. In fact, Chatfield measured that "digital fire can, however, be fought with fire."[46] In this case, the digital fire started by Trump and his young, far-right supporters was characterized by "an extreme subcultural snobbishness toward the masses and mass culture."[47] How fitting, then, that certain members of the opposition would fight back using memorable figures (particularly women) from pop culture, using memes of already familiar dialogue to amplify, in a playful way, the desired serious message.

The decision to use the familiar words and images of popular characters to respond to political issues also suggests a savvy understanding of how social media platforms can amplify some voices over others. In theory, sites such as Twitter and Instagram present everyone with an equal opportunity to have their views and/or images shared with the masses. In reality, the likelihood of any given tweet or image going viral through the process of likes and/or retweets increases significantly for those with substantial numbers of followers and—on Twitter—a "verified" blue tick status. This hierarchy favors pop culture celebrities and even characters, as well as a smaller number of those who received fame through social media, including alt-right figures such as Milo Yiannopoulos. For non-famous users, creating content that is linked to celebrities is one strategy for tapping into their substantial cultural capital. On Twitter or Instagram, this may involve tagging them in a post in the hopes that they will share it. Indeed, three of the actresses from *Sex and the City* have endorsed the everyoutfitonSATC Instagram, including Kristin Davis (who played Charlotte), who posted a picture of herself wearing a "We Should All Be Mirandas" shirt.[48] Similarly, in February 2017, Alicia Silverstone shared a version of the subtitled *Clueless* speech on her Instagram along with a caption reading, "Who knew Cher would be leading the way?"[49]

Jenkins also acknowledged the importance of questions of voice to digital politics. Considering the diversification of communication channels, he explained that this development was politically important because "it expands the range of voices that can be heard: though some voices command greater prominence than others, no one voice speaks with unquestioned authority."[50] This brings us back to his dismay at the 2004 mashup video that positioned Trump as a populist spokesman who could help challenge President Bush. At this point, Bush's authority was being threatened by the remediation of Trump's authoritative vocal presence as "the boss" on *The Apprentice*, and his corresponding power to tell contestants (or Bush), "You're fired!" Given that Trump's subsequent rise to political power was, in many respects, due to his ability to extend his authoritative voice to other, non-business-related topics (on which he knew much less), it was fitting that he would eventually be placed in opposition to *Clueless*'s protagonist. Like Trump in his reality show, Cher speaks passionately and authoritatively to other characters and the broader audience (partly through omniscient narration)—even about subjects she knows little about. Yet, on the subjects of US civil liberties and tolerance toward immigrants, she knows what to say to someone like Trump, who similarly relies on verbose hyperbole.

Part of what can make slacktivism ineffective is the way it combines wasted effort with false reassurance, all the while alienating individuals from more effective forms of activism. However, the links between subtitled memes and the historical practice of creating protest signs provide another reason for why this trend should not be dismissed as ineffective.[51] As Tufekci noted of the Montgomery bus boycott in 1955, producing and distributing over fifty thousand pamphlets requires a lot of time and effort. Pamphlets had to be copied in secret in the middle of the night, and then handed out by a team of volunteers.[52] Compare this with *Bust* magazine's strategy of creating a high-quality PDF featuring Rizzo's face from *Grease* and a reworked line of her film dialogue. The content served double duty as a social media meme and an easily printed protest sign for the women's marches. So it was not a wasted effort: *Bust* activists had devised a way to save their followers from having to spend time making individual physical posters, by offering them three they could download for free. Their message could thus be spread more easily and with less financial and physical cost. Indeed, political memes—more generally—can be considered the digital incarnation of political cartoons, such as those that appeared in the long-running British magazine *Punch* (1841–1992). The relationship between satirical cartoons and subtitled memes is apparent with a cursory glance: the cartoons coupled a drawn illustration with a caption beneath it, and subtitled screenshot memes depend on pairing text with image to bring an idea to life.

RESPONDING TO THE "BECHDEL TEST," "MANSPLAINING," AND INTERSECTIONALITY

To fully understand the benefits and limitations of subtitled voices to gender and representation, it is necessary to invite male characters (beyond Trump) back into the conversation, as well as to consider the racial dimensions at work in these subtitled memes. It is also necessary to go beyond US politics and online communities with a left- or right-wing slant. The use of female screen characters as social commentators, for example, seems tied to two high-profile reference points for gendered verbal dynamics in digital culture: the "Bechdel test" and discourse around "mansplaining."

The Bechdel test originated in a comic strip by Alison Bechdel, where one character stipulates that to pass the test, a film must: (1) include at least two women, (2) who have at least one conversation, (3) about something other than a man or men.[53] Though it dates to 1985, it started to reemerge as a digital sensation in around 2012. According to Google Trends, interest in the term peaked in December 2015, and it continues to be subject to sudden spikes in interest.[54] Blogs and websites have increasingly measured films using these simplistic parameters. In the period between May 2014 and November 2015, for instance, the number of films analyzed on the "Bechdel Test Movie List" website (bechdeltest.com) more than doubled, from approximately three thousand to over six thousand.[55] Meanwhile, in Sweden in 2013, cinemas began to rate films according to their ability to pass the test.[56] The test's popularity would seem to partly explain the heavy recycling of female characters' speech around this time, including the "Feminist Lisa Simpson" Tumblr, which effectively recast Lisa as the show's main protagonist by foregrounding her (subtitled) voice over those of the other characters. Given the general discourse surrounding the test—that female characters are being "crowded out" of scripts—sharing subtitled stills and GIFs allows for another form of consciousness raising. Such memes highlight the value and quality of dialogue spoken by women in audiovisual media.

Though less strictly tied to film and television than the Bechdel test, the concept of "mansplaining" is also increasingly discussed and illustrated online using examples from screen media. According to Merriam-Webster, mansplaining is "what occurs when a man talks condescendingly to someone (especially a woman) about something he has incomplete knowledge of, with the mistaken assumption that he knows more about it."[57] The concept is generally discussed in relation to real-world exchanges. Although the writer Rebecca Solnit is often cited as bringing the concept (if not the term) to US popular culture, through a 2008 essay, subsequent digital discourse

You think that, because you don't know any better.

Figure 5.6. Screenshot from a *Pocahontas* (1995) GIF that has been used to explain "mansplaining."

uses GIFs from popular film and television to illustrate the concept.[58] In this way, recycled speech can have a purpose apart from promoting characters or dialogue considered to have a positive message: it can also be used to critique scripted speech seen as damaging. Disney films are seen to provide good source material. In *Pocahontas* (Mike Gabriel and Eric Goldberg, 1995), John Smith tells the title character, "You think that, because you don't know any better," while leaning into her with his elbow on his knee, literally wagging his finger at her (figure 5.6).[59] In the GIF, we then see a close-up of Pocahontas raising her eyebrow, frustrated, in reaction to Smith's (body) language. The full GIF is crucial to the dynamic. In order for it to function as an example of mansplaining it is significant that the line lacks specificity: we don't know what she thinks, or what he thinks, for that matter, because of the ambiguity of the pronoun—"that"—which lends the moment a certain universality. Yet Smith is an Englishman, and Pocahontas a Native American. The GIF is thus loaded as much with racial and colonial politics as with gender inequality. Smith's willingness to talk down to her is tied to his privileged status as both a man and a white colonizer. As such, the example can be seen as a rare example of an intersectional subtitled GIF, though the racial dimension tends to be ignored when the GIF is embedded as a general illustration of mansplaining.

This disregard for racial dynamics has been observed as a widespread problem. The term "digital blackface" denotes the use of reaction GIFs and other online tools featuring Black subjects by white internet posters to "embody blackness." This variation on minstrel performance (in which white performers used blackface makeup in the nineteenth and early twentieth centuries) has been considered particularly insidious because it can offer "a more seamless transformation" than in minstrelsy—as when white people use reaction GIFs of Black people to express themselves.[60] In 2017, the dominant GIF platform,

GIPHY, revealed that the most popular GIFs for expressing #happiness and #sadness in the United States were short clips of Black women—the former a moment from *The Oprah Winfrey Show* (Harpo Studios, 1986–2011), in which Winfrey screams with joy, her outstretched arms shaking two microphones at the audience and camera. Indeed, GIFs of Black people often depend on gestures and facial expressions rather than dialogue; they thus generally rely on body language, rather than spoken language, to gain traction. And, as the journalist Amanda Hess explained in the *New York Times*, the widespread popularity of such GIFs captures how, "on the internet, white people outsource their emotional labor to black people."[61] The *Pocahontas* mansplaining GIF demonstrates how the experience of minorities, or characters belonging to such minorities, can become subsumed by white people willing to share these expressive moments as though they were their own. In this respect, it is a reminder that one of the inherent flaws of the Bechdel test is its disregard for the potential hierarchy among women's screen voices (on the basis of race, age, or class) in addition to the typical gender hierarchy.

The female characters considered here, and those used as politicized digital spokeswomen more generally, tend to be white and to lack awareness of their privilege. No doubt the relative rarity of pop cultural spokeswomen of color reflects the fact that the casting departments of US television, and especially film, have historically overlooked women of color.[62] The lack of women of color in mainstream audiovisual media means that the world of memes can perpetuate long-standing inequalities. Rather than offering an intersectional form of feminism, women of color can be subjected to a secondary form of digital silencing. This is only slowly beginning to change, with shows such as *The Mindy Project* (Fox; Hulu, 2012–2017), *How to Get Away with Murder* (ABC, 2014–), and *Fresh off the Boat* (ABC, 2015–) featuring, respectively, Indian American, Black, and Taiwanese American leads. And dialogue by such female characters is making its way to social media in the form of subtitled screenshots and GIFs. Given the issues around "digital blackface" in reaction GIFS, however, it seems clear that turning characters played by women of color into meme-able digital spokeswomen for political or social issues could be problematic. Such women cannot, or should not, be used to speak for all women.

Although there is no clear solution to these problems, there have been some purposeful critical responses, such as a series of "Woke Charlotte" posts on the everyoutfitonSATC Instagram.[63] By rescripting the dialogue of particular characters via subtitles, Fairless and Garroni have attempted to draw attention to—and undo—some of the damaging speech in the original dialogue for *Sex and the City*. Building on online practices of "fansubbing," which have grown rapidly since late in the twentieth century, they scripted critical comebacks in which Charlotte corrects the other characters for their racist, classist, or transphobic remarks.[64] Charlotte's new responses highlight how, despite *Sex and the City*'s initial reception as a celebration of female sexuality and independence, the show's disregard for intersectionality and gender fluidity seems intolerant, and at times offensive, when viewed through the lens of the identity politics of the late 2010s. Through the more inclusive and self-aware figure of "Woke Charlotte," Fairless and Garroni highlight the complicity of white women (or at least white female characters) in perpetuating racist, classist, homophobic, and transphobic discourse and stereotypes. The rescripting of scenes encourages fans of the show to reflect on how they responded to these sentiments, both at the time of the show's airing and subsequently. They also provide a model, and literal lines of dialogue, for how women with relative privilege (based on race, class, sexual orientation, or gender identification) might use their voices to become allies of those with less privilege. And all this is done in a satirical way that can persuade, or even educate, their followers via an entertaining format.

Audiences have long engaged with media, particularly cult films like *Clueless*, by talking back to the screen. Trends within digital culture, including political memes and remixed media more generally, now allow social media users to repurpose characters' speech when quoting them in the public theaters of the internet. As part of a gendered political discourse, this strategy can allow women's groups to more easily and playfully "talk back" to public figures. In particular, it allows social media users to voice their dissatisfaction in ways that may not explicitly change the status quo, but that nonetheless help to fight digital fire with fire, as well as serving a therapeutic function by allowing users to unite around a shared message and fictional messenger. In relation to the secondary lives of dialogue outside of its original narrative, it is significant that these are generally one-sided conversations. In a departure from the intertitle precursors of silent cinema, we rarely see the people being addressed in the fictional world; nor do we hear their responses. The new addressee is determined by the new context, with real-world events providing a new narrative that the old dialogue is selected to match. In the *Clueless* and *Sex and the City* examples, we might identify former president Trump as the new addressee, one interpolated into the existing story-world as the person to whom the words are now directed. Yet presumably the poster of the subtitled imagery knew that Trump was unlikely to see the meme, or to listen to the message even if he did. The more important addressee was the collective digital audience, particularly those people who agreed with, or at least appreciated, the sentiment conveyed by the words.

Repurposing familiar scripted dialogue can be an effective strategy for spreading a desired political message. Although the underlying message is likely serious, by presenting it in a playful, pop cultural package, the likelihood that the silent sound-bite will be "heard" is increased. Precisely who hears it, however, is likely to be a subset of the larger population, most likely digital natives—for whom memes and their related, remixed digital objects are a go-to means of shorthand communication. The ability of subtitled screenshots and GIFs to function as a kind of voice is part of a digital media landscape in which audiovisual media are broken down into their constituent parts (sound, image, text) and remixed in new combinations. Much as film podcasts can remediate screen voices without the presence of the visible body, memes can remediate the components of the speaking screen body (its image and its words) without the presence of the audible voice. And this is not a new phenomenon. It returns us to early cinema, to silent films that communicated characters' voices via a combination of intertitles and unheard moving lips. What has changed is that the audience is now much more likely to read these titles in a particular voice, to mentally enunciate the words with a particular performer's voice in mind.

CHAPTER 6

RUPAUL'S DRAG RACE AND THE QUEERED REMEDIATION OF WOMEN'S VOICES

WHEN HOLLYWOOD MUSICAL STAR DEBBIE REYNOLDS APPEARED as a guest judge on the second season of *RuPaul's Drag Race* (Logo TV, 2009–2016; VH1 2017–), her feedback included notable praise for the quality of one of the drag queen's lip-synced performances during a challenge: "Your lip sync was very, very good . . . which I noticed right away because in films that's what we always did. . . . It's not easy to lip-sync correctly and you did a super job." Though Reynolds doesn't name-drop any films, her role as Kathy Selden in *Singin' in the Rain* (Gene Kelly and Stanley Donen, 1952) immediately comes to mind. After all, the film includes the most renowned dramatization of lip syncing in Hollywood film history. Reynolds's character provided the pleasing voice to replace that of silent film star Lina Lamont (Jean Hagen) when Lina's voice was deemed an unacceptable match for her body in the film-within-a-film (figure 6.1). Unbeknownst to Reynolds in 2010, perhaps, was the aptness of her comments within the context of *RuPaul's Drag Race* (*RPDR*) and media scholarship more broadly.

Reynolds's performance as a dubbing artist in *Singin' in the Rain* has frequently been analyzed in influential scholarship on cisgender woman's voices, including Kaja Silverman's *The Acoustic Mirror*.[1] Furthermore, lip syncing is a central component of every episode of *RPDR*. As part of the reality show's sustained interest in popular culture, it makes a frequent focus of cis women's voices in screen media—from RuPaul's own verbal-vocal impersonations of actresses to challenges such as "Kardashian: The Musical," wherein contestants lip-sync to a musical parody of life under Kris Jenner's matriarchy. Most significantly, each episode ends with a "Lip Sync for Your Life" challenge between the episode's two weakest contestants. In an attempt

171

Figure 6.1. Screenshot of a scene where Kathy Selden (Debbie Reynolds) provides the voice to replace that of silent film star Lina Lamont (Jean Hagen) in *Singin' in the Rain* (1952). Produced by Metro-Goldwyn-Mayer.

to be saved by RuPaul—the mononymous head judge and communal "drag mother"—they battle it out to a predetermined song by a cis musical diva.[2]

In her judging, Reynolds praises a performance by the drag queen Raven for its precise execution. She focuses on Raven's technical skills over what I argue are the more complex elements at play in every lip-sync performance on *RPDR*: the liminal performance of gender and sexuality when a cis woman's voice is combined with the expressive body of a lip-syncing drag performer.[3] Indeed, as John Mercer, Charlie Sarson, and Jamie Hakim noted in their introduction to a special issue of *Celebrity Studies* on *RuPaul's Drag Race*, despite preconceptions around its assumed majority gay male audience, the show provides "a space to consider performances of gender and identity that are not confined to expressions of gay male sexuality."[4] *RPDR* is just one recent iteration of the long tradition of cross-gender performance, which dates back at least to the thirteenth century, and includes well-known examples, such as the young men who performed as female characters in William Shakespeare's England.[5] The substantial body of scholarship on drag queens is somewhat divided over the degree to which they subvert gender binaries as provocateurs or gender-anarchists.[6] As Steven P. Schacht and Lisa Underwood have explained, drag queens can be interpreted as "symbolic representatives of the cultural ideals associated with the feminine and women and how they have changed over time."[7]

Here I consider how *RPDR* offers a rich symbolic commentary on cis women's voices, in particular, and how the show updates the historical role of the voice in acts of drag performance by providing hypermediated lip syncs that suit twenty-first-century audiences' appetite for YouTube's style of spectacle-based "attractions." Alongside the show's deployment of an intensified style of editing, its contestants create high-impact movements, or "body talk," that allow them to express what Roland Barthes termed "vocal grain." This is achieved through the use of props and gymnastics and in ways that reflect contemporary identity politics, including an increased acceptance of gender fluidity.[8] Given my interest in the cisgender female voice, I only address performances of feminine drag, while acknowledging that there exists a much broader spectrum of drag performance.

The ways that the female voice in *RPDR* relate to Teresa Rizzo's conception of YouTube as a return to early film's "cinema of attractions" are significant.[9] More than any other element of the show, the lip-sync performances gain millions of independent views, alongside actual music videos, on YouTube. From the start, the show has encouraged live tweeting, with hashtags appearing on screen and RuPaul uttering them directly to the camera. The contestants also orient themselves toward social media (through carefully crafted posts and profiles). Moreover, the short moments of dramatic movement in lip-sync performances lend themselves particularly well to resharing via short looping GIFs. Such performances can be uncannily similar to early cinema's "Serpentine Dances," one of the definitive examples of modernist cinema as a non-narrative spectacle.[10] As signaled in the images here, of Loïe Fuller in 1902 and *RPDR* contestant Coco Montrese in 2013, the swirling fabric of a female-presenting body in motion is offered to the audience as a hypnotic vision (figure 6.2). And while both performances were initially presented in traditional media (Fuller on film strip; Montrese on television), they now coexist on YouTube and in GIF databases.

As Mark Edward and Stephen Farrier noted in *Contemporary Drag Practices and Performers*, "The power of *RuPaul's Drag Race* in any discussion of drag, though resistible, is undeniable," given its popularity and its "gravitational pull" on current discussions of contemporary drag performance, leading to what they described as a "colonization of drag through a dominant form."[11] *RuPaul's Drag Race* has been critiqued for its exclusion of drag king performers and its promotion of a polished and often commodified form of drag. One of the show's redeeming features, however, is its consistent amplification of cis women's voices across historical

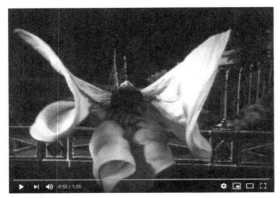

"Serpentine Dance", Loïe Fuller (1902).

Alyssa Edwards VS Coco Montrese - Cold Hearted Lipsync HD | Rupaul Season 5 Episode 9

Figure 6.2. Screenshots from YouTube showing the spectacle of swirling fabric in motion in both a Loïe Fuller serpentine dance (1902) and a *RuPaul's Drag Race* (2013) lip sync.

and contemporary Western music, film, and television. I argue here that the show's self-referential approach to women's voices in popular culture is what allows it to contribute to critical and creative discourse on the voices of women in audiovisual media. Even if *RPDR* can be generative in this regard, many in the drag community have taken issue with how the *RPDR* empire (made up of several television shows, a podcast, a web series, drag conferences, and more) has eclipsed the much longer history of drag performance as well as the contemporary drag scene on both sides of the Atlantic.[12] Before examining the specifics of lip syncing and gendered vocal dynamics on the show, it is thus necessary to revisit this rich drag history as it relates to vocal embodiment.

But first, a word on gendered pronouns. RuPaul has repeatedly stated that he has no preference with regard to masculine or feminine pronouns. Within the context of *RPDR*, the judge and cisgender male contestants generally use feminine pronouns when in drag (alluding to their female personae) and masculine pronouns when out of drag. And while a small (but growing) number of contestants identify as transgender women, since the vast majority identify as men (including those under focus in this chapter), I refer to those queens using male pronouns throughout, with the exception of contestants who have publically expressed a preference for gender-neutral or feminine pronouns.

HISTORICIZING THE VOICE IN DRAG PERFORMANCE

RPDR is not the first queer screen production to tap into the uncanny pleasure of a drag queen miming to a woman's voice. The practice extends on the tradition of theatrical drag shows and on the legacy of films such as *The Adventures of Priscilla, Queen of the Desert* (Stephan Elliott, 1994) and *Wigstock: The Movie* (Barry Shils, 1995). More directly, the show's lip-sync battles are modeled on the career of the titular judge, which included RuPaul's experimental lip-sync music video to Dionne Warwick's "Heartbreaker" for *The American Music Show* (People TV, 1981–2005) in the early 1980s.[13] In the subsequent *Wigstock*, drag queen Lypsinka restages a scene from *Mommie Dearest* (Frank Perry, 1981) at the New York drag festival of the same name. This recording, for a film documentary, is an important antecedent to the central role that lip syncing plays on *RPDR*.[14] Yet, even though Lypsinka's recording found its way to screen audiences via documentary, it was not designed for a camera to the same extent as the *RPDR* performances. What is remarkable about *RPDR*'s foregrounding of lip-sync performances is how they are being recorded and edited in new ways by the show's producers, as well as by fans of the show, who create lip-sync compilations and "best ofs" for redistribution on YouTube, in addition to short looping GIFs of notable moments from the lip-sync battles. Given the silent format of the GIF, seeing lip-sync moments remediated in this way is a reminder that the voice itself was never really attached to drag queens' bodies. Instead, the women's prerecorded voices enable the queens to demonstrate other, very visual physical skills.

In her discussion of lip sync in *Mother Camp: Female Impersonators in America*, first published in 1979, cultural anthropologist Esther Newton noted that almost all drag acts were done to some kind of musical accompaniment and featured "'feminine' vocalization, either sung or spoken." Yet she identified a clear hierarchy, wherein lip-syncing performers were "paid less [than performers who sing live] since it is disparagingly said in the profession that 'anybody can mouth a record.'" Newton similarly dismissed the lip syncer, whose performances she described as "record acts." She thus added her support to the generally derogatory view of such a performance method. She wrote, for example, "The record vocalist exercises creativity only in the choice of songs he will perform and in his visual appearance during the set."[15] And yet, as the remainder of this chapter explores, in the four decades since Newton's critique, lip syncing has been reappraised as a skill that celebrates a talented performer's ability to visualize vocal grain and to serve as an emotional conduit for a given song. My analysis of film, televisual, and online examples of lip syncing unpacks the creative and performance skills which Newton unfairly dismissed.

The treatment of cis women's voices in *RuPaul's Drag Race* intersects in remarkable ways with existing literature on queer musical voices, cis women's screen voices, and the voice from a psychoanalytic perspective. Wayne Koestenbaum, for example, explored the significance of the castrato and psychoanalysis to what he termed "the queen's throat" as part of a poetic theorization of the complex relationship between voice culture and queer culture. He surmised that "taking 'voice' to mean self-expression, contemporary gay subcultures have equated vociferousness with the refusal to remain closeted."[16] This observation, that self-expression and the open embrace of homosexuality are uniquely intertwined, certainly seems to apply to the ritualized lip-sync performances in *RPDR*—even if the voice being expressed is not the drag queen's own.

More recently, with a focus on the voice as it relates to gender rather than sexuality, Jennifer Fleeger developed the concept of the "mismatched woman," whose singing body and voice do not seem to "fit." Her analysis has points of connection with drag queens who lip-sync to cisgendered women's voices—in that there will always be a mismatch despite any illusion to the contrary, though this is something that can also be noted of most lip-syncing performances. Fleeger noted how "media producers work hard to ensure that women will sound as they look." She provided case studies of women who have deviated from this norm, such as US recording performer and radio emcee Kate Smith, as well as Susan Boyle, the Scottish singer whose performance in a reality singing show audition went viral. Relatedly, the lip-sync challenges of *RPDR* depend on them mimicking how the singer's face and body might look during a staged performance, particularly in terms of the expressiveness that accompanies the delivery of emotional songs. As such they align somewhat with Fleeger's description of Smith, who she said served as a "musical conduit," someone who could "[transmit] the affective content from composer to listener." Smith, in Fleeger's words, used her body "as an instrument that could resonate with feelings without necessarily adopting that emotion herself."[17]

In light of all this, I contend that the unrestrained body language of the drag queens on *RPDR* serves to communicate the emotions of given songs—albeit ones that they are miming to and not singing. Furthermore, I note that editors can play an important strategic role in constructing an impressive lip-sync performance. This corresponds to what Fleeger wrote about the importance of media producers in ensuring that female singers on screen would sound as they looked.[18] The selective use of slow-motion, along with cutaway shots of the judges' reactions, help to establish the value of lip syncing as measure of a drag queen's talent. This is particularly the case when the judging panel includes the singer whose voice is being heard (for example, the likes of Natalie Cole or Olivia Newton-John responding to their own voices being reanimated by cross-gender drag performers).

Fleeger's book-length study of the mismatched woman is a substantial theoretical development in the study of women's screen voices—a topic that received a burst of critical attention at the end of the twentieth century and the turn of the twenty-first.[19] As detailed earlier in this book, the topic remains relatively underexplored in relation to contemporary screen media. Fleeger emphasized the impact of recording technology, whereas earlier theories of women's screen voices—such as Silverman's *Acoustic Mirror*—instead relied on psychoanalysis. Indeed, the psychoanalytic take on the "maternal voice" will help me explore various conceptions of the drag queen as a maternal figure. Thinking about how *RuPaul's Drag Race* brings together various concepts of mothering and the voice will thus provide an entry point to the show's thematic focus on the expressive potential of combining cis women's voices with drag queens' bodies.

THE MATERNAL VOICE, FROM *MOTHER CAMP* TO "MAMA RU"

The figurative weight of RuPaul's own singing and speaking voice is often overlooked in image-focused analyses of the drag superstar and his series. For example, in Jim Daems's *The Makeup of RuPaul's Drag Race*, the first edited collection about the show, various chapters focus on visual makeovers: the show's creation of perfect womanly "images," for example, and its "visions" of feminine beauty and play.[20] Referred to affectionately as "Mama Ru" by many of the contestants, RuPaul draws ironically on the vocal inflections of the crazed mother from the film *Mommie Dearest*, as well as from the notion of the teacher as a maternal figure in *The Prime of Miss Jean Brodie* (Ronald Neame, 1969).[21] Faye Dunaway's cult classic portrayal of Joan Crawford in *Mommie Dearest* is verbally referenced in a number of episodes, including the first show in Season 6, which begins with RuPaul's homage to Dunaway's campy performance. Indeed, David J. Fine and Emily Shreve have made a compelling case for reading RuPaul's verbal and vocal channeling of Jean Brodie (Maggie Smith) as part of the show's broader pedagogic aim of narcissistically reproducing RuPaul in his drag daughters.[22]

These references may initially seem incidental, but each show's "Lip Sync for Your Life" segment reinforces the weight of the maternal voice construct as related to RuPaul. The challenge is framed by his power to dictate the queens' fate. With melodramatic *Mommie Dearest* relish, he repeats the now famous line: "Ladies, this is your last chance to impress me and save yourself from elimination. Good luck, and don't fuck it up." After each performance, and without consulting any of the other judges, RuPaul issues his verdict to the safe queen: the performer's name, followed by "Shantay, you stay" (drawing on a line from RuPaul's breakthrough 1992 song "Supermodel [You Better Work]").[23] At various points the queens are required to lip-sync to songs from RuPaul's own career. These are almost the only times when the lip-sync battle is soundtracked to the voice of someone who is not a cisgender woman. By association, however, such moments effectively equate RuPaul's androgynous voice (considered in greater detail below) with that of a cisgender woman. RuPaul's status as a communal drag mother has developed in tandem with the show's success, leading to his 2017 single "Call Me Mother."

The presentation of RuPaul's voice as that of a nurturing but unconventional mother also recalls and reworks the crucial role that psychoanalysis attributes to the mother's voice in the formation of subjectivity and identity. For psychoanalyst Guy Rosolato—whose idea of "the acoustic mirror" Silverman subsequently developed in relation to women's voices in classical Hollywood cinema—a baby's own sense of self emerges before the Lacanian mirror stage, specifically when the father's speech interrupts the voice of the mother. In this moment, the baby's identification with the mother's voice (as his or her own) is lost.[24] In a symbolic sense, RuPaul's voice on the show can be seen to provide a queer return to the idealized and symbolically loaded maternal voice. As a drag mother to the show's many contestants, it is fitting that RuPaul lends his own voice to the contestants when they lip-sync to his prerecorded songs. In this variation of the return to the acoustic mirror scene, the drag queens, RuPaul's de facto children, are encouraged to identify the mother's voice as their own (see figure 6.3). Moreover, in achieving the status of a communal celebrity drag mother, RuPaul, as a gay Black man, seems to build on the legacy of Black women as a major influence in drag culture.

In these ways, RuPaul's self-aware appropriation of the power associated with the maternal voice complicates a parallel media discourse that ties gay men to voices that are stigmatized as a result of female gender markings. The

Figure 6.3. Screenshot of the finale of Season 9 of *RuPaul's Drag Race* (Logo TV, 2017), complete with a mouth-based stage production as RuPaul determines the pairs for the lip-sync battles.

documentary *Do I Sound Gay?* (David Thorpe, 2014), an exploration of so-called gay voices, examines how gay men negotiate their identification with women through vocal inflections. At one point in the film, a speech training expert suggests that the filmmaker, David Thorpe, may have picked up certain vocal intonations as a child "by listening to more women than men." Indeed, this point relates to long-standing questions in academic studies of speech and phonetics. Some such studies have questioned whether gay men's voices tend to be more "dynamic" in intonation, and if this is why such voices can be stereotyped as being similar to, or imitative of, women's voices.[25] Within *RPDR*, to sound like a woman is a positive thing. The emulated women are not necessarily ones the performers know personally; they are women, such as Joan Crawford or Maggie Smith, whom they have chosen to mimic. But with the lip-sync performances, it is as though the image of the singing woman and surrogate mother is being erased in order to provide the drag-child with the opportunity to self-actualize.

The timing of the recurring lip-sync performances—the "Lip Sync for Your Life" segment is generally at the end of each episode—is also significant. Like the acoustic mirror scene, this is a key threshold point for the competing drag queens. Although each queen is expected to prepare for the performance in advance of every judging, the vast majority of them are never called on to perform in this segment. Lip syncing is presented as a kind of transformative cleansing for a queen who has performed poorly during the episode: if he wins the battle and is not sent home, then it provides a form of rebirth. The queen who has been given another chance often expresses gratitude for the chance to redeem themself.[26]

The high stakes involved in lip syncing necessitates further discussion of what kind of vocal embodiment constitutes a strong performance within the confines of the show's logic, and why. By removing the role of the microphone and foregrounding the role of the camera, editing, props, and gymnastics, *RPDR*'s spectacular lip-sync performances can make the voice appear more present in the body. Such representations invert Barthes's off-quoted concept of the presence of the body in the grain of the voice. For Barthes, an individual's vocal grain emerges from the audible traces of the body (including teeth, tongue, and lungs) in that person's voice.[27] In my analysis, it is partly the specifics of this vocal embodiment that create a symbiosis between the lip-syncing drag performer and the powerful cisgender female singer. This vocal re-embodiment creates a twenty-first-century style of spectacle that raises questions about essentialist approaches to the voice, gender, and the body.

VISUALIZING THE GRAIN OF THE VOICE THROUGH "BODY TALK"

Early in 2009, RuPaul premiered the single "Cover Girl," alongside a promotional video for the first season of *RPDR*. One of its directional lyrics—"Let your whole body talk"—signals how a successful drag queen must perform during the lip-sync segment of the show he would later host. "Body Talk" is also the title of one of Silverman's key chapters in *The Acoustic Mirror*—a chapter in which she discusses how *Singin' in the Rain* reveals the "very high stakes . . . involved in the alignment of the female voice with the female image."[28] Though Silverman focused on postproduction dubbing (postdubbing) rather than lip syncing, she nonetheless referred to skills that are required in both processes. These skills are grounded in precise timing, with a view to hiding the seams of a voice that is synced with a distinct body. Silverman described how postdubbing, in this and other films, "juxtaposes voices with images after the latter have been produced and (usually) edited, so bringing momentarily together in the studio the shadow play of celluloid and the actual voice of flesh-and-blood actors. The latter speak the lines assigned to them while closely observing the lip movements represented on screen."[29] With lip-sync performances, such as those on *RPDR*, this relationship and its very purpose is flipped: the voices are recorded first, the images second. Lip syncers do not closely observe singers' corresponding movements on screen; rather, they must attend to the voice in order to mimic the movements of the lips (and other body parts). When lip syncing is performed for the camera, it is not a question of these disparate factors being brought together "momentarily in the studio": instead, the "shadow play" becomes the main event, the purpose and crux of the entertainment.[30]

The most significant difference between postdubbing and *RPDR*'s "live" lip syncing is the value attributed to the secondary performer. In the world of postdubbing, the work of the postdubber (who provides the voice) tends to be undervalued relative to that of the original, and later silenced, performer. Indeed, as noted in chapter 1, it is not uncommon for dubbing artists to go entirely uncredited. In explicitly celebrating the skills of the talented lip-syncing performer, *RPDR* intensifies the associations, from the traditions of postdubbing, of the voice as less central than the image in audiovisual performances where the image of the singer is also being recorded. Furthermore, *RPDR* makes it clear that to describe this skill as one confined to the singer's *lips* would be an undervaluation. To be sure, as Freya Jarman-Ivens observed, "watching a lip-synched performance, the perception of accuracy is highly dependent on a good match between phonemes and mouth movements."[31] And yet, as Jarman-Ivens also explained, as part of her study on voice and identification, "there are numerous other subtle bodily movements that may determine the perceived accuracy of any given act of lip-synching. Such movements may include those in any direction of the head (which may coincide, in song particularly, with changes of pitch), or tensions perceptible in the neck (specifically including movements with the larynx, visible through the neck, and which may coincide not only with pitch but with volume), or movements of the chest that indicate the amount of air held within the lungs and the rate of its expulsion."[32] In other words, and much as RuPaul directs us through the lyrics of "Cover Girl," lip-sync performers may be silent, but they let the "whole body talk." Removing the voice from the equation could be seen to acknowledge the glut of singing-based talent shows (and the key role that stage presence and image end up playing in competitors' trajectories), as though the producers of *RPDR* know that if viewers wanted a singing-based reality television show, they would watch *American Idol* (Fox, 2002–2016; ABC, 2002–) or *The Voice* (NBC, 2011–) instead.

Perhaps more importantly, the value of *silently* communicating a song is that it can make visible Barthes's concept of vocal grain. For the queens of *RPDR*, a winning performance is often one that seems to visualize elements of the singer's grain—for example, when a wide-open mouth reveals a tongue visibly contorting in a way that kinesthetically fits the soundtrack. Similarly, a skilled queen can allow audiences to see the deep inhalation of breath that comes before an extended note, and the tilting back of the head as the performer reaches for the note. This process thus involves a kind of reverse engineering based on sound: the lip syncer listens for components of grain and decides how a given body part might appear when making a given sound. Such decisions may be made in advance (when rehearsing for a given song) or instinctively during a performance. This is not to say that the drag queens strive for realism, with the excessive performativity of drag also extending to an excessive embodiment of the prerecorded voice. A drag performer's overdrawn lips are often matched by moments of overenunciation. To better understand how perceptions of vocal grain can change when visualized, it is worth considering a recent trend in online videos that display people singing in magnetic resonance imaging (MRI) machines. This trend coexists with *RPDR* lip-sync clips on platforms such as YouTube, with the two spectacles sharing the novelty of making the voice's unseen properties more perceptible.

Increasingly, researchers of singing are using recordings from MRI scanners to analyze bodily differences tied to singing qualities such as volume and pitch. By making MRI recordings of singers with different voice classifications (i.e., soprano, alto, bass), such research can identify trends in terms of sound qualities and the specifics of, say, lip opening and pharynx width.[33] Though the initial motivations for such recordings were grounded in scientific research, videos of people singing in MRI machines have gained broad popularity online, leading some singers to make them for entertainment purposes. Take, for example, a video about opera singer Michael Tolle posted by the British newspaper *The Telegraph*, which is described as "incredible footage reveal[ing] the contorting vocal tract." The paper urges us to watch the video "to see someone singing like you never have before."[34] Despite different motivations behind such videos and even different formats, the interest in them relates well to lip-sync performances and to how they highlight the vocal grain of the singers whose voices the queens attempt to embody.

Both spectacles depend on the voice's enigmatic properties. We generally recognize and accept that a given voice emerges from a given body, even though the physical processes that produce the voice are largely hidden. When one watches an MRI video of someone singing, the close correspondence between the moving skeletal human image and the full sound of the voice can be hypnotizing. A lip-sync performance that pays close attention to visualizing grain can similarly hypnotize, by creating a close correspondence between the moving human and the sound of the prerecorded voice. Even if the correspondence is merely an illusion in lip sync, both types of spectacles take their audiovisual impact from the mystifying properties of the embodied voice.

Figure 6.4. Screenshot of Sasha Velour releasing a flood of petals from their wig during a song's climax in the finale of Season 9 of *RuPaul's Drag Race* (Logo TV, 2017).

Whereas the MRI videos have a natural means of visualizing the voice, the process used by *RPDR*'s queens often depends on the well-timed use of expressive props. When it comes to the release of props, or dramatic dance moves, the lip syncer is not subject to the same pressure as the singer when releasing the breath, but the importance of a controlled deployment remains. We see this in the Season 9 finale of *RPDR*, when Sasha Velour releases a flood of red petals from under their wig during the passionate climax of Whitney Houston's "So Emotional" (figure 6.4). The cascade of petals both enhances the emotions expressed by Houston's powerful melisma and draws the audience's attention to Velour and away from their competitor.

Velour's strategy of hiding props within their costume signals the importance of a balance between concealing and revealing the illusion of drag performance. Drag queens generally aim to maintain their characters, but the sheer energy expended throughout a performance often dislodges the very masking devices (such as wigs and padding) that typically uphold the drag character's image. As such, some of the most powerful lip-sync moments in *RPDR* history are those in which a queen preempts the disintegration of coherence and purposefully turns a masking device into an expressive prop. We see this in a number of the most digitally circulated performances (in the form of YouTube best-of lists and mashups). For example, during Season 2, makeup maven Raven uses an escaping breast pad to direct attention back to his face when he dabs his face with it toward the end of the performance. As though powdering away moisture from his jawline, Raven turns what could have been a performance flaw into a reminder that his drag persona is known for flawless makeup.

So pushing at the boundaries of the lip-sync illusion can be an important aspect of screened lip-sync performances that feature a "mismatch" between the gender of the two respective bodies, but it can also be an important

Figure 6.5. Screenshot of the performance by the "Crying Woman from Los Angeles" in *Mulholland Drive* (2001), in which the lip-syncing woman falls flat. Produced by Les Films Alain Sarde.

aspect of those that do *not* feature such a mismatch. This is the case with a scene in *Mulholland Drive* (David Lynch, 2001), wherein Rebekah Del Rio's character of "la Llorona de Los Ángeles" (the Crying Woman from Los Angeles) destroys the illusion of her passionate live performance when she collapses mid-song and the track keeps playing (figure 6.5).[35] In fact, Season 7 *RPDR* contestant Katya revealed that it was this scene, as well as the film's use of dubbing as "a thematic tool," that inspired him to start drag: "The woman sings 'Crying' by Roy Orbison in Spanish. And it's a recording, and she falls flat."[36]

This scene impacted Katya's early song selections, none of which were in English. Furthermore, they were by performers whose careers had spanned film and music, such as Brigitte Bardot and Alla Pugacheva. Like Debbie Reynolds's guest judging comments, which made a direct comparison between the drag queens' lip-syncing and her own film performances, Katya's description of their initiation into lip syncing provided evidence that lip syncing in *RPDR* builds as much on the historical representation of women's voices in audiovisual media as it does on the tradition of theatrical drag lip syncing. For Katya and other drag queens, the aspiration is not necessarily to lip-sync well *for a drag performer* but to lip-sync as well as formerly screened female singers—from Reynolds to Bardot to Del Rio—virtually all of whom have had to lip-sync to their own voices, or to someone else's, for the camera. The drag queen's aspiration can be toward a certain ventriloquial spectacle: a moment that will go down in screen history, whether film history, as in

Singin' in the Rain and *Mulholland Drive*, or television and viral YouTube history, as it is for *RPDR* clips.

LIP SYNC AS SCREEN SPECTACLE

Beyond a careful use of props, drag queens' navigation of the illusion of female vocal masquerade can depend on well-timed dance moves of a gymnastic nature. This is similar to what happened in *Mulholland Drive*, where the scene described above derives impact from the character's "falling flat." Indeed, literally hitting the stage can equally be important to *RPDR*'s presentation of lip sync as spectacle. Across the many seasons of *RPDR*, various forms of "splits," for example, have proven particularly popular as a way of attracting the judges' attention—especially when timed so that the execution provides a high-impact punctuation to the beat of the music. When someone performs a split, the lines extending from his or her pelvis to inner thighs and lower leg form an angle of roughly 180 degrees. The impact of very sudden "drop splits" arises in part from the dramatic line of the legs, as well as from the attention this move draws to many of the contestants' tucking of their penises, as part of their cross-gender drag aesthetic. We are frequently shown the dropped-jaw expressions of the *RPDR* judges after a performer lands in a drop split.[37] The performative significance of the moment can be further reinforced by voice-over comments by the performing queen (overlaid on the soundtrack after postrecording interviews), as well as by the mass of fan-made GIFs of splits available online.

The drag queens seem to embrace the symbolic and performative potential of tucking their penises. We see this in drag queen Katya's performance of Olivia Newton-John's "Twist of Fate" in Season 7. Speaking over his own lip-sync performance, one in which a split is accompanied by perfectly enunciated miming, the comedic drag queen explains, "I just try to pound my vagina into the stage so hard that the building shakes" (figure 6.6). Given that Katya has no actual song to force out, he forcibly expresses with his legs what the singer would express with her breath.

RPDR's mediation of Katya's "vagina-pounding" performance is significant for several reasons, including a number of stylistic choices on the part of the show's editing team. First, Katya's first drop split (a side split where the legs extend to the left and right of the torso) plays in a slightly slowed motion, a technique the producers frequently employ to add emphasis to such a move. After the moment of impact, we cut back to guest judge Newton-John, who vocalizes her shock and admiration with a drawn-out "whoahoa!" The show's postproduction team highlighted Katya's first split

Figure 6.6. Screenshots of Katya's performance of Olivia Newton-John's "Twist of Fate" in Season 7 of *RuPaul's Drag Race* (Logo TV, 2015), with post-performance attention to the discomfort caused by doing splits.

through a selective use of slow motion, but Katya intentionally delivers a second split (a front split where one leg extends in front of the torso and the other behind) very slowly, mimicking Newton-John's drawn-out vocal embellishments at this point of the song. The judges are shown laughing in response to this embodiment, wherein Katya's legs and lips match the speed and phonemes, respectively, of the song. He maintains expressive coherence until the end of the number, and once it ends (and he and Sasha Belle return to their places to hear which of them RuPaul will allow to proceed to the next stage), Katya is shown pulling comically at the crotch region under his short skirt—reminding viewers of the uncomfortable consequences of the gymnastic pounding. This bodily vulnerability becomes palpable at such moments—which are common across *RPDR*'s lip-sync segments—and reverberate further online when turned into short looping GIFs.

It is common to see guest judges—such as Newton-John, Lady Gaga, Ariana Grande, Paula Abdul, and Faith Evans—take great pleasure in the experience of having their voices re-embodied by a drag queen. For example, in Season 4, guest judge Natalie Cole engages in a call-and-response duet with drag queen Dida Ritz as he expertly performs to Cole's classic "This Could Be (an Everlasting Love)." Cole was ultimately in a duet *with herself*, but it was Dida Ritz's embodiment of her voice that led to this extraordinary event, wherein Cole used her knowledge of her own song to adlib, gospel-style, verbal and nonverbal embellishments during the breaks in the track's vocals. Dida Ritz's high-energy performance was virtually flawless in terms of his miming, wide-eyed expressions (signifying muscularly the straining for notes, for example), and rhythmic dancing (responding perfectly to the changing beats). Cole's response to the performance can be read as a validation that such perfected lip syncing, with its corresponding "body talk," takes real skill. As Cole's impassioned response to Dida-Ritz-as-Natalie-Cole suggests, when singers are repositioned as listeners they can hear their own voices anew, perhaps appreciating them in a way that is not possible when singing. Cole, of course, could easily listen to her own recordings, but *seeing* the energetic passion that Dida Ritz brought to the embodiment may have, paradoxically, provided her with the necessary distance to really hear herself. Cole's obvious pleasure is frequently seen when guest judges' songs are chosen for the lip-sync battle. Rather than regarding the contestants as appropriative, or as competition, these singers tend to experience a well-executed lip sync as a flattering spectacle—particularly when the drag queen provides the nimble physical strength to visualize the cisgender woman's vocal grain.

VOCAL IDENTITY POLITICS

This discussion of the relationship between drag contestants and cisgender women singers leads us closer to addressing one of the key questions presented by *RuPaul's Drag Race*'s engagement with cis women's voices: Does the show generally empower or disempower those cisgender women whose famous voices are "put on" by the drag queen contestants? This question is especially complex if the voice is understood to provide the kind of sonic costume implied by Koestenbaum in *The Queen's Throat*, where he asserts that "a voice is like a dress; playing a record is sonic drag."[38] Some might argue that the practice of lip syncing on *RuPaul's Drag Race* is ultimately a form of patriarchal cultural appropriation. After all, these singers' voices are being remediated by other performers, generally cis men, and in many cases without their permission. The singers could be described as unknowing ventriloquists whose voices are thrown into a dummy they did not approve. Yet to focus on the fact that the drag queens temporarily take possession of cis women's voices is to ignore the various ways in which they are also disempowered by the norms of white, gender- and hetero-normative patriarchy. As we learn from their back stories, many of the queens use (or initially used) drag as a form of therapy when they were bereaved or alienated from family members, or even when dealing with deeper bodily changes, such as

HIV seropositivity or gender transitioning. The casts are also racially diverse, with many Black and Latinx competitors, and a significant number of Asian heritage. If we take an intersectional approach to identity politics, we see there is perhaps less of a case for reading lip syncing as appropriation: for the most part, these are relatively disempowered people borrowing the voices of relatively empowered cis women.

The potential for lip syncing to open up a space for identity exploration and fluidity extends to the relative unimportance of there being a "match" between the race of the original singer and the lip-sync performer. This is made clear from even a quick review of *RPDR*'s early seasons. Sasha Velour's winning performance of Whitney Houston's "So Emotional" came in spite of, not because of, any physical similarity between the bald white drag queen and the soulful Black diva. Velour's masterful display of props allowed them to be crowned over Shea Couleé, their Black competitor. And vice versa with Season 9's runner-up, Peppermint, whose performance as Britney Spears in a musical challenge impressed the judges in part because it captured Spears's "essence" *despite* Peppermint being Black and looking nothing like her. Similarly, it was a Filipino American queen, Manila Luzon, who managed to capture the bizarre melodrama of Donna Summer's "MacArthur Park." Luzon's theatricality lent itself perfectly to the manic moments of Summer's disco arrangement of the song. In this regard, *RPDR*'s lip-syncing battles can be considered one element of what Kai Kohlsdorf has described as the show's post-race and postfeminist landscape, wherein "the queens must be able to become anyone, across racial identification, gender presentation, and style."[39]

Kohlsdorf highlights the potentially problematic nature of the show's emphasis on universal sameness as it relates to the contestants: that is, by downplaying the ongoing structural discrimination faced by people of color and women for the sake of entertainment, it potentially helps to sustain such inequalities. One only has to look to lip-sync battles on other shows, however—say, on *The Tonight Show Starring Jimmy Fallon* (NBC, 2014–)—to see more extreme and racially appropriative examples. When actor Paul Rudd lip-syncs to Tina Turner on *Jimmy Fallon*, the performance could seem to displace the Black woman's body from her hard-won place in musical culture, substituting a privileged straight white man. Rudd received extensive praise for the lip sync, which relied on Turner's distinctive performance of her 1984 song "Better Be Good to Me." A white man using lip sync to appropriate a Black woman's performance as though it were his own could be seen as downplaying the Black woman's authorial agency.[40] The lip-synced songs in *RuPaul's Drag Race* are chosen long before RuPaul determines which two drag queens—the weakest contestants in that episode—will perform to them. There is thus no opportunity to contrive a situation wherein certain contestants will be chosen, or more closely "match" the body of the singer whose voice they must embody. With the *Tonight Show* segments, on the other hand, there is a problematic tendency for white actors to lip-sync to Black singers, a trend that extends on a long history of racial mimicry in the US film and music industries.

While combining a drag queen's body with a diva's voice may result in gender frisson, in other respects they create a perfect union. Certain artists whose music is featured on *RuPaul's Drag Race*—such as Madonna, Cher, Lady Gaga, Annie Lennox, and Liza Minnelli—have been described as "masculine women," suggesting that they, too, resist normative gender roles.[41] *RPDR* has paid extensive homage to both Madonna and Lady Gaga, in the form of runway challenges ("The Night of 1000 Madonnas," in Seasons 8 and 9, and "The Night of 1000 Gagas," in Season 9). Such women are known for navigating the music industry on their own terms, rather than having their voices and images overly manipulated by record executives. Significantly, some of these "masculine" women are also considered to be dependent on, or even appropriators of, queer culture.

Communication scholar Mary Marcel, for example, noted how Madonna's "voguing" "coopted [a style] from gay and transgender people," suggesting that she mass-marketed their dance moves while they "remained culturally, economically and socially marginalized."[42] Interpreted this way, when queens "borrow" the voices of cisgender women they are merely reaping delayed benefits from a musical culture they themselves helped to shape. However, this issue does raise the question of whether there is a lack of space (both on *RPDR* and on screen more generally) for women who would like to perform lip syncs to male voices. While *The Tonight Show* fares better than most in this regard, the fact that men's voices are less frequently ventriloquized signals how aspects of the vocal playing field remain uneven. In fact, as Merrie Snell observed in her book *Lipsynching*, critical responses to singers who lip-sync to their own voices can be distinctly gendered and "patriarchal," with the most vicious attacks often aimed at performers who are young and female, or whose primary audience is seen as young and female or queer.[43]

RPDR's celebration of women who resist certain normative gender roles gains further significance when considered in light of feminist debate around the figure of the *androgyne* (a term Barthes used to describe a composite of both man and woman).[44] In her feminist critique of Barthes's *The Pleasure of the Text*, literary theorist Jane Gallop argued that a desire to escape sexual difference can be seen as "just another mode of denying women."[45] Expanding on this concept in her study of the castrato, musicologist Joke Dame made a number of comments that are worth reflecting on in relation to the drag queens of *RPDR*: "Male interest in the androgyne has been unmasked as a strategy of annexation, as a one-sided appropriation of the female by men. For only male subjects can enrich and complete themselves by adopting female properties. As soon as women show male characteristics they are, in dominant male discourse, immediately classified negatively, that is, as castrating women and phallic mothers."[46] In certain circumstances, drag queens can reasonably be described as temporarily adopting female properties to enrich themselves, if only to performative effect. However, in *RPDR*, such a relationship should not be considered a "one-sided appropriation of the female by men," but a symbiotic exchange, whereby both parties have their liminal gendered status highlighted through an association with the voice and body of someone else. In the performative space of a *RPDR* lip-sync battle, the parallels and tensions of this exchange are played out for entertainment, with the setup also calling into question essentialist approaches to voice and gendered bodies more generally, by making a consistent and celebratory feature of mismatched singing women.

Fleeger's concept of the mismatched woman depends on the relationship between her recorded voice and her recorded image. The gender fluidity of *RPDR*'s queens suggests that they can drift between these labels, particularly during lip-sync performances to cis women's voices and while performing in cross-gender drag. When embodying a diva's song, they have the power to turn her (as well as themselves) into a temporarily mismatched woman. In certain cases, however, the songs chosen for the lip-sync battles are sung by women who might already be considered as "mismatched," or at least androgynous, from the perspective of body and/or voice. One stand-out example is Jinkx Monsoon's and Detox's performances of Yma Sumac's "Malambo No. 1" in Season 5. Fleeger described Sumac, a cult Peruvian singer with a range of five and a half octaves, as a "tantalizing" mismatched woman.[47] Though Fleeger did not consider Sumac further, the *RPDR* embodiment of "Malambo No. 1" reveals certain connections between Sumac and drag queens in terms of the combination of exotic image and uncategorizable voice. Much as a gender-bending lip sync can evoke uncanny pleasure in an audience, Sumac's performances evoked what Francesco Adinolfi described as "infinite wonder" for Americans in the Cold War period.[48]

Adinolfi wrote of the various legends surrounding the career of the woman known for having "the voice of birds and earthquakes." Sumac could reproduce any number of natural sounds that are not normally expressed through the human voice. She enhanced her performances through her animalistic body language, feeding the legend that shamans "tried to coax evil spirits of the jaguar and the *chiwako*, or nightingale, from her throat."[49] Like the lip-syncing queens, Sumac built her career around a sense of incongruous sound: the throat that produces the song—or seems to produce it, in the case of the queen—is defying nature. In the Sumac lip sync, Jinkx Monsoon successfully channels their overtly theatrical persona into the schizophrenic structure of the song, as when Sumac alternates between whooping shrieks and deep *wow-oh-ow-oh-ows*.

The Yma Sumac example is one of various instances when the songs or artists selected for the "Lip Sync for Your Life" segment seem to be in a self-conscious dialogue with more essentialist views on gender, voice, and embodiment. This is also the case with Season 4's use of Aretha Franklin's "(You Make Me Feel Like) A Natural Woman." Lip-sync "best-of" lists on digital media frequently cite contestant Latrice Royale's performance of this song.[50] And the impact of the performance no doubt rested in part on some physical similarities between Royale and Franklin in terms of body size, skin tone, and hair style. Yet the performance avoided overt campiness, instead tapping into the genuine sense of female personation already present in the lyrics that Franklin made famous. Judith Butler has previously discussed the song in relation to *heterosexual* drag, explaining that the lyric implies that the singer previously did *not* feel like a natural woman:[51] "Aretha sings, you make me feel *like* a natural woman, suggesting that this is a kind of metaphorical substitution, an act of imposture, a kind of sublime and momentary participation in an ontological illusion produced by the mundane operation of heterosexual drag."[52] How fitting, then, that a cross-gender drag performer whose body naturally approximates Franklin's should embody her voice while miming these lyrics. Latrice Royale thus provides a different but related metaphorical substitution and act of imposture to that described by Butler. In this moment, on the stage of *RPDR*, he makes us believe that he feels like one natural woman in particular: Aretha Franklin. There is a certain sublimity to the moment, given that Royale's performance happened somewhat by chance: had he not been in the bottom two that week, then another queen would have embodied Franklin's voice instead. Given that none of the other contestants that season resembled Franklin—not to mention that Royale's competitor in the lip sync thought it appropriate to do gymnastics throughout the emotional ballad—we can reasonably assume the performance would not have provided as strong an illusion had it been done by someone else. Put differently, while divas' songs and voices are generally used because they provide a temporary, verbal-vocal script for idealized womanhood, in this case the script enabled an especially close match.

In the Yma Sumac and Aretha Franklin examples, it becomes apparent that lip sync on *RuPaul's Drag Race* can use discordances between voices and performers to underscore broader complexities of what makes a voice categorizable as male or female, or what makes a voice "natural." Sumac's voice could produce natural sounds associated with animal expressions rather than the human voice; Franklin was commonly referred to as the "the *Queen* of Soul," while also being famous for singing a song that implied she did not necessarily feel like "a natural woman." In these ways, drag queens' lip-sync performances can destabilize vocal ground that was already unsteady, and so productively undermine more essentialist approaches to the gendered voice. At the same time, to do so potentially disregards long-standing intersectional issues related to race and gender: Franklin's song potentially speaks to how, historically, Black women have often been excluded from conceptions of femininity.[53]

THE ILLUSION OF COHERENCE AND THE SPEAKING VOICE

The focus thus far has been on lip-synced musical performances, and yet *RPDR* also incorporates considerable commentary on gendered conceptions of the speaking voice. The vocal identity politics can be less progressive in this regard, with a certain tendency to reinforce damaging discourse on how women, and drag queens, should sound when they speak. Season 2 is notable in this respect, owing to the constant mocking leveled at Tyra Sanchez for his low and unquestionably masculine voice. Sanchez, a twenty-one-year-old Black man, was unwilling to alter his voice, and that was a point of criticism for several of the judges and fellow contestants. Most of the show's drag queens speak with at least a slightly elevated, and thus effeminate, pitch. But I would argue that the issue that some had with Sanchez's voice ultimately came down to his hyperfeminine appearance—a detail that recalls the kind of pressure historically placed on actresses to sound as they looked (as in Fleeger's concept of "matching" more broadly), particularly as silent cinema transitioned into sound. For many drag queens on the show, the image of the woman will always reveal signs of masculinity—a result either of nature, or, more often, design: almost no contestants aim to "pass" as cisgender women. Sanchez's gender performance was so verisimilar, however, that one guest judge referred to him as looking "like a china doll." No one seems to mind the relatively masculine voice of Bianca Del Rio in Season 6, perhaps because Del Rio is not aiming for verisimilitude. (Del Rio is also an insult comic and was the season's eventual winner.) Sanchez's comparatively realistic approach to cis female drag, however, led to unrelenting pressure for him to create a correspondingly feminine sound. In this respect, Sanchez suffered from the same gendered expectations as the Lina Lamont character in *Singin' in the Rain*, to whom a publicist explained, "You're a beautiful woman; audiences think you've got a voice to match."

In what can be seen as another maternal speech act by "Mama Ru," RuPaul refrained from critiquing Tyra Sanchez for his voice.[54] Deliberating over Sanchez with the panel, he comments on the entwined relationship between the drag artist's sound and image, explaining that while he himself doesn't alter his voice when dressed in drag, people often believe that he does: "People perceive [my voice] differently." It is important to note that what RuPaul refers to as his natural register is relatively high-pitched for a man—and considerably more effeminate than Tyra Sanchez's bass tones. At the same time, RuPaul's comment points to the importance of visual presentation to the perception of vocal presentation. With a relatively androgynous voice, RuPaul can vocally "pass" as a man, as a drag queen, or potentially even as a cisgender woman, depending on how he looks. For Sanchez, however, the voice is too unquestionably male to sustain the illusion that he is a cisgender woman—a mismatch that seemed to evoke disappointment in certain judges and fellow competitors. Sanchez was being criticized for an unwillingness to deliver the "full package," much as Lina Lamont and various other film and television characters have since. This trope is particularly common in US sit-coms, wherein conventionally attractive women are presented as unappealing on account of a nasal or high-pitched voice—examples include the characters of Janice in *Friends* and Karen in *Will & Grace* (NBC, 1998–2020).

At other points across *RPDR*'s history, its contestants have delivered more conventional combinations of speaking voice and body, with some challenges requiring the performers to demonstrate vocal versatility. From Season 2 onward, the show has included "Snatch Game"—a parody of the NBC game show *The Match Game* (1962–1969, 1973–1979), where each contestant had to impersonate a celebrity of his or her choice while answering fill-in-the-blank questions. In their quest to score laughs, the contestants in this segment of *RPDR* mimic their celebrity's appearance in an exaggerated way and improvise clever responses from that woman's point of view. For a truly successful impersonation, the voice must also resemble the star's. Perhaps unsurprisingly, then, some of the most stand-out "Snatch Game" performances have been those in which the chosen celebrity has a distinctive voice that the drag queen effectively conveys. For instance, contestants have successfully channeled television's Judge Judy's emphatic Brooklyn delivery, or the drawn-out vowels of "Little Edie" Beale from *Grey Gardens* (Albert and David Maysles, 1975). While each "Lip Sync for Your Life" performance gives body to a very audible female singing voice (albeit a prerecorded play-back version), each "Snatch Game" gives voice to a collection of entirely absent female celebrities as contestants alter and rerecord new androgynous versions of the celebrities' familiar vocal signatures. As such, the drag queens revise the sounds of female celebrities in a ritual that, when successful, serves as a celebration of the range of women's voices and their distinctive vocal traits. The segment's reliance on vocal impersonation can put some of the more androgynous elements of the voice on display, as when the cisgender male queens successfully emulate the pitch of various cisgender women.

Yet the show's tongue-in-cheek approach to pop culture can lead to a parodying of female voices in a way that could be seen as misogynistic. Season 9's "Kardashian: The Musical" is a case in point, one that captures the fine line between playful humor and problematic stereotyping. For this challenge, the contestants were required to lip-sync to a six-minute-long theatrical number that dramatized the rise of the Kardashian-Jenner family empire. The production, though set to music, mostly involved lip-syncing to a speech-singing-styled soundtrack. Notably, a number of the prerecorded voices sizzled with "vocal fry" in a way that could be seen as contributing to a discourse in the media that mocks the way these women speak. For example, an *Elle* article, "Kim Kardashian's Voice May Prevent Her from Getting a Job," blamed a variety of well-known women for spreading the "vocal fry" phenomenon: "Women who *don't* naturally have vocal fry are starting to imitate it willingly, thanks to celebs like Kardashian and movies like *Mean Girls*."[55] Although these traits are not specific to cis women—the linguist Mark Liberman has even used a waveform visualization to demonstrate the traits of "creak" and "fry" in Bruce Willis's voice—popular media discourse often suggests that they are.[56]

It appears, then, that even an overtly liberal show such as *RuPaul's Drag Race* finds ways to police voices that do not sound sufficiently feminine, as when the judges and fellow contestants critiqued Tyra Sanchez's voice for what they perceived as unquestionably masculine elements. In related ways, the show has also intensified existing discourse that mocks the speaking traits of some cisgender women. For example, by mimicking Faye Dunaway's melodramatic performance as Joan Crawford, RuPaul renders the materi-ality of the female voice excessive and entertaining, also contributing to the ongoing trend for cis women's vocal qualities to be critiqued in popular discourse. On the other hand, when contestants (and RuPaul himself) speak using an exaggerated form of "vocal fry," both in and out of drag, they draw attention to its use across various gender identifications. As such, they can disrupt the damaging discourse suggesting that women can fall prey to vocal trends more easily than men, who are instead suggested to have more stable "natural" voices. By producing sounds more frequently associated with the sonics of women's voices (as in the "Snatch Game" impersonations), the queens highlight overlaps between the sound properties of cis men's and cis women's voices. To imitate the voices of female celebrities, they purposely take advantage of their own voices' expressive and performative potential. Indeed, their ability to do so supports the idea that, as Elvira Mendoza and colleagues have explained, "differences in voice qualities across sexes may be due more to sociocultural than physiological factors." These sociocultural factors, as well as vocal traits that cannot be divided using a simple gender binary, are often downplayed in anatomical studies around difference (and some of which are also increasingly recognized as exclusionary to transgender individuals). Frequency-based studies of gender and pitch, for example, have shown that the average woman's pitch can be higher than the average man's by up to an octave, resulting from the greater length of male vocal folds.[57] And yet, while the natural pitch of a voice may be largely beyond an individual's control, other traits—such as breathiness—that are perceived as "feminine" can be learned and performed.[58] Indeed, a queen like Season 9's Farrah Moan reproduces the kind of iconic breathy sound that is associated with Marilyn Monroe, whose appearance Farrah Moan equally works to emulate.

LIP SYNC AS DIGITAL SPECTACLE

Writing in 1979, Esther Newton asserted that a lip-syncing drag queen "exercises creativity" only in relation to his choice of songs and his visual appearance during a set.[59] Yet, in the four decades since Newton's influential *Mother Camp* was first published, the skills involved in creatively re-embodying a voice, particularly for the camera, have come to be seen in a new light. They have come to the fore in particular in *RuPaul's Drag Race*. This show, which, for better or worse, has brought drag culture into the mainstream, appearing both on television and on the secondary screens of the internet, emphasizes the power and pleasure of visualizing the grain of women's voices in novel ways. Here, the seams between the body of the original female performer and that of the drag performer re-embodying her voice are made visible. Unlike Newton's queens, those on *RPDR* have no choice about song selection during each episode's "Lip Sync for Your Life" segment. Their choices instead relate to creative reinterpretation and performative impact: knowing when to release a prop, or when to jump into a split, so that they hit the stage on the correct musical beat. It is these dynamics that lend such performances well to the culture of online sharing on platforms such as YouTube and via the GIF and other micromedia formats. The show has updated female vocal impersonation for the digital era's return to an exhibitionist style of non-narrative-based spectacle.

As presented on the show, lip-sync battles suggest an underlying symbiosis between the drag queen and the singing diva, one that increases the value of these cisgender women's voices to the queens' self-actualization as cross-gender drag performers. The chosen songs provide the queens with a temporary verbal-vocal script for idealized versions of womanhood, while simultaneously allowing for women's voices to be remediated in ways that destabilize essentialist approaches to voice, gender, and body. And underlying the remediation of cis women's voices on *RuPaul's Drag Race* is the central figure of RuPaul himself, whose body of work demonstrates a sustained interest in women's voices, and especially in the figurative weight attached to the maternal voice.

RuPaul's position as "Mama Ru" to various drag daughters complicates the symbolic weight attached to the maternal voice in both psychoanalysis and drag culture. While the show sometimes disrupts this discourse, in other cases it reinforces long-standing prejudices—as when the contestants' speaking voices are subject to the same kinds of critiques as those of cisgender women in film and television history. RuPaul refrains from such judgments, however. When RuPaul impersonates the voices and delivery of famous cisgender female performers, he accepts the performers' inherited and performed vocal traits.

THE VOCAL LANDSCAPE FOR WOMEN WILL CONTINUE to evolve in tandem with developments in digital technologies and culture as well as in relation to broader social issues. Over time, certain speculative elements of my analysis may either be confirmed or disproved. Indeed, the evolving nature of these issues is in keeping with my theorization of the screen voice as indeterminable in chapter 1. Will the voices of women of color continue to be largely excluded as the models for screen-activated voice technologies? Will the activist use of female characters' voices continue to play a role in US presidential elections, as they did in 2016? To what degree will my somewhat dystopian predictions regarding actresses' vocal recordings being appropriated to create "deepfake" voices come true? How will the narrative of the (probable) first known recording of Frida Kahlo's voice develop—and if turns out *not* to be her voice, will the many sites that disseminated the audio recording, alongside familiar imagery of Kahlo, update these digital artifacts? One thing is clear: even as the technologized female voice moves forward—occupying or accessed through an ever-increasing number of screen types and devices—scholars aiming to better understand these manifestations must continue to look back through media history and scholarship. Although advances in software and hardware (and individuals' engagement with both) will continue to impact the representation, reception, and remediation of women's screen voices, most of these trends have analog precursors, and so an awareness and understanding of these will remain crucial.

In my native city of Dublin, the tourist board, Fáilte Ireland, launched a program of "talking statues" in 2018. Well-known writers and performers—including Academy Award nominee Ruth Negga and Screen Actors Guild nominee Maria Doyle Kennedy—were commissioned to provide voices for some of the city's best-known statues, to be accessed via QR codes on smart devices. These statues then "call you back," a setup that seems to update John Giorno's Dial-A-Poem service in the late 1960s (whereby people could access at random—via a rotary phone—recordings of famous poets, such as Allen Ginsberg and Frank O'Hara, reading selections of their poetry).[1] In Ireland, the appeal of the talking statues was likewise tied to the novelty of a "live" one-on-one encounter with a familiar prerecorded voice. The selection of statues reflected the patriarchal trappings of official historical commemoration, as male Irish writers were particularly well represented. Yet the fact that Negga and Doyle Kennedy were chosen to voice statues offered hope, not least because the inclusion of Ethiopian-born Negga meant the talking statues were not as exclusively white as their original subjects.

Of the eleven statues based on people, three of the people were women. Negga provided the voice for "Fidelity," one of four women at the base of the O'Connell Monument (with a script written by the local poet Paula Meehan). Doyle Kennedy provided the voice for Molly Malone, the fictional fishmonger made famous in the folk song of the same name, in which she is described as "crying 'Cockles and mussels, alive, alive, oh.'" This script was written by a student, Michaela McMahon, one of some 150 entrants to Fáilte Ireland's open call for this particular statue. Giving the statue a voice goes some way to redressing problems with the design of the Malone statue—which emphasizes her physicality, particularly her amble bosom, which is frequently subject to a "male gaze" and groped in tourist photos.[2]

Launching the talking statue initiative on its website, the tourist board asserted that "Molly Malone's voice" would "echo over the streets of Dublin." As at various other times in this book, an echoing female voice was thus offered up to the masses, although here in ways that downplayed the technology, and the facts, in favor of further mythologizing. Malone's voice, as performed by Doyle Kennedy, would not actually *echo over* the streets (a description that summons images of a loudspeaker system, or at least a resonant megaphone) so much as it would emanate from individual smart devices, most often, probably, via headphones or earbuds. Not minding the inaccuracy, the Lord Mayor of the city playfully commented that Dubliners and visitors alike would "once again hear her voice ring through the streets of Dublin."[3] Molly Malone was a fishmonger, and fishmongers' voices did at one time ring out in the streets. But she was fictional, and his statement rendered her as "real." Moreover, her voice would not be ringing out in the streets, but experienced by individuals via their smartphones.

Other details of the talking statues project gestured back to some of the findings in this book as well, including the fact that the recordings were produced in partnership with Audible, the leading streaming platform for audiobooks, a company owned by Amazon (which is also the proud parent of virtual assistant "Alexa"). The casting of Negga and Doyle Kennedy was likely tied to their broader acting accomplishments, particularly on screen,

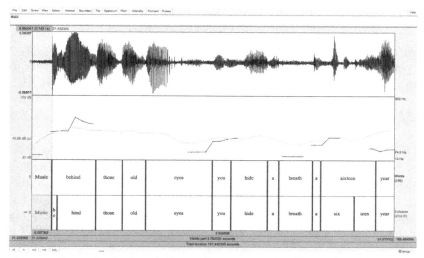

Figure 7.1. Screenshot by Georgia Brown showing a sample of her analysis of Vivien Leigh's voice in *Ship of Fools* (1965), as rendered using PRAAT speech analysis software.

including Negga's various high-profile award nominations for *Loving* (Jeff Nichols, 2016) in 2017, and Doyle Kennedy's increasingly international presence owing to her role on the Canadian series *Orphan Black* (BBC America, 2013–). These choices fit with my analysis of the expanded, transmedial spaces occupied by the voices of actresses such as Geena Davis, Sarah Jessica Parker, and Joanna Lumley (as museum guides or in virtual reality). Public familiarity with Negga and Doyle Kennedy as embodied presences has enabled their voices to travel to more disembodied formats. The choices also recall Milena Droumeva's research into women's voices in video games.[4] Negga, before the statues project was announced, had already performed for that format—in 2015, she had been nominated for a "Behind the Voice Actors Award" for her role in the 2014 game *Dark Souls II*.

As this book concludes, it feels safe to say that the trends I have examined will not remain static. And while perhaps biased, I do not see this as a limitation of the study so much as an inevitable aspect of contemporary media development in general and their relationship to digital technologies in particular. It was with delight that I recently learned of Georgia Brown's current doctoral project at Queen Mary, University of London, for example, where she is using speech analysis software to analyze Vivien Leigh's on-screen performances, identifying quantitative vocal differences across her lengthy acting career (figure 7.1).[5] This interdisciplinary study, being conducted between the department of film studies and the school of electronic engineering and computer science, is a timely reminder that we now have the tools to revisit historical screen voices with fresh eyes and ears, and with the benefit of extra expertise resulting from cross-disciplinary collaborations. Furthermore, as with Droumeva's use of spectrograms to analyze gendered vocal tropes in video games, or the 3D optical scanning system recently used to resurrect the recordings of Thomas Edison's talking twentieth-century dolls, the role of the screen and imagery as a framing device remains key.[6]

Digital technologies continue to raise the stakes of the technologized female voice in terms of privacy, data, and dependence. Since Edison's day, talking dolls, such as Genesis Toys' "My Friend Cayla," have become increasingly problematic. Between 2015 and 2017, various consumer groups filed complaints about "Cayla" with the European Commission's Directorate-General for Justice and Consumers once it became apparent that vulnerabilities in the doll's software made it possible for it to record conversations and for its voice controls to be hacked. In Germany, an official watchdog organization warned parents to destroy the dolls.[7] Such incidents can ultimately underscore broader suspicions about the latent unruliness and uncanniness of the technologized female voice. Such fears circulate frequently online, as in viral YouTube videos of "Evil Alexas": rogue speech assistants who laugh maniacally, invoking Hélène Cixous's image of the laughing Medusa in the process.[8] Yet digital artists themselves, too, are now dwelling on the optics of unruly female screen voices. Recall Björk's virtual reality music video for "Mouth Mantra," described in the Introduction to this book, and the vortex-like shots recorded inside a 3D printed replica of the singer's mouth. Here, shots of Björk with lipstick bleeding onto her teeth and skin give materiality to an unapologetically nonconforming female voice.

Female screen voices are no longer coloring within the lines—or the lips—as they instead push the boundaries between formats and media. As in the immersive "Mouth Mantra" video, digital technologies are primed to offer—and can even encourage—visual and vocal presentations of women's voices that go beyond the traditional focus on voice-over and embodiment. In doing so, they can revisit and revise earlier iconography of the speaking and singing mouth as well as the diverse media formats in which the female voice has been presented: silent film intertitles map onto GIFs and memes; radio performances map onto podcasts; voice-overs map onto virtual reality headsets.

The concrete acoustic mirrors built in the United Kingdom in the 1920s and 1930s can inform analysis of the functioning of female screen voices in the digital era. Indeed, this wartime technology—and the subsequent use of parabolic acoustic mirrors in surveillance and outdoor events—are just as revealing as psychoanalysis's subsequent deployment of the acoustic mirror as an audio adaptation of the "mirror stage" in child development, if not more so. The concrete structures worked by reflecting sound waves, with their acoustic walls channeling sounds through a complex system of microphones into a control room, where they were monitored and analyzed in tandem with data from other acoustic mirrors. Parabolic acoustic mirrors are still in use today. They frequently appear in pairs in science exhibitions and museums, where their ability to transmit a conversation—even a whisper—from one person to another across a large room or plaza is put on display. They are often termed "listening vessels" or "whisper galleries."[9] As those who read the accompanying copy on museum signage will discover, it is their shape, which reflects the sound waves to a focal point, that allows the incoming voice to be amplified and heard by the person sitting at the center of one of the parabolic dishes.

Digital technologies can function in analogous ways, allowing screen voices to be recorded and monitored as part of a complex network. Much as parabolic microphones allow sounds to be picked up from very far away and amplified, women's screen voices can travel across screen mediums and formats, though they often reverberate in distinctly different ways when heard again. This is the case with Jane Fonda's historical activist voice, which spoke to soldiers in Vietnam via radio address, and now speaks in remediated form to contemporary audiences through the *You Must Remember This* podcast series. It is the case with memes of twentieth-century female film characters, who now speak out on twenty-first-century politics in subtitled film stills or GIFs. The now shattered "acoustic mirror" of classical Hollywood and psychoanalysis cannot be pieced back together. And now, more than ever, the screen's sound mirror is grounded in a technological network that allows it to reflect ever more voices, which can travel even greater distances. These diffuse vocal shards register and resonate as both distorted and uncannily familiar. We must continue to listen to them, analyze them, and then listen again. Because, as times and technologies change, so, too, do the voices.

My sincerest thanks to Sarah McGavick and Jim Burr at the University of Texas Press for their enthusiastic support and careful development of this book project. The manuscript benefited greatly from Sarah's deep interest in, and knowledge of, gender and media, as well as from careful copyediting by Kathy Streckfus. I am equally grateful to the two peer reviewers, whose detailed, perceptive, and constructive feedback was invaluable to the process and the final shaping of the book. Thanks to both, especially for finding the time and concentration to complete this task in the middle of a pandemic.

I extend my gratitude to the Carnegie Trust, Scotland, for providing me with a Research Incentive Grant in 2018 to facilitate a visit to the Margaret Herrick Library in Los Angeles. My work on this book began in earnest during my time at the University of St Andrews, where it was also supported by a Gender, Diversity and Inclusivity funding award as well as by a Research Assistant Internship, whereby India Basagni conducted some helpful research into the dubbing of women's voices.

Earlier versions of several sections of this book have appeared in article format: an earlier version of Chapter 5 was published in *The Velvet Light Trap* 82 (Fall 2018); an earlier version of Chapter 6 was published in *Journal of Cinema and Media Studies* 61, no. 1 (Fall 2021); and sections of Chapter 4 were published in "Remixing Actresses' Voices on the *You Must Remember This* Podcast," as part of my coedited "In Focus" dossier on "Revoicing the Screen," *Journal of Cinema and Media Studies* 59, no. 4 (Summer 2020). My thanks to the respective editors and peer reviewers, whose input was also very valuable to developing my ideas.

Finally, thanks to my colleagues at both Trinity College Dublin and St Andrews, as well as to family and friends for their support throughout.

INTRODUCTION

1. For further discussion of these advertisements and their relationship to touch in the digital era, see David Parisi, "Fingerbombing, or 'Touching Is Good': The Cultural Construction of Technologized Touch," *Senses and Society* 3, no. 3 (2008): 307–328.

2. The ad can be viewed on YouTube. See "Nesplayer," "Nintendo DS Commercial Promo #1," October 25, 2007, YouTube video, www.youtube.com/watch?v=ULMjlig6Imo.

3. "Comedy Dynamics," "Mike O'Brien—Sexy Bible (feat. Scarlett Johansson, Jorma Taccone)," October 28, 2015, SoundCloud recording, https://soundcloud.com/comedydynamics/mike-obrien-sexy-bible.

4. Joceline Andersen, "Now You've Got the Shiveries: Affect, Intimacy, and the ASMR Whisper Community," *Television and New Media* 16, no. 8 (December 2015): 692.

5. See Frederick S. Lane, "Phone Sex: The First National Pornography Network," in *Obscene Profits: Entrepreneurs of Pornography in the Cyber Age* (New York: Routledge, 2001), 153–154.

6. "Hear Scarlett Johansson Read Sexy Bible Verses on New Mike O'Brien Track," *Rolling Stone*, October 28, 2015, www.rollingstone.com/music/music-news/hear-scarlett-johansson-read-sexy-bible-verses-on-new-mike-obrien-track-64070; C. Barnett, "Scarlett Johansson Reads the 'Sexy Bible' with SNL's Mike O'Brien," World Religion News, October 29, 2015, www.worldreligionnews.com/religion-news/christianity/the-bible-just-got-sexy-scarlett-johansson-reads-the-bible-with-snls-mike-obrien.

7. Lisa Guernsey, "The Desktop That Does Elvis," *New York Times*, August 9, 2001, www.nytimes.com/2001/08/09/technology/the-desktop-that-does-elvis.html.

8. Helen Harper in "MonoThyratron," "The Voder—Homer Dudley (Bell Labs) 1939," July 9, 2011, YouTube video, www.youtube.com/watch?v=5hyI_dM5cGo.

9. See Jacob Smith, "Erotic Performance on Record," in *Vocal Tracks: Performance and Sound Media* (Berkeley: University of California Press, 2008), 53–60.

10. In a related analysis of musical item numbers in Hindi cinema, Silpa Mukherjee identifies a trend for "sonic eroticism" that is conjured via a hypersexualized female scream that signposts "an invisible moment of female pleasure," with the unseen nature resulting from a continued system of censorship in the country. Crucially, the excessively erotic sounds are achieved via digitally enabled pitch correction and the infinite stretching of volume. See Silpa Mukherjee, "High-Octave Soprano to Auto-Tuned Rapper: Item Numbers and Technologies of Sonic Eroticism," *The Soundtrack* 9, nos. 1–2 (2016): 59–71.

11. Paul Flaig, "Yesterday's Hadaly: On Voicing a Feminist Media Archaeology," *Camera Obscura* 33, no. 2 (2018): 120. For further details of the process, see Vitaliy Fadeyev and Carl Haber, "Reconstruction of Mechanically Recorded Sound

by Image Processing," *Lawrence Berkeley National Library Report* 51983, March 26, 2003, www-cdf.lbl.gov/~av/JAES-paper-LBNL.pdf.

12. PBS NewsHour, "Edison's Talking Dolls: Child's Toy or Stuff of Nightmares," May 6, 2015, YouTube video, www.youtube.com/watch?v=_bgXH7U2Ja0.

13. Andersen, "Now You've Got the Shiveries," 689.

14. Susan Sontag, "The Decay of Cinema," *New York Times*, February 25, 1996.

15. Will Straw, "Proliferating Screens," *Screen* 41, no. 1 (Spring 2000): 116. Straw's reference to the dissolution of boundaries is here in reference to "the future of audiovisual media" rather than digital media per se.

16. Jen Kirby, "Why You Hear 'Laurel' or 'Yanny' in That Viral Audio Clip, Explained," Vox, May 16, 2018, www.vox.com/2018/5/16/17358774/yanny-laurel -explained.

17. Katy Steinmetz, "Meet the Voice Behind That 'Laurel' (or 'Yanny') Clip That's Driving Everyone Nuts," *Time*, May 17, 2018, https://time.com/5281287 /jay-aubrey-jones-laurel-yanny-voice.

18. See Jennifer O'Meara, "What 'The Bechdel Test' Doesn't Tell Us: Examining Women's Verbal and Vocal (Dis)empowerment in Cinema," *Feminist Media Studies* 16, no. 6 (2016): 1120–1123.

19. Laura Mulvey, "Visual Pleasure and Narrative Cinema," *Screen* 16, no. 3 (1975): 6–18.

20. Kaja Silverman, *The Acoustic Mirror: The Female Voice in Psychoanalysis and Cinema* (Bloomington: Indiana University Press, 1988); Amy Lawrence, *Echo and Narcissus: Women's Voices in Classical Hollywood Cinema* (Berkeley: University of California Press, 1991).

21. As Sjogren put it, "An orientation that presumes and insists that the woman cannot speak or be heard in the classical cinema may bar us from perceiving ways in which the feminine is represented, eventually suppressing what we seek to find." Britta H. Sjogren, *Into the Vortex: Female Voice and Paradox in Film* (Urbana: University of Illinois Press, 2006), 1.

22. Sjogren, *Into the Vortex*, 15.

23. Rick Altman, "Moving Lips: Cinema as Ventriloquism," *Yale French Studies* 60 (1980): 67–79.

24. This is the "mixing board" aesthetic that Carol Vernallis described in *Unruly Media: YouTube, Music Video, and the New Digital Cinema* (New York: Oxford University Press, 2013), 4.

25. Joanna Clay, "Actress Anna Faris Brings Her Podcast Skills to the Front of the Class," *USC News*, October 16, 2017, https://news.usc.edu/129883/actress -anna-faris-brings-her-podcast-skills-to-the-front-of-the-class.

26. I have previously discussed this as part of an *In Media Res* theme week I curated on women's politicized screen voices. Jennifer O'Meara, "Eroticizing Margot Robbie's Voice through ASMR Whispers," *In Media Res*, September 24, 2018, http://mediacommons.org/imr/content/eroticizing-margot-robbies-voice-through -asmr-whispers.

27. Aurora Mitchell, "Behind the Scenes of Björk's 360-Degree 'Mouth Mantra' Video," *Dazed Digital*, September 16, 2016, www.dazeddigital.com/music/article /32826/1/behind-the-scenes-of-bjork-s-360-degree-mouth-mantra-video.

28. Lawrence, *Echo and Narcissus*, 1, 3, 9–10.

29. Lawrence, *Echo and Narcissus*, 10. For the description of the telephone operators' voices, see C. E. McCluer, "Telephone Operators and Operating Room Management," *American Telephone Journal* 6, no. 2 (July 12, 1902), quoted by Lawrence and formerly in Lana F. Rakow, "Women and the Telephone: The Gendering of a Communications Technology," in *Technology and Women's Voices: Keeping in Touch*, ed. Cheris Kramarae (London: Routledge, 1988), 214–215.

30. See, for example, Pablo Barberá, John T. Jost, Jonathan Nagler, Joshua Tucker, and Richard Bonneau, "Tweeting from Left to Right: Is Online Political Communication More Than an Echo Chamber?," *Psychological Science* 26, no. 10 (October 2015): 1531–1542.

31. Silverman, *Acoustic Mirror*, 80. See also Jacques Lacan, "The Mirror Stage as Formative of the Function of the I as Revealed in Psychoanalytic Experience," in *Écrits: A Selection*, trans. Alan Sheridan (London: Tavistock, 1977), 1–7; Guy Rosolato, "La voix: Entre corps et langage," *Revue française de psychanalyse* 37, no. 1 (1974): 81.

32. Alan Wright and Peter Kendall, "The Listening Mirrors," *Journal of Architectural Conservation* 14, no. 1 (2008): 36. For a detailed account of these acoustic mirrors, see Richard N. Scarth, *Echoes from the Sky: A Story of Acoustic Defence* (Kent, UK: Hythe Civic Society, 1999).

33. Steven Connor, *Dumbstruck: A Cultural History of Ventriloquism* (Oxford: Oxford University Press, 2000), 40.

34. As Martin Shingler explained, "In the absence of a subtle and sophisticated vocabulary to describe non-musical sounds and the speaking voice, the attraction of musical terms and concepts remains irresistible." Shingler, "Fasten Your Seatbelts and Prick Up Your Ears: The Dramatic Human Voice in Film," *Scope* 5 (2016): 7.

35. See Milena Droumeva, "Voice and Gender in Video Games: What Can We Do with Spectrograms," Field Guide: A Media Commons Project, March 9, 2018, http://mediacommons.org/fieldguide/question/how-do-digital-media-and -technologies-allow-closer-critique-and-analysis-sound-what-relat-0.

36. Droumeva's use of spectrograms furthers insights provided in Norie Neumark, Ross Gibson, and Theo van Leeuwen's timely collection *VØ1CE: Vocal Aesthetics in Digital Arts and Media* (Cambridge, MA: MIT Press, 2010). Their volume begins to map out the transformative properties of digital media for voice culture, albeit without a focus on gender, and it, too, informs my approach in several of the chapters to follow.

37. In this regard, my study aligns with Jacqueline Warwick and Allison Adrian's collection *Voicing Girlhood in Popular Music: Performance, Authority, Authenticity* (New York: Routledge, 2016), which goes beyond audio recordings and stage performances to examine girls' musical voices across a range of media spaces, including YouTube, music videos, and transmedia franchises.

38. Mary R. Desjardins, *Recycled Stars: Female Film Stardom in the Age of Television and Video* (Durham, NC: Duke University Press, 2015).

39. *W* magazine's series of ASMR videos included thirty-four other women and just five men. See *W* magazine, *Celebrity ASMR*, Seasons 1 and 2, https://video .wmagazine.com/series/asmr.

40. Dwyer gets beneath the surface of Paramount's smear campaign against Brooks—after she refused to lend her voice to the sound version of *The Canary Murder Case* (1929)—by exploring the reception of her muteness both at the time

of these films and much more recently, including but not privileging Brooks's own account of the dubbing in her memoir *Lulu in Hollywood*, published some fifty years later. See Tessa Dwyer, "Mute, Dumb, Dubbed: Lulu's Silent Talkies," in *Politics, Policy and Power in Translation History*, ed. Lieven D'hulst, Carol O'Sullivan, and Michael Schreiber (Berlin: Frank and Timme, 2016), 157–186; Mulvey, "Visual Pleasure and Narrative Cinema."

41. Pooja Rangan, "In Defense of Voicelessness: The Matter of the Voice and the Films of Leslie Thornton," *Feminist Media Histories* 1, no. 3 (Summer 2015): 96, 95–97, 103.

42. Najmeh Moradiyan-Rizi also provides a productive revisiting of earlier theories of the (dis)embodied female voice in relation to *Shirin* (Abbas Kiarostami, 2008). See Moradiyan-Rizi "The Acoustic Screen: The Dynamics of the Female Look and Voice in Abbas Kiarostami's *Shirin*," *Synoptique* 5, no. 1 (Summer/Fall 2016): 44–56.

43. See, for example, Wendy Haslem, *From Méliès to New Media: Spectral Projections* (Bristol: Intellect, 2019).

44. Wayne Koestenbaum, *The Queen's Throat: Opera, Homosexuality, and the Mystery of Desire* (New York: Poseidon Press, 1993); Jennifer Fleeger, *Mismatched Women: The Siren's Song through the Machine* (New York: Oxford University Press, 2014).

45. There has been substantial research into voice and transgender people, including how the development of gendered vocal traits can impact quality of life. Although the description of "women's voices" is inclusive of such voices, this book is ultimately focused on cisgender women's voices, as almost none of the screen media case studies relate to transgender women, although *RuPaul's Drag Race*, discussed in Chapter 6, has included a small number of trans contestants. For further information on this topic, see, for example, Emma McNeill, "Management of the Transgender Voice," *Journal of Laryngology and Otology* 120, no. 7 (July 2006): 521–523; Adrienne B. Hancock, Julianne Krissinger, and Kelly Owen, "Voice Perceptions and Quality of Life of Transgender People," *Journal of Voice* 25, no. 5 (2011): 553–558.

46. See Helen M. Hanson and Erika S. Chuang, "Glottal Characteristics of Male Speakers: Acoustic Correlates and Comparison with Female Data," *Journal of the Acoustical Society of America* 106, no. 2 (1999): 1064.

47. Elvira Mendoza, Nieves Valencia, Juana Muñoz, and Humberto Trujillo, "Differences in Voice Quality between Men and Women: Use of the Long-Term Average Spectrum (LTAS)," *Journal of Voice* 10, no. 1 (1996): 59–60.

CHAPTER 1. FILM VOICES + TIME

1. Thorsten Fleisch, *Wound Footage*, May 20, 2009, Vimeo video, https://vimeo.com/4741823. As well as streaming online, the glitch work has been displayed at some forty festivals worldwide.

2. Jihoon Kim, *Between Film, Video, and the Digital: Hybrid Moving Images in the Post-Media Age* (New York: Bloomsbury, 2018), 101.

3. Josh Morrall, "Wound Footage Film Review," *Eye for Film*, June 8, 2019, www.eyeforfilm.co.uk/review/wound-footage-film-review-by-josh-morrall.

4. For confirmation of this dubbing see, for example, Gene Blottner, *Columbia Noir: A Complete Filmography, 1940–1962* (Jefferson, NC: McFarland, 2015), 89.

I specify that this is *most likely* Ellis's voice because she dubbed all but one of Hayworth's songs in the film, the first jazz version of this song—which is partly speech-sung. The version Fleisch used sounds like the version with Ellis's voice, but, due to his distortion, it is difficult to be absolutely certain. See Adrienne L. McLean, *Being Rita Hayworth: Labor, Identity, and Hollywood Stardom* (New Brunswick, NJ: Rutgers University Press, 2004), 237n22.

5. Morrall, "Wound Footage."

6. McLean, *Being Rita Hayworth*, 234n83.

7. "Golden Hollywood Fan," "Rita Hayworth (Voice of Anita Ellis)—Put the Blame on Mame (Gilda, 1946)," August 26, 2018, YouTube video, www.youtube .com/watch?v=-EaQtT4eLNw.

8. Barbara Klinger, "Film History Terminable and Interminable: Recovering the Past in Reception Studies," *Screen* 38, no. 2 (Summer 1997): 107–128, 108, 109.

9. See, for example, Richard Maltby, "New Cinema Histories," in *Explorations in New Cinema History: Approaches and Case Studies*, ed. Richard Maltby, Daniel Biltereyst, and Philippe Meers (Chichester, UK: Wiley-Blackwell, 2011), 8.

10. Klinger, "Film History," 126. Klinger is citing the pioneering work of Henry Jenkins. See Jenkins, *Textual Poachers: Television Fans and Participatory Culture* (New York: Routledge, 1992).

11. Klinger, "Film History," 128; Sigmund Freud, "Analysis Terminable and Interminable," *International Journal of Psycho-Analysis* 18 (1937): 373–405.

12. Klinger, "Film History," 128.

13. Tony Bennett, "Text and Social Process: The Case of James Bond," *Screen Education* 41 (1982): 3. Bennett is drawing here on ideas by Pierre Macherey, *A Theory of Literary Production* (London: Routledge and Kegan Paul, 1978).

14. While analysis of fan-site comments is increasingly common in fan studies, and media studies more broadly, scholars such as Siddhartha Menon have conceived of this in relation to the voice in particular. See Menon, "A Participation Observation Analysis of the *Once and Again* Internet Message Bulletin Boards," *Television and New Media* 8, no. 4 (2007): 341–374.

15. For an insightful account of vocal fry as it relates to the historical lineage of feminized "noise," see Marie Thompson, "Creaking, Growling: Feminine Noisiness and Vocal Fry in the Music of Joan La Barbara and Runhild Gammelsæter," *N. Paradoxa* 37 (2016): 5–11.

16. Klinger, "Film History," 128.

17. Marcus's poem, dated April 3, 1939, which cannot be reproduced due to copyright, is located in the Margaret Herrick Library, Academy of Motion Picture Arts and Sciences, Los Angeles, in "Katharine Hepburn Papers," folder 629.

18. Katharine Hepburn, "Voice," in *Me: Stories of My Life* (New York: Ballantine Books, 1991), 359–371.

19. Michael Ausiello, "It's Here: Lauren Graham's Final Gilmore Girls Interview," *TV Guide*, May 7, 2007, www.tvguide.com/news/lauren-grahams-final -8429. Attesting to Graham's famously fast speech in the series, her 2016 book is titled *Talking as Fast as I Can: From Gilmore Girls to Gilmore Girls* (London: Virago Press, 2016).

20. "PIPPA," "Watch a film before you start," September 21, 2012, Amazon review, www.amazon.co.uk/gp/customer-reviews/R35NRRBN8621QF/ref=cm_cr _arp_d_rvw_ttl?ie=UTF8&ASIN=0345410092.

21. For example, see David Scott Diffrient and David Lavery, eds., *Screwball*

Television: Critical Perspectives on Gilmore Girls (Syracuse, NY: Syracuse University Press, 2010).

22. "PIPPA," "Watch a film before you start."

23. Ralph Marcus, "In Praise of Katharine Hepburn's Voice," fan mail poem dated October 28, 1950. According to the New York Public Library's archival entry for this record, part of the Katharine Hepburn Papers, Hepburn replied by letter on December 29, 1950. See Camille Croce Dee, "Guide to the Katharine Hepburn Papers, ca. 1854–1997 and Undated (Bulk Dates 1928–1994)," New York Public Library, December 2007, 30, www.nypl.org/sites/default/files /archivalcollections/pdf/thehepbu.pdf.

24. Dee, "Guide to the Katharine Hepburn Papers," 30.

25. Hepburn, *Me*, 359.

26. Henry Jenkins, *Convergence Culture: Where Old and New Media Collide* (New York: NYU Press, 2006), 4; Pierre Lévy, *Collective Intelligence: Mankind's Emerging World in Cyberspace* (New York: Plenum Trade, 1997).

27. Nikki van der Zyl, *For Your Ears Only: The Voice of the Stars* (Holland-on-Sea, UK: Apex Publishing, 2011).

28. "Zerominus," "Why Were They Dubbed?," Commander Bond, July 20, 2009, http://debrief.commanderbond.net/topic/55347-why-were-they-dubbed.

29. "Tybre," "Why Were They Dubbed?" Commander Bond, July 20, 2009, http://debrief.commanderbond.net/topic/55347-why-were-they-dubbed/page -1.html#entry1040399.

30. "Tybre," "Why Were They Dubbed?"

31. "barryt007," "Nikki van der Zyl—Voice Dubber Extraordinaire," MI6 Community, March 14, 2011, www.mi6community.com/discussion/105/nikki-van -der-zyl-voice-dubber-extraordinaire.

32. "Desi," "Voice Dubber Extraordinaire," MI6 Community, April 30, 2012; "TheWizardofIce," "Voice Dubber Extraordinaire," MI6 Community, December 13, 2012, www.mi6community.com/discussion/105/nikki-van-der-zyl-voice-dubber -extraordinaire.

33. "JBFan626," "Voice Dubber Extraordinaire," MI6 Community, December 13, 2012, www.mi6community.com/discussion/105/nikki-van-der-zyl-voice-dubber -extraordinaire.

34. See "Nikki van der Zyl," British Film Institute, no date, www.bfi.org.uk /films-tv-people/4ce2bd1b22d3e (accessed July 8, 2019). For a full list of her claimed Bond voice roles, see Nikki van der Zyl, "Official Website of Nikki van der Zyl," archived at Internet Archive, Wayback Machine, https://web.archive.org/web /20200131235735/http://nikkivanderzyl.co.uk.

35. Chris Fellner, *The Encyclopedia of Hammer Films* (London: Rowman and Littlefield, 2018), 481.

36. Van der Zyl, "Official Website of Nikki van der Zyl."

37. Stephen Wright and Claire Ellicott, "The Secret Bond Girl: Unknown Artist Dubbed the Voices of 007's Best-Known Beauties—but Now She's Banned from the Movies <*sic*> Spy's 50th Birthday Party!," *Daily Mail*, September 21, 2012, www .dailymail.co.uk/femail/article-2206882/Bonds-secret-girl-Unknown-artist-dubbed -voices-007s-best-known-beauties–know-shes-banned-movies-spys-50th-birthday -party.html; Reed Tucker, "Bond's Secret Weapon," *New York Post*, October 4, 2012, https://nypost.com/2012/10/04/bonds-secret-weapon.

38. "thelivingroyale," "The Mystery of Shirley Eaton's Voice Being Dubbed in Goldfinger," MI6 Community, February 27, 2013, www.mi6community.com /discussion/comment/223173/#Comment_223173.

39. For example, see p. 4 of the "Voice Dubber Extraordinaire," MI6 Community, March 2013, www.mi6community.com/discussion/105/nikki-van-der-zyl -voice-dubber-extraordinaire/p4.

40. "Roots66," "Ursula Andress on 'What's My Line?,'" December 1, 2009, YouTube video, www.youtube.com/watch?v=0Rof1W3HcUs.

41. Howard Maxford, *Hammer Complete: The Films, the Personnel, the Company* (Jefferson, NC: McFarland, 2018), 15.

42. See comments by "David Williamson" and "hyun ahn," on "Roots66," "Ursula Andress on 'What's My Line?'"

43. "haranoe synechism," on "Roots66," "Ursula Andress on 'What's My Line?'"

44. Marni Nixon is perhaps the most famous female dubbing artist in cinema, but her voice work was generally confined to singing parts.

45. Ronald Bergan, "Mercedes McCambridge: Big-Screen Actor Whose Tough Personality—and Voice—Matched Her Roles," *Guardian*, March 19, 2004, www .theguardian.com/news/2004/mar/19/guardianobituaries.film.

46. Ron Lackmann, *Mercedes McCambridge: A Biography and Filmography* (Jefferson, NC: McFarland, 2005), 115.

47. Jay Beck, "William Friedkin's *The Exorcist* and the Proprietary Nature of Sound," *Cinephile* 6, no. 1 (Spring 2010): 8–9, www.cinephile.ca/files/vol6no1 -complete-withbleed.pdf.

48. Lackmann, *Mercedes McCambridge*, 116.

49. "Obituaries: Spirited McCambridge Had Big Voice," *Variety*, March 22–28, 2004, 59.

50. "McCambridge, 85, Had Wickedly Good Voice," *USA Today*, March 18, 2004.

51. Bergan, "Mercedes McCambridge."

52. Beck, "William Friedkin's *The Exorcist*," 8–9.

53. "Xspawn13," "The Exorcist—Mercedes McCambridge Raw Audio Tracks," December 14, 2018, YouTube video, www.youtube.com/watch?v= QUmyeNcld5M.

54. "Xspawn13," "The Exorcist."

55. "DarkLight90," "The Exorcist: Scenes with Linda Blair and Mercedes Mc-Cambridge's Voice as the Demon," April 16, 2010, YouTube video, www.youtube .com/watch?v=VtApL7Ddvgo.

56. Tessa Dwyer, "Mute, Dumb, Dubbed: Lulu's Silent Talkies," in *Politics, Policy and Power in Translation History*, ed. Lieven D'hulst, Carol O'Sullivan, and Michael Schreiber (Berlin: Frank and Timme, 2016), 170–172.

57. Laura Mulvey, "Visual Pleasure and Narrative Cinema," *Screen* 16, no. 3 (1975): 6–18.

58. Dwyer, "Mute, Dumb, Dubbed," 175, 161; Louise Brooks, *Lulu in Hollywood* (New York: Knopf, 1982).

59. In relation to film dubbing, the focus has tended to be on interlingual rather than intralingual dubbing. See, for example, Hans Vöge, "The Translation of Films: Sub-Titling versus Dubbing," *Babel* 23, no. 3 (1977): 120–125; Antje Ascheid,

"Speaking Tongues: Voice Dubbing in the Cinema as Cultural Ventriloquism," *Velvet Light Trap* 40 (Fall 1997): 31–41; Colleen Montgomery, "Double Doublage: Vocal Performance in the French-Dubbed Versions of Pixar's Toy Story and Cars," in *Locating the Voice in Film: Critical Approaches and Global Practices*, ed. Tom Whittaker and Sarah Wright (Oxford: Oxford University Press, 2017), 83–100.

60. "filmclips," "Louise Brooks in a Talkie," November 20, 2008, YouTube video, www.youtube.com/watch?v=C6oTprKNeVU. As of July 5, 2021, this video had roughly 94,000 views and 190 comments.

61. Dwyer, "Mute, Dumb, Dubbed," 171.

62. In this regard, van der Zyl may have been influenced by dubbing singer Marni Nixon's autobiography. See Nixon, *I Could Have Sung All Night: My Story* (New York: Billboard Books, 2006).

63. Andrew Roberts, "Nikki van der Zyl: The Bond Girl You've Never Seen Who Voiced Some of the Films' Best Known Heroines," *Independent*, October 11, 2015, www.independent.co.uk/arts-entertainment/music/features/nikki-van-der-zyl-the-bond-girl-youve-never-seen-who-voiced-some-of-the-films-best-known-heroines-a6689701.html.

64. Kaja Silverman, *The Acoustic Mirror: The Female Voice in Psychoanalysis and Cinema* (Bloomington: Indiana University Press, 1988); Amy Lawrence, *Echo and Narcissus: Women's Voices in Classical Hollywood Cinema* (Berkeley: University of California Press, 1991).

65. Mulvey, "Visual Pleasure."

66. Saige Walton and Nadine Boljkovac, "Introduction: Materialising Absence," *Screening the Past* 43 (April 2018), www.screeningthepast.com/2018/02/introduction-materialising-absence.

67. Norman Wanstall, "Foreword by Norman Wanstall, Supervising Sound Editor," reproduced from van der Zyl, *For Your Ears Only*, 2011, Van der Zyl, "Official Website of Nikki van der Zyl."

68. These statistics are based on global internet traffic and engagement over the past ninety days as of July 9, 2019. See "IMDb.com," Alexa, www.alexa.com/siteinfo/imdb.com (accessed July 9, 2019).

69. "Nikki van der Zyl," IMDb, www.imdb.com/name/nm0886424/?ref_=nv_sr_1?ref_=nv_sr_1 (accessed July 8, 2019).

70. Despite the name, the podcast also includes video footage. "James Bond Radio," "Bond Behind the Scenes: Nikki van der Zyl Interview. James Bond Radio Podcast #047," July 31, 2015, YouTube video, www.youtube.com/watch?v=IfpTeEgHkg4.

71. "Film Clip—Nikki van der Zyl from A Bond for Life: How James Bond Changed My Life," August 31, 2016, IMDb, www.imdb.com/videoplayer/vi3484988953.

72. "Golden Hollywood Fan," "Adele Jergens (Voice of Virginia Rees)—I'm So Crazy for You," April 24, 2019, YouTube video, www.youtube.com/watch?v=rFKWMhQRWjM; "Golden Hollywood Fan," "Donald O'Connor and Vera-Ellen (Voice of Carole Richards)—It's a Lovely Day Today," May 10, 2019, YouTube video, www.youtube.com/watch?v=kGfzBL9Zn_Q.

73. Laura Wagner, "Adele Jergens: A Lot of Woman," in *Killer Tomatoes: Fifteen Tough Film Dames*, ed. Ray Hagen and Laura Wagner (Jefferson NC: McFarland: 2004), 92, 95.

74. For example, in McLean's *Being Rita Hayworth*, details of Hayworth's dubbing by Anita Ellis is included in a footnote. See McLean, *Being Rita Hayworth*, 234n83.

75. "My Interview with Ray Hagen about Ann Sheridan," Remembering Ann Sheridan, January 26, 2011, www.ann-sheridan.com/Ann_Sheridan_Interviews /Ray_Hagen_Interview.html.

76. Approximately one hundred hours of Greta Garbo's private telephone calls with art curator Sam Green were similarly recorded (by Green and apparently with Garbo's permission). After Green's death, the tapes were donated to the film archives at Wesleyan University. The tapes have also been transcribed and incorporated into writing on Garbo. See Guy Trebay, "A Collector of People along with Art," *New York Times*, April 6, 2011, www.nytimes.com/2011/04/07/fashion /07GREEN.html.

77. "jmster 46," "Ann Sheridan and Ronald Reagan," June 16, 2017, YouTube video, www.youtube.com/watch?v=Dh0aWkXSyMc.

78. "The Noir Escapade," "Nora Prentiss—1947 with Ann Sheridan," July 4, 2019, YouTube video, www.youtube.com/watch?v=Di8C_8goUoM.

79. "About," Remembering Ann Sheridan, no date, www.ann-sheridan.com /about/index.html (accessed July 8, 2019).

80. "Ray Hagen Ann Sheridan Interview," Remembering Ann Sheridan, no date, www.ann-sheridan.com/Ann_Sheridan_Interviews/Listen_to_Ann_Sheridan _Ray_Hagen_Interview.html (accessed July 8, 2019).

81. Frida Kahlo, "Portrait of Diego," essay published in the exhibition catalog for *Diego Rivera, 50 Years of Artistic Work*, Palace of Fine Arts, Mexico City, 1949.

82. Audie Cornish and Mary Louise Kelly, "Archivists Say Voice Discovered in Mexico's National Library May Be Frida Kahlo," NPR, podcast transcript from *All Things Considered*, June 14, 2019, www.npr.org/2019/06/14/732863516 /archivists-say-voice-discovered-in-mexicos-national-library-may-be-frida-kahlo-s.

83. Guardian News, "Is This the Voice of Frida Kahlo?—Audio," June 13, 2019, YouTube video, www.youtube.com/watch?v=HjTA2Dd8U9o.

84. IMER-NOTICIAS (Instituto Mexicano de la Radio), "Frida Kahlo voz," June 12, 2019, SoundCloud recording, https://soundcloud.com/antena-radio-imer /frida_kahlo_voz.

85. Alex Marshall and Mark A. Walsh, "You Know Frida Kahlo's Face. Now You Can (Probably) Hear Her Voice," *New York Times*, June 13, 2019, www .nytimes.com/2019/06/13/arts/design/frida-kahlo-voice.html.

86. Daniel Vázquez, comment on "Frida Kahlo voz," June 20, 2019, Sound-Cloud recording, https://soundcloud.com/antena-radio-imer/frida_kahlo_voz.

87. Marshall and Walsh, "You Know Frida Kahlo's Face."

88. Thomas Elsaesser, "Trapped in Amber: The New Materialities of Memory," *Framework: The Journal of Cinema and Media* 60, no. 1 (Spring 2019): 26–28. See also Pierre Nora, *Les Lieux de Mémoire* (Paris: Gallimard, 1984).

89. Elsaesser, "Trapped in Amber," 28.

90. Klinger, "Film History," 107; Tony Bennett, "Text and Social Process," 3.

91. Elsaesser, "Trapped in Amber," 29 (emphasis in original).

92. Elsaesser, 33 (emphasis in original).

93. McLean, *Being Rita Hayworth*, 234n83.

CHAPTER 2. THE (POST)HUMAN VOICE AND FEMINIZED MACHINES
IN *ANOMALISA, THE CONGRESS,* AND *HER*

1. "The Making of The Congress Using Toon Boom Harmony," Toon Boom, no date, www.toonboom.com/community/success-stories/ari-folman-yoni -goodman (accessed September 30, 2019).

2. For a thorough examination of theories of posthumanism, see Cary Wolfe, *What Is Posthumanism?* (Minneapolis: University of Minnesota Press, 2010). See also Joel Garreau, *Radical Evolution: The Promise and Peril of Enhancing Our Minds, Our Bodies—and What It Means to Be Human* (New York: Doubleday, 2005), 231–232.

3. Brandon Griggs, "Why Computer Voices Are Mostly Female," CNN, October 21, 2011, https://edition.cnn.com/2011/10/21/tech/innovation/female-computer -voices/index.html.

4. Debra Kelly, "This Is Why Voice Assistants Are All Female," Grunge, no date, www.grunge.com/136184/this-is-why-voice-assistants-are-all-female (accessed December 1, 2019).

5. See, for example, Joan K. Peters, "The 'Robettes' Are Coming: Siri, Alexa, and My GPS Lady," *Hyperrhiz: New Media Cultures*, no. 15 (2016), http:// hyperrhiz.io/hyperrhiz15/reviews/peters-the-robettes-are-coming.htm.

6. Andrea Virginás, "Gendered Transmediation of the Digital from S1m0ne to Ex Machina: 'Visual Pleasure' Reloaded?," *European Journal of English Studies* 21, no. 3 (2017): 288, 289.

7. Jennifer Fleeger, "When Robots Speak on Screen: Imagining the Cinemechanical Ideal," in *The Oxford Handbook of Voice Studies*, ed. Nina Eidsheim and Katherine Meizel (Oxford: Oxford University Press, 2019), 426.

8. Stanisław Lem, *The Futurological Congress* (New York: Seabury Press, 1974), first published in Polish as *Ze wspomnien Ijona Tichego Kongres Futurologiczny* (1971).

9. Maurice Ratcliff, *Leonard Cohen: The Music and the Mystique* (London: Omnibus Press, 2012), 44.

10. For a technical account of the 3D printing of the film, see Michael A. Parker, "Anomalisa: 3D Printed People with Real Human Issues," 3Dprint, January 14, 2016, https://3dprint.com/115151/anomalisa-3d-printed-people.

11. Joceline Andersen, "Now You've Got the Shiveries: Affect, Intimacy, and the ASMR Whisper Community," *Television and New Media* 16, no. 8 (December 2015): 692–694.

12. Laura Mulvey, "Visual Pleasure and Narrative Cinema," *Screen* 16, no. 3 (1975): 6–18.

13. David L. Smith, "Six Ways of Looking at Anomalisa," *Journal of Religion and Film* 20, no. 3 (2016), https://digitalcommons.unomaha.edu/jrf/vol20/iss3/12.

14. Nick Chen, "Your Guide to Movies That Also Work as ASMR," *Dazed Digital*, June 25, 2019, www.dazeddigital.com/film-tv/article/45016/1/your-guide -to-the-best-asmr-in-films. See also "Soft Xquare [ASMR]," "Anomalisa—Mirror [ASMR] [LOOP]," July 10, 2018, YouTube video, www.youtube.com/watch?v= gtkH4zDC-8E.

15. Andersen, "Now You've Got the Shiveries," 690.

16. See Nick Chen, "Peter Strickland Discusses In Fabric, His New Film about

a Killer Red Dress," *Dazed Digital*, June 24, 2019, www.dazeddigital.com/film-tv
/article/44975/1/peter-strickland-in-fabric-interview-bjork-fashion-asmr.

17. See, for example, Smith, "Six Ways of Looking."

18. See Donal Henahan, "Opera: Computer Love," *New York Times*, April 9,
1975, www.nytimes.com/1975/04/09/archives/opera-computer-love.html.

19. Joseph Olive is quoted in Horatia Harrod, "How Do You Teach a Computer to Speak Like Scarlett Johansson?," *Telegraph*, February 15, 2014, www
.telegraph.co.uk/culture/film/10624631/How-do-you-teach-a-computer-to-speak
-like-Scarlett-Johansson.html.

20. Laura Tunbridge, "Scarlett Johansson's Body and the Materialization of
Voice," *Twentieth-Century Music* 13, no. 1 (2016): 142.

21. Beyond Samantha Morton's unused voice work, *Her* also has a potentially
appropriative relationship to the work of artist and filmmaker Lynn Hershman
Leeson. Hershman Leeson had shared her interactive digital companion "Agent
Ruby" with Jonze back in 1999, with a view to a potential collaboration. See
"R.U. Sirius," "Long before the Spike Jonze Film *Her* There Was *Teknolust*,"
Kurzweilai, March 6, 2014, www.kurzweilai.net/long-before-the-spike-jonze-film
-her-there-was-teknolust. While Jonze didn't end up committing to a project with
Hershman Leeson, who would tackle these issues in her low-budget film *Teknolust*
(2002), the similarities between Hershman Leeson's body of work—which includes
the "Dollie Clones," Tillie and CyberRoberta (1995–1998)—is cause for concern.

22. Fleeger, "When Robots Speak on Screen," 426.

23. Kaja Silverman, *The Acoustic Mirror: The Female Voice in Psychoanalysis
and Cinema* (Bloomington: Indiana University Press, 1988).

24. Tunbridge, "Scarlett Johansson's Body," 145–147, 150.

25. Karthika Vijayan, Haizhou Li, and Tomoki Toda, "Speech-to-Singing Voice
Conversion: The Challenges and Strategies for Improving Vocal Conversion Processes," *IEEE Signal Processing Magazine* 36 (January 2019): 96.

26. Vijayan et al., "Speech-to-Singing Voice Conversion," 96.

27. Nina Power, "Soft Coercion: The City and the Recorded Female Voice,"
Nina Power website, December 7, 2017, https://ninapower.net/2017/12/07/soft
-coercion-the-city-and-the-recorded-female-voice. A version of Power's essay was
published in Matthew Gandy and B. J. Nilsen, eds., *The Acoustic City* (Berlin:
JOVIS Publishers, 2014).

28. Virginás, "Gendered Transmediation," 293.

29. Harrod, "How Do You Teach a Computer to Speak Like Scarlett Johansson?"

30. Zack Sharf, "Deepfake Porn Videos Are Using Scarlett Johansson's
Face, but She Says It's Useless to Fight Back," Indiewire, January 2, 2019,
www.indiewire.com/2019/01/scarlett-johansson-deepfakes-face-porn-videos
-1202031678.

31. April Glaser, "The Scarlett Johansson Bot Is the Robotic Future of Objectifying Women," *Wired*, April 4, 2016, www.wired.com/2016/04/the-scarlett
-johansson-bot-signals-some-icky-things-about-our-future.

32. "Voice Creation FAQ," CereProc, no date, www.cereproc.com/support/faqs
/voicecreation (accessed July 10, 2020).

33. See Natasha Lomas, "Lyrebird Is a Voice Mimic for the Fake News Era,"
TechCrunch, April 25, 2017, http://tcrn.ch/2osyU9H.

34. Matthew Gault, "After 20 Minutes of Listening, New Adobe Tool Can Make You Say Anything," *Vice*, November 5, 2016, www.vice.com/en_us/article/jpgkxp/after-20-minutes-of-listening-new-adobe-tool-can-make-you-say-anything.

35. Reena Gupta, "When Actors Are Hoarse—Tips to Preserve Your Voice," Osborne Head and Neck Institute, no date, www.ohniww.org/lindsay-lohan-emma-stone-voice-preservation (accessed October 2, 2019).

36. James A. Koufman and P. David Blalock, "Vocal Fatigue and Dysphonia in the Professional Voice User: Bogart-Bacall Syndrome," *Laryngoscope* 98, no. 5 (1988): 493–498.

37. Donna Kornhaber, "From Posthuman to Postcinema: Crises of Subjecthood and Representation in *Her*," *Cinema Journal* 56, no. 4 (2017): 8.

38. See also Kyle Buchanan, "Emma Stone, Jennifer Lawrence, and Scarlett Johansson Have an Older-Man Problem," Vulture, June 1, 2015, www.vulture.com/2015/05/emma-jlaw-and-scarletts-older-man-problem.html.

39. Roland Barthes, "The Grain of the Voice," in *Music, Image, Text*, trans. Stephen Heath (New York: Hill and Wang, 1977), 179–190.

40. Janet Cahn, quoted in Harrod, "How Do You Teach a Computer to Speak Like Scarlett Johansson?"

41. Barthes, "Grain of the Voice," 179–190.

42. Power, "Soft Coercion."

43. A. A. Dowd, "Charlie Kaufman and Duke Johnson on the Soulful Stop-Motion of *Anomalisa*," AV Club, December 14, 2015, https://film.avclub.com/charlie-kaufman-and-duke-johnson-on-the-soulful-stop-mo-1798287269.

44. Kornhaber, "From Posthuman to Postcinema," 7.

45. Power, "Soft Coercion."

46. Kornhaber, "From Posthuman to Postcinema," 7–8.

47. Scott Balcerzak, "Andy Serkis as Actor, Body and Gorilla: Motion Capture and the Presence of Performance," in *Cinephilia in the Age of Digital Reproduction: Film, Pleasure and Digital Culture*, ed. Jason Sperb and Scott Balcerzak (London: Wallflower, 2009), 196, 206–207.

48. Balcerzak, "Andy Serkis as Actor," 196.

49. This quotation appears in Matt Patches's review for *Esquire*, and it was foregrounded in much of *Anomalisa*'s promotional materials. See Matt Patches, "People Are Obsessed with Charlie Kaufman's Stop-Motion Sex Drama," *Esquire*, September 16, 2015, www.esquire.com/entertainment/movies/reviews/a37997/anomalisa-charlie-kaufman.

50. The viral spreading of the "ghost" of Mariah Carey's voice in a Musical Instrument Digital Interface (MIDI) version of her song "All I Want for Christmas Is You" is another notable example of listeners experiencing a technological effect as a kind of ghosting. See Max Pearl, "This Terrifying MIDI Version of 'All I Want for Christmas' Will Keep You Awake at Night," *Vice*, December 18, 2015, www.vice.com/en_us/article/ez7zv4/this-terrifying-midi-version-of-all-i-want-for-christmas-will-keep-you-awake-at-night. For a direct reference to the ghostly nature of the Mariah Carey example, see Sam Downey, "Can You Hear the Ghost of Mariah Carey in This Bizarre Auditory Illusion?," Nine.com, no date, www.nine.com.au/entertainment/viral/mariah-carey-illusion/3edf8190-8337-42e2-9525-d7e2f685dc4a (accessed September 20, 2019).

51. Peters, "The 'Robettes' Are Coming."

52. Thao Phan, "Amazon Echo and the Aesthetics of Whiteness," *Catalyst: Feminism, Theory, Technoscience* 5, no. 1 (2019): 1–39, 4.

53. Pooja Rangan, "In Defense of Voicelessness: The Matter of the Voice and the Films of Leslie Thornton," *Feminist Media Histories* 1, no. 3 (Summer 2015): 116–117.

54. See Renee E. Tajima, "Lotus Blossoms Don't Bleed: Images of Asian Women," in *Making Waves: An Anthology of Writing by and about Asian American Women*, ed. Asian Women United of California (Boston: Beacon, 1989), 308–317.

55. Power, "Soft Coercion."

56. For example, as Jennifer Lynn Stoever examined to powerful effect in *The Sonic Color Line*, both the voice and the cultural politics of listening are shaped by race. Focusing on sounds of blackness in relation to US slavery, for instance, Stoever explored how vocalizations such as screams, grunts, and groans were perceived by white elites as overly emotional and overly corporeal. See Stoever, *The Sonic Color Line: Race and the Cultural Politics of Listening* (New York: NYU Press, 2016), 38–41.

57. Fleeger, "When Robots Speak on Screen," 433.

58. Freya Jarman-Ivens, *Queer Voices: Technologies, Vocalities, and the Musical Flaw* (New York: Palgrave Macmillan, 2011), 161, 88–89. Jarman-Ivens focuses on singer Karen Carpenter.

59. Jason Guerrasio, "An Actor Explains How He Spent Years Voicing Hundreds of Characters in the Trippy Charlie Kaufman Movie, 'Anomalisa,'" Business Insider, March 15, 2016, www.businessinsider.com/tom-noonan-voicing-anomalisa -characters-2016-3?r=US&IR=T.

60. Kornhaber, "From Posthuman to Postcinema," 3.

61. Jarman-Ivans, *Queer Voices*, 161, 88–89.

62. Aristotle, *De Anima*, Book II, Chapter 8 (c. 350 BC); Steven Connor, *Dumbstruck: A Cultural History of Ventriloquism* (Oxford: Oxford University Press, 2000), 24.

63. Connor, *Dumbstruck*, 24.

64. Walter J. Ong, *The Presence of the Word: Some Prolegomena for Religious and Cultural History* (Minneapolis: University of Minnesota Press, 1981), 168.

65. Stephen Prince, "Actors and Algorithms," in *Digital Visual Effects in Cinema* (New Brunswick, NJ: Rutgers University Press, 2011), 123.

66. Prince, "Actors and Algorithms," 122.

CHAPTER 3. THE EXPANDED AND IMMERSIVE VOICE-OVER

1. Kaja Silverman, *The Acoustic Mirror: The Female Voice in Psychoanalysis and Cinema* (Bloomington: Indiana University Press, 1988), 57–58.

2. These include sources drawn on in the remainder of the chapter: Gene Youngblood, *Expanded Cinema* (New York: E. P. Dutton, 1970); Gene Youngblood, "Cinema and the Code," *Leonardo* 22, no. 5 (1989): 27–30; A. L. Rees, Duncan White, Steven Ball, and David Curtis, eds., *Expanded Cinema: Art, Performance, Film* (London: Tate Publishing, 2011); Haidee Wasson, "The Networked Screen: Moving Images, Materiality, and the Aesthetics of Size" in *Fluid Screens, Expanded Cinema*, ed. Janine Marchessault and Susan Lord (Toronto: University of Toronto Press, 2008), 74–95.

3. Youngblood, *Expanded Cinema*.

4. Reflecting a broader devaluation of sound in cinema during that period, *Expanded Cinema* chooses an odd moment to acknowledge the verbal-vocal for the first time: nearly one hundred pages in, Will Hindle's *Billabong* (1968) is described as a "wordless impressionistic 'documentary.'" The film's wordlessness is deemed significant—a sign of its experimental approach—but considering how dialogue or voices generally function in relation to the increasingly immersive, interactive, and interconnected forms of cinema is not. Youngblood, *Expanded Cinema*, 95. See also Youngblood, "Cinema and the Code," 27.

5. Rees et al., *Expanded Cinema: Art, Performance, Film*.

6. The only exceptions to this are a chapter related to music and a section of the book's final chapter, by the Austrian artist Valie Export, on her 2007 Venice Binnennale performance titled *The Voice as Performance, Act and Body*. See Valie Export, "Expanded Cinema: Expanded Reality," in Rees et al., *Expanded Cinema*, 297–298.

7. Rees et al., *Expanded Cinema: Art, Performance, Film*, 6.

8. Youngblood, *Expanded Cinema*, 65.

9. Sarah Kozloff, "About a Clueless Girl and Boy: Voice-Over in Romantic Comedy Today," *Cinephile* 8, no. 1 (2012): 5 (original emphasis). Here she cites her earlier work: Sarah Kozloff, *Invisible Storytellers: Voice-Over Narration in American Fiction Film* (Berkeley: University of California Press, 1988).

10. For a detailed study of voice-over in the films of Jane Campion, see Kathleen McHugh, "'Sounds that Creep Inside You': Female Narration and Voiceover in the Films of Jane Campion," *Style* 35, no. 2 (2001): 193–218.

11. Kozloff, "About a Clueless Girl and Boy," 10–11. For Kozloff, the significance of Dedee's narration is "the way in which the narrator's position straddles the line between the first-person and third, or intra- and extra-diegetic, creating an ironic frisson."

12. Kozloff, "About a Clueless Girl and Boy," 11.

13. Paula J. Massood, "Street Girls with No Future: Black Women Coming of Age in the City," in *Contemporary Black American Cinema: Race, Gender and Sexuality at the Movies*, ed. Mia Mask (New York: Routledge, 2012), 235.

14. Mekado Murphy, "25 Years after a Breakthrough at Sundance, Trying to Break through Again," *New York Times*, January 24, 2018, www.nytimes.com/2018/01/24/movies/leslie-harris-sundance-interview.html.

15. Massood, "Street Girls with No Future," 235.

16. For further discussion of voice-over in *Precious*, see Alessandra Raengo, "Shadowboxing. Lee Daniels's Non-Representation Cinema," in Mask, *Contemporary Black American Cinema*, 200–216.

17. Marisa Meltzer, "How Busy Philipps Became the Breakout Star of Instagram Stories," *New Yorker*, September 28, 2017, www.newyorker.com/culture/persons-of-interest/how-busy-philipps-became-the-breakout-star-of-instagram-stories.

18. Anna Swartz, "Busy Philipps Is Getting a Talk Show, Joining a Small Group of Women in Late-Night TV," Mic, May 1, 2018, www.mic.com/articles/189156/busy-philipps-is-getting-a-talk-show-joining-a-small-group-of-women-in-late-night-tv.

19. @Vanity Fair, "We talked to all the titans of late-night television, and found

out why it's better than ever," Twitter, September 14, 2015, https://twitter.com
/VanityFair/status/643459713561141248.

20. For an overview of such attention-grabbing vocal techniques, see Julie
Beck, "The Linguistics of the 'YouTube' Voice," *Atlantic*, December 7, 2015,
www.theatlantic.com/technology/archive/2015/12/the-linguistics-of-youtube-voice
/418962.

21. The psychological thriller *Gone Girl* (David Fincher, 2014) also employs
an unreliable female narrator. Adapted by Gillian Flynn based on her 2012 novel,
Fincher's adaptation includes Amy's (Rosalind Pike) narration throughout, switch-
ing from a voice-over based on her diary (later revealed to be a work of fiction) to
her omniscient commentary.

22. Clem Bastow, "Fleabag's Feminist Rethinking of Tired Screenwriting
Tools," *The Conversation*, July 31, 2019, https://theconversation.com/fleabags
-feminist-rethinking-of-tired-screenwriting-tools-121104.

23. "Metropolitan Museum Audio Guide Introduces *Costume: The Art of
Dress* Narrated by Sarah Jessica Parker," The Met, November 10, 2008, www
.metmuseum.org/press/news/2008/metropolitan-museum-audio-guide-introduces
-icostume-the-art-of-dressi-narrated-by-sarah-jessica-parker.

24. Jamie Beckman, "10 Awesome Celebrity-Narrated Audio Tours," Budget
Travel, January 27, 2015, www.budgettravel.com/article/10-awesome-celebrity
-narrated-audio-tours_51830.

25. "Sarahjessicaparker," April 23, 2019, Instagram video, www.instagram
.com/p/BwnBG0oFOnk.

26. "Sarahjessicaparker," September 1, 2016, Instagram video, www.instagram
.com/p/BJ0KIC3DdQs/?hl=en.

27. Parker's Instagram usage, including the "Rabbit, Rabbit" series of videos,
was explored in *In Style* magazine in April 2019. See Isabel Jones, "We Need
to Talk about Sarah Jessica Parker's Instagram," *In Style*, April 12, 2019, www
.instyle.com/news/sarah-jessica-parker-instagram-weird.

28. For other examples, see "Sarahjessicaparker," October 1, 2017, Instagram
video, www.instagram.com/p/BZtfPTTjy2N; "Sarahjessicaparker," August 1,
2019, Instagram video, www.instagram.com/p/B0nsaWuFx3q.

29. See Joceline Andersen, "Now You've Got the Shiveries: Affect, Intimacy,
and the ASMR Whisper Community," *Television and New Media* 16, no. 8 (December 2015): 692–694.

30. See Laird Borrelli-Persson, "Sarah Jessica Parker Narrates the History
of '70s Fashion in *Vogue*," *Vogue*, June 5, 2017, www.vogue.com/article/125
-anniversary-video-seventies-fashion-history-sarah-jessica-parker. See also *Vogue*,
Vogue by the Decade, last updated January 18, 2019, YouTube playlist, www
.youtube.com/playlist?list=PLztAHXmlMZFQzxmXfTAFxgbolYcO4uTDD.

31. Youngblood, *Expanded Cinema*, 54, 65.

32. Youngblood, 347–348.

33. The term "transmedia storytelling" has been used by Henry Jenkins since
2003 in pieces for the *MIT Technology Review*. He also used it in his discipline-
shifting book, *Convergence Culture: Where Old and New Media Collide* (New
York: NYU Press, 2006), particularly chapter 3, "Searching for the Origami Uni-
corn: *The Matrix* and Transmedia Storytelling," 93–130.

34. See Chapter 1 of Mary R. Desjardins, *Recycled Stars: Female Film Stardom*

in the Age of Television and Video (Durham, NC: Duke University Press, 2015), 13–55.

35. In Season 4, Episode 14, of *Family Guy*, "PTV" (2005), central character Peter Griffin critiques the over-censoring of television shows yet suggests that Parker should not be allowed on television because "she looks like a foot."

36. The meme emerged in around 2008. See "Sarah Jessica Parker Looks Like a Horse," Know Your Meme, no date, https://knowyourmeme.com/memes/sarah-jessica-parker-looks-like-a-horse (accessed September 10, 2019).

37. Tracy McVeigh, "Joanna Lumley: Never Mess with an Old Avenger," *Guardian*, May 10, 2009, www.theguardian.com/world/2009/may/10/profile-joanna-lumley-gurkhas-rights.

38. These series might be critiqued for their disavowed colonialist angle, with the Kashmir-born Lumley visiting exotic locations and often interacting with relatively disadvantaged people of color.

39. "St Andrew Launches New Museum Guide," University of St Andrews, November 12, 2012, https://news.st-andrews.ac.uk/archive/st-andrew-launches-new-museum-guide.

40. "St Andrew Launches New Museum Guide."

41. Richard Barry, "This Sounds Absolutely Fabulous," *Independent*, January 29, 1996, www.independent.co.uk/life-style/this-sounds-absolutely-fabulous-1326423.html (emphasis added).

42. These include the short documentary *La Mama: An American Nun's Life in a Mexican Prison* (Jody Hammond, 2010) and *School of the American Assassins* (Robert Richter, 1994).

43. "@SusanSarandon," "Happy to have narrated the audio tour of Frida Kahlo @TheDali. Check it out started 12/17. http://thedali.org/exhibit/frida-kahlo-dali/ #FridaDali," Twitter, December 13, 2016, https://twitter.com/SusanSarandon/status/808789399613964289.

44. Twitter user "@stephsanola" commented that "you sold out POC bcs u don't 'vote with your vagina.' U were an extremely poor choice by @TheDali for anything Mexican." User @dr_bruin was similarly critical and attempted to speak for Kahlo, asserting that "Frida is turning in her grave. She'd have boycotted a 'malinchista' like you!" Twitter, December 17, 2016, https://twitter.com/dr_bruin/status/810056826201010176.

45. Earlier uses of VR include artist David Em's production of virtual worlds for NASA's Jet Propulsion Laboratory, where Em was artist-in-residence from 1977 to 1984. For an overview of NASA's use of VR to train astronauts, see Erin Carson, "NASA Shows the World Its 20-Year Virtual Reality Experiment to Train Astronauts: The Inside Story," Tech Republic, September 17, 2017, www.techrepublic.com/article/nasa-shows-the-world-its-20-year-vr-experiment-to-train-astronauts.

46. Silverman, *Acoustic Mirror*, 57–58.

47. Kyle Melnick, "Five Emotionally Draining VR Films," VR Scout, March 30, 2019, https://vrscout.com/news/five-emotionally-draining-vr-films.

48. Julie Woletz, "Interfaces of Immersive Media," *Interface Critique Journal* 1 (2018): 97, 101.

49. Steven Connor, *Dumbstruck: A Cultural History of Ventriloquism* (Oxford: Oxford University Press, 2000), 12, 38.

50. Adi Robertson, "Dear Angelica Might Be the Most Beautiful Virtual Reality

I've Ever Seen," The Verge, January 23, 2017, www.theverge.com/2017/1/23 /14345316/dear-angelica-oculus-vr-story-studio-sundance-2017-review.

51. On horror, see, for example, Amy Roberts, "Lights Out: The Scariest VR Horror Movie Experiences," Film Daily, no date, https://filmdaily.co/obsessions /scariest-vr-horror-movie-experiences/ (accessed September 20, 2019). See also Linda Williams, "Film Bodies: Gender, Genre, and Excess," *Film Quarterly* 44, no. 4 (Summer 1991): 2–13.

52. Duncan Bell, "Oculus Rift's Dear Angelica: Is This Short Animated Film the Saddest Use of VR Ever?," T3, January 20, 2017, www.t3.com/news/oculus-rifts -dear-angelica-is-this-short-film-the-saddest-use-of-vr-ever.

53. Jacob Smith, "The Nearness of You; or The Voice of Melodrama," *Vocal Tracks: Performance and Sound Media* (Berkeley: University of California Press, 2008), 81–114.

54. Smith cites Simon Frith, *Performing Rites: On the Value of Popular Music* (Oxford: Oxford University Press, 1996), 187.

55. Smith, *Vocal Tracks*, 103. See also Morgan Wilcock, "Rep Diary: Barbara Stanwyck on Lux Radio Theatre," *Film Comment*, January 2, 2014, www .filmcomment.com/blog/rep-diary-barbara-stanwyck-on-lux-radio-theatre.

56. Angela Watercutter, "*Dear Angelica* Is the Film—and Filmmaking Tool— VR Needs," *Wired*, January 20, 2017, www.wired.com/2017/01/oculus-dear -angelica-premiere.

57. Watercutter, "*Dear Angelica*."

58. Robertson, "Dear Angelica."

59. Sarah Kozloff, *Overhearing Film Dialogue* (Berkeley: University of California Press, 2000), 235, 238, 239, 242.

60. Smith, *Vocal Tracks*, 101. Smith also cites Josh Hutchen's descriptions of "the barely suppressed sob" of 1940 radio melodramas. Hutchen, no title, *New York Times*, March 28, 1943.

61. Geena Davis Institute on Gender in Media, "About Us," https://seejane.org /about-us (accessed September 10, 2019).

62. The producers also considered Sandra Bullock, whose role as an astronaut who speaks to her dead daughter in *Gravity* (Alfonso Cuarón, 2013) reverses elements of *Dear Angelica*.

63. Geena Davis, cited in Watercutter, "*Dear Angelica*."

64. Janko Roettgers, "'Tomb Raider' Star Alicia Vikander Goes Virtual Reality with 'Arden's Wake: Tide's Fall,'" *Variety*, April 18, 2018, https://variety.com/2018 /digital/news/alicia-vikander-tides-fall-vr-penrose-1202756199.

65. Daniel Kreps, "See Cat Power React to Emotional Janis Joplin Letters in Doc Clip," *Rolling Stone*, April 21, 2016, www.rollingstone.com/music/music -news/see-cat-power-react-to-emotional-janis-joplin-letters-in-doc-clip-200697.

66. For an in-depth account of how *Lemonade* reworks traditional representations of the female voice on screen, see Ciara Barrett, "'Formation' of the Female Author in the Hip Hop Visual Album: Beyoncé and FKA Twigs," *The Soundtrack* 9, no. 1/2 (2016): 41–57.

67. Wasson, "Networked Screen," 74–95, 86.

68. "Beyond Animation: 'Dear Angelica' Premieres at Sundance," Oculus Story Studio Blog, Oculus, January 20, 2017, www.oculus.com/story-studio/blog/beyond -animation-dear-angelica-premieres-at-sundance/?locale=en_US.

69. Wasson, "Networked Screen," 76.

CHAPTER 4. KARINA LONGWORTH AND THE REMIXING OF
ACTRESSES' VOICES ON THE *YOU MUST REMEMBER THIS* PODCAST

1. The "Jean and Jane" series comprises episodes 106–114 of the podcast. See Karina Longworth, host, "Jean and Jane," *You Must Remember This*, June 27–August 21, 2017, produced by Karina Longworth, podcast, https://podcasts.apple .com/us/podcast/you-must-remember-this/id858124601?mt=2.

2. Karina Longworth, "Peg Entwistle (Dead Blondes Episode 1)," *You Must Remember This*, January 30, 2017, show notes, www.youmustrememberthispodcast .com/episodes/2017/1/26/peg-entwistle-dead-blondes-episode-1?rq=dead%20 blondes.

3. Longworth explains that, privately, Preminger seemed to feel guilty, but that publicly he said that this was precisely the kind of accident that a director hopes for. They shot extra footage and he said that the crowds' reactions to the real-life burning of Seberg were brilliant.

4. Jane Fonda, "Television," *New York Times*, October 31, 1971, www.nytimes .com/1971/10/31/archives/jane-fonda-i-want-to-work-with-women.html.

5. See Patricia Bosworth, *Jane Fonda: The Private Life of a Public Woman* (Boston: Houghton Mifflin Harcourt, 2011), 379.

6. See, for example, Frances Kindon and Alistair McGeorge, "Age-Defying Jane Fonda, 79, Shows Off Youthful Figure as She Owns the Catwalk at Paris Fashion Week," *Mirror*, October 1, 2017, www.mirror.co.uk/3am/celebrity-news/jane -fonda-defies-age-loreal-11269983.

7. Such impersonations are largely confined to early podcasts—those prior to Longworth's wide-scale inclusion of archival audio materials—and so I do not consider them in this chapter.

8. Virginia Madsen and John Potts, "Voice-Cast: The Distribution of the Voice via Podcasting," in *VØ1CE: Vocal Aesthetics in Digital Arts and Media*, ed. Norie Neumark, Ross Gibson, and Theo van Leeuwen (Cambridge, MA: MIT Press), 50, 33.

9. Madsen and Potts, "Voice-Cast," 33.

10. Michel Chion, *The Voice in Cinema*, trans. Claudia Gorbman (New York: Columbia University Press, 1999), 21, 22.

11. Karina Longworth, host, "Star Wars Episode III: Hedy Lamarr," *You Must Remember This*, January 14, 2015, produced by Karina Longworth, podcast, www .youmustrememberthispodcast.com/episodes/youmustrememberthispodcastblog /2015/1/14/star-wars-episode-iii-hedy-lamarr-ymrt-29. Relatedly, in Chapter 3 I use Jacob Smith's comparison of Barbara Stanwyck's radio and film performances for *Stella Dallas*, another instance where, in lending their voices to radio, Hollywood actresses have provided precursors for Longworth's remediation of film soundtracks.

12. Kaja Silverman, *The Acoustic Mirror: The Female Voice in Psychoanalysis and Cinema* (Bloomington: Indiana University Press, 1988).

13. Helen Macallan and Andrew Plain, "Filmic Voices," in Neumark et al., *VØ1CE: Vocal Aesthetics in Digital Arts and Media*, 243–266.

14. Kelly Faircloth, "A Chat with the Creator of Can't-Miss Classic Hollywood Podcast You Must Remember This," *Jezebel*, June 21, 2016, https://pictorial .jezebel.com/a-chat-with-the-creator-of-cant-miss-classic-hollywood-1782364338.

15. Karina Longworth, host, "Star Wars Episode VII: Lena Horne," *You Must*

Remember This, February 17, 2015, produced by Karina Longworth, podcast, https://megaphone.link/KL9647868971.

16. Allison Graham, *Framing the South: Hollywood, Television and Race during the Civil Rights Struggle* (Baltimore: John Hopkins University Press, 2001), 39.

17. Jeff Smith, "Black Faces, White Voices: The Politics of Dubbing in Carmen Jones," *Velvet Light Trap* 51 (Spring 2003): 31, 39.

18. For a summary of Longworth's six-part series on the history and subsequent legacy of the racist Disney feature, see E. J. Dickson, "New 'You Must Remember This' Season Explores History of Racist Disney Cartoon," *Rolling Stone*, October 22, 2019, www.rollingstone.com/culture/culture-features/you-must-remember-this-song-of-the-south-karina-longworth-interview-901814.

19. Natalie Baker, "'2 Dope Queens' Is the Hands-Down Funniest Podcast I've Ever Heard," *Bitch Media*, April 21, 2016, www.bitchmedia.org/article/2-dope-queens-hands-down-funniest-podcast-ive-ever-heard.

20. "About 2 Dope Queens," WNYC Studios, no date, www.wnycstudios.org/podcasts/dopequeens/about (accessed December 10, 2019).

21. Mimi Chan, "Sifu Mimi Chan," no date, www.sifumimichan.com/sifu-mimi-chan (accessed May 26, 2021).

22. "Behind the Mic," "Spotify Opens Doors for More Underrepresented Podcasters through New Sound Up Programs," Spotify, March 31, 2021, https://newsroom.spotify.com/2021-03-31/spotify-opens-doors-for-more-underrepresented-podcasters-through-new-sound-up-programs; Todd Spangler, "Spotify Reprising 'Sound Up' Podcasting Boot Camp for Women of Color," *Variety*, June 7, 2019, https://variety.com/2019/digital/news/spotify-sound-up-podcast-women-of-color-1203235654.

23. Kevin L. Jones, "Karina Longworth Talks You Must Remember This before Going on Hiatus," KQED, September 13, 2016, www.kqed.org/arts/12061768/karina-longworth-talks-you-must-remember-this-before-going-on-hiatus.

24. Macallan and Plain, "Filmic Voices," 252.

25. Scott Porch, "How Karina Longworth Is Reimagining Classic Hollywood and the Podcast in You Must Remember This," Longreads, March 17, 2015, https://longreads.com/2015/03/17/how-karina-longworth-is-reimagining-classic-hollywood-and-the-podcast-in-you-must-remember-this.

26. For a summary of the different subscription plans, see Karina Longworth, "Become a You Must Remember This Patron, Won't You?," You Must Remember This, June 13, 2019, www.youmustrememberthispodcast.com/episodes/2019/6/13/become-a-you-must-remember-this-patron-wont-you.

27. Author's email correspondence with Lindsey D. Schoenholtz, *You Must Remember This* research and production assistant, June 13, 2018.

28. Porch, "How Karina Longworth Is Reimagining Classic Hollywood."

29. Monica Dall'Asta and Alessandra Chiarini, "Editors Introduction, Found Footage: Women without a Movie Camera," *Feminist Media Histories* 2, no. 3 (Summer 2016): 1, 3–4.

30. Dall'Asta and Chiarini, "Editors Introduction, Found Footage," 4–5.

31. Alessandra Chiarini, "'Feeling-Images': Montage, Body and Historical Memory in Barbara Hammer's Nitrate Kisses," *Feminist Media Histories* 2, no. 3 (Summer 2016): 92.

32. Dall'Asta and Chiarini, "Editors Introduction, Found Footage," 6.

33. Barbara Hammer, *Hammer! Making Movies out of Sex and Life* (New York: Feminist Press, 2010), 204, quoted in Chiarini "Feeling-Images," 91.

34. Brent Lang, "'You Must Remember This' Podcast Brings Showbiz History to Life," *Variety*, March 3, 2016, https://variety.com/2016/digital/news/you-must-remember-this-podcast-1201721155.

35. Nell Frizzell, "You Must Remember This: The Woman Spilling Hollywood Secrets," *Guardian*, July 5, 2016, www.theguardian.com/tv-and-radio/2016/jul/05/you-must-remember-this-the-woman-spilling-hollywood-secrets-marilyn-monroe-charlie-chaplin.

36. Michele Hilmes, "The Disembodied Women," in *Radio Voices: American Broadcasting, 1922–1952* (Minneapolis: University of Minnesota Press, 1997), 135–136.

37. Jennifer Hyland Wang, "Producing a Radio Housewife: Clara, Lu 'n' Em, Gendered Labor, and the Early Days of Radio," *Feminist Media Histories* 4, no. 1 (Winter 2018): 64, 75–76.

38. "celmartinart," Instagram comment, January 28, 2018, www.instagram.com/p/Bee7mbFhgOV/?taken-by=karinalongworth.

39. "sabrinastent," Instagram comment, January 4, 2018, www.instagram.com/p/BdiikpGh8JO/?taken-by=karinalongworth.

40. Sophie Gilbert, "Karina Longworth Makes Old Hollywood New," *The Atlantic*, November 14, 2018, www.theatlantic.com/entertainment/archive/2018/11/karina-longworth-old-hollywoods-most-vital-historian/575728.

41. The fascination with Longworth's voice is similar to the interest in the voice of Sarah Koenig, coproducer and narrator of the *Serial* podcast (2014–). Koenig's distinctive podcast voice has led to, among other things, a cameo appearance as a ringtone on *BoJack Horseman* (Netflix, 2014–2020), and to T-shirts with the text "Sarah Koenig's Voice." See "sarah koenig's voice shirt," baddkneests.com, no date, https://badkneests.com/products/sarah-koenigs-voice-t-shirt (accessed October 29, 2019).

42. Justin Ravitz, "You Must Remember This Podcast: New Season Explores Radical Women in Hollywood," *Rolling Stone*, June 27, 2017, www.rollingstone.com/culture/culture-features/you-must-remember-this-podcast-new-season-explores-radical-women-in-hollywood-201578.

43. Calen Cross, "History Podcasts Made by Women," Bello Collective, October 6, 2016, https://bellocollective.com/history-podcasts-made-by-women-87dc6dbd980b.

44. Brent Lang, "'You Must Remember This' Podcast Brings Showbiz History to Life."

45. Scott Porch, "How Karina Longworth Is Reimagining Classic Hollywood." See also Hyland Wang, "Producing a Radio Housewife," 62–65.

46. Jacqueline Warwick and Allison Adrian, "Introduction" to *Voicing Girlhood in Popular Music: Performance, Authority, Authenticity* (New York: Routledge, 2016), 2.

47. See Raechel Tiffe and Melody Hoffman, "Taking Up Sonic Space: Feminized Vocality and Podcasting as Resistance," *Feminist Media Studies* 17, no. 1 (2017): 115–118.

48. Nora Caplan-Bricker, "Um, No, to Ummo and All Speech 'Improvement'

Apps," *Slate*, May 10, 2016, https://slate.com/human-interest/2016/05/speech
-improvement-apps-like-ummo-are-sexist-and-support-inequality.html.

49. Karina Longworth, "Star Wars Episode II: Carol Lombard and Clark
Gable," *You Must Remember This*, January 13, 2015, produced by Karina Longworth, podcast, www.youmustrememberthispodcast.com/episodes/youmustremem
berthispodcastblog/2015/1/13/star-wars-episode-ii-carole-lombard-and-clark-gable
-ymrt-28.

50. Judith Mayne, *The Woman at the Keyhole: Feminism and Women's Cinema*
(Bloomington: Indiana University Press, 1990), 2.

51. Mayne, *The Woman at the Keyhole*, 2.

52. Frizzell, "You Must Remember This."

53. For examples of such hard-boiled male narration, see Frank Krutnik, *In a
Lonely Street: Film Noir, Genre, Masculinity* (London: Routledge, 2006), 47, 107,
126, 169.

54. Allison Burnett, "Fame! Ain't It a Bitch: Confessions of a Reformed Gossip
Columnist," *Variety*, March 6, 2001, https://variety.com/2001/more/reviews/fame
-ain-t-it-a-bitch-confessions-of-a-reformed-gossip-columnist-1117797992.

55. Faircloth, "Chat with the Creator."

56. Julie Shapiro, "Why Are 70 Percent of the Most Popular Podcasts Hosted
by Men?," *Bitch Media*, February 28, 2013, www.bitchmedia.org/post/why-are-70
-percent-of-the-most-popular-podcasts-hosted-by-men.

57. Tiffe and Hoffman, "Taking Up Sonic Space," 117, 118.

58. John L. Sullivan, "Podcast Movement: Aspirational Labour and the Formalization of Podcasting as a Culture Industry," in *Podcasting: New Aural Cultures
and Digital Media*, ed. Dario Llinares, Neil Fox, and Richard Berry (London:
Palgrave Macmillan, 2019), 48, 49. The findings here are drawn from Brooke Erin
Duffy and Urszula Pruchniewska, "Gender and Self-Enterprise in the Social Media
Age: A Digital Double Bind," *Information, Communication and Society* 20, no. 6
(2017): 843–859.

CHAPTER 5. MEME GIRLS VERSUS TRUMP

1. "@bubbaprog" (Timothy Burke), Twitter, January 20, 2017, https://twitter
.com/bubbaprog/status/822495850899374080; Kenny Herzog, "Trump Plagiarized Bane in Inauguration Speech," *Death and Taxes*, January 20, 2017, www
.deathandtaxesmag.com/315851/trump-bane-plagiarized-inauguration-speech.

2. Lindsey Bever, "Trump's 'Game of Thrones'-Style Poster Makes Cryptic Cameo at Cabinet Meeting," *Washington Post*, January 2, 2019, www.washingtonpost
.com/politics/2019/01/02/trumps-game-thrones-style-poster-makes-cryptic-cameo
-cabinet-meeting; Emily Stewart, "Watch the 'Movie Trailer' Trump Showed Kim
Jong Un about North Korea's Possible Future," Vox, June 12, 2018, www.vox.com
/world/2018/6/12/17452876/trump-kim-jong-un-meeting-north-korea-video.

3. See Julia Alexander, "HBO Still Doesn't Like Trump Using Game of Thrones
Memes to Promote Himself," The Verge, April 18, 2019, www.theverge.com/2019
/4/18/18485473/mueller-report-donald-trump-meme-game-of-thrones-got-season
-8-final-hbo-statement.

4. "The Wing," Instagram post, January 29, 2017, www.instagram.com
/p/BP3NOsggodN/?taken-by=the.wing.

5. Jordan Bassett, "Cher from 'Clueless' Nailed the Refugee Debate in One Minute," NME, February 6, 2017, www.nme.com/blogs/the-movies-blog/1968370 -1968370.

6. As Banet-Weiser eloquently wrote in the introduction to *Empowered: Popular Feminism and Popular Misogyny*, "We are living in a moment in North America and Europe in which feminism has become, somewhat incredibly, popular. It feels as if everywhere you turn, there is an expression of feminism—on a T-shirt, in a movie, in the lyrics of a pop song, in an inspirational Instagram post, in an awards ceremony speech." Sarah Banet-Weiser, *Empowered: Popular Feminism and Popular Misogyny* (Durham, NC: Duke University Press, 2018), 1.

7. According to a November 2017 report by the *Guardian*, twenty women have accused Trump of sexual misconduct. Lucia Graves and Sam Morris, "The Trump Allegations," *Guardian*, November 29, 2017, www.theguardian.com/us-news/ng -interactive/2017/nov/30/donald-trump-sexual-misconduct-allegations-full-list.

8. Hampus Hagman, "The Digital Gesture: Rediscovering Cinematic Movement through GIFs," *Refractory: A Journal of Entertainment Media* 21 (December 2012), http://refractory.unimelb.edu.au/2012/12/29/hagman; Michael Z. Newman, "GIFs: The Attainable Text," *Film Criticism* 40, no. 1 (January 2016).

9. Michel Chion briefly discussed endophony in relation to texts embedded in films in *Film, a Sound Art* (New York: Columbia University Press, 2009), 175–176.

10. According to the "Know Your Meme" database, "Read this in my voice" memes began to appear in 2009. See "Read This in My Voice," Know Your Meme, no date, http://knowyourmeme.com/memes/read-this-in-my-voice (accessed July 10, 2017).

11. Hagman, "Digital Gesture."

12. Jessalynn Marie Keller, "Virtual Feminisms: Girls' Blogging Communities, Feminist Activism, and Participatory Politics," *Information, Communication and Society* 15, no. 3 (2012): 430.

13. See Sarah Banet-Weiser, *Authentic™: The Politics of Ambivalence in a Brand Culture* (New York: NYU Press, 2012).

14. Keller, "Virtual Feminisms," 430.

15. The term "spreadable" here is used as per that of Henry Jenkins, Sam Ford, and Joshua Green in *Spreadable Media: Creating Value and Meaning in a Networked Culture* (New York: NYU Press, 2013). Beyond the focus on gender activism explored in this chapter, there are a wide range of other kinds of online activism, including those related to race and abolition, that incorporate the sharing of related memes. See, for example, the Twitter handle @abolitionmemes.

16. Jenkins, *Convergence Culture*, 206, 207.

17. See Ana Teixeira Pinto, "Capitalism with a Transhuman Face: The Afterlife of Fascism and the Digital Frontier," *Third Text* 33, no. 3 (2019): 324; and Florian Cramer in the panel "Proto-Post-Fascism?," The White West: The Resurgence of Fascism as Cultural Force, Paris, May 9, 2018, www.lacolonie.paris/agenda/the -white-west-la-resurgence-du-fascisme-comme-force-culturelle.

18. The "Pussy grabs back" response received considerable attention in the popular media, including on websites aimed at girls such as *Teen Vogue*. See Alli Maloney, "#PussyGrabsBack Creators Amanda Duarte and Jessica Bennett Interview," October 21, 2016, www.teenvogue.com/story/pussygrabsback-creators -amanda-duarte-jessica-bennett-interview.

19. See Teixeira Pinto, "Capitalism with a Transhuman Face," 324, for discus-

sion of this conference paper by Cramer.

20. For a detailed account of the Trump campaign's use of digital media in the election campaign, see Nathaniel Persily, "The 2016 U.S. Election: Can Democracy Survive the Internet?," *Journal of Democracy* 28, no. 2 (April 2017): 63–67.

21. Angela Nagle, *Kill All Normies: Online Culture Wars from 4Chan and Tumblr to Trump and the Alt-Right* (Hants, UK: Zero Books, 2017), 7–8, 14, 30.

22. Teixeira Pinto, "Capitalism with a Transhuman Face," 326.

23. Nagle, *Kill All Normies*, 107.

24. For a broader discussion of dialogue in the film, see Jennifer O'Meara, "'We've Got to Work on Your Accent and Vocabulary'—Characterization through Verbal Style in Clueless," in "In Focus: Clueless," *Cinema Journal* 53, no. 3 (Spring 2014): 138–145.

25. Nicole Puglise, "'Pussy Grabs Back' Becomes Rallying Cry for Female Rage against Trump," *Guardian*, October 10, 2016, www.theguardian.com/us-news /2016/oct/10/donald-trump-pussy-grabs-back-meme-women-twitter.

26. Anonymous Tumblr blog, https://feministlisasimpson-blog.tumblr.com (accessed July 20, 2019).

27. Repost from Tumblr user "fyspringfield," June 28, 2015, https:// feministlisasimpson-blog.tumblr.com/post/122669313462.

28. The scene is from Season 5, episode 14, titled "Lisa vs. Malibu Stacy." See the repost from Tumblr user "kateordie," August 27, 2014, https:// feministlisasimpson-blog.tumblr.com/post/95891296666/genevieve-ft-kateordie -i-know-its-been-said.

29. Ednie Kaeh Garrison, "U.S. Feminism-Grrrl Style! Youth (Sub)Cultures and the Technologics of the Third Wave," in *No Permanent Waves: Recasting Histories of US Feminism*, ed. N. Hewitt (Piscataway, NJ: Rutgers University Press, 2010), 187.

30. "everyoutfitonSATC," Instagram account, June 2016, www.instagram.com /everyoutfitonsatc.

31. Followers listed on the Instagram account as of October 5, 2019.

32. "everyoutfitonSATC," Instagram post, November 7, 2016, www.instagram .com/p/BMhkd6MD_9V/?taken-by=everyoutfitonsatc.

33. "everyoutfitonSATC," Instagram post, February 20, 2017, www.instagram .com/p/BQvo-YyDyqg/?taken-by=everyoutfitonsatc.

34. This is the name given to the montage effect demonstrated by Lev Kuleshov in the 1910s and 1920s. The effect refers to a cognitive process whereby viewers can derive different meanings from single shots depending on the shot with which it is combined.

35. For a summary of insults centered on Trump's appearance, see Sidney Switzer, "We Shouldn't Mock Trump for His Appearance," Huffington Post, August 10, 2017, www.huffingtonpost.com/entry/we-shouldnt-mock-trump-for-his -appearance_us_598cae03e4b0ed1f464c0967.

36. Carolyn L. Todd, "Remember That Time Trump Flirted with Samantha on *Sex and the City*?," Refinery29, April 28, 2017, www.refinery29.com/2017/04 /152242/sex-and-the-city-donald-trump-cameo-samantha-jones-flirt.

37. Jay Owens, "Post-Authenticity and the Ironic Truths of Meme Culture," in *Post Memes: Seizing the Memes of Production*, ed. Alfie Bown and Dan Bristow (Goleta, CA: Punctum Books, 2019), 105.

38. Channing Hargrove, "Reminder: We Should All Be Mirandas—and Wear

This T-Shirt," Refinery29, September 5, 2017, www.refinery29.com/2017/09/170977/sex-and-the-city-miranda-shirt.

39. Adichie's essay was subsequently published in book form in 2014. Chimamanda Ngozi Adichie, *We Should All Be Feminists* (London: Harper Collins, 2014).

40. Jamie Feldman, "'We Should All Be Mirandas' Is the Feminist 'SATC' Mantra We Deserve,'" Huffington Post, September 6, 2017, www.huffpost.com/entry/miranda-hobbes-t-shirts-feminist_n_59afed9de4b0b5e531027de3.

41. "Membership," *The Wing*, no date, www.the-wing.com/memberships (accessed on January 3, 2018).

42. Banet-Weiser, *Authentic*, 5, 8.

43. For example, alongside an image of the Rizzo posters, the caption reads, "What would Rizzo do? Protest!! This plus the Nasty Women Unite and Joan Crawford images are available for full download over at bust.com." See Bust Magazine, Instagram post, January 19, 2017, www.instagram.com/p/BPdPFJrA0op/?taken-by=bust_magazine.

44. Tom Chatfield, *Activism or Slactivism? The Future of Digital Politics* (London: Vintage Digital, 2011), 1.

45. Zeynep Tufekci, "Adventures in the Trump Twittersphere," *New York Times*, March 31, 2016, www.nytimes.com/2016/03/31/opinion/campaign-stops/adventures-in-the-trump-twittersphere.html.

46. Chatfield, *Activism or Slacktivism?*, 12.

47. Nagle, *Kill All Normies*, 102.

48. Davis posted the picture as a disappearing Instagram story. It was captured and reposted as an "everyoutfitonSATC," Instagram post, December 4, 2017, www.instagram.com/p/BcTDt1mjwpi/?taken-by=everyoutfitonsatc.

49. "aliciasilverstone," Instagram post, February 1, 2017, www.instagram.com/p/BP9RKdHFbAA/?taken-by=aliciasilverstone.

50. Jenkins, *Convergence Culture*, 208.

51. There are, however, examples when the uses of memes as a form of online protest appears not just as ineffective but in bad taste. These include the way in which the phrase "Arrest the cops who killed Breonna Taylor" began to be attached, often ironically, to a wide range of social media posts in the summer of 2020, after the young Black woman's death. As journalist Palmer Haasch put it, "Coy references to the phrase may be well-intentioned, [but] many feel that the tone of the memes—and the use of Taylor's death seemingly as a punchline—is disrespectful to Taylor and detracts from the call for justice." Palmer Haasch, "Calls to 'Arrest the Cops Who Killed Breonna Taylor' Have Been Turned into an Online Meme That Some Say Has Gone Too Far," Business Insider, June 26, 2020, www.insider.com/arrest-the-cops-who-killed-breonna-taylor-memes-stop-2020-6.

52. Zeynep Tufekci, "After the Protests," *New York Times*, March 19, 2014, www.nytimes.com/2014/03/20/opinion/after-the-protests.html.

53. Alison Bechdel, "The Bechdel Test," in *Dykes to Watch Out For* (Ann Arbor, MI: Firebrand Books, 1986). The original comic strip can be viewed at a multitude of places online, including http://bechdeltestfest.com/about.

54. "Google Trends" search, July 15, 2017, https://trends.google.com/trends/explore?date=all&q=bechdel%20test.

55. I have written previously about the problems with using the test as a measure of gendered verbal representation. See O'Meara, "What 'The Bechdel

Test' Doesn't Tell Us: Examining Women's Verbal and Vocal (Dis)empowerment in Cinema," *Feminist Media Studies* 16, no. 6 (2016): 1120–1123.

56. Associated Press, "Swedish Cinemas Take Aim at Gender Bias with Bechdel Test Rating," in the *Guardian*, November 6, 2013, www.theguardian.com/world /2013/nov/06/swedish-cinemas-bechdel-test-films-gender-bias.

57. "Words We're Watching: Mansplaining," Merriam Webster, no date, www .merriam-webster.com/words-at-play/mansplaining-definition-history (accessed July 10, 2017).

58. Rebecca Solnit, "Men Explain Things to Me: Facts Didn't Get in Their Way," Tom Dispatch, April 13, 2008, www.tomdispatch.com/post/174918/rebecca _solnit_the_archipelago_of_arrogance.

59. For an example of the *Pocahontas* GIF being used to illustrate mansplaining, see Jessica Chandra, "Sweden Has a 'Mansplaining' Hotline So People Can Complain about Their Condescending Male Colleagues," *Elle Australia*, November 18, 2016, www.elle.com.au/news/sweden-mansplaining-hotline-6761.

60. Lauren Michele Jackson, "We Need to Talk about Digital Blackface in Reaction GIFs," *Teen Vogue*, August 2, 2017, www.teenvogue.com/story/digital -blackface-reaction-gifs.

61. Amanda Hess and Shane O'Neill, "The White Internet's Love Affair with Digital Blackface," *New York Times*, December 22, 2017, www.nytimes.com/video /arts/100000005615988/the-white-internets-love-affair-with-digital-blackface.html.

62. There are some exceptions, such as the frequently shared candidness and confidence of Sandra Oh's character Cristina Yang on *Grey's Anatomy* (2005–). See the following GIF-based listicle: BuzzFeed contributor "kk09," "Everything You Felt when You Found Out Sandra Oh Was Leaving 'Grey's Anatomy,'" Buzz-Feed, August 18, 2013, www.buzzfeed.com/kk09/everything-you-felt-when-you -found-out-sandra-oh-w-dowv#.lme2xJZzB.

63. For a collection of sample posts, see Nick Levine, "The #WokeCharlotte Meme Is Rewriting *Sex and the City*'s Problematic Past," Refinery29, December 23, 2017, www.refinery29.com/en-us/2017/12/186231/woke-charlotte-meme-sex-city.

64. See Tessa Dwyer, "Fansubbing and Abuse: Anime and Beyond," in *Speaking in Subtitles: Revaluing Screen Translation* (Edinburgh: Edinburgh University Press, 2017), 135.

CHAPTER 6. *RUPAUL'S DRAG RACE* AND THE QUEERED REMEDIATION OF WOMEN'S VOICES

1. Kaja Silverman, *The Acoustic Mirror: The Female Voice in Psychoanalysis and Cinema* (Bloomington: Indiana University Press, 1988), 45–47.

2. RuPaul's birthname is RuPaul Andre Charles, though the drag queen is known by first name only.

3. Not all the contestants on *RuPaul's Drag Race* identify as men; a number of trans and nonbinary drag queens have been on the show. As such, these dynamics and terms are being used strictly to refer to those who do identify as men. Where known, contestants' preferred pronouns are used throughout.

4. John Mercer, Charlie Sarson, and Jamie Hakim, "'Charisma, Uniqueness, Nerve and Talent': *RuPaul's Drag Race* and the Cultural Politics of Fame," *Celebrity Studies* 11, no. 4 (2020): 384.

5. For example, see Roger Baker, "Acting Style and the Sound of Juliet," in *Drag: A History of Female Impersonation in the Performing Arts* (New York: NYU Press, 1994), 46–55.

6. For example, see Judith Butler's discussion of drag in "Subversive Bodily Acts," in *Gender Trouble: Feminism and the Subversion of Identity* (London: Routledge, 1990), 79–141. See also Jeffrey Hilbert, "The Politics of Drag," in *Out in Culture: Gay, Lesbian and Queer Essays on Popular Culture*, ed. Cory Creekmur and Alexander Doty (London: Cassell, 1995), 463–469.

7. Steven P. Schacht and Lisa Underwood, *The Drag Queen Anthology: The Absolutely Fabulous but Flawlessly Customary World of Female Impersonators* (Binghamton, NY: Haworth Press, 2004), 1.

8. Roland Barthes, "The Grain of the Voice," in *Music, Image, Text*, trans. Stephen Heath (New York: Hill and Wang, 1977), 179–190.

9. Teresa Rizzo, "YouTube: The New Cinema of Attractions," *Scan: Journal of Media Arts Culture 5*, no. 1 (May 2008), http://scan.net.au/scan/journal/display .php?journal_id=109.

10. For example, see Ann Cooper Albright, *Traces of Light: Absence and Presence in the Work of Loïe Fuller* (Middletown, CT: Wesleyan University Press, 2007): 188.

11. Mark Edward and Stephen Farrier, preface to *Contemporary Drag Practices and Performers: Drag in a Changing Scene*, vol. 1, ed. Mark Edward and Stephen Farrier (London: Bloomsbury, 2020), xxi–1.

12. For an examination of the influence of *RuPaul's Drag Race* on the contemporary UK drag scene, see Joe Parslow, "Dragging the Mainstream: *RuPaul's Drag Race* and Moving Drag Practices between the USA and the UK," in Edward and Farrier, ed., *Contemporary Drag Practices*, 19–31.

13. "misterrichardson," "RuPaul's First Lip Sync on TV," from a performance televised on *The American Music Show* (People TV, 1981–2005), posted March 15, 2013, YouTube video, www.youtube.com/watch?v=kaAmlrafH8s.

14. For a discussion of Lypsinka's Wigstock performance, see David Halperin, *How to Be Gay* (Cambridge, MA: Harvard University Press, 2012), 168–175.

15. Esther Newton, *Mother Camp: Female Impersonators in America* (Chicago: University of Chicago Press, 1979), 43–44, 46.

16. Wayne Kostenbaum, "The Queen's Throat: (Homo)sexuality and the Art of Singing," in *Inside/Out: Lesbian Theories, Gay Theories*, ed. Diana Fuss (London: Routledge, 1991), 205.

17. Fleeger, *Mismatched Women*, 7, 138, 142.

18. Fleeger, 7.

19. See Silverman, *Acoustic Mirror*; Amy Lawrence, *Echo and Narcissus: Women's Voices in Classical Hollywood Cinema* (Berkeley: University of California Press, 1991); Maria DiBattista, *Fast-Talking Dames* (New Haven, CT: Yale University Press, 2001); Britta H. Sjogren, *Into the Vortex: Female Voice and Paradox in Film* (Urbana: University of Illinois Press, 2006).

20. Visually grounded makeovers are discussed by Carolyn Chernoff in "Of Women and Queens: Gendered Realities and Re-education in RuPaul's Drag Empire," in *The Makeup of RuPaul's Drag Race: Essays on the Queen of Reality Shows*, ed. Jim Daems (Jefferson, NC: McFarland, 2014), 148–167. The same collection has pieces on the womanly image, by Kai Kohlsdorf ("Policing the Proper Queer Subject: *RuPaul's Drag Race* in the Neoliberal 'Post' Moment"), 80–81, and

on "visions" of feminine beauty, by Mary Marcel ("Representing Gender, Race and Realness: The Television World of America's Next Drag Superstars"), 25. An exception in Daems's collection is Libby Anthony's discussion of linguistic barriers and stereotypes on the show ("Dragging with an Accent: Linguistic Stereotypes, Language Barriers and Translingualism"), 49–66.

21. For a thorough analysis of the connections between the matrilineal discourse of RuPaul as "Mama Ru" and the promotion and commodification of him as a brand, see Hazel Collie and Gemma Commane, "'Assume the Position: Two Queens Stand before Me': RuPaul as Ultimate Queen," *Celebrity Studies* 11, no. 4 (2020): 402–416. Collie and Commane argue that, despite contestants' references to RuPaul as "Mama Ru," RuPaul is positioned more as the "Ultimate Queen" than a traditional drag mother, as a result of the transactional relationship presented between the show's head judge and its contestants.

22. David J. Fine and Emily Shreve, "The Prime of Miss RuPaul Charles: Allusion, Betrayal and Charismatic Pedagogy," in Daems, *The Makeup of RuPaul's Drag Race*, 168–187.

23. The term "shantay" originated in *Paris Is Burning* (Jennie Livingston, 1990), a documentary on the New York drag scene in the 1980s. The documentary is heavily referenced by RuPaul throughout the various seasons of *RPDR*.

24. Guy Rosolato, "La voix: Entre corps et langage," *Revue française de psychanalyse* 38 (1974): 75–94. This is explained by Silverman in *Acoustic Mirror*, 79–81.

25. Rudolf P. Gaudio, "Sounding Gay: Pitch Properties in the Speech of Gay and Straight Men," *American Speech* 69, no. 1 (Spring 1994): 31. For a more recent examination of the topic, see Ron Smyth, Greg Jacobs, and Henry Rogers, "Male Voices and Perceived Sexual Orientation: An Experimental and Theoretical Approach," *Language in Society* 32, no. 3 (2003): 329–350.

26. Ramey Moore suggests something similar in his brief discussion of the show's lip-sync battles in "Everything Else Is Drag: Linguistic Drag and Gender Parody on RuPaul's Drag Race," *Journal of Research in Gender Studies* 3, no. 2 (2013): 22.

27. Barthes, "The Grain of the Voice," 183, 188.

28. Silverman, *Acoustic Mirror*, 46.

29. Silverman, 47.

30. Silverman, 47.

31. Jarman-Ivens, *Queer Voices*, 27. Here she cites Irene Albrecht, Jorg Haber, and Hans-Peter Seidel, "Speech Synchronization for Physics-Based Facial Animation," *Proceedings of WSCG* (February 2002): 9–16.

32. Jarman-Ivens, *Queer Voices*, 27.

33. See Matthias Echternach, Fabian Burk, Michael Burumy, Louisa Traser, and Bernhard Richter, "Morphometric Differences of Vocal Tract Articulators in Different Loudness Conditions in Singing," *PLOS One* 11, no. 4 (2016).

34. "Real-Time MRI Captures Incredible Video of Opera Singer Performing during Scan," *Telegraph*, May 4, 2016, www.telegraph.co.uk/science/2016/05/04/real-time-mri-captures-incredible-video-of-opera-singer-performi. (This video was later no longer available on the *Telegraph*'s website, but it still appeared on You-Tube. See "Infinite Quotes," "Look Inside the Head of a [*sic*] Opera Singer as He Performs Wagner Live as He Performs [*sic*]," May 8, 2016, YouTube video, www.youtube.com/watch?v=f5SUhhfwxEI, accessed July 15, 2021.)

35. For a more detailed discussion of this scene, including broader references to *Singin' in the Rain* and women's voices, see Liz Greene, "Speaking, Singing, Screaming: Controlling the Female Voice in American Cinema," *The Soundtrack* 2, no. 1 (2009): 63–76.

36. RuPaul and Michelle Visage, "Episode 76: Katya," *RuPaul: What's the Tee with Michelle Visage*, December 14, 2016, produced by The Paragon Collective, podcast, https://soundcloud.com/rupaul/episode-76-katya.

37. Fleeger, *Mismatched Women*, 6.

38. Wayne Koestenbaum, *The Queen's Throat: Opera, Homosexuality, and the Mystery of Desire* (New York: Poseidon Press, 1993), 49.

39. Kohlsdorf, "Policing the Proper Queer Subject," 73, 77.

40. For a more in-depth exploration of this topic, see Jennifer O'Meara, "Identity Politics and Vocal 'Whitewashing' in Celebrity Lip-Syncs," in *Media Ventriloquism: How Audiovisual Technologies Transform the Voice-Body Relationship*, ed. Jaimie Baron, Jennifer Fleeger, and Shannon Wong Lerner (Oxford: Oxford University Press, 2021), 117–132.

41. Judith Peraino uses the term masculine women in reference to Liza Minnelli in *Listening to the Sirens: Musical Technologies of Queer Identity from Homer to Hedwig* (Berkeley: University of California Press, 2006). Due to the extravagance of their aesthetic, Cher and Lady Gaga are often discussed as female drag queens, or "faux queens," including on *RuPaul's Drag Race*.

42. Marcel, "Representing Gender, Race and Realness," 13–14.

43. Merrie Snell, *Lipsynching* (New York: Bloomsbury, 2020), 49. Snell's study also includes some discussion of *RuPaul's Drag Race* as part of a chapter on "Lipsynching to Express," with a focus on how lip syncing in drag is both an expressive identificatory practice and a means of claiming a space for marginalized queer voices. See Snell, *Lipsynching*, 90–94.

44. Roland *Barthes* discusses the androgyne in relation to Balzac's novel *Sarrasine* (1830) in Barthes, *S/Z* (Paris: Editions du Seuil, 1970).

45. Jane Gallop, "Feminist Criticism and the Pleasure of the Text," in *Critical Essays on Roland Barthes*, ed. Diana Knight (New York: G. K. Hall, 2000), 188–201, 198.

46. Joke Dame, "Unveiled Voices: Sexual Difference and the Castrato," in *Queering the Pitch: The New Gay and Lesbian Musicology*, ed. Philip Brett, Gary Thomas, and Elizabeth Wood (New York: Routledge, 2006), 142.

47. Fleeger, *Mismatched Women*, 5.

48. Francesco Adinolfi, *Mondo Exotica: Sounds, Visions, Obsessions of the Cocktail Generation* (Durham, NC: Duke University Press, 2008), 107.

49. Adinolfi, *Mondo Exotica*, 106, 107.

50. For example, see Amy Rose Spiegel, "The 6 Most Glorious Lip Syncs on 'RuPaul's Drag Race' Ever," BuzzFeed, April 23, 2013, www.buzzfeed.com /verymuchso/the-6-most-glorious-lip-syncs-on-rupauls-drag-race-ever?utm_term= .sel7LQNGA#.feebx4pmn. See also Chris Spargo, "RuPaul's Drag Race: 5 Best Lip Syncs Of All Time," New Now Next, January 3, 2013, www.newnownext.com /rupauls-drag-race-best-lip-syncs-of-all-time/01/2013.

51. This particular phrasing of Butler's argument is that of Judith Peraino in *Listening to the Sirens*, 189.

52. Judith Butler, "Imitation and Gender Insubordination," in *The New Social*

Theory Reader: Contemporary Debates, ed. Steven Seidman and Jeffrey C. Alexander (London: Routledge, 2001), 344.

53. For example, as Angela Davis explored in her influential study *Women, Race and Class*, the "alleged benefits of the ideology of femininity did not accrue" to the Black female slave, who was expected to work for as long and as hard as her male counterparts. See Davis, "The Legacy of Slavery: Standards for a New Womanhood," in *Women, Race and Class* (New York: Random House, 1981), 7.

54. Similarly, in Season 9 RuPaul embraced the otherwise mocked lisp of contestant Kim Chi, reminding the Korean American queen, "My empire was built on a lisp."

55. Alicia Brunker, "Kim Kardashian's Voice May Prevent Her from Getting a Job," *Elle*, May 31, 2014, www.elle.com/culture/career-politics/news/a19295/kim-kardashians-voice-may-prevent-her-from-getting-a-job.

56. Mark Liberman, "Male Vocal Fry," Language Log, July 23, 2015, https://languagelog.ldc.upenn.edu/nll/?p=20155.

57. Elvira Mendoza, Nieves Valencia, Juana Muñoz, and Humberto Trujillo, "Differences in Voice Quality between Men and Women: Use of the Long-Term Average Spectrum (LTAS)," *Journal of Voice* 10, no. 1 (1996): 59–60.

58. See John Van Borsel, Joke Janssens, and Marc De Bodt, "Breathiness as a Feminine Voice Characteristic: A Perceptual Approach," *Journal of Voice* 23, no. 3 (2008): 291–294. Technically, the breathiness of women's voices is largely due to a physiological difference: men tend to have a more complete glottal closure, leading to less energy loss at the glottis and thus less "aspiration noise"—the breathy quality. See Helen M. Hanson and Erika S. Chuang, "Glottal Characteristics of Male Speakers: Acoustic Correlates and Comparison with Female Data," *Journal of the Acoustical Society of America* 106, no. 2 (1999): 1064.

59. Newton, *Mother Camp*, 46.

CONCLUSION

1. See Nicholas Zurbrugg and John Giorno, "Poetry, Entertainment, and the Mass Media: An Interview with John Giorno," *Chicago Review* 40, no. 2/3 (1994): 83–101.

2. Amy O'Connor, "It's Official: Tourists Can't Keep Their Hands Off Molly Malone's Boobs," Daily Edge, July 28, 2015, www.dailyedge.ie/molly-malone-tourists-boobs-2240994-Jul2015.

3. "Statue Comes 'Alive Alive O' as Molly Malone Speaks Out," *Fáilte Ireland*, August 15, 2018, www.failteireland.ie/Utility/News-Library/Statue-Comes-'Alive-Alive-O'-as-Molly-Malone-Speak.aspx.

4. Milena Droumeva, "Voice and Gender in Video Games: What Can We Do with Spectrograms," Field Guide: A Media Commons Project, March 9, 2018, http://mediacommons.org/fieldguide/question/how-do-digital-media-and-technologies-allow-closer-critique-and-analysis-sound-what-relat-0.

5. Screenshot, shared with permission by Georgia Brown, email correspondence, December 20, 2019.

6. Other recently published research on the topic of women's voices includes Jilly Boyce Kay's book *Gender, Media and Voice: Communicative Injustice in Public Speech* (London: Palgrave Macmillan, 2020).

7. "German Parents Told to Destroy Cayla Dolls over Hacking Fears," BBC, February 17, 2017, www.bbc.com/news/world-europe-39002142.

8. See, for example, Paola Mattola, "Playing with Amazon Echo: Evil Alexa," YouTube video, May 29, 2016, www.youtube.com/watch?v=o5Qp1jVObiY, and "Beyond Science," "CREEPY and EVIL LAUGHTERS Coming from Amazon's ALEXA?! Device Malfunction or POSSESSED," YouTube video, August 24, 2014, www.youtube.com/watch?v=cozs0nRznNg. Hélène Cixous, "The Laugh of the Medusa," trans. Keith Cohen and Paula Cohen, *Signs* 1, no. 4 (Summer 1976): 875–893.

9. See, for example, "Listening Vessels," Exploratorium, no date, www.exploratorium.edu/exhibits/listening-vessels (accessed August 9, 2020).

About a Boy (Chris Weitz and Paul Weitz, 2002)
À bout de souffle (Jean-Luc Godard, 1960)
Absolutely Fabulous (BBC, 1992–2012)
Adventures of Priscilla, Queen of the Desert, The (Stephan Elliott, 1994)
Adynata (Leslie Thornton, 1983)
All the King's Men (Robert Rossen, 1949)
American Beauty (Sam Mendes, 1999)
American Idol (ABC, 2002–)
American Psycho (Mary Harron, 2000)
Anna May Wong: In Her Own Words (Yunah Hong, 2013)
Anomalisa (Charlie Kaufman and Duke Johnson, 2015)
Apocalypse Now (Francis Ford Coppola, 1979)
Arden's Wake: Tide's Fall (Eugene Chung, 2017)
As the Clouds Roll By (various, 1946)
Audition, The (Daniel Cohen, 2006)
Awkward Black Girl (Issa Rae, YouTube, 2011–2013)
Badlands (Terrence Malick, 1973)
Barbarella (Roger Vadim, 1968)
Battle of Britain (Guy Hamilton, 1969)
Beowulf (Robert Zemeckis, 2007)
Big Short, The (Adam McKay, 2015)
Billabong (Will Hindle, 1968)
Blade Runner (Ridley Scott, 1982)
Blue (Derek Jarman, 1993)
Blue Max, The (John Guillermin, 1966)
BoJack Horseman (Netflix, 2014–2020)
Bonjour Tristesse (Otto Preminger, 1958)
Bringing up Baby (Howard Hawks, 1938)
Busy Tonight (E!, 2018–2019)
Canary Murder Case, The (Malcolm St. Clair and Frank Tuttle, 1929)
Capote (Bennett Miller, 2005)
Chamber Mystery, The (Abraham S. Schomer, 1920)
Clara, Lu 'n' Em (WGN-AM; NBC Blue Network; CBS, 1931–1937)
Clueless (Amy Heckerling, 1995)
Coming Home (Hal Ashby, 1978)
Congress, The (Ari Folman, 2013)

Dark Knight Rises, The (Christopher Nolan, 2012)
Dark Souls II (Bandai Namco Games, 2014)
Daughters of the Dust (Julie Dash, 1996)
Days of Heaven (Terrence Malick, 1978)
Dear Angelica (Saschka Unseld, 2017)
Desperate Housewives (ABC, 2004–2012)
Do I Sound Gay? (David Thorpe, 2014)
Dr. No (Terence Young, 1962)
E! True Hollywood Stories (E!, 1996–)
Ed Wood (Tim Burton, 1994)
Ex Machina (Alex Garland, 2014)
Exorcist, The (William Friedkin, 1973)
Family Guy (Fox, 1999–)
Fight Club (David Fincher, 1999)
(500) Days of Summer (Marc Webb, 2009)
Fleabag (BBC, 2016–2019)
For Your Eyes Only (John Glen, 1981)
Fresh off the Boat (ABC, 2015–2020)
Frida (Julie Taymor, 2002)
Friends (NBC, 1994–2004)
Galaxina (William Sachs, 1980)
Game of Thrones (HBO, 2011–2019)
Gilda (Charles Vidor, 1946)
Gilmore Girls (Warner Brothers, 2000–2007)
Girl, Interrupted (James Mangold, 1999)
Goldfinger (Guy Hamilton, 1964)
Gone Girl (David Fincher, 2014)
Good Girl, The (Miguel Arteta, 2002)
Gossip Girl (The CW, 2007–2012)
Gravity (Alfonso Cuarón, 2013)
Grease (Randal Kleiser, 1978)
Grey Gardens (Albert and David Maysles, 1975)
Her (Spike Jonze, 2013)
High Fidelity (Stephen Frears, 2000)
How to Get Away with Murder (ABC, 2014–2019)
Hunger Games, The (Gary Ross and Francis Lawrence, 2012–2015)
I Married a Witch (René Clair, 1942)
In a World . . . (Lake Bell, 2013)
Ingrid Goes West (Matt Spicer, 2017)
Insecure (HBO, 2016–)
Janis: Little Girl Blue (Amy J. Berg, 2015)

Just Another Girl on the I.R.T. (Leslie Harris, 1992)

La Mama: An American Nun's Life in a Mexican Prison (Jody Hammond, 2010)

Ladies of the Chorus (Phil Karlson, 1948)

Last and First Men (Jóhann Jóhannsson, 2017)

Late Show Starring Joan Rivers, The (Fox Network, 1986–1987)

Lemonade (HBO, 2016)

Letter from America (BBC, 1946–2004)

Letter to Jane (Jean-Luc Godard and Jean-Pierre Gorin, 1972)

Lobster, The (Yorgas Lanthimos, 2015)

Lucy (Luc Besson, 2014)

Made in U.S.A. (Jean-Luc Godard, 1966)

Mean Girls (Mark Waters, 2004)

Mermaids (Richard Benjamin, 1990)

Metropolis (Fritz Lang, 1927)

Mike Wallace Interview, The (ABC, 1957–1958)

Mindy Project, The (Fox; Hulu, 2012–2017)

Mommie Dearest (Frank Perry, 1981)

Moonraker (Lewis Gilbert, 1979)

Mulholland Drive (David Lynch, 2001)

News from Home (Chantal Akerman, 1978)

Nitrate Kisses (Barbara Hammer, 1992)

Nora Prentiss (Richard Sherman, 1947)

Notting Hill (Roger Michell, 1999)

One Million Years B.C. (Don Chaffey, 1965)

One Women, One Vote (Public Broadcasting System, 1995)

Opposite of Sex, The (Don Roos, 1998)

Paris Is Burning (Jennie Livingston, 1990)

Pendulum (George Schaefer, 1969)

Phil Donahue Show, The (WLWD; NBC, 1970–1996)

Piano, The (Jane Campion, 1993)

Pierrot le Fou (Jean-Luc Godard, 1965)

Pocahontas (Mike Gabriel and Eric Goldberg, 1995)

Precious: Based on the Novel "Push" by Sapphire (Lee Daniels, 2009)

Prime of Miss Jean Brodie, The (Ronald Neame, 1969)

Prix de Beauté (Augusto Genina, 1930)

Punk Singer, The (Sini Anderson, 2013)

Regarding Susan Sontag (Nancy Kates, 2014)

Restore the Earth (Luke Bradford, 2010)

RuPaul's Drag Race (Logo TV, 2009–2016; VH1 2017–)

Saint Joan (Otto Preminger, 1957)

Scandals and Mysteries (E!, 1998–2001)

School of the American Assassins (Robert Richter, 1994)

Secretary (Steven Shainberg, 2002)

Sex and the City (HBO, 1998–2004)

She (Robert Day, 1964)

Shine on Harvest Moon (David Butler, 1944)

Shirin (Abbas Kiarostami, 2008)

Show Boat (George Sidney, 1951)

S1m0ne (Andrew Niccol, 2002)

Simpsons, The (Fox, 1989–)

Singin' in the Rain (Gene Kelly and Stanley Donen, 1952)

Sois Belle et Tais-toi / Be Pretty but Shut Up (Delphine Seyrig, 1981)

Song of the South (Wilfred Jackson, 1946)

Soul Calibur (Bandai Namco Entertainment, 1995–2018)

Stella Dallas (Lux Radio Theater, 1937)

Stella Dallas (King Vidor 1947)

Stepford Wives, The (Bryan Forbes, 1975)

Suitcase of Love and Shame (Jane Gillooly, 2013)

Sunset Boulevard (Billy Wilder, 1950)

Teknolust (Lynn Hershman Leeson, 2002)

Thelma and Louise (Ridley Scott, 1991)

Tonight Show Starring Jimmy Fallon, The (NBC, 2014–)

Tout Va Bien / All's Well (Jean-Luc Godard and Jean-Pierre Gorin, 1972)

2001: A Space Odyssey (Stanley Kubrick, 1968)

Under the Skin (Jonathan Glazer, 2010)

Vertigo (Alfred Hitchcock, 1958)

Vogue by the Decade (Condé Nast, 2017)

Voice, The (NBC, 2011–)

What's My Line? (CBS, 1950–1967)

When Björk Met Attenborough (Louise Hooper, 2013)

Wigstock: The Movie (Barry Shils, 1995)

Will & Grace (NBC, 1998–2020)

Wolf of Wall Street, The (Martin Scorsese, 2013)

"About 2 Dope Queens." WNYC Studios, no date. www.wnycstudios.org /podcasts/dopequeens/about.

Adichie, Chimamanda Ngozi. *We Should All Be Feminists*. London: Harper Collins, 2014.

Adinolfi, Francesco. *Mondo Exotica: Sounds, Visions, Obsessions of the Cocktail Generation*. Durham, NC: Duke University Press, 2008.

Alexander, Julia. "HBO Still Doesn't Like Trump Using Game of Thrones Memes to Promote Himself." The Verge, April 18, 2019. www.theverge.com/2019/4/18 /18485473/mueller-report-donald-trump-meme-game-of-thrones-got-season -8-final-hbo-statement.

Altman, Rick. "Moving Lips: Cinema as Ventriloquism." *Yale French Studies* 60 (1980): 67–79.

Andersen, Joceline. "Now You've Got the Shiveries: Affect, Intimacy, and the ASMR Whisper Community." *Television and New Media* 16, no. 8 (December 2015): 683–700.

Anthony, Libby. "Dragging with an Accent: Linguistic Stereotypes, Language Barriers and Translingualism." In *The Makeup of RuPaul's Drag Race: Essays on the Queen of Reality Shows*, ed. Jim Daems, 49–66. Jefferson, NC: McFarland, 2014.

Aristotle. *De Anima*. c. 350 BC.

Ascheid, Antje. "Speaking Tongues: Voice Dubbing in the Cinema as Cultural Ventriloquism." *Velvet Light Trap* 40 (Fall 1997): 31–41.

Ausiello, Michael. "It's Here: Lauren Graham's Final Gilmore Girls Interview." *TV Guide*, May 7, 2007. www.tvguide.com/news/lauren-grahams-final-8429.

Baker, Natalie. "'2 Dope Queens' Is the Hands-Down Funniest Podcast I've Ever Heard." *Bitch Media*, April 21, 2016. www.bitchmedia.org/article/2-dope -queens-hands-down-funniest-podcast-ive-ever-heard.

Baker, Roger. *Drag: A History of Female Impersonation in the Performing Arts*. New York: NYU Press, 1994.

Balcerzak, Scott. "Andy Serkis as Actor, Body and Gorilla: Motion Capture and the Presence of Performance." In *Cinephilia in the Age of Digital Reproduction: Film, Pleasure and Digital Culture*, ed. Jason Sperb and Scott Balcerzak, 195–214. London: Wallflower, 2009.

Banet-Weiser, Sarah. *Authentic™: The Politics of Ambivalence in a Brand Culture*. New York: NYU Press, 2012.

———. *Empowered: Popular Feminism and Popular Misogyny*. Durham, NC: Duke University Press, 2018.

Barberá, Pablo, John T. Jost, Jonathan Nagler, Joshua A. Tucker, and Richard Bonneau. "Tweeting from Left to Right: Is Online Political Communication More

Than an Echo Chamber?" *Psychological Science* 26, no. 10 (October 2015): 1531–1542.

Barnett, C. "Scarlett Johansson Reads the "Sexy Bible" with SNL's Mike O'Brien." *World Religion News*, October 29, 2015. www.worldreligionnews.com/religion -news/christianity/the-bible-just-got-sexy-scarlett-johansson-reads-the-bible -with-snls-mike-obrien.

Barrett, Ciara. "'Formation' of the Female Author in the Hip Hop Visual Album: Beyoncé and FKA Twigs." *The Soundtrack* 9, no. 1/2 (2016): 41–57.

Barry, Richard. "This Sounds Absolutely Fabulous." *Independent*, January 29, 1996. www.independent.co.uk/life-style/this-sounds-absolutely-fabulous -1326423.html.

Barthes, Roland. "The Grain of the Voice." In *Music, Image, Text*, trans. Stephen Heath, 179–190. New York: Hill and Wang, 1977.

———. *S/Z.* Paris: Editions du Seuil, 1970.

Bassett, Jordan. "Cher from 'Clueless' Nailed the Refugee Debate in One Minute." NME, February 6, 2017. www.nme.com/blogs/the-movies-blog/1968370 -1968370.

Bastow, Clem. "Fleabag's Feminist Rethinking of Tired Screenwriting Tools." *The Conversation*, July 31, 2019. https://theconversation.com/fleabags-feminist -rethinking-of-tired-screenwriting-tools-121104.

Bechdel, Alison. "The Bechdel Test." In *Dykes to Watch Out For*. Ann Arbor, MI: Firebrand Books, 1986.

Beck, Jay. "William Friedkin's *The Exorcist* and the Proprietary Nature of Sound." *Cinephile* 6, no. 1 (Spring 2010). www.cinephile.ca/files/vol6no1-complete -withbleed.pdf.

Beck, Julie. "The Linguistics of the 'YouTube' Voice." *The Atlantic*, December 7, 2015. www.theatlantic.com/technology/archive/2015/12/the-linguistics-of -youtube-voice/418962.

Beckman, Jamie. "10 Awesome Celebrity-Narrated Audio Tours." Budget Travel, January 27, 2015. www.budgettravel.com/article/10-awesome-celebrity -narrated-audio-tours_51830.

Bell, Duncan. "Oculus Rift's Dear Angelica: Is This Short Animated Film the Saddest Use of VR Ever?" T3, January 20, 2017. www.t3.com/news/oculus-rifts -dear-angelica-is-this-short-film-the-saddest-use-of-vr-ever.

Bennett, Tony. "Text and Social Process: The Case of James Bond." *Screen Education* 41 (1982): 3–14.

Bergan, Ronald. "Mercedes McCambridge: Big-Screen Actor Whose Tough Personality—and Voice—Matched Her Roles." *Guardian*, March 19, 2004. www .theguardian.com/news/2004/mar/19/guardianobituaries.film.

Bever, Lindsey. "Trump's 'Game of Thrones'–Style Poster Makes Cryptic Cameo at Cabinet Meeting." *Washington Post*, January 2, 2019. www.washingtonpost .com/politics/2019/01/02/trumps-game-thrones-style-poster-makes-cryptic -cameo-cabinet-meeting.

Blottner, Gene. *Columbia Noir: A Complete Filmography, 1940–1962.* Jefferson, NC: McFarland, 2015.

Borrelli-Persson, Laird. "Sarah Jessica Parker Narrates the History of '70s Fashion

in Vogue." Vogue, June 5, 2017. www.vogue.com/article/125-anniversary-video
-seventies-fashion-history-sarah-jessica-parker.

Bosworth, Patricia. *Jane Fonda: The Private Life of a Public Woman.* Boston:
Houghton Mifflin Harcourt, 2011.

Brooks, Louise. *Lulu in Hollywood.* New York: Knopf, 1982.

Brunker, Alicia. "Kim Kardashian's Voice May Prevent Her from Getting a Job."
Elle, May 31, 2014. www.elle.com/culture/career-politics/news/a19295/kim
-kardashians-voice-may-prevent-her-from-getting-a-job.

Buchanan, Kyle. "Emma Stone, Jennifer Lawrence, and Scarlett Johansson Have an
Older-Man Problem." Vulture, June 1, 2015. www.vulture.com/2015/05/emma
-jlaw-and-scarletts-older-man-problem.html.

Burnett, Allison. "Fame! Ain't It a Bitch: Confessions of a Reformed Gossip Columnist." *Variety,* March 6, 2001. https://variety.com/2001/more/reviews/fame
-ain-t-it-a-bitch-confessions-of-areformed-gossip-columnist-1117797992.

Butler, Judith. "Imitation and Gender Insubordination." In *The New Social Theory
Reader: Contemporary Debates*, ed. Steven Seidman and Jeffrey C. Alexander,
333–345. London: Routledge, 2001.

———. "Subversive Bodily Acts." In *Gender Trouble: Feminism and the Subversion
of Identity*, 79–141. London: Routledge, 1990.

Caplan-Bricker, Nora. "Um, No, to Ummo and All Speech 'Improvement'
Apps." Slate, May 10, 2016. https://slate.com/human-interest/2016/05/speech
-improvement-apps-like-ummo-are-sexist-and-support-inequality.html.

Carson, Erin. "NASA Shows the World Its 20-Year Virtual Reality Experiment to
Train Astronauts: The Inside Story." Tech Republic, September 17, 2017. www
.techrepublic.com/article/nasa-shows-the-world-its-20-year-vr-experiment-to
-train-astronauts.

Chan, Mimi. "Sifu Mimi Chan." www.sifumimichan.com/sifu-mimi-chan.

Chandra, Jessica. "Sweden Has a 'Mansplaining' Hotline So People Can Complain
about Their Condescending Male Colleagues." *Elle Australia*, November 18,
2016. www.elle.com.au/news/sweden-mansplaining-hotline-6761.

Chatfield, Tom. *Activism or Slactivism? The Future of Digital Politics.* London:
Vintage Digital, 2011.

Chen, Nick. "Peter Strickland Discusses *In Fabric*, His New Film about a Killer
Red Dress." *Dazed Digital*, June 24, 2019. www.dazeddigital.com/film-tv
/article/44975/1/peter-strickland-in-fabric-interview-bjork-fashion-asmr.

———. "Your Guide to Movies That Also Work as ASMR." *Dazed Digital*, June
25, 2019. www.dazeddigital.com/film-tv/article/45016/1/your-guide-to-the-best
-asmr-in-films.

Chernoff, Carolyn. "Of Women and Queens: Gendered Realities and Re-education
in RuPaul's Drag Empire." In *The Makeup of RuPaul's Drag Race: Essays on
the Queen of Reality Shows*, ed. Jim Daems, 148–167. Jefferson, NC: McFarland, 2014.

Chiarini, Alessandra. "'Feeling-Images': Montage, Body and Historical Memory in
Barbara Hammer's Nitrate Kisses." *Feminist Media Histories* 2, no. 3 (Summer
2016): 90–101.

Chion, Michel. *Film, a Sound Art.* New York: Columbia University Press, 2009.

——. *The Voice in Cinema*, trans. Claudia Gorbman. New York: Columbia University Press, 1999.

Cixous, Hélène. "The Laugh of the Medusa," trans. Keith Cohen and Paula Cohen. *Signs* 1, no. 4 (Summer 1976): 875–893.

Clay, Joanna. "Actress Anna Faris Brings Her Podcast Skills to the Front of the Class." *USC News*, October 16, 2017. https://news.usc.edu/129883/actress-anna-faris-brings-her-podcast-skills-to-the-front-of-the-class.

Collie, Hazel, and Gemma Commane. "'Assume the Position: Two Queens Stand before Me': RuPaul as Ultimate Queen." *Celebrity Studies* 11, no. 4 (2020): 402–416.

Connor, Steven. *Dumbstruck: A Cultural History of Ventriloquism*. Oxford: Oxford University Press, 2000.

Cooper Albright, Ann. *Traces of Light: Absence and Presence in the Work of Loïe Fuller*. Middletown, CT: Wesleyan University Press, 2007.

Cornish, Audie, and Mary Louise Kelly. "Archivists Say Voice Discovered in Mexico's National Library May Be Frida Kahlo." NPR, June 14, 2019, podcast transcript from *All Things Considered*. www.npr.org/2019/06/14/732863516/archivists-say-voice-discovered-in-mexicos-national-library-may-be-frida-kahlo-s.

Cramer, Florian. "Proto-Post-Fascism?" (panel). The White West: The Resurgence of Fascism as Cultural Force, Paris, May 9, 2018. www.lacolonie.paris/agenda/the-white- west-la-resurgence-du-fascisme-comme-force-culturelle.

Croce Dee, Camille. "Guide to the Katharine Hepburn Papers, ca. 1854–1997 and Undated (Bulk Dates 1928–1994)." New York Public Library, December 2007. www.nypl.org/sites/default/files/archivalcollections/pdf/thehepbu.pdf.

Cross, Calen. "History Podcasts Made by Women." Bello Collective, October 6, 2016. https://bellocollective.com/history-podcasts-made-by-women-87dc6dbd980b.

Dall'Asta, Monica, and Alessandra Chiarini. "Editors Introduction, Found Footage: Women without a Movie Camera." *Feminist Media Histories* 2, no. 3 (Summer 2016): 1–10.

Dame, Joke. "Unveiled Voices: Sexual Difference and the Castrato." In *Queering the Pitch: The New Gay and Lesbian Musicology*, ed. Philip Brett, Gary Thomas, and Elizabeth Wood, 139–153. New York: Routledge, 1994.

Davis, Angela. *Women, Race and Class*. New York: Random House, 1981.

Desjardins, Mary R. *Recycled Stars: Female Film Stardom in the Age of Television and Video*. Durham, NC: Duke University Press, 2015.

de Villiers, Nicholas. "RuPaul's Drag Race as Meta-Reality Television." *Jump Cut: A Review of Contemporary Media* 54 (Fall 2012). www.ejumpcut.org/archive/jc54.2012/deVilRuPaul/text.html.

Dickson, E. J. "New 'You Must Remember This' Season Explores History of Racist Disney Cartoon." *Rolling Stone*, October 22, 2019. www.rollingstone.com/culture/culture-features/you-must-remember-this-song-of-the-south-karina-longworth-interview-901814.

Diffrient, David Scott, and David Lavery, eds. *Screwball Television: Critical Perspectives on Gilmore Girls*. Syracuse, NY: Syracuse University Press, 2010.

Dowd, A. A. "Charlie Kaufman and Duke Johnson on the Soulful Stop-Motion of *Anomalisa*." AV Club, December 14, 2015. https://film.avclub.com/charlie -kaufman-and-duke-johnson-on-the-soulful-stop-mo-1798287269.

Downey, Sam. "Can You Hear the Ghost of Mariah Carey in This Bizarre Auditory Illusion?" Nine.com, no date. www.nine.com.au/entertainment/viral/mariah -carey-illusion/3edf8190-8337-42e2-9525-d7e2f685dc4a.

Droumeva, Milena. "Voice and Gender in Video Games: What Can We Do with Spectrograms." Field Guide: A Media Commons Project, March 9, 2018. http:// mediacommons.org/fieldguide/question/how-do-digital-media-andtechnologies -allow-closer-critique-and-analysis-sound-what-relat-0.

Droumeva, Milena, Kaeleigh Evans, Nesan Furtado, and Renita Bangert. "It Gets Worse . . . The Female Voice in Video Games." *First Person Scholar*, November 1, 2017. www.firstpersonscholar.com/it-gets-worse.

Duffy, Brooke Erin, and Urszula Pruchniewska. "Gender and Self-Enterprise in the Social Media Age: A Digital Double Bind." *Information, Communication and Society* 20, no. 6 (2017): 843–859.

Dwyer, Tessa. "Fansubbing and Abuse: Anime and Beyond." In *Speaking in Subtitles: Revaluing Screen Translation*, 135–163. Edinburgh: Edinburgh University Press, 2017.

———. "Mute, Dumb, Dubbed: Lulu's Silent Talkies." In *Politics, Policy and Power in Translation History*, ed. Lieven D'hulst, Carol O'Sullivan, and Michael Schreiber, 157–186. Berlin: Frank and Timme, 2016.

Echternach, Matthias, Fabian Burk, Michael Burumy, Louisa Traser, and Bernhard Richter. "Morphometric Differences of Vocal Tract Articulators in Different Loudness Conditions in Singing." *PLOS One* 11, no. 4 (2016).

Edward, Mark, and Stephen Farrier, eds. *Contemporary Drag Practices and Performers: Drag in a Changing Scene*, vol. 1. London: Bloomsbury, 2020.

Elsaesser, Thomas. "Trapped in Amber: The New Materialities of Memory." *Framework: The Journal of Cinema and Media* 60, no. 1 (Spring 2019): 26–41.

Export, Valie. "Expanded Cinema: Expanded Reality." In *Expanded Cinema: Art, Performance, Film*, ed. A. L. Rees, Duncan White, Steven Ball, and David Curtis, 297–298. London: Tate Publishing, 2011.

Fadeyev, Vitaliy, and Carl Haber. "Reconstruction of Mechanically Recorded Sound by Image Processing." Lawrence Berkeley National Library Report 51983, March 26, 2003. www-cdf.lbl.gov/~av/JAES-paper-LBNL.pdf.

Faircloth, Kelly. "A Chat with the Creator of Can't-Miss Classic Hollywood Podcast You Must Remember This." Jezebel, June 21, 2016. https://pictorial.jezebel .com/a-chat-with-the-creator-ofcant-miss-classic-hollywood-1782364338.

Fellner, Chris. *The Encyclopedia of Hammer Films*. London: Rowman and Littlefield, 2018.

Fine, David J., and Emily Shreve. "The Prime of Miss RuPaul Charles: Allusion, Betrayal and Charismatic Pedagogy." In *The Makeup of RuPaul's Drag Race*, ed. Jim Daems, 168–187. Jefferson, NC: McFarland, 2014.

Flaig, Paul. "Yesterday's Hadaly: On Voicing a Feminist Media Archaelogy." *Camera Obscura* 33, no. 2 (2018): 104–137.

Fleeger, Jennifer. *Mismatched Women: The Siren's Song through the Machine*. New York: Oxford University Press, 2014.

———. "When Robots Speak on Screen: Imagining the Cinemechanical Ideal." In *The Oxford Handbook of Voice Studies*, ed. Nina Eidsheim and Katherine Meizel, 419–436. Oxford: Oxford University Press, 2019.

Fonda, Jane. "Television." *New York Times*, October 31, 1971. www.nytimes.com /1971/10/31/archives/jane-fonda-i-want-to-work-with-women.html.

Freud, Sigmund. "Analysis Terminable and Interminable." *International Journal of Psycho-Analysis* 18 (1937): 373–405.

Frith, Simon. *Performing Rites: On the Value of Popular Music*. Oxford: Oxford University Press, 1996.

Frizzell, Nell. "You Must Remember This: The Woman Spilling Hollywood Secrets." *Guardian*, July 5, 2016. www.theguardian.com/tv-and-radio/2016 /jul/05/you-must-rememberthis-the-woman-spilling-hollywood-secrets-marilyn -monroe-charlie-chaplin.

Gallop, Jane. "Feminist Criticism and the Pleasure of the Text." In *Critical Essays on Roland Barthes*, ed. Diana Knight, 188–201. New York: G. K. Hall, 2000.

Garreau, Joel. *Radical Evolution: The Promise and Peril of Enhancing Our Minds, Our Bodies—and What It Means to Be Human*. New York: Doubleday, 2005.

Garrison, Ednie Kaeh. "U.S. Feminism—Grrrl Style! Youth (Sub)Cultures and the Technologics of the Third Wave." In *No Permanent Waves: Recasting Histories of US Feminism*, ed. Nancy A. Hewitt, 141–170. Piscataway, NJ: Rutgers University Press, 2010.

Gaudio, Rudolf P. "Sounding Gay: Pitch Properties in the Speech of Gay and Straight Men." *American Speech* 69, no. 1 (Spring 1994): 30–57.

Gault, Matthew. "After 20 Minutes of Listening, New Adobe Tool Can Make You Say Anything." *Vice*, November 5, 2016. www.vice.com/en_us/article/jpgkxp /after-20-minutes-of-listening-new-adobe-tool-can-make-you-say-anything.

Geena Davis Institute on Gender in Media. "About Us." https://seejane.org/about -us/.

Gilbert, Sophie. "Karina Longworth Makes Old Hollywood New." *The Atlantic*, November 14, 2018. www.theatlantic.com/entertainment/archive/2018/11 /karina-longworth-old-hollywoods-most-vital-historian/575728.

Glaser, April. "The Scarlett Johansson Bot Is the Robotic Future of Objectifying Women." *Wired*, April 4, 2016. www.wired.com/2016/04/the-scarlett -johansson-bot-signals-some-icky-things-about-our-future.

Graham, Allison. *Framing the South: Hollywood, Television and Race during the Civil Rights Struggle*. Baltimore: John Hopkins University Press, 2001.

Graham, Lauren. *Talking as Fast as I Can: From Gilmore Girls to Gilmore Girls*. London: Virago Press, 2016.

Graves, Lucia, and Sam Morris. "The Trump Allegations." *Guardian*, November 29, 2017. www.theguardian.com/us-news/ng-interactive/2017/nov/30/donald -trump-sexual-misconduct-allegations-full-list.

Greene, Liz. "Speaking, Singing, Screaming: Controlling the Female Voice in American Cinema." *The Soundtrack* 2, no. 1 (2009): 63–76.

Griggs, Brandon. "Why Computer Voices Are Mostly Female." CNN, October 21, 2011. https://edition.cnn.com/2011/10/21/tech/innovation/female-computer-voices/index.html.

Guernsey, Lisa. "The Desktop That Does Elvis." *New York Times*, August 9, 2001. www.nytimes.com/2001/08/09/technology/the-desktop-that-does-elvis.html.

Guerrasio, Jason. "An Actor Explains How He Spent Years Voicing Hundreds of Characters in the Trippy Charlie Kaufman Movie, 'Anomalisa,'" Business Insider, March 15, 2016. www.businessinsider.com/tom-noonan-voicing-anomalisa-characters-2016-3?r=US&IR=T.

Gupta, Reena. "When Actors Are Hoarse—Tips to Preserve Your Voice." Osborne Head and Neck Institute, no date. www.ohniww.org/lindsay-lohan-emma-stone-voice-preservation.

Haasch, Palmer. "Calls to 'Arrest the Cops Who Killed Breonna Taylor' Have Been Turned into an Online Meme That Some Say Has Gone Too Far." Business Insider, June 26, 2020. www.insider.com/arrest-the-cops-who-killed-breonna-taylor-memes-stop-2020-6.

Hagen, Ray, and Laura Wagner, eds. *Killer Tomatoes: Fifteen Tough Film Dames*. Jefferson NC: McFarland, 2004.

Hagman, Hampus. "The Digital Gesture: Rediscovering Cinematic Movement through GIFs." *Refractory: A Journal of Entertainment Media* 21 (December 2012). http://refractory.unimelb.edu.au/2012/12/29/hagman/.

Halperin, David. *How to Be Gay*. Cambridge, MA: Harvard University Press, 2012.

Hammer, Barbara. *Hammer! Making Movies Out of Sex and Life*. New York: Feminist Press, 2010.

Hancock, Adrienne B., Julianne Krissinger, and Kelly Owen. "Voice Perceptions and Quality of Life of Transgender People." *Journal of Voice* 25, no. 5 (2011): 553–558.

Hanson, Helen M., and Erika S. Chuang. "Glottal Characteristics of Male Speakers: Acoustic Correlates and Comparison with Female Data." *Journal of the Acoustical Society of America* 106, no. 2 (1999): 1064–1077.

Hargrove, Channing. "Reminder: We Should All Be Mirandas—and Wear This T-Shirt." Refinery29, September 5, 2017. www.refinery29.com/2017/09/170977/sex-and-the-city-miranda-shirt.

Harrod, Horatia. "How Do You Teach a Computer to Speak Like Scarlett Johansson?" *Telegraph*, February 15, 2014. www.telegraph.co.uk/culture/film/10624631/How-do-you-teach-a-computer-to-speak-like-Scarlett-Johansson.html.

Haslem, Wendy. *From Méliès to New Media: Spectral Projections*. Bristol: Intellect, 2019.

"Hear Scarlett Johansson Read Sexy Bible Verses on New Mike O'Brien Track." *Rolling Stone*, October 28, 2015. www.rollingstone.com/music/music-news/hear-scarlett-johansson-read-sexy-bible-verses-on-new-mike-obrien-track-64070.

Henahan, Donal. "Opera: Computer Love." *New York Times*, April 9, 1975. www
.nytimes.com/1975/04/09/archives/opera-computer-love.html.

Hepburn, Katharine. "Voice." In *Me: Stories of My Life*, 359–371. New York:
Ballantine Books, 1991.

Herzog, Kenny. "Trump Plagiarized Bane in Inauguration Speech." *Death and
Taxes*, January 20, 2017. www.deathandtaxesmag.com/315851/trump-bane
-plagiarized-inauguration-speech.

Hess, Amanda, and Shane O'Neill. "The White Internet's Love Affair with Digital
Blackface." *New York Times*, December 22, 2017. www.nytimes.com/video
/arts/100000005615988/the-white-internets-love-affair-with-digital-blackface
.html.

Hilbert, Jeffrey. "The Politics of Drag." In *Out in Culture: Gay, Lesbian and
Queer Essays on Popular Culture*, ed. Cory Creekmur and Alexander Doty,
463–469. London: Cassell, 1995.

Hillsberg, Alex, and David Adelman. "Most Popular Social Media Sites Review:
Why Women Are the Real Power behind the Huge Success of Pinterest and
Tumblr." Finances Online, March 2014. https://reviews.financesonline.com
/most-popular-social-media-sites-review.

Hilmes, Michele. "The Disembodied Women." In *Radio Voices: American Broadcasting, 1922–1952*, 130–150. Minneapolis: University of Minnesota Press,
1997.

Hyland Wang, Jennifer. "Producing a Radio Housewife: Clara, Lu 'n' Em, Gendered Labor, and the Early Days of Radio." *Feminist Media Histories* 4, no. 1
(Winter 2018): 58–83.

Jackson, Lauren Michele. "We Need to Talk about Digital Blackface in Reaction GIFs." *Teen Vogue*, August 2, 2017. www.teenvogue.com/story/digital
-blackface-reaction-gifs.

Jarman-Ivens, Freya. *Queer Voices: Technologies, Vocalities, and the Musical Flaw*.
New York: Palgrave Macmillan, 2011.

Jenkins, Henry. *Convergence Culture: Where Old and New Media Collide*. New
York: NYU Press, 2006.

——. *Textual Poachers: Television Fans and Participatory Culture*. New York:
Routledge, 1992.

Jenkins, Henry, Sam Ford, and Joshua Green. *Spreadable Media: Creating Value
and Meaning in a Networked Culture*. New York: NYU Press, 2013.

Jones, Isabel. "We Need to Talk about Sarah Jessica Parker's Instagram." *In Style*,
April 12, 2019. www.instyle.com/news/sarah-jessica-parker-instagram-weird.

Jones, Kevin L. "Karina Longworth Talks *You Must Remember This* before Going
on Hiatus." KQED, September 13, 2016. www.kqed.org/arts/12061768/karina
-longworth-talks-youmust-remember-this-before-going-on-hiatus.

Kahlo, Frida. "Portrait of Diego." In the exhibition catalog for *Diego Rivera, 50
Years of Artistic Work*, Palace of Fine Arts, Mexico City, 1949.

Kay, Jilly Boyce. *Gender, Media and Voice: Communicative Injustice Public
Speech*. London: Palgrave Macmillan, 2020.

Keller, Jessalynn Marie. "Virtual Feminisms: Girls' Blogging Communities, Feminist Activism, and Participatory Politics." *Information, Communication and Society* 15, no. 3 (2012): 429–447.

Kelly, Debra. "This Is Why Voice Assistants Are All Female." *Grunge*, no date. www.grunge.com/136184/this-is-why-voice-assistants-are-all-female.

Kim, Jihoon. *Between Film, Video, and the Digital: Hybrid Moving Images in the Post-Media Age.* New York: Bloomsbury, 2018.

Kindon, Frances, and Alistair McGeorge. "Age-Defying Jane Fonda, 79, Shows Off Youthful Figure as She Owns the Catwalk at Paris Fashion Week." *The Mirror*, October 1, 2017. www.mirror.co.uk/3am/celebrity-news/jane-fonda-defies-age-loreal-11269983.

Kirby, Jen. "Why You Hear 'Laurel' or 'Yanny' in That Viral Audio Clip, Explained." Vox, May 16, 2018. www.vox.com/2018/5/16/17358774/yanny-laurel-explained.

Klinger, Barbara. "Film History Terminable and Interminable: Recovering the Past in Reception Studies." *Screen* 38, no. 2 (Summer 1997): 107–128.

Koestenbaum, Wayne. "The Queen's Throat: (Homo)sexuality and the Art of Singing." In *Inside/Out: Lesbian Theories, Gay Theories*, ed. Diana Fuss, 205–234. London: Routledge, 1991.

Kohlsdorf, Kai. "Policing the Proper Queer Subject: *RuPaul's Drag Race* in the Neoliberal 'Post' Moment." In *The Makeup of RuPaul's Drag Race: Essays on the Queen of Reality Shows*, ed. Jim Daems, 67–87. Jefferson, NC: McFarland, 2014.

Kornhaber, Donna. "From Posthuman to Postcinema: Crises of Subjecthood and Representation in *Her.*" *Cinema Journal* 56, no. 4 (2017): 3–25.

Koufman, James A., and P. David Blalock, "Vocal Fatigue and Dysphonia in the Professional Voice User: Bogart-Bacall Syndrome." *The Laryngoscope* 98, no. 5 (1988): 493–498.

Kozloff, Sarah. "About a Clueless Girl and Boy: Voice-Over in Romantic Comedy Today." *Cinephile* 8, no. 1 (2012): 5–13.

——. *Invisible Storytellers: Voice-Over Narration in American Fiction Film.* Berkeley: University of California Press, 1988.

——. *Overhearing Film Dialogue.* Berkeley: University of California Press, 2000.

Kreps, Daniel. "See Cat Power React to Emotional Janis Joplin Letters in Doc Clip." *Rolling Stone*, April 21, 2016. www.rollingstone.com/music/music-news/see-cat-power-react-to-emotional-janis-joplin-letters-in-doc-clip-200697.

Krutnik, Frank. *In a Lonely Street: Film Noir, Genre, Masculinity.* London: Routledge, 2006.

Lacan, Jacques. "The Mirror Stage as Formative of the Function of the I as Revealed in Psychoanalytic Experience." In *Écrits: A Selection*, trans. Alan Sheridan 1–7. London: Tavistock, 1977.

Lackmann, Ron. *Mercedes McCambridge: A Biography and Filmography.* Jefferson, NC: McFarland, 2005.

Lane, Frederick S. "Phone Sex: The First National Pornography Network." In *Obscene Profits: Entrepreneurs of Pornography in the Cyber Age, 149–182. New York: Routledge, 2001.

Lang, Brent. "'You Must Remember This' Podcast Brings Showbiz History to Life." Variety, March 3, 2016. https://variety.com/2016/digital/news/you-must-remember-this-podcast-1201721155.

Lawrence, Amy. Echo and Narcissus: Women's Voices in Classical Hollywood Cinema. Berkeley: University of California Press, 1991.

Lem, Stanisław. The Futurological Congress. New York: Seabury Press, 1974.

Levine, Nick. "The #WokeCharlotte Meme Is Rewriting Sex and the City's Problematic Past." Refinery29, December 23, 2017. www.refinery29.com/en-us/2017/12/186231/woke-charlotte-meme-sex-city.

Lévy, Pierre. Collective Intelligence: Mankind's Emerging World in Cyberspace. New York: Plenum Trade, 1997.

Liberman, Mark. "Male Vocal Fry." Language Log, July 23, 2015. https://languagelog.ldc.upenn.edu/nll/?p=20155.

Lomas, Natasha. "Lyrebird Is a Voice Mimic for the Fake News Era." TechCrunch, April 25, 2017. http://tcrn.ch/2osyU9H.

Longworth, Karina. "Become a You Must Remember This Patron, Won't You?" You Must Remember This, June 13, 2019. www.youmustrememberthispodcast.com/episodes/2019/6/13/become-a-you-must-rememberthis-patron-wont-you.

——. "FAQ." You Must Remember This, no date. www.youmustrememberthispodcast.com/faq.

——. "Peg Entwistle (Dead Blondes Episode 1)." You Must Remember This, January 30, 2017. Show notes. www.youmustrememberthispodcast.com/episodes/2017/1/26/peg-entwistle-dead-blondesepisode-1?rq=dead%20blondes.

Macallan, Helen, and Andrew Plain. "Filmic Voices." In VØ1CE: Vocal Aesthetics in Digital Arts and Media, ed. Norie Neumark, Ross Gibson, and Theo van Leeuwen, 243–266. Cambridge, MA: MIT Press, 2010.

Macherey, Pierre. A Theory of Literary Production. London: Routledge and Kegan Paul, 1978.

Madsen, Virginia, and John Potts. "Voice-Cast: The Distribution of the Voice via Podcasting." In VØ1CE: Vocal Aesthetics in Digital Arts and Media, ed. Norie Neumark, Ross Gibson, and Theo van Leeuwen, 33–59. Cambridge, MA: MIT Press.

"The Making of The Congress Using Toon Boom Harmony." Toon Boom, no date. www.toonboom.com/community/success-stories/ari-folman-yoni-goodman.

Maloney, Alli. "#PussyGrabsBack Creators Amanda Duarte and Jessica Bennett Interview." Teen Vogue, October 21, 2016. www.teenvogue.com/story/pussygrabsback-creators-amanda-duarte-jessica-bennett-interview.

Maltby, Richard. "New Cinema Histories." In Explorations in New Cinema History: Approaches and Case Studies, ed. Richard Maltby, Daniel Biltereyst, and Philippe Meers, 1–40. Chichester, UK: Wiley-Blackwell, 2011.

Marcel, Mary. "Representing Gender, Race and Realness: The Television World of America's Next Drag Superstars." In The Makeup of RuPaul's Drag Race:

Essays on the Queen of Reality Shows, ed. Jim Daems, 13–30. Jefferson, NC: McFarland, 2014.

Marcus, Ralph. "The Apocryphal Story of Katharine Hepburn's Metallic Voice." In Katharine Hepburn Papers, folder 629. Los Angeles: Margaret Herrick Library, Academy of Motion Picture Arts and Sciences.

Marshall, Alex, and Mark A. Walsh. "You Know Frida Kahlo's Face. Now You Can (Probably) Hear Her Voice." *New York Times*, June 13, 2019. www .nytimes.com/2019/06/13/arts/design/frida-kahlo-voice.html.

Massood, Paula J. "Street Girls with No Future: Black Women Coming of Age in the City." In *Contemporary Black American Cinema: Race, Gender and Sexuality at the Movies*, ed. Mia Mask, 232–250. New York: Routledge, 2012.

Maxford, Howard. *Hammer Complete: The Films, the Personnel, the Company.* Jefferson, NC: McFarland, 2018.

Mayne, Judith. *The Woman at the Keyhole: Feminism and Women's Cinema.* Bloomington: Indiana University Press, 1990.

McBane, Barbara. "Walking, Talking, Singing, Exploding . . . and Silence: Chantal Akerman's Soundtracks." *Film Quarterly* 70, no. 1 (Fall 2016). https:// filmquarterly.org/2016/09/16/walking-talking-singingexploding.

McCluer, C. E. "Telephone Operators and Operating Room Management." *American Telephone Journal* 6, no. 2 (July 12, 1902).

McHugh, Kathleen. "'Sounds That Creep Inside You': Female Narration and Voice-Over in the Films of Jane Campion." *Style* 35, no. 2 (2001): 193–218.

McLean, Adrienne L. *Being Rita Hayworth: Labor, Identity, and Hollywood Stardom.* New Brunswick, NJ: Rutgers University Press, 2004.

McNeill, Emma. "Management of the Transgender Voice." *Journal of Laryngology and Otology* 120, no. 7 (July 2006): 521–523.

McVeigh, Tracy. "Joanna Lumley: Never Mess with an Old Avenger." *Guardian*, May 10, 2009. www.theguardian.com/world/2009/may/10/profile-joanna -lumley-gurkhas-rights.

Melnick, Kyle. "Five Emotionally Draining VR Films." VR Scout, March 30, 2019. https://vrscout.com/news/five-emotionally-draining-vr-films.

Meltzer, Marisa. "How Busy Philipps Became the Breakout Star of Instagram Stories." *New Yorker*, September 28, 2017. www.newyorker.com/culture/persons -of-interest/how-busy-philipps-became-the-breakout-star-of-instagram-stories.

Mendoza, Elvira, Nieves Valencia, Juana Muñoz, and Humberto Trujillo. "Differences in Voice Quality between Men and Women: Use of the Long-Term Average Spectrum (LTAS)." *Journal of Voice* 10, no. 1 (1996): 59–66.

Menon, Siddhartha. "A Participation Observation Analysis of the *Once and Again* Internet Message Bulletin Boards." *Television and New Media* 8, no. 4 (2007): 341–374.

Mercer, John, Charlie Sarson, and Jamie Hakim. "'Charisma, uniqueness, nerve and talent': *RuPaul's Drag Race* and the cultural politics of fame." *Celebrity Studies* 11, no. 4 (2020): 383–385.

"Metropolitan Museum Audio Guide Introduces *Costume: The Art of Dress*

Narrated by Sarah Jessica Parker." The Met, November 10, 2008. www
.metmuseum.org/press/news/2008/metropolitan-museum-audio-guide
-introduces-icostume-the-art-of-dressi-narrated-by-sarah-jessica-parker.

Mitchell, Aurora. "Behind the Scenes of Björk's 360-Degree 'Mouth Mantra' Video." *Dazed Digital*, September 16, 2016. www.dazeddigital.com/music/article
/32826/1/behind-the-scenes-of-bjork-s-360-degree-mouth-mantravideo.

Montgomery, Colleen. "Double Doublage: Vocal Performance in the French-Dubbed Versions of Pixar's Toy Story and Cars." In *Locating the Voice in Film: Critical Approaches and Global Practices*, ed. Tom Whittaker and Sarah Wright, 83–100. Oxford: Oxford University Press, 2017.

Moor, Ramey. "Everything Else Is Drag: Linguistic Drag and Gender Parody on RuPaul's Drag Race." *Journal of Research in Gender Studies* 3, no. 2 (2013): 15–26.

Moradiyan-Rizi, Najmeh. "The Acoustic Screen: The Dynamics of the Female Look and Voice in Abbas Kiarostami's *Shirin*." *Synoptique* 5, no. 1 (Summer/Fall 2016): 44–56.

Morrall, Josh. "Wound Footage Film Review." *Eye for Film*, June 8, 2019. www
.eyeforfilm.co.uk/review/wound-footage-film-review-by-josh-morrall.

Mukherjee, Silpa. "High-Octave Soprano to Auto-Tuned Rapper: Item Numbers and Technologies of Sonic Eroticism." *The Soundtrack* 9, no. 1–2 (2016): 59–71.

Mulvey, Laura. "Visual Pleasure and Narrative Cinema." *Screen* 16, no. 3 (October 1975): 6–18.

Murphy, Mekado. "25 Years after a Breakthrough at Sundance, Trying to Break through Again." *New York Times*, January 24, 2018. www.nytimes.com/2018
/01/24/movies/leslie-harris-sundance-interview.html.

"My Interview with Ray Hagen about Ann Sheridan." Remembering Ann Sheridan, January 26, 2011. www.annsheridan.com/Ann_Sheridan_Interviews/Ray
_Hagen_Interview.html.

Nagle, Angela. *Kill All Normies: Online Culture Wars from 4Chan and Tumblr to Trump and the Alt-Right*. Hants, UK: Zero Books, 2017.

Neumark, Norie, Ross Gibson, and Theo van Leeuwen. *VØ1CE: Vocal Aesthetics in Digital Arts and Media*. Cambridge, MA: MIT Press, 2010.

Newman, Michael Z. "GIFs: The Attainable Text." *Film Criticism* 40, no. 1 (January 2016).

Newton, Esther. *Mother Camp: Female Impersonators in America*. Chicago: University of Chicago Press, 1979.

Nixon, Marni. *I Could Have Sung All Night: My Story*. New York: Billboard Books, 2006.

Nora, Pierre. *Les Lieux de Mémoire*. Paris: Gallimard, 1984.

"Obituaries: Spirited McCambridge Had Big Voice." *Variety*, March 22–28, 2004.

O'Meara, Jennifer. "Body Talk and the Remediation of Women's Voices in *RuPaul's Drag Race*." *Journal of Cinema and Media Studies* 61, no. 1 (forthcoming, 2021).

——. "Eroticizing Margot Robbie's Voice through ASMR Whispers." *In Media Res*, September 24, 2018. http://mediacommons.org/imr/content/eroticizing -margot-robbies-voice-through-asmr-whispers.

——. "Identity Politics and Vocal 'Whitewashing' in Celebrity Lip-Syncs." In *Media Ventriloquism: How Audiovisual Technologies Transform the Voice-Body Relationship*, ed. Jaimie Baron, Jennifer Fleeger, and Shannon Wong Lerner, 117–132. Oxford: Oxford University Press, 2021.

——. "Meme Girls versus Trump: Digitally Recycled Screen Dialogue as Political Discourse." *Velvet Light Trap* 82 (2018): 28–42.

——. "'We've Got to Work on Your Accent and Vocabulary'—Characterization through Verbal Style in Clueless." In "In Focus: Clueless," *Cinema Journal* 53, no. 3 (Spring 2014): 138–145.

——. "What 'The Bechdel Test' Doesn't Tell Us: Examining Women's Verbal and Vocal (Dis)empowerment in Cinema." *Feminist Media Studies* 16, no. 6 (2016): 1120–1123.

Ong, Walter J. *The Presence of the Word: Some Prolegomena for Religious and Cultural History*. Minneapolis: University of Minnesota Press, 1981.

Owens, Jay. "Post-Authenticity and the Ironic Truths of Meme Culture." In *Post Memes: Seizing the Memes of Production*, ed. Alfie Bown and Dan Bristow, 77–114. Goleta, CA: Punctum Books, 2019.

Parisi, David. "Fingerbombing, or 'Touching Is Good': The Cultural Construction of Technologized Touch." *Senses and Society* 3, no. 3 (2008): 307–328.

Parker, Michael A. "Anomalisa: 3D Printed People with Real Human Issues." 3DPrint, January 14, 2016. https://3dprint.com/115151/anomalisa-3d-printed -people.

Parslow, Joe. "Dragging the Mainstream: *RuPaul's Drag Race* and Moving Drag Practices between the USA and the UK." In *Contemporary Drag Practices and Performers: Drag in a Changing Scene*, vol. 1, ed. Mark Edward and Stephen Farrier, 19–31. London: Bloomsbury, 2020.

Patches, Matt. "People Are Obsessed with Charlie Kaufman's Stop-Motion Sex Drama." *Esquire*, September 16, 2015. www.esquire.com/entertainment/movies /reviews/a37997/anomalisa-charlie-kaufman.

Pearl, Max. "This Terrifying MIDI Version of 'All I Want for Christmas' Will Keep You Awake at Night." *Vice*, December 18, 2015. www.vice.com/en_us/article /ez7zv4/this-terrifying-midi-version-of-all-i-want-for-christmas-will-keep-you -awake-at-night.

Peraino, Judith. *Listening to the Sirens: Musical Technologies of Queer Identity from Homer to Hedwig*. Berkeley: University of California Press, 2006.

Persily, Nathaniel. "The 2016 U.S. Election: Can Democracy Survive the Internet?" *Journal of Democracy* 28, no. 2 (April 2017): 63–67.

Peters, Joan K. "The 'Robettes' Are Coming: Siri, Alexa, and My GPS Lady." *Hyperrhiz: New Media Cultures*, no. 15 (2016). http://hyperrhiz.io/hyperrhiz15 /reviews/peters-the-robettes-are-coming.htm.

Phan, Thao. "Amazon Echo and the Aesthetics of Whiteness." *Catalyst: Feminism, Theory, Technoscience* 5, no. 1 (2019): 1–39.

Porch, Scott. "How Karina Longworth Is Reimagining Classic Hollywood and the Podcast in *You Must Remember This*." Longreads, March 17, 2015. https://longreads.com/2015/03/17/howkarina-longworth-is-reimagining-classic -hollywood-and-the-podcast-in-you-must-remember-this.

Power, Nina. "Soft Coercion: The City and the Recorded Female Voice." Nina Power website, December 7, 2017. https://ninapower.net/2017/12/07/soft -coercion-the-city-and-the-recorded-female-voice.

Prince, Stephen. "Actors and Algorithms." In *Digital Visual Effects in Cinema*, 99–145. New Brunswick, NJ: Rutgers University Press, 2011.

Puglise, Nicole. "'Pussy Grabs Back' Becomes Rallying Cry for Female Rage against Trump." *Guardian*, October 10, 2016. www.theguardian.com/us-news /2016/oct/10/donald-trump-pussy-grabs-back-meme-women-twitter.

Raengo, Alessandra. "Shadowboxing. Lee Daniels's Non-Representation Cinema." In *Contemporary Black American Cinema: Race, Gender and Sexuality at the Movies*, ed. Mia Mask, 200–216. New York: Routledge, 2012.

Rakow, Lana F. "Women and the Telephone: The Gendering of a Communications Technology." In *Technology and Women's Voices: Keeping in Touch*, ed. Cheris Kramarae, 207–229. London: Routledge, 1988.

Rangan, Pooja. "In Defense of Voicelessness: The Matter of the Voice and the Films of Leslie Thornton." *Feminist Media Histories* 1, no. 3 (Summer 2015): 95–126.

Rapold, Nicholas. "Interview: Charlie Kaufman and Duke Johnson." *Film Comment*, December 16, 2015. www.filmcomment.com/blog/interview-charlie -kaufman-and-duke-johnson.

Ratcliff, Maurice. *Leonard Cohen: The Music and the Mystique*. London: Omnibus Press, 2012.

Ravitz, Justin. "You Must Remember This Podcast: New Season Explores Radical Women in Hollywood." *Rolling Stone*, June 27, 2017. www.rollingstone.com /culture/culturefeatures/you-must-remember-this-podcast-new-season-explores -radical-women-in-hollywood-201578.

Reagan, Gillian. "Roger Ebert Samples Amazing New Voice Synthesiser on Oprah." Business Insider, March 3, 2010. www.businessinsider.com.au/watch -roger-ebert-sample-new-voice-technology-on-oprah-2010-3.

Rees, A. L., Duncan White, Steven Ball, and David Curtis, eds. *Expanded Cinema: Art, Performance, Film*. London: Tate Publishing, 2011.

Rizzo, Teresa. "YouTube: The New Cinema of Attractions." *Scan: Journal of Media Arts Culture* 5, no. 1 (May 2008). http://scan.net.au/scan/journal/display .php?journal_id=109.

Roberts, Amy. "Lights Out: The Scariest VR Horror Movie Experiences." Film Daily, no date. https://filmdaily.co/obsessions/scariest-vr-horror-movie -experiences.

Roberts, Andrew. "Nikki van der Zyl: The Bond Girl You've Never Seen Who Voiced Some of the Films' Best Known Heroines." *Independent*, October 11, 2015. www.independent.co.uk/arts-entertainment/music/features/nikki-van-der -zyl-the-bond-girl-youve-never-seen-who-voiced-some-of-the-films-best-known -heroines-a6689701.html.

Robertson, Adi. "Dear Angelica Might Be the Most Beautiful Virtual Reality I've Ever Seen." The Verge, January 23, 2017. www.theverge.com/2017/1/23 /14345316/dear-angelica-oculus-vr-story-studio-sundance-2017-review.

Roettgers, Janko. "'Tomb Raider' Star Alicia Vikander Goes Virtual Reality with 'Arden's Wake: Tide's Fall.'" Variety, April 18, 2018. https://variety.com/2018 /digital/news/alicia-vikander-tides-fall-vr-penrose-1202756199.

Rosolato, Guy. "La voix: Entre corps et langage." Revue française de psychanalyse 38 (1974): 75–94.

"sarah koenig's voice shirt." Badkneests.com, no date. https://badkneests.com /products/sarah-koenigs-voice-t-shirt.

Scarth, Richard N. Echoes from the Sky: A Story of Acoustic Defence. Kent, UK: Hythe Civic Society, 1999.

Schacht, Steven P., and Lisa Underwood. The Drag Queen Anthology: The Absolutely Fabulous but Flawlessly Customary World of Female Impersonators. Binghamton, NY: Haworth Press, 2004.

Shapiro, Julie. "Why Are 70 Percent of the Most Popular Podcasts Hosted by Men?" Bitch Media, February 28, 2013. www.bitchmedia.org/post/why-are-70 -percent-of-the-most-popular-podcasts-hosted-by-men.

Sharf, Zack. "Deepfake Porn Videos Are Using Scarlett Johansson's Face, but She Says It's Useless to Fight Back." Indiewire, January 2, 2019. www.indiewire .com/2019/01/scarlett-johansson-deepfakes-face-porn-videos-1202031678.

Shingler, Martin. "Fasten Your Seatbelts and Prick Up Your Ears: The Dramatic Human Voice in Film." Scope 5 (2016): 1–12.

Silverman, Kaja. The Acoustic Mirror: The Female Voice in Psychoanalysis and Cinema. Bloomington: Indiana University Press, 1988.

"Sirius, R.U." "Long before the Spike Jonze Film Her There Was Teknolust." Kurzweilai, March 6, 2014. www.kurzweilai.net/long-before-the-spike-jonze- film-her-there-was-teknolust.

Sjogren, Britta H. Into the Vortex: Female Voice and Paradox in Film. Urbana: University of Illinois Press, 2006.

Smith, David L. "Six Ways of Looking at Anomalisa." Journal of Religion and Film 20, no. 3 (2016). https://digitalcommons.unomaha.edu/jrf/vol20/iss3/12.

Smith, Jacob. Vocal Tracks: Performance and Sound Media. Berkeley: University of California Press, 2008.

Smith, Jeff. "Black Faces, White Voices: The Politics of Dubbing in Carmen Jones." Velvet Light Trap 51 (Spring 2003): 29–42.

Smyth, Ron, Greg Jacobs, and Henry Rogers. "Male Voices and Perceived Sexual Orientation: An Experimental and Theoretical Approach." Language in Society 32, no. 3 (2003): 329–350.

Snell, Merrie. Lipsynching. New York: Bloomsbury, 2010.

Solnit, Rebecca. "Men Explain Things to Me: Facts Didn't Get in Their Way." Tom Dispatch, April 13, 2008. www.tomdispatch.com/post/174918/rebecca _solnit_the_archipelago_of_arrogance.

Sontag, Susan. "The Decay of Cinema." New York Times, February 25, 1996.

Spargo, Chris. "RuPaul's Drag Race: 5 Best Lip Syncs of All Time." New Now

Next, January 3, 2013. www.newnownext.com/rupauls-drag-race-best-lip-syncs -of-all-time/01/2013.

Spiegel, Amy Rose. "The 6 Most Glorious Lip Syncs on 'RuPaul's Drag Race' Ever." BuzzFeed, April 23, 2013. www.buzzfeed.com/verymuchso/the-6-most -glorious-lip-syncs-on-rupauls-drag-race-ever.

"St. Andrew Launches New Museum Guide." University of St Andrews, November 12, 2012. https://news.st-andrews.ac.uk/archive/st-andrew-launches-new -museum-guide.

Steinmetz, Katy. "Meet the Voice behind That 'Laurel' (or 'Yanny') Clip That's Driving Everyone Nuts." *Time*, May 17, 2018. https://time.com/5281287/jay -aubrey-jones-laurel-yanny-voice.

Stewart, Emily. "Watch the 'Movie Trailer' Trump Showed Kim Jong Un about North Korea's Possible Future." Vox, June 12, 2018. www.vox.com/world /2018/6/12/17452876/trump-kim-jong-un-meeting-north-korea-video.

Stoever, Jennifer Lynn. *The Sonic Color Line: Race and the Cultural Politics of Listening*. New York: NYU Press, 2016.

"Story Studio." "Beyond Animation: 'Dear Angelica' Premieres at Sundance." Oculus, January 20, 2017. www.oculus.com/story-studio/blog/beyond-animation -dear-angelica-premieres-at-sundance.

Straw, Will. "Proliferating Screens." *Screen* 41, no. 1 (Spring 2000): 115–119.

Sullivan, John L. "Podcast Movement: Aspirational Labour and the Formalization of Podcasting as a Culture Industry." In *Podcasting: New Aural Cultures and Digital Media*, ed. Dario Llinares, Neil Fox, and Richard Berry, 35–56. London: Palgrave Macmillan, 2019.

Swartz, Anna. "Busy Philipps Is Getting a Talk Show, Joining a Small Group of Women in Late-Night TV." Mic, May 1, 2018. www.mic.com/articles/189156 /busy-philipps-is-getting-a-talk-show-joining-a-small-group-of-women-in-late -night-tv.

Switzer, Sidney. "We Shouldn't Mock Trump for His Appearance." Huffington Post, August 10, 2017. www.huffingtonpost.com/entry/we-shouldnt-mock -trump-for-his-appearance_us_598cae03e4b0ed1f464c0967.

Tajima, Renee E. "Lotus Blossoms Don't Bleed: Images of Asian Women." In *Making Waves: An Anthology of Writing by and about Asian American Women*, ed. Asian Women United of California, 308–317. Boston: Beacon, 1989.

Teixeira Pinto, Ana. "Capitalism with a Transhuman Face: The Afterlife of Fascism and the Digital Frontier." *Third Text* 33, no. 3 (2019): 315–336.

Thompson, Marie. "Creaking, Growling: Feminine Noisiness and Vocal Fry in the Music of Joan La Barbara and Runhild Gammelsæter." *N. Paradoxa* 37 (2016): 5–11.

Tiffe, Raechel, and Melody Hoffman. "Taking Up Sonic Space: Feminized Vocality and Podcasting as Resistance." *Feminist Media Studies* 17, no. 1 (2017): 115–118.

Todd, Carolyn L. "Remember That Time Trump Flirted with Samantha on Sex and the City?" Refinery29, April 28, 2017. www.refinery29.com/2017/04/152242 /sex-and-the-city-donald-trump-cameo-samantha-jones-flirt.

Trebay, Guy. "A Collector of People along with Art." *New York Times*, April 6, 2011. www.nytimes.com/2011/04/07/fashion/07GREEN.html.

Tufekci, Zeynep. "Adventures in the Trump Twittersphere." *New York Times*, March 31, 2016. www.nytimes.com/2016/03/31/opinion/campaign-stops /adventures-in-the-trump-twittersphere.html.

———. "After the Protests." *New York Times*, March 19, 2014. www.nytimes.com /2014/03/20/opinion/after-the-protests.html.

Tunbridge, Laura. "Scarlett Johansson's Body and the Materialization of Voice." *Twentieth-Century Music* 13, no. 1 (2016): 139–152.

Van Borsel, John, Joke Janssens, and Mark De Bodt. "Breathiness as a Feminine Voice Characteristic: A Perceptual Approach." *Journal of Voice* 23, no. 3 (2008): 291–294.

van der Zyl, Nikki. *For Your Ears Only: The Voice of the Stars*. Holland-on-Sea, UK: Apex Publishing, 2011.

Vanity Fair. "We talked to all the titans of late-night television, and found out why it's better than ever." Twitter, September 14, 2015. https://twitter.com /VanityFair/status/643459713561141248.

Vernallis, Carol. *Unruly Media: YouTube, Music Video, and the New Digital Cinema*. New York: Oxford University Press, 2013.

Vijayan, Karthika, Haizhou Li, and Tomoki Toda. "Speech-to-Singing Voice Conversion: The Challenges and Strategies for Improving Vocal Conversion Processes." *IEEE Signal Processing Magazine* 36 (2019): 95–102.

Virginás, Andrea. "Gendered Transmediation of the Digital from S1m0ne to Ex Machina: 'Visual Pleasure' Reloaded?" *European Journal of English Studies* 21, no. 3 (2017): 288–303.

Vöge, Hans. "The Translation of Films: Sub-Titling versus Dubbing." *Babel* 23, no. 3 (1977): 120–125.

"Voice Creation FAQ." CereProc, no date. www.cereproc.com/support/faqs /voicecreation.

Walton, Saige, and Nadine Boljkovac. "Introduction: Materialising Absence." *Screening the Past* 43 (April 2018). www.screeningthepast.com/2018/02 /introduction-materialising-absence.

Wanstall, Norman. "Foreword by Norman Wanstall, Supervising Sound Editor." Reproduced from Nikki van der Zyl, *For Your Ears Only: The Voice of the Stars*, Holland-on-Sea, UK: Apex Publishing, 2011. Nikki van der Zyl website, 2011. www.nikkivanderzyl.co.uk/page1_10.htm.

Warwick, Jacqueline, and Allison Adrian, eds. *Voicing Girlhood in Popular Music: Performance, Authority, Authenticity*. New York: Routledge, 2016.

Wasson, Haidee. "The Networked Screen: Moving Images, Materiality, and the Aesthetics of Size." In *Fluid Screens, Expanded Cinema*, ed. Janine Marchessault and Susan Lord, 74–95. Toronto: University of Toronto Press, 2008.

Watercutter, Angela. "Dear Angelica Is the Film—and Filmmaking Tool—VR Needs." *Wired*, January 20, 2017. www.wired.com/2017/01/oculus-dear -angelica-premiere.

Williams, Linda. "Film Bodies: Gender, Genre, and Excess." *Film Quarterly* 44, no. 4 (Summer 1991): 2–13.

"The Wing." Instagram post, January 29, 2017. www.instagram.com /p/BP3NOsggodN/?taken-by=the.wing.

Woletz, Julie. "Interfaces of Immersive Media." *Interface Critique Journal* 1 (2018): 96–110. https://interfacecritique.net/journal/volume-1/woletz -interfaces-of-immersive-media.

Wolfe, Cary. *What Is Posthumanism?* Minneapolis: University of Minnesota Press, 2010.

Woolf, Virginia. *To the Lighthouse.* London: Hogarth Press, 1927.

Wright, Alan, and Peter Kendall. "The Listening Mirrors." *Journal of Architectural Conservation* 14, no. 1 (2008): 33–54.

Wright, Stephen, and Claire Ellicott. "The Secret Bond Girl: Unknown Artist Dubbed the Voices of 007's Best-Known Beauties—But Now She's Banned from the Movies (*sic*) Spy's 50th Birthday Party!" *Daily Mail*, September 21, 2012. www.dailymail.co.uk/femail/article-2206882/Bonds-secret-girl-Unknown-artist -dubbed-voices-007s-best-known-beauties–know-shes-banned-movies-spys-50th -birthday-party.html.

Youngblood, Gene. "Cinema and the Code." *Leonardo* 22, no. 5 (1989): 27–30.

———. *Expanded Cinema.* New York: E. P. Dutton, 1970.

Björk. "Mouth Mantra." 2015. Directed by Jesse Kanda. Virtual Reality music video.

"Caroline ASMR." "ASMR Super Slowwww Hand Movements and Trigger Words for Sleep," June 14, 2020. YouTube video. https://www.youtube.com/watch?v=QbiKtyrU1Ko&t=148s.

Chan, Mimi, host. *Culture Chat with Mimi Chan*. 2017–present. Produced by Mimi Chan. Podcast. www.culturechatpodcast.com.

"Comedy Dynamics." "Mike O'Brien—Sexy Bible (feat. Scarlett Johansson, Jorma Taccone)." October 28, 2015. SoundCloud recording. https://soundcloud.com/comedydynamics/mike-obrien-sexy-bible.

"DarkLight90." "The Exorcist: Scenes with Linda Blair and Mercedes McCambridge's Voice as the Demon." April 16, 2010. YouTube video. www.youtube.com/watch?v=VtApL7Ddvgo.

Faris, Anna, host. *Anna Faris Is Unqualified*. 2015–present. Produced by Michael Barrett, Jeph Porter, and Rob Holysz. Podcast. www.unqualified.com.

"Film Clip—Nikki van der Zyl from A Bond for Life: How James Bond Changed My Life." August 31, 2016. IMDb. www.imdb.com/videoplayer/vi3484988953.

"filmclips." "Louise Brooks in a Talkie." November 20, 2008. YouTube video. www.youtube.com/watch?v=C6oTprKNeVU.

Fleisch, Thorsten. *Wound Footage*. May 20, 2009. Vimeo video. https://vimeo.com/4741823.

"Golden Hollywood Fan." "Adele Jergens (Voice of Virginia Rees)—I'm So Crazy for You." April 24, 2019. YouTube video. www.youtube.com/watch?v=rFKWMhQRWjM.

——. "Donald O'Connor and Vera-Ellen (Voice of Carole Richards)—It's a Lovely Day Today." May 10, 2019. YouTube video. www.youtube.com/watch?v=kGfzBL9Zn_Q.

——. "Rita Hayworth (Voice of Anita Ellis)—Put the Blame on Mame (Gilda, 1946)." August 26, 2018. YouTube video. www.youtube.com/watch?v=-EaQtT4eLNw.

Guardian News. "Is This the Voice of Frida Kahlo?—Audio." June 13, 2019. YouTube video. www.youtube.com/watch?v=HjTA2Dd8U9o.

IMER-NOTICIAS (Instituto Mexicano de la Radio). "Frida Kahlo voz." June 12, 2019. SoundCloud recording. https://soundcloud.com/antena-radio-imer/frida_kahlo_voz.

Jacobson, Abbi, host. *A Piece of Work*. 2017. Produced by Tony Phillips, Rachel Neel, Sarah Sandbach, Hannis Brown, Tania Ketenjian, Amanda Aronczyk,

and Matt Frassica. WNYC Studios. Podcast. www.wnycstudios.org/podcasts
/pieceofwork.

"James Bond Radio." "Bond behind the Scenes: Nikki van der Zyl Interview.
James Bond Radio Podcast #047." July 31, 2015. YouTube video. www
.youtube.com/watch?v=IfpTeEgHkg4.

"jmster 46." "Ann Sheridan and Ronald Reagan." June 16, 2017. YouTube video.
www.youtube.com/watch?v=Dh0aWkXSyMc.

Longworth, Karina, host. "Jean and Jane." *You Must Remember This*. June 27–
August 21, 2017. Produced by Karina Longworth. Podcast. https://podcasts
.apple.com/us/podcast/you-must-rememberthis/id858124601?mt=2.

———. "Star Wars Episode II: Carol Lombard and Clark Gable." *You Must Remember This*. January 13, 2015. Produced by Karina Longworth. Podcast. www
.youmustrememberthispodcast.com/episodes/youmustrememberthispodcastblog
/2015/1/13/star-wars-episode-ii-carole-lombard-and-clark-gable-ymrt-28.

———. "Star Wars Episode III: Hedy Lamarr." *You Must Remember This*.
January 14, 2015. Produced by Karina Longworth. Podcast. www
.youmustrememberthispodcast.com/episodes/youmustrememberthispodcastblog
/2015/1/14/star-wars-episode-iii-hedy-lamarr-ymrt-29.

———. "Star Wars Episode VII: Lena Horne." *You Must Remember This*. February
17, 2015. Produced by Karina Longworth. Podcast. https://megaphone.link
/KL9647868971.

"misterrichardson." "RuPaul's First Lip Sync on TV," from a performance televised on *The American Music Show* (People TV, 1981–2005). Posted March 15,
2013. YouTube video. www.youtube.com/watch?v=kaAmlrafH8s.

"MonoThyratron." "The Voder—Homer Dudley (Bell Labs) 1939." July 9, 2011.
YouTube video. www.youtube.com/watch?v=5hyI_dM5cGo.

"Nesplayer." "Nintendo DS Commercial Promo #1." October 25, 2007. YouTube
video. www.youtube.com/watch?v=ULMjlig6Imo.

"The Noir Escapadee." "Nora Prentiss—1947 with Ann Sheridan." July 4, 2019.
YouTube video. www.youtube.com/watch?v=Di8C_8goUoM.

PBS NewsHour. "Edison's Talking Dolls: Child's Toy or Stuff of Nightmares." May
6, 2015. YouTube video. www.youtube.com/watch?v=_bgXH7U2Ja0.

Powers, Melissa, and Matthew Eng, cohosts. *Asian Oscar Bait*. 2016–2017. Produced by Caroline Pinto. Podcast. www.asianoscarbait.com.

"Real-Time MRI Captures Incredible Video of Opera Singer Performing during
Scan." *Telegraph*, May 4, 2016. www.telegraph.co.uk/science/2016/05/04/real
-time-mri-captures-incredible-video-of-opera-singer-performi.

"Roots66." "Ursula Andress on 'What's My Line?'" December 1, 2009. YouTube
video. www.youtube.com/watch?v=0Rof1W3HcUs.

RuPaul, and Michelle Visage. "Episode 76: Katya." *RuPaul: What's the Tee with
Michelle Visage*. December 14, 2016. Produced by The Paragon Collective.
Podcast. https://soundcloud.com/rupaul/episode-76-katya.

"Sarahjessicaparker." April 23, 2019. Instagram video. www.instagram.com
/p/BwnBG0oFOnk.

——. September 1, 2016. Instagram video. www.instagram.com/p/BJ0KIC3DdQs/?hl=en.

Slaughter, Melissa, Rachel Liu, and Alex Chester, cohosts. *We're Not All Ninjas*. 2016–present. Podcast. https://werenotallninjas.libsyn.com.

"Soft Xquare [ASMR]." "Anomalisa—Mirror [ASMR] [LOOP]." July 10, 2018. YouTube video. www.youtube.com/watch?v=gtkH4zDC-8E.

Sow, Aminatou, and Ann Friedman, cohosts. *Call Your Girlfriend*. 2014–present. Produced by Gina Delvac. Podcast. www.callyourgirlfriend.com.

Vogue. *Vogue by the Decade*. Last updated January 18, 2019. YouTube playlist. www.youtube.com/playlist?list=PLztAHXmlMZFQzxmXfTAFxgbolYcO4uTDD.

W magazine. "Celebrity ASMR." Seasons 1 and 2. https://video.wmagazine.com/series/asmr.

Williams, Jessica, and Phoebe Robinson, cohosts. *2 Dope Queens*. 2016–2018. Produced by Joanna Solotaroff and Rachel Neel. Executive producer Jen Poyant. WNYC Studios. Podcast. www.wnycstudios.org/podcasts/dopequeens.

"XSpawn13." "The Exorcist—Mercedes McCambridge Raw Audio Tracks." December 14, 2018. YouTube video. www.youtube.com/watch?v=QUmyeNcld5M.

Note: Page numbers in italic type indicate information contained in images or image captions.

À bout de souffle (film, French), 122, 123
Absolutely Fabulous (television series, British), 104
accents in vocals. *See under* language
acousmatic voice, 127
Acoustic Mirror, The (Silverman), 171, 180. *See also* acoustic mirrors, examples of and concepts around
acoustic mirrors, examples of and concepts around, 11–12, 171, 178, 179, 200–201
activism: digital, and recycled dialogue, 153–159; digital, commodification of, 159–163; pop culture and social media activism, 147, 163–165; sociopolitical, 119, 124–125, 126. *See also* memes in modern culture
Activism or Slacktivism? (Chatfield), 163–164
Adaptation (film), 88
Adichie, Chimamanda Ngozi, 161
Adinolfi, Francesco, 190–191
Adobe Audition (software), 13
Adobe VoCo (vocal cloning), 73, 84
Adrian, Allison, 140
Adventures of Priscilla, Queen of the Desert, The (film), 175
Adynata (film), 77
age issues: ageism, 57, 74; mature voices, advantages and authority of, 38, 73–74, 79–80, 104–105, 114–115
A.I. (film), 78
"Alexa" (virtual assistant), 16, 41, 55, 72, 77, 200
Alexa.com, 41
Allsbrook, Wesley, 110, 111
All the King's Men (film), 34

All Things Considered (radio show), 46–47
Altman, Rick, 8
alt-right, 155–156, 164
Amazon, 26–27, 198
American Beauty (film), 90
American Music Show, The (television show), 175
American Psycho (film), 155–156
Andersen, Joceline, 2, 64
Andress, Ursula, 30, 31–34
androgynous figures/voices, 82, 178, 189–190, 193, 194
Angelica (character). *See Dear Angelica* (VR animation short)
animation: ensouled voice in digital animations, 83–84, 108–109; stop-motion, 16, 56, 61; in VR films, 106–112, *110*. *See also* GIFs and subtitled stills
Aniston, Jennifer, 89
Anna May Wong (documentary film), 105
Anomalisa (film), 15–16, 60–65, 68–70, 71, 74, 75–76, 79–80
AOL, 78, 102, 103–104
Apocalypse Now (film), 128
"Apocryphal Story of Katharine Hepburn's Metallic Voice, The" (Marcus), 26–27
appearance (visual "beauty") and freedoms of digital media, 7, 101, 136–139
Apple, 2, 133
Apprentice, The (television show), 154, 165
Arden's Wake: Tide's Fall (VR short), 103, 106, 113
Aristotle, 82
artificial intelligence, female standard for, 15, 53–54, 56, 68, 77
Asian Oscar Bait (No More Excuses, Hollywood) (podcast), 131

Asians: as lip-sync performers, 188; scarcity of in mainstream digital media, 105, 131; and vocalized racism, 77–78
#AskHerMore (twitter campaign), 7
ASMR (autonomous sensory meridian response) videos. *See* autonomous sensory meridian response (ASMR) videos
athletic moves in lip-sync performance, 183, 185–187
Atlantic, The, 138
Aubrey, Jay, 6–7
Audible (audio book platform), 27, 198
Audition, The (film short), 102
Ausiello, Michael, 26
Authentic (Banet-Weiser), 162
autonomous sensory meridian response (ASMR) videos: development and popularity of, 1–2, 5; and embodiment *vs.* disembodiment, 99; sexualized/fetishized voices, 3, 9, 11, 62, 64–65. *See also* whispered vocalizations/narrations
Awkward Black Girl (web series), 91, 94

Bacall, Lauren, 73
Bajarin, Tim, 55
Bakhtin, Mikhail, 155
Balcerzak, Scott, 75
Bale, Christian, 155
Bane (character, *The Dark Knight Rises*), 147
Banet-Weiser, Sarah, 149, 162
Bangert, Renita, *13*
Barbarella (film), 122
barkers, silent film, 87, 115
Barthes, Roland, 74, 173, 180, 189
"basic bitch" figures, 156
Bassett, Jordan, 148–149
Bastow, Clem, 97
Bechdel, Alison, 166
Bechdel test, 7, 166–170
Beck, Jay, 35, 36
Bell, Duncan, 108
Bell, Kristen, 97
Bell, Lake, 92–93, 115. *See also In a World . . .* (film)
Bell Telephone Laboratories, 2

Bennett, Jessica, 155
Bennett, Tony (scholar), 24–25, 50
Benza, A. J., 142–143
Beowulf (film, 2007), 83
"Better Be Good to Me" (song), 188
Beyoncé, 91, 114
Bianca Del Rio (drag queen), 192
Big Short, The (film), 9
Billabong (film), 216n4
Bitch Media (magazine), 163
Bitwa o Anglię (*Battle of Britain*, film), 42
Bizet, Georges, 130
Björk (performer), 9–10, 200
Black voices. *See* people of color, voices of
Blade Runner (film), 56
Blair, Linda, 31, 34–36
Blalock, P. David, 73
blondness, stigmatization of, 121, 135–136
Blue (film), 89
"blue discs," 2
Blue Max, The (film), 32
"body in the voice" concept, 67–68, 74–77, 75–76. *See also* humanness and posthuman feminized technology
body talk/body language in lip syncing, 171, 173, 176–177, 180–185
body/voice mismatch. *See* mismatched voice/appearance expectations
Bogart, Humphrey, 73
Bogart-Bacall syndrome (voice disorder), 73
Boljkovac, Nadine, 41
Bond for Life, A (fan documentary), 43
"Bond girls," dubbing of, 28–34, 36. *See also* van der Zyl, Nikki
Bonjour Tristesse (film), 121
Bosworth, Patricia, 125
Bringing Up Baby (film), 26
British Film Institute, 30–31
British voices, 78
Broad City (television series), 131
Brodie, Jean (film character), 178
Brooks, Louise, 14, 39, 205–206n40
Brown, Georgia, 199
bubbles, speech, 151
Bullock, Sandra, 219n62

Burke, Timothy, 147
Bush, George W., 154, 165
Bust (magazine), 163, 165
Busy Tonight (television show), 93–94, 95
"butch noir," 142–143
Butler, Judith, 191

Cahn, Janet, 72, 74
"Call Me Mother" (song), 178
Call Your Girlfriend (podcast), 140
"cameraless" cinema, 132–136. *See also* found-footage cinema
Canary Murder, The (film), 39, 40, 205–206n40
Capote (film), 127
Capote, Truman, 127
Carey, Mariah, 214n50
Carmen (opera), 130
Carmen Jones (film), 130
Carol (character, *In a World*), 92–93, 113
Caroline ASMR (ASMR video artist, YouTube channel), 5
Carothers, Isobel, 137
Carrie Bradshaw (character, *Sex and the City*), 97, 99, 160
cartoons, political, 165
Casino Royale (film), 32
castrato voices, 176, 190
Cattrall, Kim, 160
celebrity culture. *See* pop culture
Celebrity Studies (journal), 172
CereProc (vocal cloning), 72–73
Cerf, Bennett, 32, 33
Chamber Mystery, The (silent film), 151, 152
Chan, Mimi, 131
Chantel (character, *Just Another Girl on the I.R.T.*), 91–92
Charlotte (character, *Sex and the City*), 168–169
Chatfield, Tom, 163–164
Cher Horowitz (character, *Clueless*), 88, 148–149, 150, 153–157, 161–162, 164
Chester, Alex, 131
Chiarini, Alessandra, 134, 135, 136
Chion, Michel, 127–128

Chung, Eugene, 113
"cinema of attractions" concept, 173, *174*
Cixous, Hélène, 200
Clara, Lu 'n' Em (radio show), 137–138, 139
Clarkson, Patricia, 89
Clinton, Hillary Rodham, 104, 148, 154, 155, 163
Clueless (film), 8, 148–149, 150, 153–157, 161–162. *See also* Cher Horowitz (character, *Clueless*)
Coco Montrese (drag queen), 173, *174*
Cohen, Leonard, 60, 84
Cole, Natalie, 186–187
collage films, 120, 134
"collective intelligence" and internet community, 28–31, 34, 39–40, 41–44. *See also* cultural memory
Commander Bond (website), 28
computer-generated imagery (CGI), 57–58
concatenation in digitized voices, 70–71
Congress, The (film), 57–60, 70, 71–72, 74–75, 81, 82–84
Connor, Steven, 12, 82, 107
Contemporary Drag Practices and Performers (Edward and Farrier, eds.), 173
Cooke, Alistair, 123
copyright issues, 132
Cornish, Audie, 46–47
"Cover Girl" (song), 180
Cramer, Florian, 155
Crawford, Joan, 177–178, 194
Cross, Calen, 139
cross-gender performances. *See RuPaul's Drag Race* (*RPDR*) (television series)
cultural memory, 49–52. *See also* "collective intelligence" and internet community
Culture Chat with Mimi Chan (podcast), 131
"culture wars, online," 149

Daems, Jim, 177
Daily Show, The (television series), 131
Dali Museum, Florida, 102, 104
Dall'Asta, Monica, 134, 136

Daly, John Charles, 32
Dame, Joke, 190
dance moves in lip-sync performance, 185–187
Dandridge, Dorothy, 129, 130
Dark Knight Rises, The (film), 147
Dark Souls II (video game), 199
Dash, Julie, 91, 114
Daughters of the Dust (film), 91, 114
Davis, Angela, 231n53
Davis, Bette, 143
Davis, Geena, 85, 105, 106, 109, 112–113, 114–115. *See also Dear Angelica* (VR animation short)
Davis, Kristin, 164
Dazed (magazine), 64
"Dead Blondes" (thirteen-part series from *YMRT*), 121, 135–136
Deadspin (website), 147
Dear Angelica (VR animation short), 85, 87, 88, 103, 106–112, 113, 115
Dedee (character, *The Opposite of Sex*), 88, 89–91
Delibes, Léo, 80
Del Rio, Rebekah, 184
Desjardins, Mary R., 13, 101
Desperate Housewives (television series), 97
Detox (drag queen), 190
Dial-A-Poem service, 197
Dida Ritz (drag queen), 186–187
"digital blackface," 164–168
digital text: and endophony process, 150–151, 157; subtitled screen images, 47, 148, 150–153. *See also* GIFs and subtitled stills; superimposed text
digitization of female voices, overviews, 4–7, 197–201
Dior, 161
disembodied voices. *See* embodiment/disembodiment concepts
distortion effects. *See* glitch videos
diversity. *See* people of color, voices of; racial issues
Do I Sound Gay? (documentary film), 179
dolls, talking, 2, 3, 4–5

Doyle Kennedy, Maria, 197–199
drag kings, 173
drag queens. *See RuPaul's Drag Race (RPDR)* (television series)
Dr. No (film), 29, 30, 32–34
Droumeva, Milena, *13*, 199, 200
dual roles, challenges of, 58–59
Duarte, Amanda, 155
dubbing of film voices, 14, 21–23, 28–36, 38, 39, 41–44, 181
Dublin, Ireland, 197–199
Dudley, Homer, 2–3
Dulac, Germaine, 134
Dunaway, Faye, 177–178, 194
Dwyer, Tessa, 14, 38–40
dysphonia (voice disorder), 73

Eaton, Shirley, 29
Ebert, Roger, 72–73
Echo and Narcissus (Lawrence), 10–11
Edison, Thomas, 2. *See also* dolls, talking
Edward, Mark, 173
Edwards, Elwood, 102
Ed Wood (film), 101
El Bachiller (radio show), 46
Elle (magazine), 194
Ellis, Anita, 22, 51–52
Elsaesser, Thomas, 49–51
embodiment/disembodiment concepts: and cross-gender performers, 174, 180, 186–187; and ghosting phenomena, 74–77; "male gaze" concept and gender bias, 7–9, 40–41, 56, 61–62, 81; and narration perspectives, 97–99, 116–117, 199; scholarship and perspectives on, 7–9, 14, 16–17; and voicing in Virtual Reality, 102–103. *See also* visual *vs.* vocal presence of women
emotion, vocal expression of, 108–112, 135. *See also* vocal delivery permutations
emotive voice. *See* emotion, vocal expression of
endophony (mental enunciation), 150–151, 157, 170
E! network, 93–94, 142–143

Eng, Andrew, 131
"ensouled" voices, 82–83
Entwistle, Peg, 121
Eon Productions, 31, 42
erotic voicing, 1–2
ethnic voices. *See* people of color, voices
of
E! True Hollywood Story, 142–143
European Commission's Directorate-
General for Justice and Consumers, 200
"everyoutfitonSATC" Instagram account,
149, 159–163, 164
"Evil Alexas" (YouTube video), 200
Exhibition of the Wonders of Electricity
(1890), 3
Ex Machina (film), 56
Exorcist, The (film), 31, 34–36, 36–38
*Expanded Cinema: Art, Performance,
Film* (Rees et al., eds.), 87, 216n4
expanded cinema concept, 85–88, 100,
103, 114–117
expanded voice-overs: affective voice and
Virtual Reality, 105–113; evolution
of in contemporary culture, 114–117;
Instagram medium, 93–96; modern
trends and perspectives, 88–93;
overview, 85–88; in Virtual Reality,
102–105. *See also* narration/
narratives
Export, Valie, 216n6

Fáilte Ireland (National Tourism Development Authority), 197
Faircloth, Kelly, 128
Fairless, Chelsea, 159–163, 168–169
"fake news" contentions of Trump camp,
155–156
Family Guy (television show), 101
fan input and communications, 25–28
"fansnubbing," 168–169
Faris, Anna, 8–9, 120
Farrah Moan (drag queen), 195
Farrier, Stephen, 173
fascism and far right social media use, 156
Fellner, Chris, 30
feminine voice and gendered identity
expectations, 189, 191–192, 194–195

"Feminist Lisa Simpson" Tumblr page,
149, 157–159, 166
fetishization of women. *See* sexualization/
fetishization of women
Fey, Tina, 93–94
Fight Club (film), 155–156
film history, approaches to, 23–28
Fine, David J., 178
Flaig, Paul, 4
Fleabag (television series, British), 97
Fleeger, Jennifer, 56, 67, 79, 176–177,
190. *See also* mismatched voice/
appearance expectations
Fleisch, Thorsten, 21–23, 40, 51
Flynn, Gillian, 217n21
Fonda, Henry, 123
Fonda, Jane, 119–120, 121–126
foreign accents/language. *See under*
language
For Your Ears Only (van der Zyl), 28, 40
found-footage cinema, 120, 132–136, 141
4chan (imageboard website), 155
Franklin, Aretha, 191–192
Freeman, Morgan, 150, *151*
"Fregoli Delusion," 61
Fresh off the Boat (television show), 168
Freud, Sigmund, 24
Frida (film), 46–47
Friedkin, William, 34–36
Frizzell, Nell, 137, 138, 142
fry, vocal. *See* vocal fry
Fuller, Loïe, 173, *174*
Furtado, Nesan, *13*
Futurological Congress, The (Lem), 57

Gable, Clark, 140–141
Galaxina (film), 136
Gallop, Jane, 189–190
Game of Thrones (television drama
series), 147
"Gamergate," 7
GarageBand software, 133
Garbo, Greta, 211n76
Gardner, Ava, 129–130
Garrido, Amparo, 48–49
Garrison, Ednie Kaeh, 159
Garroni, Lauren, 159–163, 168–169

Gault, Matthew, 73
Gayson, Eunice, 29
Geena Davis Inclusion Quotient (GD IQ), 113
Geena Davis Institute on Gender in Media, 113
gendered dynamics and identity politics: artificial intelligence, female standard for, 15, 53–54, 56, 77; Bechdel test, 7, 166–170; gender bias in media, 92, 112–113; normative gender roles, queering of, 189–192; overview, 13–14; perpetuation of Victorian standards, 11–12; pleasure formats (listening), 3; technologized voices and gendered roles, 55–56; vocal gender markers, 18–19, 79–82, 175, 176, 178–179, 206n45. *See also* identity politics; male perspective, predominance of; mismatched voice/appearance expectations; sexism
Genesis Toys, 200
"ghosting" phenomena, 38, 74–77
GIFs and subtitled stills: and cross-gender performances, 173, 175, 185, 186; and cultural commentary, 148, 149, 150, 151–152, 152–153, 158, 166–168. *See also* memes in modern culture
Gilbert, Sophie, 138
Gilda (film), 21–23, 40, 51
Gilmore Girls (television series), 26
Giorno, John, 197
GIPHY (GIF platform), 168
Girl, Interrupted (film), 89
"Girls Just Want to Have Fun" (song), 62, 69
glitch videos, 21–23
Gloria Swanson Hour, The (television show), 101
Godard, Jean-Luc, 123–124, 125
Gone Girl (film), 217n21
Good Girl, The (film), 89
Google Trends, 166
Gorin, Jean-Pierre, 125
Gossip Girl (television series), 97
Graham, Lauren, 26, 27
Gravity (film), 219n62

Grease (film), 163, 165
Green, Sam, 211n76
Grey's Anatomy (television series), 227n62
Guardian (newspaper), 47–48, 102, 137, 156–157
guides, narrated, 85, 97, 98, 102–103
Gupta, Reena, 73
Gyllenhaal, Maggie, 89

Haasch, Palmer, 226n51
Hagen, Jean, 171, *172*
Hagen, Ray, 44, 45
Hagman, Hampus, 150, 151
Haitian refugees, 148–149, 154
Hakim, Jamie, 172
HAL 9000 computer voice, 55, 84
Hammer, Barbara, 134, 135
Hammer Film Productions, 30
Hammerstein, Oscar, 130
Hanks, Tom, 79
Harper, Helen, 2–3
Harris, Leslie, 91
Hayek, Salma, 46–47
Hayworth, Rita, 21–23, 43, 51–53
"Heartbreaker" (song), 175
Heathers (film), 89
Heckerling, Amy, 88, 148, 156
Hepburn, Katharine, 25–28
Her (film), 2, 65–68, 70, 76, 81
Hershman Leeson, Lynn, 213n21
Hess, Amanda, 168
heteronormative patterns of sexualized voices, 2, 62. *See also under* sexualization/fetishization of women
Hilmes, Michele, 137
Hindi cinema, 203n10
Hindle, Will, 216n4
historical topographies and cultural memory, 49–52
Hoffmann, Melody, 144
Hoffmann, Philip Seymour, 127
Honey Rider (Bond girl), 31–34
Hopper, Hedda, 129, 142
Horne, Lena, 129–130
Horne, Marilyn, 130
Houston, Whitney, 183, 188

How to Get Away with Murder (television series), 168

humanness and posthuman feminized technology: *Anomalisa*, 60–65; *The Congress*, 57–60; and embodiment of soul, 82–84; *Her*, 65–68; and normalization of white female voices, 77–79; overview, 53–57; queering of, 79–82; singing and digital voices, 74–77

Hunter, Holly, 89

Hyland Yang, Jennifer, 137–138

identity politics: dynamics of in digital era, 13–15, 18–19; and gendered speaking voices, 192–195; and gender fluidity, 173; gender normative vocals, queering of, 187–192; and political media, 149, 155, 159, 169. *See also* gendered dynamics and identity politics

"If It Be Your Will" (song), 60, 84

I Married a Witch (film), 121, 136

IMDb (website and database), 41–43

immersion (media), degrees of, 107, 108

immigration and refugee issues, 148–149, 154

"I'm So Crazy for You" (song), 43

#ImWithHer movement, 155

In a World . . . (film), 88, 92–93, 95, 113

Independent (magazine), 40

Ingrid Goes West (film), 95–96, 111

"In Praise of Katharine Hepburn's Voice" (Marcus), 27

Insecure (television series), 94

Instagram, use of. *See* expanded voiceovers; podcasts, medium overviews; *You Must Remember This* (*YMRT*) (podcast)

Instituto Mexicano de la Radio, 46

intermediality and narration, 86, 87–88, 97–102, 104, 114

interminable/terminable concepts, 23–25

intertitles in silent films, 15, 150–153, 169–170

Into the Vortex (Sjogren), 7–8

Invisible Histories Trilogy (film), 135

Invisible Storytellers (Kozloff), 88–89

Jacobson, Abbi, 120

James Bond films, 28–31

James Bond Radio (podcast series), 42–43

Janis: Little Girl Blue (documentary film), 114

Januszczak, Waldemar, 49

Jarman, Derek, 89

Jarman-Ivens, Freya, 79, 81, 181

Jason Leigh, Jennifer, 60–62, 63, 64, 65

"Jean and Jane" (nine-part series from *YMRT*), 120–126, 127–128, 135, 145

Jenkins, Henry, 28, 154, 164–165

Jenner, Kris, 171

Jergens, Adele, 43

Jezebel (magazine), 128, 142–143

Jinkx Monsoon (drag queen), 190, 191

Jóhannsson, Jóhann, 89

Johansson, Scarlett: and de facto standards for voice technology, 72, 73–74, 76; and sexualization of women's voices, 1–2; vocal gender markers, 81; as voice in *Her*, 19, 65–68

Johnson, Ariyan, 91

Johnson, Rian, 138

Jonze, Spike, 65, 67, 76, 213n21

Joplin, Janis, 114

Just Another Girl on the I.R.T. (film), 91–92

Kahlo, Frida, 46–49, 102, 104–105

Kanda, Jesse, 9–10

"Kardashian: The Musical" (*RPDR* segment), 171, 194

Katya (drag queen), 184, 185–186

Kaufman, Charlie, 60–61, 88

Keller, Jessalynn Marie, 153

Kendrick, Anna, 27

Kim, Jihoon, 21

Kim Jong-un, 147

Klinger, Barbara, 23–25, 50

Koda, Harold, 98

Koenig, Sarah, 222n41

Koestenbaum, Wayne, 18, 176, 187

Kohlsdorf, Kai, 188

Kornhaber, Donna, 73, 74, 80

Koufman, James, A., 73

Kozloff, Sarah, 88–89, 111
"Kuleshov effect," 160

Lacan, Jacques/Lacanian theory, 11–12, 178
Lackmann, Ron, 35
Ladies of the Chorus (film), 43
Lake, Veronica, 121, 136
Lakmé (opera), 80
Lamarr, Hedy, 15, 128
Lamont, Lina (character), 171, *172*, 193
Lang, Brent, 139
language: affected social dialects, 93, 140, 150; foreign accents, stigmatization of, 34, 64, 77–78; regional dialectic accents, stigmatization of, 121
Last and First Men (film), 89
late-night television, 93–94
Late Show Starring Joan River, The (television show), 94
Latrice Royale (drag queen), 191
Lauper, Cyndi, 62, 69
Lawrence, Amy, 7, 10–11, 40, 86, 90
Lee, Gypsy Rose, 32
Leigh, Vivien, 199
Lem, Stanislaw, 57
Lemonade (film), 91, 114
Leonard, Gloria, 2
Letter from America (radio weekly, British), 123, 124
Letter to Jane (film, French), 124, 125
Lévy, Pierre, 28
Liberman, Mark, 194
lieux de mémoire (sites of memory), 49–50
"Lip Sync for Your Life" (*RPDR* segment), 171–172, 178, 179–180, 194
Lipsynching (Snell), 189
lip syncing. *See RuPaul's Drag Race* (*RPDR*) (television series)
Lisa (Simpson) (character, *The Simpsons*), 156, 157–159
"listening ears" devices, 12
Liu, Rachel, 131
Lobster, The (film), 89
Loden, Barbara, 121
Lohan, Lindsay, 73

Lombard, Carole, 140–141
Longworth, Karina: and mismatched voice/appearance, 136–143; overviews, 17, 119–120; on revising narrative framing, 128–129; techniques and strategies, 132–136. *See also You Must Remember This* (*YMRT*) (podcast)
looped media, 150. *See also* GIFs and subtitled stills
Los Angeles Free Press, 100
"Louise Brooks in a Talkie" (video), 39–40
Loving (film), 199
Lulu in Hollywood (Brooks), 39
Lumley, Joanna, 78, 85, 102–104, 105
Ly, Doan, 105
Lypsinka (drag queen), 175
Lyrebird (vocal cloning), 73, 84

Macallan, Helen, 128, 132
"MacArthur Park" (song), 188
Made in U.S.A. (film, French), 124
Madonna, 189
Madsen, Virginia, 127
magnetic response imaging (MRI), 182
Makeup of RuPaul's Drag Race, The (Daem), 177
"Malambo No. 1" (song), 190
"male gaze" concept and gender bias, 7–9, 40–41, 56, 61–62, 81. *See also* embodiment/disembodiment concepts
male perspective, predominance of, 49, 128–131, 132. *See also* "male gaze" concept and gender bias
Malone, Molly (folk character), 198
"Mama Ru," 177
Manila Luzon (drag queen), 188
"mansplaining," 166–167, 168
Marcel, Mary, 189
Marcus, Ralph, 26–28, 50
Mar-ir-ia-a (opera), 66, 67
Marker, Chris, 133–134
Marshall, Chan "Cat Power," 114
Martin, Lynn, 44
masculine voice and gendered identity expectations, 189, 194–195
Match Game, The (television show), 193

materialization of unseen voices, 40–41, 43

maternal voice and mothering, 177–180, 193, 196

mature voices, advantages and authority of, 38, 73–74, 79–80, 104–105, 114–115

Mayne, Judith, 141–142

McCambridge, Mercedes, 31, 34–38

McClure, Troy, 150

McDaniel, Hattie, 129

McLean, Adrienne, 22, 51

McMahon, Michaela, 198

McQueen, Alexander, 98

McVeigh, Tracy, 102

media immersion, degrees of, 107

Meehan, Paula, 198

melodrama, qualities of, 106, 107–112, 140–142

Meltzer, Marisa, 93

"meme-magick" phenomenon, 155

memes in modern culture: benefits and limitations of, 163–165; and gender politics, 166–170; overviews, 8–9, 147–149; and recontextualization of favorite media characters, 159–163; in social and political activism, 153–159; voice-as-text effects, 150–153. See also GIFs and subtitled stills

memory, cultural, 49–52. See also "collective intelligence" and internet community

Mendoza, Elvira, 18, 195

Mercer, John, 172

Mermaids (film), 89

Me: Stories of My Life (Hepburn), 26

Metamorphoses (Ovid), 10–11

#MeToo movement, 112, 135, 144

Metropolis (film), 55–56

Metropolitan Museum of Art (The Met), 98

MI6 Community (website), 28–30, 31

Mike Wallace Interview, The (television series), 122

Mindy Project, The (television show), 168

Miranda Hobbes (character, Sex and the City), 161

mismatched voice/appearance expectations: concept overview, 18–19; and gender fluidity, 176–177, 183–184, 190, 192–195; Karina Longworth and YMRT, 136–143. See also embodiment/disembodiment concepts

Mismatched Women (Fleeger), 18. See also mismatched voice/appearance expectations

misogyny, 2, 121–122, 123, 143, 155

Mitchell, Aurora, 9–10

"mixing board" aesthetic, 204n24

Mommie Dearest (film), 163, 175, 177–178

Monroe, Marilyn, 195

Morgan, Henry, 32

Morrall, Josh, 21–22

Morton, Samantha, 65, 67–68, 76–77

Moskowitz, Blaire, 98

Mother Camp (Newton), 175–176, 195

motion capture technology, 16, 56, 57–58, 75–76

"Mouth Mantra" (VR video), 9–10, 200

Mukherjee, Silpa, 203n10

Mulan (film), 131

Mulholland Drive (film), 184

Mulvey, Laura, 7, 14, 39, 40, 81

Murch, Walter, 128

museum guides, narrated, 85, 97, 98, 102–103

Museum of Modern Art (MoMA), 120

Museum of the University of St Andrews (MUSA), 85, 102–103

musical voices, 114

"My Friend Cayla" (doll), 200

Mysteries & Scandals (television show), 142–143

Nagle, Angela, 155, 156

narration/narratives: embodiment/disembodiment concepts, 97–99, 116–117, 199; and intermediality, 86, 87–88, 97–102, 104, 114; museum guides, narrated, 85, 97, 98, 102–103; and white male perspective, 128–131. See also expanded voice-overs

National Immigration Law Center, 161

National Public Radio (NPR), 46–47
National Sound Library, Mexico (La Fonoteca Nacional), 46
"nearness" experience, 108, 112. *See also* whispered vocalizations/narrations
Negga, Ruth, 197–199
"Networked Screen, The" (Wasson), 115
Newman, Michael Z., 150
Newton, Esther, 175–176, 195
Newton-John, Olivia, 185–186
New Yorker, 93
New York Public Radio, 120
New York Times, 49, 168
Nintendo, 1
Nistor, Margareta, 30
Nitrate Kisses (film), 134, 135
Nixon, Cynthia, 161
Nixon, Marnie, 209n44
Nixon, Richard, 125
NME (British website/magazine), 148–149
noir film narration style, 88–89, 90, 97, 142–143
Noonan, Tom, 61, 62, 77, 79–80
Nora, Pierre, 49–50
Nora Prentiss (film), 44
Norton, Edward, 155
Nouvelle Vague (film), 125
Novak, Kim, 59

O'Brien, Mike, 2
O'Connell (Daniel) monument, 198–199
Oculus VR, 85, 105–106, 110. *See also Dear Angelica* (VR animation short)
Oculus VR presentations and headsets, 105–106
Oh, Sandra, 227n62
Olive, Joseph, 66
Olsen, Elizabeth, 95–96
One Million Years B.C. (film), 30
Ong, Walter, 82
open feedback systems, 100
Opposite of Sex, The (film), 88, 89–91
Oprah Winfrey Show, The (television show), 168
Orphan Black (television series, Canadian), 199

Ovid, 10–11
Owens, Jay, 161

Panoply podcast network, 133
Paramount, 40
Paris is Burning (documentary film), 229n23
Parker, Sarah Jessica, 87–88, 97–101, 114, 115, 116
Patreon platform, 133
patriarchal culture and female disempowerment, 79, 120–126, 187. *See also* sexualization/fetishization of women
PBS News Hour, 4
Pendulum (film), 122
penis tucking in drag queen performance, 185–186
Penrose Studios, 106, 113. *See also Arden's Wake: Tide's Fall* (VR short)
people of color, voices of: cross-gender performers, 188–189; digital media scarcity of, 168; ethnic voices, silencing/appropriation of, 77–78, 105, 168–169; voice-overs by, scarcity of, 105, 114. *See also* women of color
Peppard, George, 122
Peppermint (drag queen), 188
Peraino, Judith, 230n41
Peters, Joan K., 77, 78
Phan, Thao, 77
Phil Donahue Show, The (television show), 123
Philipps, Busy, 27, 87, 93–96, 98–99, 101, 111, 115, 116
Phoenix, Joaquin, 65, 76
physicality of digital characters, 74–77. *See also* embodiment/disembodiment concepts
physical response to VR, 107, 108
Piano, The (film), 89
Piece of Work, A (podcast), 120
Pierrot le Fou (film, French), 124
Pike, Rosalind, 214n21
Pitt, Brad, 155
Plain, Andrew, 128, 132
Plaza, Aubrey, 95
Pleasure of the Text (Barthes), 189

Pocahontas (film), 167, 168
Podcast Movement convention, 145
podcasts, medium overviews, 17, 119–120, 126–128, 144–145
Polar Express, The (film), 79
politics. *See* activism; gendered dynamics and identity politics
pop culture: and celebrity culture, 164, 167–168, 194; and social media activism, 147, 163–165
Poppins, Mary, 75, 76
"popular feminism," 149
Porch, Scott, 139, 141
pornography and sexualized voices, 2, 72, 84
postdubbing *vs.* lip syncing, 180–181
posthuman voice and feminized technology. *See* humanness and posthuman feminized technology
Potts, John, 127
Power, Nina, 70–71, 74, 75, 78
Powers, Melissa, 131
Precious: Based on the Novel "Push" by Sapphire (film), 91
Preminger, Otto, 121–122, 130
Prime of Miss Jean Brodie, The (film), 177–178
Prince, Stephen, 83
Prix de Beauté (film), 39
pronouns for cross-gender performers, 174–175
props and sets in lip-sync performance, 185–187
psychoanalytical perspective on drag queens, 176
puppets, 3D-printed, 16, 56, 61, 63, 74–75, 76
#pussygrabsback campaign against Trump, 155, 157
"Put the Blame on Mame" (song), 21–23, 51
Pygmalion (Greek myth), 56

Queen's Throat, The (Koestenbaum), 18, 187
queering of digitized voices, 79–82. *See also RuPaul's Drag Race (RPDR)* (television series)
"Quill" (Oculus software), 110

"Rabbit, rabbit" Instagram videos (Parker), 99–100, 115
race and choice of narrator, 104–105
racial issues: colonialist approaches, 218n38; and digital media dynamics, 166–170; discrimination in Hollywood, 129–130; and politics on social media, 155; racialized vocal hierarchies, 9, 77–79, 128–131; racial mimicry, 189. *See also* people of color, voices of
radio voices: and creation of melodrama, 108–109; and "disembodied woman" concept, 137–138; "radio-*acousmêtre*," 127–128
Rae, Issa, 91, 94
Rangan, Pooja, 14, 77
Rappaport, Mark, 133–134
Ratcliff, Maurice, 60
Raven (drag queen), 172, 183
Ravitz, Justin, 139
Reagan, Ronald, 44
Recycled Stars (Desjardins), 13
recycling and revision of vocals, overviews, 13–15, 153
Rees, A. L., 250
Rees, Virginia, 43
reflexivity. *See* self-awareness and reflexivity in female voice-overs
Regarding Susan Sontag (film), 89
Remembering Ann Sheridan (fan site), 44–45
Restore the Earth (animated film short), 102
revisionist approach to film history, 17, 97, 120, 122, 128–131, 142
revoicing. *See* dubbing of film voices
Reynolds, Debbie, 171, 172
Ricci, Christina, 88, 91
Richards, Carole, 43
Rivera, Diego, 46, 48
Rizzo (character, *Grease*), 163, 165

Rizzo, Teresa, 173
Robbie, Margot, 9
Roberts, Rachel, 71
Robertson, Adi, 107, 111
Robinson, Phoebe, 131
robots/robotic voices, 53
Rock, Chris, 78
Rolling Stone, 2, 139
Rose, Billy, 130
Rosolato, Guy, 11–12, 178
(*RPDR*) (*RuPaul's Drag Race*) (televi-sion series). *See RuPaul's Drag Race* (*RPDR*) (television series)
Rudd, Paul, 188–189
RuPaul's Drag Race (*RPDR*) (television series): body talk/body language in lip syncing, 171, 173, 176–177, 180–185; drag performance, background and perspectives, 175–177; and gender identity politics, 187–192; maternal voice and gender markers, 177–180; and mismatched voice/appearance concepts, 18–19, 192–195; overview, 171–175; and spectacle, concepts of, 185–187, 195–196; and visual gender markers, 80
rupturing of narrative, 128, 132. *See also* mismatched voice/appearance expectations
Ryder, Winona, 89

S1m0ne (film), 56, 71
Saint Joan (film), 122
Samantha Jones (character, *Sex and the City*), 160, 161
Sarandon, Susan, 102, 104–105
Sarson, Charlie, 172
Sasha Velour (drag queen), 183, 188
Schacht, Steven P., 172–173
Schoenholtz, Lindsey, 133
scholarship on women's voices, 10, 86–87, 171, 172–173, 175–177
Screen Facts (magazine), 44
Screening the Past (journal), 41
Seberg, Jean, 120. *See also* "Jean and Jane" (nine-part series from *YMRT*)

Secretary (film), 89
self-awareness and reflexivity in female voice-overs, 57–59, 88–93
Serial (podcast), 222n41
seriality, value of, 135–136
Serkis, Andy, 30
"Serpentine Dances," 173, *174*
Sex and the City (television series), 97, 99–100, 149, 159–163, 168–169
sexism: in cinema, 7, 128–131; in gamer community, 7; male perspective, predominance of, 49, 128–131, 132; misogyny, 2, 121–122, 123, 143, 155; sexist stereotyping, 132–136; and Trump's use of social media, 154–157; and vocal expectations, 28. *See also* gendered dynamics and identity politics; sexualization/fetishization of women
sexualization/fetishization of women: patriarchal culture and female disem-powerment, 79, 120–126, 187; and virtual assistants, 65–68, 70, 72; of women's voices, 1–7, 61–63. *See also* whispered vocalizations/narrations
Seyrig, Delphine, 125–126
"shantay," 229n23
She (film), 30, 32
Sheridan, Ann, 44–46
Shine on Harvest Moon (film), 44
Shingler, Martin, 205n34
Show Boat (film), 129–130
Shreve, Emily, 178
Shub, Esfir, 134
Sidibe, Gabourey, 91
Silverman, Kaja: acoustic mirror concept, 11–12, 171, 178, 180; embodiment/disembodiment concept, 7–8, 86, 90–91, 94–95
Silverstone, Alicia, 8, 148. *See also* Cher Horowitz (character, *Clueless*)
Simpsons, The (television series), 150, 156, 157–159
singing: by digital "women," 61, 62–63, 64–65, 66, 68–74, 80; and intermedial narration, 114

Singin' in the Rain (film), 171, 172, 180, 193

"Siri" (virtual assistant), 2, 16, 55, 77. *See also* virtual assistants

Sjogren, Britta H., 7–8, 9

SJWs (social justice warriors) of Tumblr, 156

Slaughter, Melissa, 131

Smith, David L., 63–64, 80

Smith, Jacob, 108–109

Smith, Jeff, 130

Smith, Kate, 176

Smith, Maggie, 178

Smith, Yeardley, 157

"Snatch Game" (*RPDR* parody segment), 193–194

Snell, Merrie, 189

"So Emotional" (song), 183, 188

softness and grain in vocals, 74–77, 173, 176, 180–185. *See also* whispered vocalizations/narrations

Sois belle et tais-toi (Be Pretty but Shut Up) (film, French), 125–126

Solnit, Rebecca, 166–167

Song of the South (film), 130

"sonic eroticism," 203n10

Sontag, Susan, 6

Soul Calibur (video game), *13*

SoundCloud (online audio distribution/ sharing), 1–2, 46–49

Sow, Aminatou, 140

Spacey, Kevin, 90

Spears, Britney, 188

spectacle, use of in lip-sync performance, 183, 185–187, 195–196

spectrographic analysis of voice, 13

speech and phonetics, study of, 13, 179, 182, 199–200

speech bubbles, 151

Spotify (streaming audio service), 131

"spreadable" digital activism, 153–154, 224n15

Stanwyck, Barbara, 108–109, 142

Stella Dallas (film/radio soap opera series), 108–109, 142

Stepford Wives, The (film), 55–56

Stewart, James, 59

Stone, Emma, 73, 74

stop-motion animation, 16, 56, 61, 83. *See also* Virtual Reality (VR)

Stratten, Dorothy, 136

Strickland, Peter, 64

subtitled screen images, 47, 148, 150–153. *See also* GIFs and subtitled stills

Sullivan, John L., 144–145

Sumac, Yma, 190–191

Summer, Donna, 188

Sunset Boulevard (film), 97

superimposed text: and mental enunciation effect, 150–151, 157; moderation of affect and movement in GIFs, 150; strategic uses of, 88, 96, 148, 150, 156. *See also* intertitles in silent films

Sutherland, Donald, 124

Swanson, Gloria, 101

Swinton, Tilda, 89

synthesized human speech, 2, 53, 66, 68–74

"talking statues" program in Dublin, 197–199

Taylor, Breonna, 226n51

technologized voices/characters: male *vs.* female, modern trends, 54–56; queering of voices, 81; synthesized human speech, 2, 53, 66, 68–74; virtual assistants, 2, 70; voice cloning, 72–73, 84. *See also* virtual assistants

technology, developments in: and diachronic analysis of female screen voice, 24; proliferation of and cultural impact, 6–7; and voice, overviews, 12–15. *See also* "collective intelligence" and internet community

Teixeira Pinto, Ana, 155

Teknolust (film), 213n21

Telegraph (newspaper, British), 182

terminable/interminable concepts, 23–25

Thelma and Louise (film), 113

Thewlis, David, 61, 80

"This Could Be (an Everlasting Love)" (song), 186–187

Thornton, Leslie, 14, 77

Thorpe, David, 179

3D technology, 4, 16, 56, 61, 63, 74–75, 76. *See also* motion capture technology; stop-motion animation
Tide's Fall (VR short). *See Arden's Wake: Tide's Fall* (VR short)
Tiffe, Raechel, 144
Till the Clouds Roll By (film), 129
"to-be-dubbed-ness" concept, 14, 38
"to-be-looked-ness" concept, 14, 39
Todd, Carolyn L., 161
Tolle, Michael, 182
Tonight Show Starring Jimmy Fallon, The (television show), 188–189
Tout va bien (*All's Well*) (film, French), 123–124
transgender vocal performers, 175, 206n45
TrueMajority (liberal advocacy group), 154
Trump, Donald, 147–149, 154–157, 160–161, 164–165
Tufekci, Zeynep, 164, 165
Tumblr (social media miniblog), 155, 156
Turnbridge, Laura, 67, 68, 75
Turner, Tina, 188
"Twist of Fate" (song), 185–186
Twitter, 164
2 Dope Queens (podcast), 131
2001: A Space Odyssey, 55, 84
Tyra Sanchez (drag queen), 192–193, 194

UbuWeb, 127
"uncanny valley" concept, 83
Underwood, Lisa, 172–173
Unqualified (podcast), 8–9, 120
Unseld, Saschka, 111
uptalk, 25, 81, 140, 144

"Valley girl" accent, 93, 140, 150
van der Zyl, Nikki, 28–31, 36, 40–43, 124
Vanity Fair, 94
Variety, 139
Vélez, Lupe, 129
ventriloquism, concepts of, 8
Vernallis, Carol, 204n24
Vertigo (film), 59, 61, 62

Vice (magazine), 73
video games, women's voices in, 13, 199–200
Vietnam War, 119, 123, 124–125
Vikander, Alicia, 105, 106, 113
Virginás, Andrea, 56, 70, 81
virtual assistants: characterizations and trends in, 2, 16, 41, 55, 72, 77, 200; fetishization of, 65–68, 70, 72
Virtual Reality (VR), 85, 102, 105–112, 116–117
visual *vs.* vocal presence of women, 1–2, 7, 9, 56–57, 67–68, 85–88. *See also* embodiment/disembodiment concepts; male perspective, predominance of; mismatched voice/appearance expectations
Vocabulary.com, 7
vocal damage and disorders, 73–74
vocal delivery permutations: affected social dialects, 93, 140, 150; control and self-manipulation of, 136–143; criticism of, 140, 144–145; expressiveness in narratives, 108–112; uptalk, 25, 81, 140, 144; vocal fry, 25, 81, 140, 194–195. *See also* autonomous sensory meridian response (ASMR) videos; softness and grain in vocals
vocal fry, 25, 81, 140, 194–195. *See also* softness and grain in vocals
vocal grain. *See* softness and grain in vocals
"vocalic space" concept, 107
vocal vortex concept, 7–8, 9–10
"Voder" (Voice Operation Demonstrator) machine, 2–3, 4
Vogue by the Decade (documentary series), 97, 99–100
"voice-cast," 127
voice cloning technology, 72–73, 84
voice-off, definition, 7
voice-only acting, career challenges of, 67–68
voice-overs: and career challenges of voice-only acting, 67–68; and disembodied voices, 128, 132, 137–139; intermediality and narration, 86,

87–88, 97–102, 104, 114. *See also* expanded voice-overs

W *(magazine)*, 9
Wagner, Laura, 43
Wallace, Mike, 122
Waller-Bridge, Phoebe, 97
Walters, Barbara, 126
Walton, Saige, 41
Wanstall, Norman, 41, 49
Warner Brothers, 35
Warwick, Dionne, 175
Warwick, Jaqueline, 140
Wasson, Haidee, 115, 116
Watercutter, Angela, 109, 110
"weaponization of carnival," 155
"weepies," 141–142
Weinstein, Harvey, 135
Weisz, Rachel, 89
Welch, Raquel, 30
Welles, Orson, 35
We're Not All Ninjas (podcast), 131
What's My Line? (television show), 32–34
When Björk met Attenborough (film), 89
whispered vocalizations/narrations, 1, 99, 108–109, 116. *See also* autonomous sensory meridian response (ASMR) videos; softness and grain in vocals
"whitewashing" (racial ventriloquism), 77
white women's voices as de facto standard, 9, 77–79
Whitman, Mae, 85, 106, 108, 109, 112
Wigstock: The Movie (film), 175
Williams, Jessica, 131
Wired (magazine), 109
"Woke Charlotte" memes, 168–169
Woletz, Julie, 107, 108
Wolf of Wall Street, The (film), 9
Women, Race and Class (Davis, A.), 231n53

Women Make Movies (distributor), 105
women of color: Black voices cast by Black creators, 91; and domination of white female voice, 9, 77, 105, 168–169; and drag culture, 178, 188–189; marginalization of in cinema, 129–130; resurrection of thru modern media, 127–131
"women's films," 141–142
"Workout, The" (exercise video), 123
World Religion News (website), 2
World's Fair, New York (1939), 3
Wound Footage (glitch video), 21–23, 33, 51–52
Wright, Robin, 53–54, 57–60, 71–72, 74–75, 81–84

"Yanny or Laurel" audio illusion, 6–7
YMRT (*You Must Remember This*) (podcast). *See You Must Remember This (YMRT)* (podcast)
"(You Make Me Feel Like) A Natural Woman" (song), 191–192
You Must Remember This (YMRT) (podcast): "Jean and Jane" series and recapturing narrative, 121–126; Longworth's techniques and strategies, 132–136; Longworth's voice/appearance mismatch, 136–143; overviews, 119–120, 143–145; podcasting medium characterization, 126–128; as reversal of screened voice dynamic, 152–153; revising the white male perspective, 128–131, 132. *See also* Longworth, Karina
Youngblood, Gene, 86–87, 86–88, 100, 116
YouTube: and *RPDR*, 18, 173, *174*, 175; and uncredited dubbing, exposure of, 15, 23, 28–34, 36–38, 39–43, 44–48; whisper videos on, 1, 5, 9, 62, 64–65